BIBLE ENCYCLOPEDIA

CHRISTIAN SCHOOL EDITION

Volume Two

K-Z

BERKELEY AND ALVERA MICKELSEN

David C. Cook Publishing Co.

ELGIN, ILLINOIS—WESTON, ONTARIO
FULLERTON, CALIFORNIA

PHOTO CREDITS

Metropolitan Museum of Art, page 8
Religious News Service, page 93
Paul M. Schrock, page 99
Toronto Star Syndicate, pages 26, 50, 53, 70, 160, 181, 189, 198

Edited by Dean Merrill, Marshall Shelley, and Sharrel Keyes
Designed by Marita Root
Cover by Kurt Dietsch
Printed in the United States of America

ISBN 0-89191-169-3

Two-Volume Set A2622/25957
(Volume II A2638/01305)

When the 12 spies came back to Kadesh, they brought back beautiful fruit from the Promised Land. But they also brought back stories of the giants they had seen.

KADESH and **KADESH-BARNEA** *(KAY-dish bar-NEE-uh)* are both names for a city about 100 miles southwest of Jerusalem in what we call the Sinai Peninsula. This city was an oasis in the wilderness.

The Israelites camped here while waiting to enter Canaan after leaving Egypt. When they reached this point, Moses sent 12 spies to scout out the Promised Land. Although the Lord wanted the people to go on in, they would not. They were afraid, because the spies reported there were giants in the land. Because they rebelled, the Lord made them wander 40 more years in the wilderness.

Moses' sister, the prophet Miriam, died at Kadesh-barnea and was buried there. Near Kadesh, Moses struck a rock from which God then gave water to the complaining Israelites. Later, Kadesh-barnea was the southern border of the kingdom of Judah.

Where to find it

The people rebel at Kadesh *Numbers 13–14;
   Deuteronomy 1: 19-28; Joshua 14: 6-8*
Water from a rock *Numbers 20: 11*
Miriam dies and is buried at Kadesh *Numbers
   20: 1*
Kadesh is southern border of Judah *Joshua 15: 3*

1

KEDAR (KEY-dar) was both the name of a son of Ishmael and the people who descended from him. They were the ancestors of modern Arabs. In Bible times they lived in the desert in black tents and wandered from place to place tending their sheep. They lived mostly in the northern part of what is now Saudi Arabia. They worshiped idols instead of God.

Where to find it

Kedar, son of Ishmael   *Genesis 25:13*
Kedarites, people of the desert   *Isaiah 42:11; 60:7*

KEEPER in Bible times was a person who guarded or watched over something. Usually he guarded cattle, vineyards, or orchards, but sometimes a keeper guarded prisons or other places as a soldier would. Keepers guarded the tomb where the body of Jesus was placed.

Keeper is also a word picture of someone guarding what his mouth or tongue says.

Where to find it

Keepers at the tomb of Jesus   *Matthew 27:66*
A word picture   *Psalms 34:13; 141:3*

KENITES (KEY-nites) were wandering metalworkers who lived in the land of Canaan during the time of Abraham. They were still there when the Israelites arrived from Egypt. They were kind to the Israelites and may have taught some of them how to work with metal. They continued to live in parts of Israel until about the time of King David. King Saul once gave them a friendly warning to get away from the scene of a battle he was about to start.

Where to find it: *Genesis 15:19; 1 Samuel 15:6; 27:10*

KETURAH (kuh-TOOR-uh) was Abraham's second wife. She married him after the death of Sarah, his first wife, and after Isaac's marriage. Keturah and Abraham had six sons: Zimran, Jokshan, Medan, Midian, Ishbak, and Shuah. These six sons were the forefathers of Arabian tribes. Abraham sent them away to the east to live and raise their families.

Where to find it: *Genesis 25:1-6*

KEY in the Bible is often a word picture for authority. This is because a key controls entrance or exit, and the person with the key can decide who comes and goes. Jesus is said to have the keys for (the authority over) death and hades. Jesus gave Peter authority. But as the only one, the true one, Jesus in Revelation 3:7 still has supreme authority over who enters heaven. With this same authority—the word picture of a key—Jesus will lock Satan in the bottomless pit at the end of time.

Where to find it

Jesus' keys   *Revelation 1:18; 3:7*
Peter's key   *Matthew 16:19*
Satan locked up   *Revelation 9:1; 20:1*

KID (see *Animals*)

KIDRON (KID-run) is a stream that begins east of Jerusalem and winds about 20 miles through a valley to the Dead Sea. Most of the time it is dry. Only after heavy rainfall does it have water in it. Kidron separates the Mount of Olives from Jerusalem, so Jesus crossed it on his way to the garden of Gethsemane.

KING is a man who rules a country and its people. Often the king was thought to be either stronger or smarter than most people.

After the people of Israel first settled in Canaan, they did not have a king. They were ruled by judges, who made necessary decisions. But all the countries—and even some of the cities—around Israel had kings. And the people complained that they wanted one too.

The prophet Samuel warned the Israelites that God did not want them to have a king. The Lord wanted to be their only ruler. An earthly king would not always serve them well. "This is how a king will act," Samuel said. "He will tell you all what to do, and he will send your sons off to war."

But the people would not listen. "No!" they said, "we will have a king over us!"

So the Lord told Samuel to appoint Saul as king. After Saul, David became king, and after David, Solomon. These three were the greatest kings of Israel. Most of the time they led the people in honoring God.

But some of the later kings of Israel and Judah became very wicked and encouraged the worship of false gods. A few kings were good, leading the people back to the worship of God, who was the true King of Israel.

In the New Testament, Jesus is called our King. He rules over all people and all of creation. He leads a battle against death that he will win. He will be the all-powerful, wise,

Israel's first king, Saul, was anointed by Samuel.

loving King of the universe through all eternity.

Where to find it

The people demand a king   *1 Samuel 8: 4-22*
Jesus shall reign   *1 Corinthians 15: 24-28*

KINGDOM OF GOD means God's rule over people and places. In the Old Testament, the people over whom God ruled was Israel. In the New Testament, the Kingdom people are Christians. When we say that Jesus is our Lord, we are saying that he is the King of our lives. Jesus taught us to pray, "Thy kingdom come, thy will be done on earth as it is in heaven." This means we are praying that all people will recognize God as King and obey him.

The words *Kingdom of God* and *Kingdom of Heaven* mean the same thing. The Jewish people said "Kingdom of Heaven" because they felt God's name was too sacred to speak.

The Bible speaks of an earthly Kingdom of God and a heavenly Kingdom. God will finally remove evil from all of his creation. Then his Kingdom (both earth and heaven) will be free from all sin.

Where to find it

Israel called the Kingdom of the Lord   *1 Chronicles 28: 5*
Jesus teaches about Kingdom of God   *Matthew 13: 31-33; Mark 4: 26-32; Luke 10: 9; 13: 18-21*
Final Kingdom of God   *Luke 22: 18; 2 Timothy 4: 18; 2 Peter 1: 11*

KINGDOM OF HEAVEN (see *Kingdom of God*)

KINGDOM OF ISRAEL (see *Northern Kingdom*)

KINGDOM OF JUDAH (see *Southern Kingdom*)

KINGS, FIRST BOOK OF, is an Old Testament book that tells the story of Israel's kings from Solomon (about 970 B.C.) to Ahab (851 B.C.). 1 Kings tells about the plan for and the building of Solomon's Temple. It includes a long dedication of the Temple as well as Solomon's prayer dedicating all the people to the worship of God.

1 Kings also tells how the kingdom of Israel was divided into two kingdoms, Israel and Judah, after the death of Solomon. The Northern Kingdom (Israel) and the Southern Kingdom (Judah) were rivals. A few of the kings who ruled the new kingdoms were good. Many were wicked and worshiped false gods.

1 Kings also tells how God sent prophets such as Elijah to call the people and the kings back to the Lord. Elijah's messages and the miracles God performed for him are recorded in 1 Kings.

Where to find it

The Temple and Solomon's dedication   *1 Kings 8: 1-61*
Division of the kingdom   *1 Kings 12: 1-20*
Elijah's conflict with King Ahab   *1 Kings 17–21*

KINGS, SECOND BOOK OF, is an Old Testament book that continues the history of the two kingdoms, Israel and Judah, from about 850 B.C. until their fall. The Northern Kingdom (Israel) was defeated and taken captive by Assyria in 722 B.C. The Southern Kngdom (Judah) fell to Babylon in 586 B.C.

Several prophets proclaimed God's judgment and warning to these kings of Judah and Israel. These prophets included Elisha, who took on Elijah's cloak as Elijah was taken into heaven. Other prophets during this time were Amos and Hosea in the Northern Kingdom and Obadiah, Joel, Isaiah, Micah, Nahum, Habakkuk, Zephaniah, and Jeremiah in the Southern Kingdom.

All these prophets repeated again and again that God's judgment was coming. The reasons were because God's people no longer worshiped the true God and because their lives were not pleasing to God. Once in a while the people repented but later slipped back to their old ways.

The prophets' warnings came true. All God's people became exiles in foreign lands.

Where to find it

Fall of the Northern Kingdom   *2 Kings 17*
Fall of the Southern Kingdom   *2 Kings 24: 8–25: 30*

KING JAMES VERSION (see *Authorized Version*)

KIN, KINSMEN are people who are family or relatives. In ancient time a kin had the right to get revenge for a wrong done to one of his relatives or to pay his debt for him. (Also see *Family*.)

KIRIATH-JEARIM *(KUR-yath JEE-o-rim)* was a fortresslike city about 12 miles west of

It was a joyful day when the ark left Kiriath-jearim.

Jerusalem. About 1050 B.C. the Philistines captured the ark of the Covenant in a battle with the Israelites. Later they returned it to Kiriath-jearim. The ark stayed in a specially built house for 20 years, until King David brought it back to Jerusalem with great pomp and ceremony.

Where to find it

The ark comes back from Kiriath-jearim   *1 Samuel 6: 21–7: 2; 2 Samuel 6: 1-15*

KISHON *(KEY-shun)*, **KISON** *(KISS-un)* are both names for a brook in the mountains of what is now northwestern Israel near Lebanon. During the winter, the melting snows from the mountains make it dangerous to cross. It must be forded only at special places.

On the banks of the Kishon, the army of Deborah and Barak defeated the Canaanites led by Sisera. Many of the Canaanite soldiers were washed away by the raging Kishon when their chariots got bogged down in the mud and water. This was proof to the Israelites that God was with them in the battle.

Where to find it: *Judges 5: 21*

KISS, in Bible times as today, was a sign of love, greeting, or respect. It was a common greeting between male relatives as well as between male and female relatives and between friends. Often one kissed on the cheek, forehead, or beard, but lips, hands, and even feet were kissed also. While kissing usually showed affection, it was sometimes a formal part of a blessing and of anointing a king in Old Testament times. In the New Testament, a kiss became the usual greeting between believers in the early church.

Probably the most famous kiss in the Bible is the one Judas gave Jesus in the Garden of Gethsemane. While it seemed to be a greeting, it really was a sign to soldiers that this was the man to arrest.

Where to find it

Kissing as a part of a blessing   *Genesis 27: 26-27*
Kissing as a formal greeting   *Romans 16: 16*
Judas's kiss   *Matthew 26: 48-49; Mark 14: 44-45; Luke 22: 47-48*

KITCHEN (see *House*)

KITE (see *Birds*)

KNEAD *(need)* means to work flour and water with the hands until it becomes dough. In Bible times kneading was always done in a kneading trough, a bowl made of wood, bronze, or clay. A small portion of the previous day's dough was always left in the trough so the next day's bread would have leavening for rising.

KNEES, KNEEL. As in our day, parents in Bible times often held their children on their knees and lap. Sometimes when a child was adopted, he was placed upon the knees of one of his new parents as a sign that he now belonged to them.

Kneeling is a posture of worship or prayer. People kneel before earthly as well as heavenly authorities. People kneeled before Jesus, and Jesus kneeled before God when he prayed in the garden of Gethsemane.

KNOWLEDGE, in the Bible, means more than just knowing facts. Knowledge also means caring about a person or thing. When we say God knows everything, we mean not only that he has all the facts about things on earth but also that he personally cares about his creation.

When we know God, we believe in him, and we begin to understand what God wants us to be. For example, we know that even though we sin, God expects us to live according to his stated will. When we avoid sin and do what God wants, we show that we know God's saving truth and that we are Jesus' disciples.

Knowing God also means realizing that he wants all the world to share salvation through Christ. This is sometimes called understanding the "mystery" of God. (See also *Mystery of God.)* Matthew 11: 27 tells us that the way to know God is to know Jesus.

The Bible also sometimes uses the word *know* to describe sexual intercourse between a husband and wife. In this way the special caring side of knowledge is shown.

Where to find it

Knowing God brings knowledge of ourselves *Psalm 51: 3*
Knowing God brings knowledge of his purposes *Colossians 1: 9*
Knowing God and Christ brings eternal life *John 17: 3*
"Knowing" in marriage *Genesis 4: 1, 25*

KNOWLEDGE, TREE OF, was a special tree in the Garden of Eden set apart by God to test the obedience of Adam and Eve. He told them not to eat its fruit, but they ate it anyway.

There was probably not much special about the fruit—the sin was in disobeying God's command. After they ate, Adam and Eve had a knowledge of evil that they did not have before.

Where to find it: *Genesis 2: 9, 17; 3: 1-19*

KOHATHITES *(KO-hath-ites)* were the descendants of Kohath, the second son of Levi, and a grandson of Jacob. The Kohathites took care of the ark, candlesticks, altars, and vessels for the Tabernacle. Moses was a Kohathite.

After the Israelites settled in the Promised Land, the priestly Kohathites lived in the cities in the hill country of southern and central Israel. Later, after David prepared a place for the ark of the Covenant in Jerusalem, Kohathites brought it into the city with much pomp and ceremony. All during the Israelites' kingdom, the Kohathites were important on the religious scene. Even after the Jews returned from exile in Babylon, the Kohathites had important religious duties.

Where to find it

Kohath, son of Levi *Exodus 6: 16, 18*
Kohathites in the Tabernacle *Numbers 4: 1-3, 34-37*

KORAH *(KOR-uh)* was the name of several people in the Bible, of which these two are the most important:

1. A Levite whose descendants were doorkeepers and musicians in the Tabernacle and the Temple. Some of the Psalms (42, 44—49, 84, 87—88) were written by Korahites and were probably sung by a Korahite choir.

2. A man who, with two of his friends, led a rebellion against Moses during the Exodus. God caused the earth to open and swallow the three men and their followers. This was a dramatic warning to the other Israelites against rebelling.

Where to find it

Korahites in the Tabernacle *Numbers 26: 9-11*
The rebellion leader *Exodus 6: 24; 1 Chronicles 6: 22*

The stranger at the well turned out to be a servant of Laban's and Rebekah's great-uncle, Abraham.

L

LABAN *(LAY-bun)* was the grand-nephew of Abraham. Laban's family had stayed near Haran when Abraham left to follow God to the Promised Land.

Years later, Abraham wanted a wife for his son Isaac. He sent his most trusted servant back to his relatives near Haran. When the servant met a young woman named Rebekah near a well, he felt she would be just the right bride for Isaac. Laban was Rebekah's brother, and when he saw the bracelets the servant had given Rebekah, he hurried the servant into his house. He gave him food and did everything he could to please him. When the servant told Laban about Abraham and Isaac, Laban quickly approved the marriage of his sister.

After many years, Jacob, the son of Rebekah and Isaac, ran away to Haran because his brother, Esau, was very angry with him. Jacob fell in love with Laban's daughter Rachel. He agreed to work for Laban seven years in order to earn Rachel as his bride. But Laban tricked Jacob and sent Leah, his older daughter, to be Jacob's wife instead. Jacob asked to work

6

seven more years in order to have Rachel as his wife also. Laban agreed, and Rachel and Jacob were married. After the second seven-year period, Jacob worked for six more years. When he decided to leave, he said to Laban, "Let me have the speckled and spotted goats and the black sheep from your flocks for my wages for these years."

Laban said, "Good! Let it be as you said." But Laban removed all the speckled and spotted goats and the black sheep before Jacob had a chance to collect them. But Jacob was just as tricky. He waited for the next generation to be born and then chose out the animals Laban had said he could have. Finally, Jacob outwitted Laban and returned to his own country.

Where to find it

Laban and Rebekah   *Genesis 24:29-50*
Laban and Jacob   *Genesis 29–30*

LABOR means the work a person does. In ancient times most people worked hard to make a living. The Bible says work is good. There is a proverb that tells the lazy man to follow the example of the ant and to get busy. Peter was a fisherman; Paul was a tentmaker. In some of his letters, Paul said he expected all Christians to work.

While most people were farmers, some were skilled craftsmen such as potters, metal workers, stone masons, scribes, dyers, weavers, tentmakers, or carpenters (see *Occupations*).

The word *labor* was also used to describe childbirth in the Bible.

Where to find it

God's labor   *Genesis 2:2*
Lazy man should work   *Proverbs 6:6*
Work is honored   *Proverbs 10:16*
Paul's labor   *Acts 18:3*
Christian's labor   *1 Thessalonians 4:11; 2 Thessalonians 3:10-12*
Childbirth   *Genesis 35:16-17*

LACHISH *(LAY-kish)* was a city 25 miles southwest of Jerusalem. Joshua and his army attacked Lachish as the Israelites were fighting to take over Canaan. Many years later, after Israel was divided into the Northern and Southern Kingdoms, King Rehoboam made Lachish into a strong fort. King Amaziah was murdered in Lachish. The prophet Micah said the chariots of Lachish were the beginning of Judah's sin. He meant that the people of Judah had to pay a lot of money for Egyptian horses to pull the chariots.

Where to find it

Joshua's attack   *Joshua 10:31-33*
King Rehoboam strengthens Lachish   *2 Chronicles 11:5*
King Amaziah's death   *2 Chronicles 25:27*
Micah's prophecy   *Micah 1:13*

LADDER is mentioned in the story of Jacob's dream at Bethel. In his dream Jacob saw a ladder between heaven and earth. Angels were going up and down the ladder, letting him know that God loved him and would take care of him. The ladder Joseph dreamed about probably looked like a wide staircase.

Where to find it: *Genesis 28:12-17*

LAKE OF GENNESARET (see *Galilee, Sea of*)

LAMB is a young sheep (see *Animals*).

Lambs were eaten only on very special occasions. Meat was scarce, and to kill an animal before it had given birth was wasteful. For that reason, a person in Bible times would show great love and respect to God by giving a lamb as an offering. Giving a lamb as a sacrifice meant giving the very best to God.

A lamb was always sacrificed as a part of the Passover feast (see *Feasts, Passover*). The Jews celebrated Passover because God freed them from slavery in Egypt.

Lamb is also a word picture for Jesus' offering himself to free us from sin. The Bible calls Jesus the Lamb of God (see *Lamb of God*).

Where to find it

Lambs as offerings   *Genesis 4:4; 22:7*
Passover lamb   *Exodus 12:3-13*

LAMB OF GOD is a New Testament name for Jesus. That name was especially meaningful to people in Jesus' day because Jews sacrificed lambs as part of many worship services (see *Lamb*). The term *Lamb of God* described Jesus' mission: to sacrifice himself for our sins.

When John the Baptist saw Jesus, he shouted, "Behold, the Lamb of God, who takes away the sin of the world!"

The apostle Peter wrote, "You were ransomed with the precious blood of Christ, like that of a lamb without blemish or spot."

In the Book of Revelation, *lamb* is often a word picture for Jesus. That book shows Jesus as the Lamb of God, who will rule heaven and earth and see that sin is forever destroyed.

Where to find it

John the Baptist calls Jesus Lamb of God *John 1:29*

Ransomed with blood of Christ *1 Peter 1:18-19*

Jesus the lamb will rule *Revelation 5:12-13; 7:14; 13:8; 22:1, 3*

LAMECH *(LAY-mek)* was the name of two men in Genesis.

The first Lamech was a descendant of Cain and a poet. He murdered a man to get even with him. Then he wrote a song about the murder.

The other Lamech was the father of Noah. Lamech believed that the Lord would use his son to bring a blessing to the world.

Where to find it

The poet who wanted revenge *Genesis 4:23*

Noah's father *Genesis 5:29*

LAMENTATION (see *Mourning*)

LAMENTATIONS *(LAM-en-TAY-shuns)* is an Old Testament book of poems. Jeremiah wrote them about 580 B.C., after Jerusalem was destroyed. Babylon had captured Judah and taken many of the people away. The people left in Jerusalem were suffering. Although they worked very hard, many were hungry. Their friends and families were far away. They didn't know what might happen next.

The prophet Jeremiah suffered with them. He put his and their feelings into words in the poems in Lamentations. Even when Jeremiah was very discouraged, he was able to write about God's great faithfulness.

Jeremiah said the people in Jerusalem knew

that their troubles were the result of their own wickedness and turning away from God. They admitted their sin. They knew God was right when he said they were bad and needed to be punished. They also had been warned by the prophets that God's judgment was coming.

Jeremiah asked God for forgiveness and mercy. He said that although nations become powerful and then get weak, God remains the same.

But thou, O Lord, dost reign forever;
Thy throne endures to all generations.
Lamentations 5:19

Jeremiah's poems were a comfort to the people.

LAMP is a container that gives light. Lamps were usually shallow bowls with one side slightly pointed to hold a wick. Some had

A stone lamp, probably from Old Testament times.

handles, and some had tops with small holes where the olive oil (used for fuel) was poured in. Lamps were made from clay or bronze. Every house had several lamps. Usually one was kept burning all the time to light the others when it became dark.

Lamp and *light* are used often in the Bible as word pictures. Christ is called a light that shines in the darkness. God's Word is called a lamp. Since lamps were very important in helping people see where to go in the darkness, these word pictures showed that Christ himself is the way to God, and God's Word helps people know what to do.

Where to find it

Gives light *Matthew 5:15*

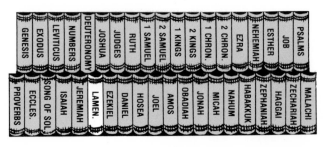

Christ is a light *John 1: 5*
God's Word a lamp *Psalm 119: 105; 2 Peter 1: 19*

LAMPSTAND was a tall holder on which a lamp was placed so it would be high and give more light. Usually lampstands in Bible times were made of pottery, but some were made of metal. Often they were decorated. A special kind of lampstand was the menorah, which had places for seven lamps or wicks. Menorahs were probably used for light in the

Temple. After the destruction of the Temple, Jewish people used menorahs to help them remember Temple worship.

In the Book of Revelation, the seven lampstands are word pictures used to make readers think of seven churches in Asia Minor.

LANCE (see *Weapons*)

LANDMARK was an object, usually a stone but sometimes a post, used to mark a boundary. Moving a landmark was a serious sin, because it meant robbing a person of his land.

Where to find it: *Deuteronomy 19: 14; 27: 17*

LANGUAGES OF THE BIBLE were Hebrew, Aramaic, and Greek. Most of the Old Testament was written in Hebrew, which was also the language spoken by the Israelites for most of that time (see *Hebrew Language*).

Parts of the Old Testament and some words of the New Testament were written in Aramaic. This was the language spoken by the people in the later periods of the Old Testament and during the time of the New Testament. It is similar to Hebrew (see *Aramaic*).

Most of the New Testament was written in Greek, the language most widely spoken in

the Roman Empire. All educated people read and spoke Greek. Greek is a complicated language and can express many ideas (see *Greek Language*).

Jesus probably knew all three languages. He probably spoke Aramaic at home, learned Greek from townspeople as he grew up, and studied Hebrew in the early religious classes all Jewish boys were given. The apostle Paul also knew those three languages.

The people in the Middle East spoke many languages. Words and phrases from Egyptian, Syrian, Persian, and Latin appear at times in the Bible. The inscription above Jesus' cross was in Hebrew, Greek, and Latin so everyone could read it.

LAODICEA *(lay-oh-dih-SEE-uh)* was a wealthy city in the land that is now Turkey. The city was on one of the busy trade routes during New Testament times. The writer of Revelation scolded Laodicea for its wealth. A church had started there, but the church people had gotten so comfortable that they lost their enthusiasm for God's work. They didn't realize that although they were rich, they had become poor spiritually. The apostle Paul wrote a letter to Laodicea. It is mentioned in Colossians 4: 16, but we do not have a copy of a letter with that name today.

Where to find it: *Revelation 3: 14-22*

LASCIVIOUSNESS *(luh-SIV-ee-us-ness)* means acting immorally and not feeling ashamed of it. The King James Version of the Bible uses this word in Galatians 5: 19 and Ephesians 4: 19 (see also *Licentiousness*).

LAST DAYS is used two ways in the New Testament. It sometimes means God's final judgment on individuals and on the earth.

In other places it means the time of history beginning with Jesus Christ.

Where to find it

God's final judgment *John 6: 40; 11: 24; 12: 48*
History since Jesus' time *Acts 2: 17; 2 Timothy 3: 1; Hebrews 1: 2; 2 Peter 3: 3*

LAST SUPPER is the name of the last meal Jesus ate with his disciples before his crucifixion.

It happened on Thursday evening of Passover Week in an upper room of a house in Jerusalem.

Almost everything about it was unusual, starting earlier in the day, when Jesus sent Peter and John to find a place for the meal. He told them to enter Jerusalem and then follow a man carrying a water pitcher. When the man got to his house, the two disciples were to ask to use one of the rooms for the evening. Everything happened as Jesus had described.

After the Passover meal was finished, Jesus gave a lesson in humility by washing the disciples' feet, which was really a slave's job. Jesus also said clearly that Judas was going to betray him. Judas then got up and left. Jesus shocked Peter, who thought of himself as one of Jesus' best friends, by telling him he would soon refuse to admit that he even knew Jesus.

Sometime during the evening, Jesus shared some broken bread and some wine with the disciples. This was a picture of his death the next day, when he himself would be broken for all people (see *Lord's Supper*).

Jesus and the disciples sat and talked together a long time that evening. They finally sang a hymn and then left for the Garden of Gethsemane.

Where to find it: *Matthew 26: 17-30; John 13–14*

LATCHET *(LACH-et)* is the King James Version word for the leather strap that held sandals on the feet. It is sometimes used as a picture of the most unimportant thing a person can own. John the Baptist said he was not worthy even to untie Jesus' latchets.

Where to find it: *John 1: 27*

LATIN, the language of the Roman people, appears a few times in the New Testament (see *Languages of the Bible*). It was one of the three languages used on the sign above Jesus' cross. Other Latin words in the Bible are military and government words people would have learned from the Romans who ruled over Israel at that time.

Where to find it: *Luke 23: 38; John 19: 20*

LATTER RAIN (see *Spring Rain*)

LATTICE *(LATT-iss)* was a window covering made by crossing narrow boards, leaving spaces between them—something like a shut-

ter. Air and light could come in, but people any distance away could not easily see through a lattice.

LAVER *(LAY-ver)* was a bowl for washing. In Old Testament times, lavers were placed between the door of the Tabernacle or Temple and the altar. Priests washed their feet and hands in the lavers before they worshiped God. This washing was to picture being cleansed from sin. In the Temple, the lavers were decorated and were so large that they

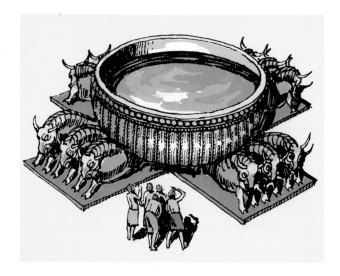

were placed on stands. Sometimes animals for sacrifice were also washed with water from these lavers.

Where to find it: *Exodus 30: 17-21; 1 Kings 7: 23-47*

LAW is a word that means several things in the Bible, depending on what the particular writer is talking about. Here are some of the meanings:

1. Instruction about God and directions for how we are to live. Psalm 119: 97 says, "Oh, how I love thy law! It is my meditation all the day." *Law* in the Psalms usually refers to all the teachings in the first five books of the Old Testament.

2. The Ten Commandments and other related laws in the Old Testament about our relationships with God and other people.

3. The Old Testament laws about sacrifices for sin and priestly offerings, as well as the Ten Commandments.

4. The New Testament, especially the Book of James, speaks of a new "law" or

principle—the law of liberty in Christ. Christians are to be controlled by this "law of liberty."

Parts of the Old Testament have detailed instructions that told how Hebrews were to eat, dress, build houses, and worship. Even today some Jewish people live by these laws. For example, one food law said they were not to eat meat and dairy products in the same meal. So if you were to order steak in a restaurant in Jerusalem, you could not have butter for your bread at the same meal (although you could have margarine).

The Old Testament Law had many rules about the religious services of the Israelites. Many of these, such as the sacrificing of lambs, were pictures of the salvation that God would provide through Jesus Christ. The New Testament Book of Hebrews says that these Old Testament sacrifices and the laws about them are no longer needed. Now we have a better way. Christ has fulfilled the Law for all who accept him.

Jesus also repeated and deepened the moral principles of the Ten Commandments. Those who follow Jesus are to obey his teachings.

Where to find it

Books of the Law   *Genesis, Exodus, Leviticus, Numbers, Deuteronomy*
Ten Commandments   *Exodus 20:3-17*
Laws about sacrifices and offerings   *Leviticus; Galatians 3:21; Hebrews 10:1*
Jesus refers to laws about our relationships with God and other people   *Matthew 22:36-40*
Law of liberty   *James 1:25; 2:12*

LAWYER (see *Occupations*)

LAYING ON OF HANDS (see *Hands, Laying on of*)

LAZARUS (*LAZZ-uh-rus*), **(PARABLE),** was a sick beggar with ugly sores on his body. He was the main character in a story Jesus told. Lazarus had been so poor that he didn't have enough to eat. He begged for food at the door of a rich man who had plenty to eat and even wasted some. The rich man never gave Lazarus a good meal and he didn't do anything about his painful sores.

Both Lazarus and the rich man died, and in the next life their places were just the oppo-

*Lazarus was a beggar
because he was too sick to work.*

site. Lazarus lived next to the father of the Jewish people, Abraham. His life was now comfortable and happy. The rich man was uncomfortable and unhappy, and he was in pain. Now the rich man became the beggar, asking Abraham to let Lazarus bring him a drink. But Abraham said, "Son, remember that in your life you received lots of good things. Lazarus had only bad things. Now you are separated from each other by too great a distance for anyone to come and help you."

The rich man wanted Abraham to send Lazarus back to warn the rich man's five brothers not to make the same mistakes he had made. Abraham refused, saying that if the brothers did not listen to the clear teachings of Moses and other prophets, they would not listen to someone who came back from the dead.

Where to find it: *Luke 16:19-31*

LAZARUS (*LAZZ-uh-rus*) **OF BETHANY** was a special friend of Jesus. He was the brother of Martha and Mary. Jesus had often visited at Lazarus's house in Bethany, a village about two miles from Jerusalem.

On one visit Jesus found Mary and Martha crying because Lazarus had died. Both Martha and Mary knew of Jesus' power, so each of them said, "Lord, if you had been here, my brother would not have died."

But Jesus told them, "I am the resurrection and the life." Then he went to the tomb of Lazarus. "Lazarus, come out!" Jesus shouted.

Lazarus came back to life after having been dead four days; he walked out of the tomb.

Later, the chief priests wanted to kill Lazarus because so many people heard about the miracle and were believing in Jesus.

Where to find it: *John 11:1-46; 12:9-11*

LEAD *(led)* was a common and important metal in Bible times. It was used to make weights, fishline sinkers, and writing tablets. Lead was also used to refine silver.

LEAH *(LEE-uh)* was Jacob's first wife. She was the mother of Reuben, Simeon, Levi, Judah, Issachar, Zebulun, and Dinah. Jacob's second wife was Rachel, Leah's younger sister. Jacob had worked for seven years in order to marry Rachel, but Laban, the women's father, sent Leah to the wedding instead. Jacob was disappointed but he worked another seven years for Rachel. Although Leah knew she was not the favorite, she was loyal to Jacob. She went with him to Canaan when he left Laban's house.

Where to find it: *Genesis 29:21-30; 35:23*

LEATHER is animal skin that has been tanned. It was widely used in Bible times. Some people, like John the Baptist and Elijah, wore leather clothes. But leather was mostly used for shoes, containers, armor, and writing materials.

LEAVEN *(LEV-un)* is the ingredient in bread that makes it rise, or expand. *Leaven* is also used in the Bible as a word picture for ideas or influences that grow or spread.

Sometimes *leaven* is used to mean a good influence. For example, Jesus compared the Kingdom of God to leaven. Silently, steadily, the Kingdom grows just as bread dough rises.

More often *leaven* is a picture of a bad influence. For example, Jesus said the wrong teaching of the Pharisees was like leaven. Keeping leaven out of bread was a picture of people keeping sin or evil out of their lives. That was one reason the Jews always ate unleavened bread at their Passover meals. The other reason for eating unleavened bread at Passover was that it reminded the Jewish people of how the Israelites had to leave Egypt in a hurry. They had to be ready to go when God commanded them. They could not wait for the bread to rise.

Jesus ate unleavened bread the night he was betrayed.

Where to find it

A good influence   *Matthew 13:33; Luke 13:20-21*
A bad influence   *Matthew 16:11*
At Passover   *Exodus 12:33-34; 13:7-10*
Jesus eats   *Mark 14:12, 22*

LEBANON was the name of a mountain range; it is now in the southern part of the country also called Lebanon. *Lebanon* means "the white" and probably refers to the snow that covers the tops of the mountains most of the year. The high, rugged peaks are famous for

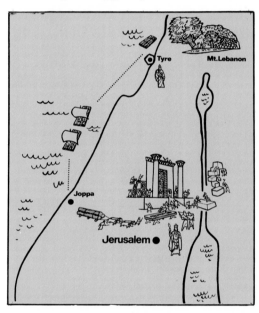

their beauty. Tall trees from these mountains, called the cedars of Lebanon, were used to build Solomon's Temple.

Where to find it: *1 Kings 5:1-18*

LEEK (see *Plants*)

LEFT HAND (see *Right Hand*)

LEGALISM means being very strict about rules. People who are legalists act as if following the rules is all they need to do in order to go to heaven. They put the emphasis on the rules instead of the idea behind the rules. In the early church some people believed they had to keep all the Jewish laws as well as believe in Christ in order to be saved. Paul wrote the books of Romans and Galatians to show that we are saved through faith, not legalism (see *Law*).

LEGION *(LEE-jun)* was a unit of the Roman army, usually 6,000 men. The word *legion* came to mean a great many, or a very large number.

Where to find it: *Matthew 26: 53; Mark 5: 9, 15; Luke 8: 30*

LENTILS (see *Plants*)

LEOPARD (see *Animals*)

LEPROSY (see *Diseases*)

LETTER is a written message. Both the Old Testament and the New Testament contain letters. Generally, letters and epistles are the same thing (see *Epistle*), but some people would say letters are written for one person, while epistles are meant to be shared and read by many people.

Letter in the Bible can also mean a single letter of the alphabet, or any small detail, as in "letter of the law."

Where to find it

Letters of information or instruction   *Esther 1: 22; 3: 13; Jeremiah 29: 1-28*
Letters of authority   *Acts 15: 22-23*

LEVI *(LEE-vie)* was Jacob and Leah's third son. His descendants were the Levites—the tribe from which all priests came. Levi took part in a bloody revenge against the men of the city of Shechem.

Levi and his brothers were jealous of their younger brother Joseph. They sold Joseph as a slave. Later, in Egypt, Levi and his brothers had to bow down to Joseph, who had become an important man (see *Joseph*).

Levi became a common Jewish name. It was the second name for the apostle Matthew.

Where to find it

Levi and Simeon's revenge   *Genesis 34: 25-31; 45: 1-7*
Levi and Joseph   *Genesis 37: 4, 28; 42: 6*

LEVIATHAN (see *Animals*)

LEVIRATE *(LEV-uh-rut)* **LAW** or **LEVIRATE MARRIAGE** was the custom of a widow marrying her dead husband's closest male relative,

usually his brother. This would make sure the widow and her children would be taken care of. The Sadducees once asked Jesus a trick question about this custom.

Where to find it: *Matthew 22: 23-33*

LEVITES *(LEE-vites)* were the descendants of Levi, the son of Jacob and Leah. During the Exodus from Egypt, when the people wanted to worship false gods, Moses asked, "Who is on the Lord's side?" Right away, the sons of Levi volunteered to help him. Moses said to them, "Today you have ordained yourselves for the service of the Lord." Moses gave them this special blessing for being loyal to him.

The Levites became the tribe from which all the priests came. All priests had to be Levites, but not all Levites were priests. Those who were priests were descended from Aaron, who was both a Levite and Moses' brother. Other Levites were religious teachers and workers in the Tabernacle or Temple.

When the Israelites settled in the Promised Land, all the tribes except the Levites were given areas of land. The Levites were given 48 cities scattered throughout the land so they could minister to all the people (see *Priests* and *Levitical Cities*).

Where to find it

The Levites' choice   *Exodus 32: 25-29*

LEVITICAL *(luh-VIT-eh-cul)* **CITIES** were the 48 cities given to the tribe of Levi when Israel took over Canaan. The cities were scattered throughout the country so the Levites could do their priestly and teaching work for all the people. But the Levites probably did not occupy all 48 as they should have.

Six of these cities were called cities of refuge. People could run to these cities for legal protection.

Where to find it: *Numbers 35:1-8; Joshua 21*

LEVITICUS *(luh-VIT-eh-cuss)*, the third book of the Old Testament, has been called "the priests' handbook," because it sets down

rules for religious ceremonies as well as for everyday life. It is named for the tribe of Levi, from which all priests of Israel came. Leviticus was written by Moses while the Israelites wandered in the wilderness before they entered the Promised Land.

The first seven chapters told the priests how to offer sacrifices for their sins and for the sins of all the other people. Other chapters gave rules about what food to eat, about keeping clean, about how to observe the Sabbath, and about doing right or wrong acts. Chapter 16 was especially important; it described what had to happen on the Day of Atonement, when the high priest entered the Holy of Holies (see *Day of Atonement*).

In Leviticus God again promised to be with his people: "I will make my abode among you. I will walk among you, and will be your God, and you shall be my people."

The word *holy* is used again and again in Leviticus to describe God and to show the people what God wanted them to be like. God told them that keeping all these commands and ceremonies were part of living as God's people should.

LEVY *(LEV-ee)* means a tax. Sometimes kings or other rulers made people pay levies with money, crops, what was captured in military battles, or even with slaves. Moses was told to

raise a levy for the Lord of what was won in battle.

Where to find it: *Numbers 31:28; 1 Kings 5:13, 15; 9:21; 2 Chronicles 8:8*

LIBATION *(LIE-bay-shun)* is a pouring out of liquids—wine, oil, water—as an offering. Libations were either poured on an altar or drunk. They were part of many Old Testament sacrifices. Libations were also made to heathen gods.

Where to find it

Part of Old Testament sacrifices *Exodus 29:40-41*
To heathen gods *Deuteronomy 32:38*

LIBERTY, the opposite of slavery, means freedom. In the Bible it can mean physical freedom from being the slave of another person, or it can mean freedom from being a slave to sin or legalism.

Slavery was common in ancient times, and the Bible treats slavery as a fact of life. A slave could be given liberty and become a free person—but this was not as common as it should have been.

Liberty from sin comes through accepting Christ as Savior and becoming free to live as he wants us to live. As Romans 6:18, 22 tells us, liberty comes from choosing a new master.

Liberty from legalism comes from realizing that right standing with God doesn't come through keeping rules and regulations. Galatians 2:4 and 5:1 say such slavery is unnecessary for the Christian.

LICENTIOUSNESS *(lie-SENT-shuss-ness)* is not controlling yourself morally or sexually. The Bible condemns licentiousness because immoral people disobey God and hurt other people as well as themselves.

Where to find it: *Romans 13:13; 2 Corinthians 12:21; Ephesians 4:17-19*

LIFE may mean either physical life or spiritual life. Both kinds of life come from God.

When God first created people, he breathed into Adam the breath of life. Physical life is God's precious gift to each person. God forbids any person to take another person's life.

While a healthy physical life is important, a healthy spiritual life is even more important. Spiritual life is a gift from God also. It is given to each person who accepts God's Son, Jesus, as Savior. This new life begins when a person commits himself in faith to Christ. It is a life of friendship with God that will last forever.

Where to find it

God breathes physical life   *Genesis 2:7*
God forbids killing   *Genesis 9:5; Exodus 20:13; Leviticus 24:17*
God gives spiritual life   *John 3:36; 5:24; Romans 6:23; 1 John 5:12*

LIFE, BOOK OF, is a word picture of the heavenly record of those who are in fellowship with God while they are on earth. The Bible says that only those whose names are in the book of life will get to enter heaven.

Where to find it: *Philippians 4:3; Revelation 20:11-15*

LIGHT AND DARKNESS are often word pictures in the Bible. *Darkness* is a word picture of sin and death. People who don't know about God live in this darkness of sin. Light is a picture of life, holiness, and purity—things that are good and necessary and are the opposite of the darkness of sin. God himself is light, and he made light. God's Word brings light, or understanding (see also *Lamp*).

Where to find it

God is light   *James 1:17; 1 John 1:5*
Jesus is the light of the world   *John 8:12; 9:5; 12:46*
God's Word is a light   *Psalm 119:105; Isaiah 8:20*

LILY (see *Plants*)

LIME is a white substance made by burning limestone, shells, or bones that contain lime. Lime was used for making plaster, for dyeing wool, and for improving the soil.

LINEN is a cloth or thread made from flax. It was fine and expensive fabric in Bible times, worn by wealthy people and by the priests in the Temple. Jesus was buried in linen and put in a rich man's tomb. When the Book of Revelation says that in heaven Christians will be dressed in fine linen, it shows they will wear the very best—probably what they could not afford on earth. Revelation also says the linen robes of the Christians stand for their good deeds.

Where to find it

Priest wears linen   *Leviticus 6:10*
Jesus' burial garment   *Matthew 27:59*
Christians will wear linen robes   *Revelation 19:8*

LINTEL *(LIN-tul)* is the board or stone across the top of a door or window. The lintel supports the wall above it. On the first Passover, every Israelite family brushed the blood of the Passover lamb on the front lintel of their house (see *Passover*).

Where to find it: *Exodus 12:22-23*

LION (see *Animals*)

LIVER is a large part inside human and animal bodies. It is part of the system that digests food. Heathen people used animal livers to try to tell the future or find out other secrets. Some Bible writers saw the liver as the place where deepest sorrows were felt.

Where to find it

Heathen try to tell future   *Ezekiel 21:21*
Place for feeling sorrow   *Lamentations 2:11 (KJV)*

LIVING CREATURES

LIVING CREATURES is a term used in Genesis 1 and 2 to refer to people and animals. *Living creatures* is used again, this time only of animals, when God made a covenant with Noah that he would never again destroy all animal life.

The prophet Ezekiel had a vision involving four living creatures. They had faces resembling those of a man, lion, ox, and eagle. They seem to have been angels.

In the Book of Revelation there are also four living creatures who worship and praise God. One looks like a lion, another an ox, a third a man, and a fourth an eagle. They seem to represent all of nature.

Where to find it

People and animals   *Genesis 1: 20, 24, 30; 2: 7, 19*
Animal life   *Genesis 9: 8-17*
Ezekiel's vision   *Ezekiel 1: 5-22; 3: 13; 10: 5-10*
Living creatures who praise God   *Revelation 4: 6-9*

LOAN (see *Debt*)

LOCUST *(LOW-cust)* is an insect much like a grasshopper. It was very common in Bible lands. Locusts would gather in large groups and travel long distances, eating everything. Locusts were the eighth plague God sent to Egypt before the Israelites were freed. Locusts were also eaten for food. The Old Testament Book of Joel was written after crops in Palestine had been destroyed by locusts.

LOD (see *Lydda*)

LODGE was a temporary dwelling place, usually for travelers, but sometimes for watchmen.

LOG is a piece of wood just as it comes from a tree. The word *log* is also the Hebrew name for a small liquid measure.

LOINS *(loynz)* are the middle part of the body, between the ribs and the hips. People wore wide belts around their loins and fastened swords there when they had to fight battles. So having your loins "girded" meant you were ready for action. Sometimes people wrapped sackcloth around their loins to show they were in mourning because someone had died

or they had sinned. Because the reproductive organs are in the loins, children were said to have come from the "loins" of their parents.

LOIS *(LOW-iss)* was the grandmother of Timothy on his mother's side of the family. She helped rear Timothy in the Christian faith.

Where to find it: *2 Timothy 1: 5*

LONGSUFFERING means having patience and not giving up when trouble comes. It is listed in the King James Version of the Bible as one of the virtues of the Christian and one of the qualities of Christ. The word is translated "patience" in the Revised Standard Version and most newer translations.

LORD in the Bible usually refers to God the Father, or Jesus Christ. However, it is sometimes used for kings, slave owners, or leaders. *Lord* is used for one who has respect, power, and authority. Men who were called lord in ancient times had to be obeyed by those under them. Sometimes any person who deserved respect would be called lord. When the word *lord* is applied to God, it shows that he is the owner and ruler of the whole earth. People who follow him are to obey and respect him.

In the Old Testament some translations print the word in capital letters—LORD—when the word is the special Covenant name (Yahweh) that the Israelites had for God. This word was so sacred to the Israelites that they did not even pronounce it. They substituted another word meaning "lord" or "master." The American Standard Version uses the word *Jehovah* for this special Covenant name for God. In Psalm 97: 5, both words for *lord* appear. You can look up this verse and see how your translation shows the difference between the two words.

Where to find it: *Isaiah 1: 24; Romans 10: 9; 1 Corinthians 6: 11*

LORD OF HOSTS is a special Old Testament name for God. It shows his control over all the angels in heaven as well as his followers on earth. Often the name gives the idea of God and all the forces of righteousness going into battle against evil.

Where to find it: *1 Samuel 1:11; Psalm 24:10; 59:5; 84:1, 3, 12*

LORD'S DAY is the day set aside to honor the Lord Jesus Christ. Because Jesus rose from the dead on the first day of the week (Sunday), many early Christians used that day to worship and remember him. Other things made this day special. After his resurrection, Jesus appeared to his disciples on the first day of the week. The coming of the Holy Spirit at Pentecost was on the first day of the week while early Christians were meeting together to honor Christ. The vision John received before he wrote the Book of Revelation came on the Lord's Day.

Where to find it

Jesus appeared on first day   *Luke 24:13-49; John 20:1-25*
Early Christians met on first day   *Acts 20:7; 1 Corinthians 16:1-2*
John's vision   *Revelation 1:10*

LORD'S PRAYER is the name Christians have given the prayer Jesus taught his disciples. They had asked, "Lord, teach us to pray."

The model prayer Jesus gave them begins, "Our Father who art in heaven." This short, beautiful prayer shows that believers may pray to their heavenly Father, asking him to complete his plans in the world and to meet their needs. This prayer shows how much we must depend on God.

Where to find it: *Matthew 6:9-13; Luke 11:2-4*

LORD'S SUPPER is a celebration when Christians proclaim Jesus' death and resurrection from the dead. It reminds us that all Christians are part of God's family and that we look forward to the time when Christ will fully rule all of the universe.

The Lord's Supper was started at the last Passover feast Jesus ate with his disciples, the night before he was crucified. As they were eating, Jesus took some bread, broke it into pieces, and told his disciples to eat it. "This is my body," he said. Then he gave them some wine and told them to drink it. "This is my blood," he said. Breaking the bread and pouring the wine were pictures of what would happen the next day, when Jesus' body was broken and his blood was shed for all people. Jesus told the disciples they should meet to-

OUR FATHER which art in heaven, Hallowed be thy name.
Thy kingdom come. Thy will be done in earth, as it is in heaven.
Give us this day our daily bread.
And forgive us our debts, as we forgive our debtors.
And lead us not into temptation, but deliver us from evil:
For thine is the kingdom, and the power, and the glory, for ever. Amen.
(Matthew 6:9-13)

Lot and his two daughters barely escaped the fire that destroyed Sodom.

gether often to share such a meal and remember him. He promised he would be present with them in a special way when they did this.

Christians through the centuries have continued to take part in the Lord's Supper. It is a time to remember what Christ has done for us and to renew our promise to obey him.

Where to find it: *Matthew 26: 26-28; Mark 14: 22-24; Luke 22: 17-19; 1 Corinthians 10: 16-17; 11: 23-34*

LOT, Abraham's nephew, went with Abraham from Ur to their new home in Canaan. They and their families and herds traveled a long way together, and they seemed to get along well. But after they reached Canaan, problems arose. Their herdsmen quarreled. Abraham decided that he and Lot must have separate land. Abraham took Lot to a high place and asked him to choose. "If you take the right hand, then I will go to the left," Abraham said.

Selfishly, Lot chose the land that looked better for his cattle. But that selfish decision led to trouble for Lot and his family. His land lay near the wicked cities Sodom and Gomorrah. Lot and his family later moved to Sodom. Lot faced many problems living there, and finally God destroyed the cities for their wickedness. But God spared Lot, leading him and his family away just in time.

Where to find it: *Genesis 11: 31; 13–14*

LOTS were objects—often stones of various colors or with markings on them—that people used to decide something by chance. The nearest things like this today would be drawing straws. Ancient peoples used lots for a variety of purposes: to decide who should get what portion of land, or to try to find out who was guilty of a crime. They also used lots for gambling.

In the Old Testament, lots were used, along with prayer, to help determine God's will in certain matters. For example, lots were used to select the first king of Israel.

When the Roman soldiers cast lots for Jesus' garment, they were adding to his humiliation by gambling for the only thing he owned.

Where to find it

To select a king   *1 Samuel 10: 20-21*
Soldiers cast lots   *Matthew 27: 35*

LOT'S WIFE ran with her husband and daughters from the wicked city of Sodom when God told them he would destroy it. Because their family had been the only righteous people in the city, God wanted to spare their lives. "Flee for your life; do not look back or stop anywhere in the valley," the angels had told them.

But Lot's wife disobeyed the angels' command. As she looked back to watch fire and brimstone fall on the cities of Sodom and Gomorrah, she was destroyed also. Her body turned into a pillar of salt.

Where to find it: *Genesis 19:15-28*

LOVE is what the Christian faith is all about. Love is more than just a feeling of being attracted to someone or of feeling happy with someone—as we do with family, friends, or pets. It means choosing to be kind and helpful to others even though we may not want to. It is doing for other people what we would like to have them do for us.

Love between a husband and wife is a promise to care for each other and do everything possible to help the other person. This love-promise brings tenderness, joy, excitement, and a sense of how good it is to be together. It also helps husbands and wives go through times of trouble together. When this attitude is shared with children, a family becomes a true place of love.

The Bible says God is love and that all real love comes from God. God shows his love for us by caring for us all the time. He also showed it by sending his son, Jesus, to take away our sins. Jesus Christ is the highest example of love, both in his life on earth and in his death for us.

God's power helps us love others. The Bible speaks of "brotherly love," which is being concerned for others who need something we can give. They may be people we have never met. Christ said we are to love even our enemies.

The Christian church is built on God's love for us and on the special love Christians have for each other. Jesus said, "By this all men will know that you are my disciples, if you have love for one another."

Where to find it

How love acts *Matthew 5:43-48; 22:37-39; 1 Corinthians 13; 1 John 3:14*
God is love *John 3:16; 17:26; 1 John 4:8, 16*
Christians love one another *John 13:35; 1 John 2:10-18*

LOVE FEAST was a meal Christians in the early church shared to show their love for each other. Often they ate these meals together before the church members took part in the

Lord's Supper (see *Lord's Supper*).

Where to find it: *1 Corinthians 11:18-22; Jude 12*

LOVINGKINDNESS is an Old Testament word for God's kindness and mercy toward us. It does not change or stop, and it shows how much he loves us.

LUCIUS *(LOO-she-us)* was the name of two New Testament men:

1. A man from Cyrene who was one of the teachers and prophets of the church at Antioch.

2. A Jew in Corinth who sent his greetings to the church at Rome.

Where to find it

Lucius of Cyrene *Acts 13:1*
Lucius in Corinth *Romans 16:21*

LUKE was a well-educated Gentile doctor. He wrote two New Testament books, the Gospel of Luke and the Acts of the Apostles. He traveled with the apostle Paul, who called him the "beloved physician" in Colossians 4:14. His writing style shows he watched for details

and was accurate, traits he may have learned as a doctor.

Scholars believe he may have come from Macedonia (northern Greece). Tradition says he was martyred in Greece.

LUKE, GOSPEL OF, is the third book in the New Testament. It is the story of the life of Jesus written about A.D. 60 by the doctor Luke. Although he was not one of the twelve disciples and probably did not know Jesus while he lived on earth, Luke was a close friend of the apostle Paul and got much information for his Gospel from him. He no doubt also talked to Mary, Jesus' mother, and probably to Mary and Martha of Bethany. He wrote his Gospel for Gentiles, because Luke himself was a Gentile and because Paul was an apostle to the Gentiles. Luke's purpose was to record in an orderly way exactly what Jesus said and did. He was writing for people who had just heard of Jesus.

After a short introduction, Luke records the life of Jesus step by step, beginning before he was born. He tells about the angel's visit to Mary, Mary's answer, and the full story of the birth of Jesus. This is the only Gospel that tells anything about the boyhood of Jesus. Then comes his baptism, his public ministry, and finally his death, resurrection, and ascension.

Throughout the book, Luke shows Jesus' concern for all people: rich and poor, Gentile and Jew. He also points out the many times Jesus prayed—at his baptism, after cleansing the leper, before calling his disciples, on the Mount of Transfiguration, on the cross, and at his death.

LUST is a strong craving or desire, often a strong sexual desire, that is out of control. Jesus said sexual lust was very bad.

Where to find it: *Matthew 5:28*

LYDDA *(LID-uh)* was a village, sometimes called Lod, about 30 miles northwest of Jerusalem. Jews returning after the Babylonian Exile settled there for a while. Peter helped the people in a church there.

Where to find it

Jews settle there after exile   *Ezra 2:33; Nehemiah 7:37*
Peter helps church   *Acts 9:32-38*

LYDIA *(LID-ee-uh)*, a well-to-do businesswoman in Philippi, was Paul's first convert in Europe. She heard about Jesus as she and other women were praying by a river. She believed what Paul told her about Christ. After her whole family and her servants believed and were baptized, she invited Paul and his traveling companions to stay at her home. The church at Philippi met at her house.

Where to find it: *Acts 16:13-15, 40*

LYING is any action or word that is meant to deceive or fool someone else. God is truth, and he expects his people to speak the truth. Satan is the father of lies, and those who tell lies are giving support to Satan. All types of lying are condemned in the Bible, but especially bad is "bearing false witness"—telling something untrue about another person in order to hurt him.

Where to find it

Don't bear false witness   *Exodus 20:16*
Satan, father of lies   *John 8:44*
God is truth   *John 1:17; 14:6; Romans 3:4*

LYSIAS, CLAUDIUS *(LISS-ee-us, CLAW-dee-us)*, was commander of the Roman troops in Jerusalem when the apostle Paul was arrested. He rescued Paul from an angry crowd, then sent him to Caesarea. When he discovered Paul was a Roman citizen, he sent a letter to the Roman governor Felix to make sure Paul got a fair trial.

Where to find it: *Acts 21:31–23:30; 24:22*

LYSTRA *(LISS-truh)* was a Roman colony in the land that is now Turkey. Paul healed a crippled man there, and came back to the city several times on his missionary journeys. Timothy came from Lystra.

Where to find it: *Acts 14:1-11; 16:1*

When God spoke to Moses from a burning bush, he gave him a difficult job: to lead the Israelites out of slavery in Egypt.

MACCABEES *(MAK-uh-beez)*, **REVOLT OF THE,** was a revolution led by Jewish patriots in 168-167 B.C. to make Syria stop persecuting the Jews in Palestine. The revolution brought some freedom for the Jews.

A priest named Mattathias and his sons were the leaders of the revolt. One of the sons, Judas, was called Maccabee (meaning "Hammerer") because of his fighting ability.

21

Later all the men in the revolt were called Maccabees. Judas and his band of Jews camped in the mountains and fought against the Syrians who occupied their country. They also fought against those Jews who sided with the Syrians. The Maccabees tore down pagan altars and asked other Jewish people to join them. Syria sent in its army, and the Maccabees insisted they would "either live nobly or die nobly." They defeated the Syrian army.

After driving away the Syrians, Judas Maccabee worked to restore true worship in Palestine. He cleansed the Temple from pagan worship and began proper sacrifices to the Lord. An eight-day celebration called Hanukkah (see *Hanukkah*) dedicated the Temple to right worship.

Their troubles did not end, but the Jewish people remember the Maccabees as heroes. Their story is told in two books called 1 and 2 Maccabees. These books are a part of the Roman Catholic Bible.

MACEDONIA *(mass-uh-DOE-nee-uh)* was a Roman province in New Testament times. A kingdom in the northern part of modern Greece, it was the first part of Europe to hear about Christ. The apostle Paul visited Macedonia many times. Paul first traveled to Macedonia after he had a vision. "Come over to Macedonia and help us," the man in the vision said. Paul left right away and landed at Philippi, the leading city in Macedonia. There he met Lydia, and when she accepted Christ, the first church in Europe began.

Where to find it: *Acts 16: 9-10*

MACH-PELAH *(mack-PEE-luh)* was a field near Hebron where Sarah, Abraham, Isaac, Rebekah, Leah, and Jacob were all buried. Abraham bought the field after Sarah died because it had a cave that could be used as a tomb.

Where to find it: *Genesis 23; 25: 10; 49: 29-31; 50: 13*

MADNESS (see *Diseases*)

MAGDALENE (see *Mary Magdalene*)

MAGI *(MAY-jie)* is a name used for the wise men from the East who came to Bethlehem to honor the baby Jesus. The wise men followed a star to Bethlehem and brought Jesus expen-

sive gifts. They honored him as a newborn king. *Magi* originally was the name of an ancient Persian religious group who predicted the future and read stars. Later any persons who seemed to have unusual ability or intelligence were called Magi.

Where to find it: *Matthew 2*

MAGIC means to make things happen by using real or make-believe supernatural powers. When the Bible mentions magic, it does *not* mean magicians' tricks. It refers more to what we call the occult. The Old Testament Law forbade magic. Early Christians turned from practicing magic and burned all their books about it.

Where to find it

Old Testament prohibitions *Exodus 22: 18;*
Leviticus 19: 26; 20: 27; Deuteronomy 18: 10-11
New Testament examples *Acts 8: 9; 13: 8; 19: 14*

MAGISTRATES *(MAJ-is-traits)* were the highest government officials in a Roman colony.

Cities often had more than one magistrate—sometimes as many as five. They ran the city and settled disputes in everyday matters. Paul and Silas were brought before the magistrates at Philippi, who put them in prison and then later decided to let them go.

Where to find it: *Acts 16:16-39*

MAGNIFICAT *(mag-NIFF-uh-kat)* was the song of praise Mary sang after the angel told her she would be the mother of the Son of God. It starts out with the beautiful phrase "My soul doth magnify the Lord." The word *magnificat* comes from *magnify*.

Where to find it: *Luke 1:46-55*

MAGOG (see *Gog and Magog*)

MAHANAIM *(MAY-huh-NAY-um)* was the town on the east side of the Jordan River where Jacob met two angels. Later it became a city of refuge and was given to the tribe of the Levites. It was the capital of Israel for a short time after the death of Saul.

Where to find it: *Genesis 32:2; 2 Samuel 2:8*

MAHLON *(MAY-lon)* was Ruth's first husband, an Israelite who married her in Moab and died about ten years later.

Where to find it: *Ruth 1:2, 5; 4:9-10*

MAID, MAIDEN means either a young unmarried woman, or a female servant, or both.

MAINSAIL (see *Ships*)

MALACHI *(MAL-uh-kie)* was the prophet who wrote the last book of the Old Testament. He lived around 450 B.C. and warned against sin and turning from God. He predicted that those who were not true to God would be judged, and he promised blessing for those who repented.

The book asked questions to make the people think about their lives. Malachi criticized priests for being careless in conducting worship. He condemned the people who were not giving God their tithes and were using defective animals for sacrifices. He asked them to return to obeying the Law.

Malachi looked forward to the Messiah, who would be God's "messenger of the Covenant" and would cleanse and purify God's people. "The Lord whom you seek will suddenly come to his temple," Malachi said in 3:1-3. "But who can endure the day of his coming, and who can stand when he appears? For he is like a refiner's fire . . . and he will purify. . . ."

Although Malachi preached about judgment, he reminded the people that the Lord cared for them. The book begins with "I have loved you, says the Lord." And it ends with a promise of the coming Messiah: "But for you who fear my name the sun of righteousness shall rise, with healing in its wings."

MALCHUS *(MAL-cuss)* was the high priest's servant whose ear was cut off by Peter in the Garden of Gethsemane. He had come with the others to arrest Jesus, but Jesus had mercy on him and healed his ear.

Where to find it: *John 18:10*

MALTA (see *Melita*)

MAMMON *(MAM-un)* was the Aramaic word for riches. Jesus said that people could not give themselves to God and also give all their energies to get rich. Mammon, or wealth, was an idol for people in Jesus' day just as in ours.

Where to find it: *Matthew 6:24; Luke 16:11, 13*

MAMRE *(MAM-ree)* was the name for:
1. An Amorite friend of Abraham.
2. A place north of Hebron where Abraham lived and built an altar. It may have been named for his friend Mamre. Close by at Mach-pelah (see also *Mach-pelah*), Abraham buried his wife Sarah and was later buried there himself. Mamre became a sacred place for the Jews because of its association with Abraham.

Where to find it
Abraham's friend   *Genesis 14:13, 24*
Place   *Genesis 13:18; 18:1*

MAN in the Bible is a word that often means all people—men and women. God made man to love and worship him. Genesis 5:2 says, "Male and female he created them, and he blessed them and named them Man when they were created."

Man can also mean a person of the male sex.

All persons—men and women—were created like God with thoughts, feelings, and a will. God made people to be his special friends. This makes people different from animals. Men and women are responsible for taking care of Planet Earth.

People cannot live complete lives by themselves—we need others and we need God. Without God's help, people are proud, selfish, and sinful. But God lets each person make a choice—to stay selfish and die that way, or to accept God's help and live with him.

Where to find it
Man includes males and females   *Genesis 5:1-2*
All are created in God's image and are to care for the earth   *Genesis 1:27-28*
Everyone sins   *Psalm 143:2; Romans 3:23*
Everyone can choose life   *Romans 1:16-17; 6:23; 1 Corinthians 15:45-50*

MAN OF LAWLESSNESS (see *Anti-Christ*)

MAN OF SIN (see *Anti-Christ*)

MAN, SON OF (see *Son of Man*)

MANASSEH *(muh-NASS-uh)* was the name of two men in the Old Testament.

1. Joseph's oldest son, who was born in Egypt. His grandfather Jacob adopted him, and he became head of one of the 12 tribes of Israel.

2. An evil king of Judah. Son of King Hezekiah, he began to rule in 687 B.C. when he was only 12 years old. At first Manasseh was too young to control the people in power, and they started the country worshiping idols. But as he grew up, Manasseh did things even worse. He built altars to Baal and to the sun, moon, stars, and planets. He put a heathen altar inside the Temple. He punished people or prophets who remained true to God. After God allowed him to be captured and taken to Babylon, he repented of his evil work. But it was too late. He had already brought his country, Judah, to its downfall.

Where to find it
Joseph's son   *Genesis 41:51; 48:5, 19*
King of Judah   *2 Kings 21:1-17; 2 Chronicles 33:1-20*

MANASSEH *(muh-NASS-uh)*, **TRIBE OF,** was one of the 12 tribes of Israel that left Egypt for Canaan. The people in the tribe were descendants of Manasseh, Joseph's son who was adopted by Jacob. When they got to Israel, half of the tribe settled east of the Jordan River and half crossed over. Those on the west side were given good land, and they were important among the 12 tribes. Their land stretched from the Jordan River to the Mediterranean Sea through the middle of Canaan. They later became part of the Northern Kingdom of Israel. Those who stayed on the east side became idol worshipers. All of the tribe of Manasseh were later taken away as prisoners to Assyria.

Where to find it: *Joshua 17:7-10*

MANDRAKE (see *Plants*)

MANGER *(MAIN-jur)* is a box built at the right height to feed cattle or horses. It was usually filled with straw, hay, or oats. The most famous manger was the one where the baby Jesus was laid when he was born in Bethlehem.

Where to find it: *Luke 2:7, 12, 16*

MANIFEST *(MAN-uh-fest)* means to show or reveal something. When the Bible says God manifests himself, it means God makes himself known to people.

MANNA *(MAN-uh)* was a food God provided for the Israelites while they wandered in the wilderness. In a miraculous way, manna appeared fresh every night on the ground so the people could gather it in the morning. They could use it in many ways. They could grind it up and make cakes, or they could boil it like cereal. The Bible says it looked like white seeds or flakes and tasted like wafers made with honey.

Where to find it: *Exodus 16: 13-21, 31-36; Numbers 11: 7-9*

MANOAH *(muh-NO-uh)* was Samson's father. He and his wife had wanted a child for a long time. One day an angel appeared to Manoah's wife and told her she would have a son, and she should dedicate him to the Lord as a Nazirite (see *Nazirite*). Manoah asked God to send the angel again so they could ask him what to do with their son. When the angel came, he repeated his instructions. He proved he was an angel by going up toward heaven in the flame of the altar Manoah prepared. The angel's word came true. A son was born, and Manoah and his wife raised him according to the strict Nazirite laws (see *Samson*).

Where to find it: *Judges 13*

MANSION *(MAN-shun)* is the word used by the King James Version in John 14: 2 to mean a place to live. Other translations use the word *room*.

MANSLAYER means a person who has killed someone else, either accidentally or on purpose. The Old Testament said that a manslayer could run to a city of refuge (see *City of Refuge*), where he would be safe until a trial could be held to determine whether he had killed accidentally or on purpose. If the killing was accidental, he could stay in the city of refuge and be safe. If the killing was on purpose, he was to be put to death. In Old Testament times, the relatives of a person who had been killed (accidentally or on purpose) considered it their duty to get revenge, to kill the person who had killed their relative.

Where to find it: *Exodus 21: 12-14; Numbers 35: 6, 9-32*

MANTLE *(MAN-tul)* was usually a loose cloak without sleeves worn like an overcoat. In 2 Kings 2: 8-14 Elijah's mantle was given to Elisha

as a sign that he would become a prophet after Elijah's death.

MARAH *(MAY-ruh)* means "bitter." It was also the name of the first place where the Israelites found water on their journey out of Egypt. After three days of travel, the people were thirsty, but the water was too bitter to drink. God showed Moses a plant that could turn the bitter water into fresh water.

Where to find it: *Exodus 15: 23-26*

MARANATHA *(MAIR-uh-NATH-uh)* means "our Lord comes" in Aramaic. It was an expression of greeting or joy used by the early Christians. Paul used this word in 1 Corinthians 16: 22 as part of his good-bye.

MARCUS *(MAR-cuss)* is the Latin or Roman form of the name *Mark* (see also *Mark, John*).

MARINER is a sailor or seaman (see also *Ships, Sailing*).

MARK is the word used in the King James Version of the Bible for a special sign or for a goal. It may mean a sign or stigma, such as the mark of Cain in Genesis 4: 15. It may mean a seal of ownership, as in Revelation 7: 2-8. It may be the signature for those who can't write, as in Job 31: 35.

Or, it may be a goal, such as the mark Paul set for himself in Philippians 3: 14.

MARK, GOSPEL OF, is the second book of the New Testament. It's the shortest of the Gospels and records Jesus' actions more than his words. John Mark wrote this Gospel in Rome about A.D. 65-70. Many scholars think that Mark wrote down much of the material that the apostle Peter used in his preaching. It was probably the first of the Gospels to be written.

Mark did not write about Jesus' birth or

childhood. The story starts with Jesus as a grown man meeting John the Baptist. This Gospel tells about Jesus' temptation, his work in his home region of Galilee, and his choosing and training his disciples. It describes many of Jesus' miracles and shows that Jesus was a helper of others as well as master of the universe.

But when Jesus' work of healing and teaching was coming to an end, he began to prepare his disciples for the future. Mark wrote what Jesus taught about the troubles that lay ahead. He recorded Jesus' last supper with his disciples, Jesus' arrest in the Garden of Gethsemane, and his death on the cross. Mark ended his Gospel with Jesus' resurrection from the dead. In the last chapter, an angel talks to Mary, Mary Magdalene, and Salome and gives this promise: "Do not be amazed; you seek Jesus of Nazareth, who was crucified. He has risen, he is not here. . . . Go, tell his disciples and Peter that he is going before you to Galilee; there you will see him, as he told you."

The last 12 verses in Mark are often printed in small type at the end of the book. This is because some of the oldest Greek copies we have of this Gospel do not include those verses. Most scholars believe the last 12 verses were added later by someone else.

MARK, JOHN, was the writer of the second Gospel and a friend of Peter. He traveled with Paul and Barnabas on their first missionary journey. John was his Jewish name; Mark or Marcus was his Roman name. In the New Testament, he is called Mark, John Mark, and John.

Mark's mother, Mary, lived in Jerusalem in a large house. She was a Christian, and when Mark was a young man, he met many of the early Christian leaders. Peter referred to him as "my son" in 1 Peter 5:13 because of their close friendship.

Mark started out with Paul and Barnabas on a missionary journey but did not finish it, perhaps because of homesickness or some disagreement with Paul. Mark went along with Barnabas on his next journey and proved himself. Later Paul highly recommended Mark as a good Christian worker. Mark spent some time with Paul in Rome, and it was prob-

ably there he wrote the Gospel that has his name.

Where to find it

MARKETPLACE was the center of town life in Bible times. People bought and sold supplies, met friends, hired workers, and gathered for meetings and discussions. Court cases were often tried in the marketplace. Paul and Silas were brought to the rulers in the marketplace in Philippi and then were attacked by the crowds gathered there.

Paul often preached in marketplaces on his missionary journeys.

Where to find it: *Acts 16:19-23; 17:17*

The Middle East today still has open marketplaces.

MARRIAGE began in the Garden of Eden as a way for human beings to give and receive love and companionship. Genesis 2:24 says, "A man leaves his father and his mother and cleaves to his wife, and they become one flesh."

Marriage also is intended to provide a loving place for children.

The model God gave in Genesis, before people sinned, was for one husband and one wife. In Old Testament times, Hebrew men, like the pagan men around them, often had more than one wife. The Bible never says this is good; it simply tells what the people did. In fact, the Old Testament tells many stories about problems that arose when men had more than one wife.

The Bible gives many instructions about marriage. Husbands and wives are to love each other; submit to each other; enjoy each other; respect each other.

Marriage is sometimes used in the Bible as a picture of God's relationship with his people. In the Old Testament, God is pictured as the husband and the Hebrew people as his wife. Christ "gave himself" for the Church as husbands are to "give themselves" for their wives. Wives are to be subject to their husbands as the Church is subject to Christ.

Where to find it

Beginning of marriage *Genesis 2: 18-24*
Marriage means oneness *1 Corinthians 7: 4*
Marriage a picture of Christ's love *Ephesians 5: 21-33*

MARS' HILL was a little hill in downtown Athens near the temple to the ancient Greek gods. The Greek council met there in New Testament times, and Paul was brought there to explain his message. Paul delivered a famous sermon there, and part of it is found in Acts 17: 16-34.

MARTHA *(MAR-thuh)* was a close friend of Jesus. She and her brother Lazarus and sister Mary lived in Bethany, just two miles outside Jerusalem. Jesus often visited them for meals, and Martha seemed to be the hostess on these occasions. John 11: 5 records that "Jesus loved Martha and her sister and Lazarus," showing how close this family was to him.

But one time Jesus had to scold Martha. Busy in her kitchen, Martha was upset because her sister wasn't helping her prepare the food. Instead, Mary was listening to Jesus teach. Jesus gently reminded Martha that it was better to listen and learn from him. The Kingdom of God is more important than anything else. "Martha, Martha," he said, "you are anxious and troubled about many things; one thing is needful. Mary has chosen the good portion, which shall not be taken away from her."

Later, when Jesus returned to Martha's

home at the death of Lazarus, he talked with her about the meaning of the Resurrection, showing that he knew she was able to understand his teaching, too.

Where to find it: *Luke 10: 38-42; John 11: 1-44*

MARTYR *(MAR-tur)* is a person who is killed or made to suffer greatly because of his beliefs. Stephen was the first Christian martyr. Most of the apostles and many other early Christians were martyred because they would not give up their faith in Christ. The Bible says many more will give their lives for Christ before the time of the final judgment.

Where to find it: *Acts 6: 8–7: 60; 22: 20; Revelation 6: 9-11*

MARVEL *(MAR-vul)* is an amazing, wonderful thing. Jesus' works were seen as marvels by the crowds who followed him.

MARY, MOTHER OF JESUS, was a godly woman. When the angel Gabriel told her she would give birth to God's Son, she asked, "How can this be?" The angel explained that God would work a miracle through her, and the child to be born would not be Joseph's son, but the Son of God. She responded with a beautiful hymn of praise (see *Magnificat*). Shortly after that she married Joseph, a carpenter to whom she was engaged. Mary remembered all the wonderful events surrounding Jesus' birth and probably shared them later with the apostles and the Gospel writers.

When Jesus was 12 years old, Mary and

Joseph were amazed that Jesus taught the teachers in the Temple.

Years later, at a wedding in the village of Cana, she asked Jesus to perform his first miracle.

When Jesus was being crucified, he took special notice of his mother, who had come to be with him at his death. He asked his disciple John to care for her. (Joseph apparently had already died.) Later, Mary seems to have been active in the early church.

Where to find it

Gives birth to Jesus *Matthew 1–2; Luke 1–2*
At Jesus' first miracle *John 2:1-11*
At Jesus' death *John 19:25-27*
Active in early church *Acts 1:14*

MARY MAGDALENE *(MAG-duh-leen)* was a woman from whom Jesus cast out seven demons. She was also the first person to whom

It was very early on Easter morning when Mary Magdalene took her spices to the tomb of Jesus.

Jesus appeared after his resurrection. She was a devoted follower of Jesus. She was called "Magdalene" because she came from the town of Magdala on the Sea of Galilee. Like Jesus, she was a Galilean.

She was one of the women who went to Jesus' tomb early Easter morning. When she saw that the tomb was empty, she ran and met Peter and John, telling them that the body of Jesus was gone.

She later returned to the tomb, where she met Jesus himself. He told her to go tell the other disciples about his resurrection.

Where to find it

Cured by Jesus *Mark 16:9; Luke 8:2*
Follows Jesus' body to the tomb *Matthew 27:56-61*
Learns of the resurrection and meets Jesus *Matthew 28:1-10; John 20:1-18*

MARY OF BETHANY, the sister of Martha and Lazarus, was a close friend of Jesus. Jesus often visited her family home in Bethany, just two miles from Jerusalem. Mary liked to sit with the disciples and listen to Jesus teach. When Martha scolded her for not helping prepare a meal, Jesus said, "Mary has chosen the good portion" (see also *Martha)*. Mary also watched as Jesus brought her dead brother Lazarus back to life.

Another time Mary was so filled with love for Jesus that she poured expensive perfume on his feet. Jesus appreciated her gift and told those around him that this was a sign he was being prepared for burial.

Where to find it

Chooses the best *Luke 10:38-42*
Sees Lazarus alive again *John 11:2-31*
Anoints Jesus *John 12:1-8*

MASON (see *Occupations)*

MASSAH *(MASS-uh)* and **MERIBAH** *(MARE-uh-buh)* were places in the Sinai desert where Moses, at the command of God, struck a rock to bring water.

Where to find it: *Exodus 17:1-7; Deuteronomy 6:16; 9:22; 33:8*

MASTER was a name for Jesus used in the New Testament, especially in the Gospel of Luke. The name showed respect for Jesus as a teacher and guide.

*Jesus ate with Matthew and his friends—
whether the Pharisees liked it or not.*

MATTHEW *(MATH-you)* was a tax collector before he became one of Jesus' disciples. He was also called Levi. He wrote the first book of the New Testament, the Gospel of Matthew. He was well prepared to write a story of Jesus' life, because tax collectors were skilled at writing and keeping records, and because Matthew was with Jesus during all of Jesus' public life.

Matthew met Jesus while he was collecting taxes for King Herod Antipas in Galilee. Tax collectors were very unpopular. They were working for the Roman Empire that loyal Jews hated. Plus, tax collectors were often dishonest, taxing more than they had to and keeping the extra money themselves.

Matthew was busy at his work when Jesus walked up to him and said, "Follow me." Matthew left his business and followed Jesus. Later he had a dinner party at his home for his tax collector friends and Jesus. Outsiders were upset that Jesus associated with such unpopular people. Jesus replied, "Those who are well have no need of a physician, but those who are sick." Matthew never went back to his tax collecting. Instead he followed Jesus.

Where to find it

Jesus calls Matthew *Matthew 9:9; Mark 2:14; Luke 5:27*
Jesus meets Matthew's friends *Matthew 9:10-13; Luke 5:29-32*

MATTHEW *(MATH-you)*, **GOSPEL OF,** is the first book of the New Testament. It is the life story of Jesus written by his apostle Matthew. It was written especially for Jewish readers.

This Gospel often shows that Jesus fulfilled the Old Testament prophecies. "That it might be fulfilled" is a common expression in Matthew. This book shows that Jesus was the King the Jewish people had been looking for.

Matthew traced Jesus' ancestors back to King David, and then back to Abraham, the father of the Hebrew people. Matthew told about the birth of Jesus and the visit of the Eastern kings to honor him.

Matthew included several collections of things Jesus taught. These are placed among the stories of his healings and other good works.

The first group of sayings is about what it means to follow Jesus. This includes the well-known Sermon on the Mount in chapters 5 to 7.

The second group of teachings is in chapter 10. Jesus told the 12 apostles what he expected of them and what they should expect when they went out to preach about Christ and his Kingdom.

The third section of sayings is about the Kingdom of God. It is a series of stories in which Jesus compared his Kingdom to seed that a farmer sows, to a hidden treasure, and to a net thrown into the sea. These stories appear in chapter 13.

Other stories and teachings about what the Kingdom of God means appear throughout the rest of the book. The largest collection is in chapters 24 and 25. Chapters 26—28 tell about the Last Supper, the arrest, the trial, death, and resurrection of Jesus. Matthew's Gospel ends with the Great Commission, given by Jesus just before he was taken to Heaven. "Go therefore and make disciples of all nations, baptizing them in the name of the Father and of the Son and of the Holy Spirit, teaching them to observe all that I have commanded you; and lo, I am with you always, to the close of the age."

MATTHIAS (muh-THIE-us) was chosen to take the place of Judas Iscariot. The 11 apostles first chose two men who met the requirements: Matthias and Joseph Justus. Both men had been with Jesus and the other apostles since the time of Jesus' baptism. Then the apostles prayed, "Lord, who knowest the hearts of all men, show which one of these two thou hast chosen to take the place in this ministry and apostleship." The Lord chose Matthias, and he began the work of an apostle. Matthias is never mentioned again in the New Testament.

Where to find it: Acts 1:15-26

MEAL is grain that has been ground. It is different from flour, because flour is made from the inner kernel only, and meal is made from the whole grain. Wheat was the most popular grain in Bible times, but barley was used more by poor people. Ground grain, or meal, was used for food and for sacrificial offerings (see Offerings).

Women would grind grain at dawn each day. Because ground meal would spoil in the hot climate, only enough was prepared to last that day.

MEAL OFFERING (see Offerings)

MEALS and eating customs varied in Bible times, but generally people ate two meals a day. Workers did not eat breakfast but often took some bread and cheese with them to work. Then one light meal was eaten sometime between 10 o'clock and noon just before a midday rest from the hot sun. Then a large meal was eaten in the evening. This was a time for fellowship and having guests. Banquets and feasts were always held in the evening. At ordinary meals women ate with the men, but only men were invited to banquets.

Meals were made up of three kinds of food: vegetables (including grains), fruits, and animal foods (lamb, calf, and milk products). The poor people, however, rarely ate meat. The main food of the poor was bread, which they ate at every meal. Sometimes honey or oil was mixed in the bread dough.

Knives, forks, or spoons were not used. Dinner was usually one main dish, with everything cooked together in the same pot. People dipped bread into the pot or used their fingers.

In Abraham's time people usually sat on the ground for meals. But in New Testament times people stretched out on the floor or on couches around three sides of a large, low, square table, leaving the fourth side free for serving. Usually guests would recline at a right angle to the table, supporting themselves on their left elbow so their right hands were free for eating.

Giving thanks before meals was expected. Jesus gave thanks before feeding the 5,000. He also gave thanks at the Last Supper.

Where to find it: *Genesis 18:8; Matthew 15:36*

MEAT OFFERING (see *Offerings*)

MEASURES were not as exact in ancient times as they are today. People then were satisfied with round numbers. They often measured things in "handfuls"—the amount one could hold in his hand. On page 32 are some of the measures mentioned in the Bible compared approximately to our measures today.

MEDES *(meeds)* were the people of the land of Media (what is today the northwest part of Iran). A fierce, warlike people, they were important during Old Testament times. They often joined with the Persians to fight the Assyrians and the Egyptians. Israel was sometimes part of their battleground.

Darius the Mede was the first ruler of the Medo-Persian Empire after it defeated Babylon. Daniel worked under Darius for about nine years, and Darius was kind to Daniel.

Where to find it: *Isaiah 13:17; Daniel 5:31; 6:8, 12; 8:20*

MEDIATOR *(MEE-dee-ay-tor)* is any person who settles differences or arguments between people. In the Bible, several people were mediators in disputes. Jonathan was mediator between David and Saul.

But *mediator* is also a special name in the Bible for Jesus, because he brings people together with God. People choose to sin; they are separated from God, who is holy. God cannot allow evil. Yet God loves the people he created and wants to fellowship with them. For this reason Jesus came to earth to bridge the wide gap that sin had put between people and God. He restored the friendship and fellowship of God with his creation. He is our mediator.

Where to find it
Jonathan *1 Samuel 19:4*
Jesus *Hebrews 8:6; 9:15; 1 Timothy 2:5*

MEDICINE (see *Disease*)

MEDIUMS *(MEE-dee-ums)* are persons who claim they can talk with the dead. Some ancient mediums claimed they could hear whispers coming from the ground. Many pagan religions had mediums, but the Old Testament and the New Testament forbade believers from trying to contact dead people through mediums.

Where to find it: *Leviticus 19:31; 20:6, 27; Isaiah 8:19*

MEEKNESS is humbly relying on God. It is the opposite of sinful pride, of rebelling against God and relying on yourself. Meek people understand that God is their Master. They are eager to do what God has in mind for them on earth. Meek people are gentle and considerate with others. Jesus was meek, and he expects his followers to be meek. He said, "The meek shall inherit the earth." The apostle Paul listed meekness as a fruit of the Spirit.

Where to find it
Jesus our example of meekness *Matthew 5:5; 11:29; 2 Corinthians 10:1*
Christians should be meek *Galatians 5:23; Ephesians 4:2; Colossians 3:12; Titus 3:2*

MEGIDDO *(muh-GID-oh)* was a fortresslike city in north central Israel. The Israelites had a hard time conquering this Canaanite city, but after it was theirs, it became a great city during the reign of King Solomon.

Because it was an important city, nations often fought to control it. Its very name began to mean "bloodshed." Ahaziah was killed there by Jehu. Josiah was killed there by the Egyptians, according to 2 Chronicles 35:22.

The word *Armageddon* means "hill of Megido." It refers to the final battle between the forces of good and the forces of evil, whenever that battle may occur.

Where to find it: *2 Kings 9:27; 2 Chronicles 35:22; Revelation 16:16*

MELCHIZEDEK *(mel-KIZZ-ih-dek)* was a priest and king of the city of Salem while Abraham was living in Canaan. His name means "king of righteousness."

❧ HEBREW MEASUREMENTS ❧

HEBREW MEASUREMENTS	U.S. MEASUREMENTS	METRIC MEASUREMENTS
Liquid Measures:		
log	2/3 pint	.313 liter
hin 12 logs	1 gallon	3.8 liters
bath 6 hins	6 gallons	22.7 liters
cor, homer 10 baths	60 gallons	226.8 liters
metretai, firkin	10 gallons	38.37 liters
Dry Measures:		
kab, cab	1.16 quarts	1.28 liters
omer, issaron 1 4/5 cabs	2.09 quarts	2.3 liters
seah 3 1/3 omers	2/3 peck	5.81 liters
ephah 3 seahs	1/2 bushel	17.6 liters
lethech	2 1/2 bushels	88.1 liters
homer, cor 2 lethech	5 bushels	176.2 liters
10 ephahs		
100 omers		
bushel	7 1/2 quarts	8.3 liters
measure	1 quart	1.1 liters
pot	1 pint	.55 liters
Distance Measures:		
finger	3/4 inch	19 millimeters
handbreadth, palm, 4 fingers	3 inches	76 millimeters
span 3 handbreadths	9 inches	.22 meters
cubit 6 handbreadths	18 inches	.44 meters
reed 6 cubits	9 feet	2.64 meters
fathom	6 feet	1.82 meters
stadium, furlong	606 feet	184.7 meters
mile	4860 feet	1.48 kilometers

Area Measures:

acre, yoke—the area oxen could plow in one day (5/8 acre)

When Melchizedek met Abraham, Melchizedek brought food to him and blessed him. Abraham, in turn, gave him one-tenth of what he had.

The Old Testament does not say any more about Melchizedek. But he is mentioned many times in the New Testament Book of Hebrews. There Melchizedek is used as a word picture of Christ. Melchizedek is said to have had "neither beginning nor end" (because the Old Testament doesn't list his parents or children) and is said to have been a great priest because he blessed Abraham and Abraham gave gifts to him. But the writer of Hebrews points out that Christ is even a greater priest "after the order of Melchizedek."

Where to find it: *Genesis 14: 18-20; Hebrews 5: 5-10; 6: 19-20; 7: 1-22*

MELITA *(muh-LEE-tuh)* is the name used in the King James Version for the island now called Malta. It is in the Mediterranean Sea about 60 miles south of Sicily, off the toe of Italy. Paul was shipwrecked on Melita.

Where to find it: *Acts 27: 27–28: 2*

MEMBERS is a word used in the Bible to mean parts of something. Sometimes it means parts of the human body and sometimes it means persons in the church, who are members of the Body of Christ.

Where to find it

Human body *Job 17: 7; James 3: 5*
Church body *1 Corinthians 12: 12-31*

MEMORIAL *(mem-ORE-ee-ul)* makes us remember something or someone. Nearly all the feasts and offerings in the Old Testament are called memorials—acts to help the Israelites remember God and what he has done. The Passover feast was a memorial to the Israelites' escape out of Egypt. The offerings that the Israelites brought helped them remember who God was and what he expected of them.

One of the meanings of the Lord's Supper is that it is a memorial to the death and resurrection of Christ. Christ said we should do it "in remembrance of me" (see *Lord's Supper).

Where to find it

Feasts and offerings were memorials *Exodus 12: 14; 13: 9; Leviticus 2: 9; 23: 24*

The Lord's Supper as memorial *1 Corinthians 11: 23-25*

MENAHEM *(MEN-uh-hem)* was a wicked king of Israel from 745 to 738 B.C. He began his reign by killing the former king. He paid bribes to the king of Assyria in order to keep peace and "did that which was evil in the sight of the Lord."

Where to find it: *2 Kings 15: 13-22*

MENE, MENE, TEKEL, AND PARSIN *(MEE-nee, TEE-kul, PAR-sun)* **(or UPHARSIN)** were mysterious Aramaic words that were suddenly written on the wall of King Belshazzar's banquet hall while he was giving a great feast. The guests were merrily drinking wine from golden cups taken from the Temple in Jerusalem. When they saw the words, they were

shocked. The terrified king called in his wise men to interpret the words, but they could not. Then the queen suggested they bring in Daniel, one of the captives from Israel. She had heard that he could interpret dreams.

Daniel told the king what the words meant:

"God has numbered the days of your kingdom and brought it to an end.

"You have been weighed in the balances and found wanting.

"Your kingdom is divided and given to the Medes and Persians."

That very night King Belshazzar was killed (see *Belshazzar*).

Where to find it: *Daniel 5*

MENORAH (*muh-NOR-uh*) is a seven-candle candlestick used in the Tabernacle, the Temple, and in synagogues. It is still used today by Jews in their homes and worship (see also *Lampstands*). It is one of the symbols of the nation of Israel.

MEPHIBOSHETH (*muh-FIB-uh-sheth*), also called Meribaal, was the crippled son of Jonathan, David's friend. Jonathan was killed in battle when Mephibosheth was five years old. A nurse grabbed the boy and ran from Jerusalem to keep him safe from the fights over who would be the next king. In her rush, she dropped him—and crippled him for life.

After David was settled on the throne, Mephibosheth was brought to him. David remembered his friendship with Jonathan and invited Mephibosheth to live in the palace. Even though he was King Saul's grandson and might have claimed to be king, Mephibosheth

Crippled Mephibosheth got to move to David's palace.

remained loyal to King David. David realized Mephibosheth's loyalty and accepted him as a friend.

Where to find it: *2 Samuel 4:4; 9; 16:1-4; 19:24-30*

MERAB (*MIR-ab*) was the oldest daughter of King Saul. Merab and her sister Michal sang praises to David after he killed Goliath. Saul promised David he could marry Merab if he would fight in the army. Actually, he hoped David would be killed in battle, because he was jealous of David.

But David never did marry Merab. Saul gave her as wife for another man. Saul's plan for David didn't work; he returned safely from battle. So Saul let David marry Michal.

Where to find it: *1 Samuel 18:19-27*

MERARITES (*MEE-ruh-rites*) were the descendants of Levi's youngest son Merari, and they worked in the Temple along with other Levites. As the Israelites traveled in the wilderness, the Merarites were responsible for carrying the wooden bases and pillars of the Tabernacle.

Where to find it: *Numbers 3:17, 33-37; Ezra 8:18-20*

MERCHANT (see *Occupations*)

MERCY means showing more love and kindness to a person than he expects or deserves. Mercy is both feelings and acts of kindness. God shows mercy in his daily care of people, in his forgiveness, and in his gift of life through Jesus Christ. Christians are to follow Jesus' example and be merciful. Those who show mercy will receive mercy.

Where to find it: *Matthew 5:7*

MERCY SEAT was a beautiful slab of gold on top of the ark of the Covenant. On it stood the two golden cherubim. The ark sat inside the Holy of Holies in the Tabernacle and Temple. On the annual Day of Atonement, the mercy seat was sprinkled with the blood of the sacrifice to wipe away the sins of the high priest and the sins of all the Israelites (see also *Tabernacle* and *Temple*).

Where to find it: *Exodus 25:17-22; 26:34; 37:6-9; Leviticus 16:2, 13-15*

MERIBAH (see *Massah and Meribah*)

MEROM *(MEE-rum)*, **WATERS OF,** was a small lake north of the Sea of Galilee. Today the lake has been drained and is some of the best farmland in modern Israel.

Where to find it: *Joshua 11: 5, 7*

MESHA *(MEE-shuh)* was a king of Moab who tried to rebel against Israel. Moab had been under Israel's control since the days of King David. The Moabites did not like paying taxes to Israel, so they tried to fight.

Mesha's side of the story was carved on a stone found east of the Dead Sea in 1868 by archaeologists. Mesha wrote about his victories against the Israelites. But later Israel, Judah, and Edom destroyed his land. And during the last battle, Mesha sacrificed his oldest son (see also *Moab*).

Where to find it: *2 Kings 3: 4-27*

MESOPOTAMIA *(mess-uh-po-TAME-ee-uh)* was the land about where Iraq is today. Babylon, an important nation in the Old Testament, was located in central Mesopotamia. The city-state of Ur, where Abraham first lived, was in southern Mesopotamia. Fierce Assyria covered the northern part. The area of Mesopotamia, sometimes called Aram, had a great influence on Old Testament people because of both trade and wars. Many Jews were carried there during their captivity. Part of the Old Testament was written in Babylon (see *Babylonia* and *Assyria*).

MESSENGER *(MESS-un-jer)* is someone with a message. In the Bible both humans and angels were messengers from God. Prophets were sometimes called messengers. Apostles were often messengers, because they were sent to tell God's message about Christ.

Where to find it: *2 Chronicles 36: 15-16; 2 Corinthians 8: 23*

MESSIAH *(muh-SIE-uh)* is the Hebrew word for "anointed one." It applies in a special way to Jesus. Old Testament priests, prophets, and kings were all anointed with oil in a ceremony dedicating them and their work to God. Even the bowls and other parts of the Tabernacle were anointed to set them apart for God's purposes.

God revealed that he would send a Mes-

siah, an "anointed one," to bring peace and to establish his Kingdom. The Jewish people looked forward to the day when this Messiah would come and deliver them.

But many Jewish people misunderstood the Messiah's work. They expected a political leader who would help them defeat their Gentile rulers. Instead, God was sending a spiritual Savior who would give meaning to life on earth and through all eternity. The Messiah was a suffering servant who would bring more than earthly blessing.

The disciples realized that Jesus Christ was the Messiah, God's special anointed one, who would fulfill God's purpose. When Andrew told his brother Peter about Jesus, he said, "We have found the Messiah."

When Jesus first began to teach and preach, he showed the people in his hometown that he was the Messiah. He went to the synagogue and read a passage about the anointed one from Isaiah 61: 1-2. Then he said, "Today this scripture has been fulfilled in your hearing."

"I am the Messiah," Jesus told a woman at a well.

Even though Jesus was careful not to give people the wrong idea that he would help overthrow the Roman government, they kept thinking he would. When he died on the cross, they could not understand what was happening. Only after Jesus rose from the dead, and after the Holy Spirit came at Pentecost, did the disciples begin to understand that Jesus was a spiritual Messiah.

Christ is the Greek word for Messiah. Whenever the New Testament refers to Jesus as Christ, it is saying that he is the Messiah.

Where to find it

The suffering servant *Isaiah 53*
Andrew's discovery *John 1:41*
Announcement at Nazareth *Luke 4:16-21*

METHUSELAH *(muh-THOO-zuh-luh)* lived longer than anyone else in the Bible. He died at age 969, just before God sent the Flood to cover the earth. Noah was his grandson.

Where to find it: *Genesis 5:21-27*

MICAH *(MY-cuh)*, **BOOK OF,** is an Old Testament book written by the prophet Micah just before the Northern Kingdom was conquered in 722 B.C. In his book, Micah preached against the sins of the people. But he also told how God would some day bless his people.

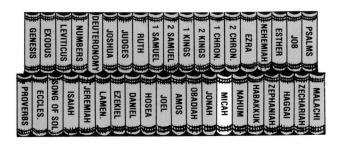

Micah said that God was angry with the people for worshiping idols, taking advantage of the poor, and refusing to obey God. He said both the Northern Kingdom (Samaria) and the Southern Kingdom (Jerusalem) would fall before their enemies.

Against this gloomy background, Micah told about God's plan for the world. The Messiah would come to fulfill God's plan. Micah 5:2 says Bethlehem would be the place where the ruler of Israel would be born. Micah reminded everyone that although God sees the sins of his people, he loves and forgives those who repent. Micah 7:18 declares, "Who is a God like thee, pardoning iniquity and passing over transgression? . . . He does not retain his anger for ever because he delights in steadfast love."

MICAH, THE EPHRAIMITE *(MY-cuh the EE-from-ite)*, was involved in a strange Old Testament story. He stole some money from his mother, then returned it to her, and she said she had decided to use it for God to make an image for her son! So Micah used the silver to make an image and set it up as an idol in his house. Then he made one of his sons priest for the idol.

A traveling Levite came to visit, and Micah asked him to be his special priest. He said, "Now I know that the Lord will prosper me, because I have a Levite as priest."

Later some Israelites came from the tribe of Dan, stole Micah's image, and asked the Levite to be their priest instead. Micah tried to fight for his image, but he did not have enough men.

The writer of Judges described all this by saying, "Every man did what was right in his own eyes."

Where to find it: *Judges 17*

MICAIAH *(muh-KAY-yuh)* was a true prophet of God during the reign of wicked King Ahab of Israel. Ahab had gathered many prophets to advise him and King Jehoshaphat of Judah about their battle plans. All the other prophets said that the kings should go to battle—they would win. But Micaiah said they would be defeated. "I see all Israel scattered upon the mountains, as sheep that have no shepherd," he said.

The king was furious. "Put this fellow in prison, and feed him with bread and water until I come back in peace," Ahab commanded.

But King Ahab did not come back in peace—he was killed in battle. The prophet of God, Micaiah, had prophesied the truth.

Where to find it: *1 Kings 22:8-28; 2 Chronicles 18:7-27*

MICHAEL *(MY-kul)* is an archangel whose name means "Who is like God?" Michael is most concerned with caring for God's people, the Jews. He fights against the wicked, even Satan himself.

Where to find it: *Daniel 10:10-21; Jude 1:9; Revelation 12:7*

MICHAL *(MY-kul)* was King Saul's second daughter. She became David's first wife. After David killed Goliath, Saul became jealous of David's popularity. When Saul learned that Michal loved David, he thought he had a way to get rid of David. He said that if David would kill 100 Philistines in battle, he could marry Michal. He hoped David would be killed. But instead, David killed 200 Philistines, and Saul had to let Michal marry David.

Saul was still jealous and tried to kill David again. When Saul sent men to kill David, Michal helped him escape by putting a dummy into his bed. After David ran away, Saul arranged for Michal to marry another man, Paltiel.

After David's victory against Saul, Michal was returned to David. But all did not go well. Michal disapproved of the way David danced when the ark of the Covenant was returned to Jerusalem. Michal had no children.

Where to find it

David wins Michal *1 Samuel 18:20-27*
Michal helps David escape *1 Samuel 19:11-17*
Their relationship broken *2 Samuel 6:16-23*

MICHMASH *(MICK-mash)*, sometimes spelled Michmas, was a city on a high hill about eight miles northeast of Jerusalem. It controlled an important pass between the Jordan valley and western Israel. In this pass, during a battle between Israel and the Philistines, Saul's son Jonathan led the Israelites to victory.

Where to find it: *1 Samuel 13–14*

MIDIAN *(MID-ee-un)* was the son of Abraham and his second wife, Keturah. The Midianites, his descendants, were wealthy nomads who lived east of the Jordan River and down into the Sinai Peninsula. Moses married a Midianite, Zipporah.

When the Israelites were in the wilderness after they left Egypt, the Midianites seemed friendly to them. Many years later they became enemies. Two hundred years after Israel settled in the Promised Land, the Midianites gained rule over them for a few years. They made life miserable for the Israelites, raiding their villages and trampling down their crops. God chose Gideon to drive the Midianites out.

Where to find it

Moses and the Midianites *Exodus 2:15-21; 18:1-11*
Gideon and the Midianites *Judges 6–7*

MIDWIFE is a woman who helps during childbirth. When a baby was born in ancient times, there usually wasn't a doctor, but there was nearly always a midwife.

MILE (see *Measure*)

MILETUS *(my-LEE-tus)* was a Greek city in what is now called Turkey. It was on the east coast of the Aegean Sea. It was a stopping place for the apostle Paul on his journeys.

Where to find it: *Acts 20:15-17*

MILK is mentioned in the Bible as food and also as a word picture for abundance. Fresh milk was not usually drunk but was used to make cheese and yogurt. Canaan was described as a land "flowing with milk and honey," meaning that it had rich soil and enough rain to grow good crops.

MILLS and **MILLSTONES** were used to grind grain into meal or flour. Two round, heavy stones rotated against each other as people (usually women) turned them with a handle. Some mills were so big that oxen were used to turn them. The sound of the mill grinding in

When the Philistines finally captured Samson, they blinded him and made him push a millstone.

the morning was the sign of prosperity, according to Jeremiah 25:10.

MILLENNIUM *(muh-LEN-ee-um)* means 1,000 years. The word *millennium* does not appear in the Bible, but *a thousand years* is found six times in Revelation 20:1-7. The phrase *a thousand years* probably means a long period of time rather than exactly 1,000 years. Revelation says that during this period Satan will not be able to deceive people. Christ will rule,

MILLET

and the people who have been martyred for Christ will receive special honor. Christ's reign will be one of righteousness and liberty.

MILLET (see *Plants*)

MIND, to ancient people, was not simply another word for *brain*. Translators often use the word *mind* to mean the center of the whole person.

Bible writers often used *heart* to refer to the center of thinking and deciding (see *Heart*).

MINES (see *Occupations*)

MINISTER *(MIN-uh-stir)* means "to serve." It also refers to a person who serves. Today it usually means a person whose life is dedicated to service for God and who earns his living in this service. The apostle Paul said that those who are called by God to spend their lives proclaiming the gospel should earn their living that way.

Paul wrote to Timothy that he had been appointed by God for this kind of service. Several places in the New Testament mention the "laying on of hands" for those who have received this special calling of God (see *Hands, Laying on of*).

Where to find it

Ministers and their living *1 Corinthians 9:14*
Paul, a minister *1 Timothy 1:12; 2 Timothy 1:11*
Laying on of hands *Acts 13:3; 2 Timothy 1:6-8*

MINISTRY *(MIN-uh-stree)* usually refers to the work of serving God. Christ had a ministry; so did the apostles.

In the New Testament *ministry* did not necessarily mean serving God as a paying job, but it could mean that (see also *Minister*).

Where to find it

Christ's ministry *Hebrews 8:6*
The apostles' ministry *Acts 1:25*

MIRACLE is a wonderful happening done by the power of God. Miracles may be beyond the known laws of nature, but they are not magic. Miracles depend on God's will and his power, not on any magic formula. The one who works the miracle does so through God's power. Miraculous displays of God's power are found throughout the Old Testament, especially during the times of Moses, of Elijah

When a wedding feast ran out of wine, Jesus miraculously made some more—out of water.

and Elisha, and of Daniel.

The greatest miracles in all of history came during the lifetime of Jesus Christ. Jesus spoke a great deal about the reign of God. The miracles Jesus worked were samples of what it will be like when God's reign in the world is complete and all evil and sin are destroyed.

The apostle John said that Jesus did many miracles that are not told in the New Testament, but that "these are written that you may believe that Jesus is the Christ, the Son of God, and that believing you may have life in his name" (John 20:31).

MIRIAM *(MEER-ee-um)* was an Old Testament prophet and poet. She was the sister of Moses and Aaron. As a young girl she looked after the baby Moses when he was hidden in a basket in the Nile River to keep him safe from the Egyptians (see *Moses*). When an Egyptian

Miriam's mother made a basket for baby Moses—and it saved his life.

princess found Moses, Miriam offered to find a nurse for the baby. The nurse was Moses' mother, so even though Moses belonged to the princess, his mother raised him as a Hebrew.

As an adult, Miriam joined Moses and Aaron on the Exodus of the Israelites from Egypt. After escaping from the Egyptians in the miraculous crossing of the Red Sea, Miriam composed a song of praise to the Lord and led the other women in celebrating the victory.

From the beginning of the Exodus, Miriam was respected as a prophet. Later prophets identified her as a leader of the Hebrews. But Miriam and her brother Aaron criticized Moses for choosing a wife they didn't think was suitable. For this unwise criticism Miriam was cursed with leprosy. But Moses prayed for her, and God said Miriam would have to stay outside the camp for seven days. The whole march was delayed because of her illness. Then the Lord healed her. When she died, she was buried at Kadesh.

Where to find it

Protects Moses   *Exodus 2:4, 7-8*
Praises the Lord   *Exodus 15:20-21*
Is rebuked   *Numbers 12:1-15*

Dies   *Numbers 20:1*
Later mention   *Micah 6:4*

MIRROR in Bible times was not glass but a polished brass surface. Mirrors were usually round with wooden or ivory handles. Only wealthy people could afford them during Old Testament times, but by New Testament times they were more common. They did not show as clear a reflection as glass mirrors. When Paul writes in 1 Corinthians 13:12 about seeing "darkly" in a mirror, he means the image was dark and indistinct.

MISSIONARY JOURNEYS were travels of Paul and other early disciples to spread the gospel throughout Greece and Asia Minor (now Turkey). Paul made three missionary journeys. On the first he went through the island of Cyprus and then to the southern coast and inland plateau of Asia Minor. On the way he began churches; on the way back to Jerusalem he visited the churches he had started, to encourage and help them.

On Paul's second trip, he went to Greece—Athens and Corinth—by way of Macedonia (today's northern Greece). He stayed in Corinth a year and a half before returning to Jerusalem and Antioch.

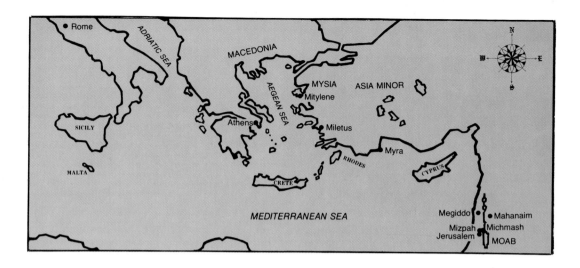

On his third journey, he visited most of the same churches again and collected money to help poor Christians at Jerusalem.

Where to find it

Paul's first missionary journey *Acts 13–14*
Paul's second missionary journey *Acts 15: 36–18: 22*
Paul's third missionary journey *Acts 18: 23–21: 16*

MITE (see *Money*)

MITYLENE (*mit-uh-LEE-nay*), also spelled *Mytilene,* was the chief city on the Greek island of Lesbos in the Aegean Sea. Paul visited this center of culture and poetry on his third missionary journey.

Where to find it: *Acts 20: 14*

MIXED MULTITUDE means people from different nations. A "mixed multitude" (not Israelites) came with the Hebrews when they left Egypt. Later they began to complain about the hard life in the wilderness.

Where to find it: *Exodus 12: 38; Numbers 11: 4-6*

MIZPAH (*MIZ-puh*), sometimes spelled *Mispeh,* was the name of several towns mentioned in the Old Testament. The most important Mizpah, in the land of Benjamin, was often visited by Samuel. Once, when the Israelites had come together with Samuel at Mizpah to worship God, the Philistines suddenly attacked them. God sent a severe thunderstorm that confused the attackers, and the Israelites were able to chase them away.

Hundreds of years later, Mizpah became the ruling city of Judah after the Babylonians conquered the land. Jeremiah moved to Mizpah when Nebuchadnezzar forced many Jews to Babylon. Archaeologists differ about the site of this Mizpah, but many think it was eight miles north of Jerusalem.

Where to find it

Samuel judges at Mizpah *1 Samuel 7: 5-17*
Judah ruled from Mizpah *2 Kings 25: 22-25; Jeremiah 40: 13–41: 18*
Jeremiah lives at Mizpah *Jeremiah 40: 6*

MNASON (*NAY-sun*) was a rich Christian from Cyprus with whom Paul stayed on his last visit to Jerusalem. He had been a Christian from the early days of the church.

Where to find it: *Acts 21: 16*

MOAB (*MOE-ab*) was the nation that descended from Lot's grandson Moab. These people lived east of the southern part of the Dead Sea, and they were constant enemies of the Israelites. When the Israelites were leaving Egypt for the Promised Land, the Moabites refused to let them pass peacefully through their land. Although they couldn't conquer Israel, they did make trouble. They sent young Moabite women into the Israelites' camp to tempt the men into worshiping idols. God was angry and sent a plague upon Israel as punishment.

Moses died on Mount Pisgah in Moab. Joshua was chosen on the nearby plains to be Israel's next leader.

Almost a hundred years later, the Moabites joined the Ammonites and the Amalekites and ruled over Israel for 18 years. Finally Ehud, a man from the tribe of Benjamin, killed the

40

Moabite king, and the Moabite army went home.

Some events in the Book of Ruth took place in Moab, and Ruth herself was a Moabite. This story took place in a time of peace between Israel and Moab.

But trouble began again around 850 B.C. King Ahab had demanded heavy tribute (a kind of tax) from Mesha, the king of Moab. Mesha rebelled, and Kings Jehoram of the Northern Kingdom and Jehoshaphat of Judah defeated Moab and ruined the land (see also *Mesha*). Moab never again became a strong nation.

Where to find it

Moab causes trouble for wandering Israelites
Judges 11:17-18; Numbers 22:1–25:9
Moab rules Israel until king is killed *Judges 3:12-25*
Moab rebels and is defeated *2 Kings 3:4-27*

MOLECH *(MOE-leck),* **MOLOCH** *(MOE-lock)* was an ugly heathen god to whom people were sometimes sacrificed. He was worshiped by the Ammonites before Israel came to Canaan. Sometimes heathen people killed their own children and placed the bodies in the arms of the idol. Moses told the Hebrews they were to have nothing to do with this horrible god.

Some Israelites still worshiped Molech. King Solomon tried to please some of his heathen wives by building a place for Molech worship. Later some Jews tried to worship both the true God and Molech. This greatly displeased God, and was one of the reasons God allowed Israel to be overcome by its enemies.

Where to find it: *Leviticus 18:21; 20:1-5; Psalm 106:35-42*

MOLTEN IMAGE (see *Graven Image*)

MONEY in very early times was pieces of metal, often in the shape of jewelry, especially bracelets. The owner could trade a piece of metal or a whole bracelet for the goods he needed. Perfumes and ointment were also used for trade.

The first coin mentioned in the Old Testament, the shekel, means "weight." The value of the metal money depended on how much it weighed.

About 700 B.C. coins with some imprint or stamp began to be used. The Hebrews at first used the coins of the Assyrians or Babylonians, but later they made their own coins of metal stamped with an official seal.

Some of the coins most often mentioned in the New Testament are:

Denarius was a Roman coin made of silver. It was about the size of our dime. It was worth a day's wages of a poor worker. Some translations use *penny* or *pence* for this coin, but it was worth much more than our modern penny. A denarius often had the picture of the Roman emperor stamped on it. In Matthew 22:15-22, Jesus said that by looking at the coin anyone could see that it belonged to Caesar.

Drachma was a Greek coin worth about the same as a denarius (see above). A drachma was usually stamped with a picture of a Greek god, animal, or other object. The drachma is the coin mentioned in Luke 15:8.

Farthing was a Greek coin of little value. It was worth two mites (see below). Some translations use *penny* for farthing. A farthing is mentioned in Matthew 10:29 and Luke 12:6.

Mite was the Jewish coin of least value. It was made of copper. Two mites were worth one farthing or one penny. This was the coin the woman placed in the Temple offering in Mark 12:42 and Luke 21:1-4.

Pound was equal to about 50 shekels, or the wages of a poor man for 50 days. When Jesus told a parable about a man giving his servants one, five, and ten pounds to invest, he was speaking of large sums of money (Luke 19:11-26).

Pence, Penny refers to the Roman denarius, worth about a day's pay for a poor working man (see *Denarius*).

The two sides of a shekel coined about 140 B.C.

Shekel was a Jewish coin about the size of a nickel. A picture of a pot of manna was imprinted on one side and the picture of a flowering rod on the other side. A shekel was worth about the same as a Roman denarius—the wages of a poor working man for one day.

Talent was worth 3,000 shekels—the wages of a working man for almost ten years. When Jesus talked about talents in his parables, he was speaking of huge sums of money (Matthew 18:23-35; 25:14-30).

MONEY CHANGER, a man who sat at a table in the Temple court during New Testament times, was like a banker in some ways. He exchanged foreign coins for the Jewish coins the priests demanded in Temple worship.

Often money changers made a large profit, because they were not afraid to cheat. Jesus said they had made the Temple a den of thieves, and he chased them out after his triumphal entry into Jerusalem.

Where to find it: *Matthew 21:12; Mark 11:15*

MOON was one of the earliest ways of measuring time. A month was measured by time from full moon to full moon. Some heathen people worshiped the moon, but Hebrews were told not to worship the sun, moon, or stars (see also *Stars*).

Where to find it: *Deuteronomy 4:19*

MORDECAI *(MOR-duh-kie)* was a Jewish hero of the Book of Esther. He was a cousin and adviser to Queen Esther. Mordecai and Esther lived in Susa, the Persian capital, about 486-465 B.C. After Esther became the king's wife,

Mordecai saved the king's life by warning him of a plot against him.

Haman, the king's chief minister, became furious with Mordecai for not bowing to him as he rode through the streets. Haman devised a plan that the king approved to have all the Jews killed, and he built a gallows especially for Mordecai. Neither Haman nor the king knew that Queen Esther was Jewish. Mordecai went into mourning for his people, wailing and wearing sackcloth and ashes. He told Esther she should reveal to the king that she was Jewish and try to get the king to give some protection to her people. When Esther told the king what Haman's plot was, Haman was hanged on his own gallows. Mordecai then replaced Haman as chief minister to the king.

Where to find it: *Esther 2–10*

MORIAH *(muh-RIE-uh)* was the place where God said Abraham should offer Isaac as a sacrifice. Isaac was spared, however, when God provided an animal for the sacrifice. The exact location is not known, but many people believe this is the same Mount Moriah on which Solomon built his Temple—a rocklike hill in the center of today's Jerusalem.

Where to find it: *Genesis 22:2; 2 Chronicles 3:1*

MORNING STAR is the planet Venus. It is the sign of dawn. The apostle Peter compared the morning star to the signs pointing to Jesus as the coming Messiah (see *Stars*).

Where to find it: *Job 38:7; 2 Peter 1:19*

MORTAL *(MOR-tul)* is having to face death someday. All people and animals have mortal bodies. But God is immortal; he lives forever and will never die.

MORTAL SIN is sin that leads to the death of the soul. It is an especially harmful sin, done knowingly, that leads to eternal separation from God. John does not say exactly what mortal sin is. He may have meant denying that Jesus Christ is God's Son.

Where to find it: *1 John 5:16-17*

MORTAR *(MOR-tur)* has two meanings.
1. A bowl made of stone or lava-rock. In this

bowl, grain or spices are pounded with a hard tool called a pestle. The manna God sent in the wilderness was ground this way.

2. A substance used to bind bricks or stones together in building. Mud or clay was the mortar in ordinary homes; a sand and lime mixture was used in more expensive houses.

MOSES *(MOE-zus)* is the man most often mentioned in the Old Testament. He was the leader of the Hebrews in their escape from Egypt. He was also the man who received the Ten Commandments and the Old Testament Law from God. He is considered the founder of the Jewish religion.

Moses was the son of Hebrew slaves in Egypt. Just after he was born, the Pharaoh ordered that all male Hebrew babies were to be killed. Moses' mother made a waterproof basket, placed her baby son in it, and hid it in the rushes near the shore of the Nile River. She told her daughter, Miriam, to watch it (see *Miriam*). The basket and baby were found by an Egyptian princess, who adopted Moses. She hired Moses' mother to take care of him while he was young. In this way, Moses grew up understanding the beliefs and customs of both the Hebrews and the Egyptians.

When Moses was 40 years old, he had to flee from Egypt because he killed an Egyptian while trying to defend an Israelite slave. Moses lived in the wilderness for another 40

years. Then God spoke to him from a bush that looked like it was on fire but never burned up. God told Moses that he was to lead the Israelites out of their slavery in Egypt to a Promised Land that God would give them.

Moses said he could not lead because he was not a good speaker. But God told him his brother Aaron would be his helper and do the speaking. It took ten terrible plagues sent by God on Egypt before the Pharaoh said the Israelites could leave. Even then he changed his mind and sent his army to bring them back. God defeated the Pharaoh by opening the Red Sea for the Israelites to go through safely, then closing it on the Egyptian army that tried to follow them. So the Israelites escaped.

During their 40 years in the wilderness, God guided the people with a cloud during the day and a pillar of fire at night. But the people constantly grumbled and complained that Moses had led them out of Egypt to die in the desert. Many times Moses was discouraged. Sometimes he disobeyed God. But he was still a great leader. He had to organize a mass of people, settle their arguments, answer their complaints, and try to teach them how to worship God. God gave Moses instructions about building a Tabernacle as a place of worship. He gave Moses laws so the people would know how to live.

Moses and all the adults who left Egypt were not permitted to enter the Promised Land because of their earlier sins of doubting and disobeying God.

Just before Moses turned over the leadership of the nation to Joshua, Moses gave a great speech. He reminded the Israelites of how God had led them through their years in the wilderness and how they had often failed to obey God. He reminded them of the Ten Commandments and other instructions God had given them. He emphasized that God expected love and obedience from them—not grumblings and complainings. He told them how important it was to keep God's Law and to teach it to their children. Most of the Book of Deuteronomy is a record of Moses' final speech (or speeches).

Moses died at age 120 and was buried in the land of Moab. Moses is often mentioned in the New Testament as the giver of the Law that Christ came to fulfill.

Where to find it

Childhood and early life *Exodus 2: 1-10*
The burning bush *Exodus 3: 2–4: 17*
Leads Israelites out of Egypt *Exodus 12*
Farewell speeches *Deuteronomy 1–33*
Death *Deuteronomy 34*

MOST HOLY PLACE (see *Temple* and *Holy of Holies*)

MOTE is a speck of straw, chaff, or wood tiny enough to get into the eye.

Where to find it: *Matthew 7: 3-5; Luke 6: 41-42*

MOUNT OF OLIVES (see *Olives, Mount of*)

MOUNT SINAI (see *Sinai, Mount*)

MOUNT TABOR (see *(Tabor, Mount*)

MOURNING (*MORN-ing*) is showing sadness or sorrow, usually at a person's death.

When people in Bible times learned of a death or other tragedy, they often tore their clothes. Sometimes mourners sprinkled dust or ashes on their heads. People often wore clothing made of coarse material (such as goat hair) as a sign of mourning. Another mourning custom was to cover your head with a heavy veil.

When people wanted to show they were sorry for their sins, they often showed it in these same ways.

After a person died, friends and relatives would mourn for a week or longer. They would cry loudly around the body. Sometimes extra mourners would be hired to help the family express grief. Musicians might play mournful music (especially on the flute) to show the family's sadness even more. Some of these customs are seen in the story of the death of Jairus's daughter.

Where to find it

Dust on the head *Joshua 7: 6*
Torn clothes *2 Samuel 1: 2*
Coarse clothing *Isaiah 22: 12*
Heavy veil *Jeremiah 14: 3*
Crying and wailing *Luke 8: 52-53*

MULBERRY (see *Plants*)

MULE (see *Animals*)

MURDER means to kill someone on purpose. It is a horrible sin, and God says in the Sixth Commandment, "Thou shalt not kill." The Living Bible properly translates this, "You must not murder."

Murder is not the same as manslaughter. Manslaughter means to kill someone accidentally. In the Old Testament a person accused of killing someone could flee to a City of Refuge. If he could prove he had not killed on purpose, or that he had not killed anyone at all, he was protected there from revenge. A person accused of murder could not be found guilty unless two witnesses had seen him do it. If a person were found guilty, he would be put to death (see also *City of Refuge*).

Where to find it

Sixth Commandment *Exodus 20:13*
Two witnesses needed *Numbers 35:30-31;
Deuteronomy 17:6-7*

MURMUR means constant complaining or grumbling. Murmuring is often spoken so low and so unhappily that the words are hard to understand.

MUSIC was an important part of life in Bible times, from birth to death. People used music to celebrate and to mourn, to praise God and to praise their heroes. Music made everyday work more pleasant.

Music was important in the worship of the Hebrews. The Temple had an orchestra. The Levites were the Temple singers and musicians. They often used singers and instruments together. Some parts of the Bible were meant to be sung. The Psalms are the best known songs, but other songs are found throughout the Old and New Testaments.

Many of the introductions to the psalms give instructions about how they are to be sung. Psalm 61 and several others use a Hebrew word that means "with stringed instruments." Psalm 5 says, "for the flutes." We aren't sure of the meaning of some of the words. *Alamoth,* in the introduction to Psalm 46, means "maidens." It probably meant that it was to be sung by women's voices only. Many psalms tell which melodies should be used. Psalm 22 says the tune should be "The Hind of the Dawn." Psalm 45 is supposed to be sung to "Lilies." These tunes, of course, were not written down, so we have no way of knowing what they were.

MUSICAL INSTRUMENTS were important in Bible times. Here are some of the most common ones:

Bells were small jingles attached to the hem of the high priest's garments. When he moved, they rang to call attention to the sacred work the high priest was doing.

Clarinet, called a flute in some translations, was something like today's clarinet but much simpler. It was used at weddings, banquets, and funerals. Matthew 9:23 shows that it was played along with the wailing of mourners at a funeral.

Cymbals, used only in religious ceremonies, were similar to today's cymbals. Psalm 150 talks about "loud cymbals" and "high-sounding cymbals." The loud cymbals were larger, played with both hands. The smaller high-sounding cymbals were played with one hand by attaching them to the thumb and middle finger.

Flute was an instrument with a shrill sound, made of a hollow reed, bone, or piece of wood. It was not considered proper for use in religious services.

45

Gong, made of brass, was used at weddings and other happy times. Paul refers to its loud noise in 1 Corinthians 13:1.

Harp was made of wood with 12 strings. The musician picked the strings with his fingers. The harp was one of the most important instruments in the Temple orchestra.

Lyre *(LIE-ur)* was a square or triangle-shaped instrument. Like the harp, it was made of wood, but it usually had 10 strings instead of 12 and was plucked with a small pick instead of the fingers. The lyre was smaller in size and higher in pitch than the harp. It made a sweet, soft sound. It was one of the Temple orchestra instruments. David played a lyre to soothe Saul in 1 Samuel 16:23.

Oboe was a double reed instrument similar to the modern oboe. It had two pipes, which could be blown separately or together. It was used for Passover festivals and other special ceremonies.

Organ was a skin-covered box with ten holes. Air was forced through to make the sound, which was regulated by the holes. It made a loud sound and was used in the Temple to call priests and Levites to their duties.

Pipe was a shepherd's pipe or flute that was played to express wild joy or great sorrow. It was not used in the Temple orchestra, but the psalmist encouraged its use in worship in Psalm 150:4.

Psaltery was another stringed instrument, but it was different from both the harp and the lyre. The psaltery had ten strings and was similar to today's zither. It was often played with the harp and lyre.

Shofar, a curved ram's horn, is still used in Jewish worship today. Shofars were part of the Temple orchestra, and a shofar was blown by the priests as a signal in religious ceremonies. It is still used that way today: to announce events such as the Jewish New Year and the beginning of each Sabbath. The Israelites blew shofar horns as the walls of Jericho fell down.

Tambourine, or *tof,* was a small drum made from a wooden hoop and animal skins. (There were no bells attached as on our modern tambourines.) It beat the rhythm for dances, joyful occasions, and religious ceremonies. Both King David and the prophet Miriam played the tambourine when they wanted to show their delight in the Lord's care for them.

Timbrel *(TIM-brul)* was a small drum, something like a tambourine but without any jingles attached. It was used to provide rhythm for dances and celebrations. It was usually played by women.

Trumpet was a straight tube about 18 inches long ending in a bell shape, made from either copper or silver. There were always at least two trumpets played at each Temple service—and sometimes as many as 120. Trumpets and shofars were blown to begin important events.

MUSTARD (see *Plants*)

MYRIAD *(MEER-ee-ud)* originally meant 10,000 but later came to mean a great or countless number.

MYSIA *(MISH-ee-uh)* was the northwest section of Asia Minor, now part of Turkey. Paul visited Mysia several times because he passed through it on his way to and from Macedonia and Greece. It was a Roman province.

MYSTERY *(MIS-ter-ee)* in the New Testament means a secret that was once hidden but now is revealed. These are important truths that God has made known through Jesus Christ.

Paul uses *mystery* to refer to several truths. For example, in Ephesians 3, the mystery is that Jews and Gentiles who believe in Christ are now part of one people—the Church. In Colossians 1:26, the mystery is that Christ lives in every believer. For Paul, Christ was the great mystery or secret that had been revealed.

NAAMAN *(NAY-uh-mun)* was a commander of Syria's army. But he had the disease of leprosy.

His wife's young Hebrew slave said there was a prophet in Israel who could heal Naaman. So he went to the home of Elisha. Elisha did not come out of his house to see Naaman. He sent a message that if Naaman would dip seven times in the Jordan River he would be healed.

Naaman was angry. He said if he was supposed to dip himself, his own country had better rivers than the Jordan. However, Naaman's servants urged him to follow Elisha's directions. He did and was healed.

He went back to Elisha and promised not to offer sacrifices to any god but the Lord. He tried to give Elisha some expensive gifts, but Elisha refused them.

Where to find it: *2 Kings 5:1-27*

Noah's building project didn't make much sense— until it started to rain.

47

NABAL (see *Abigail*)

NABOTH *(NAY-buth)* was an Israelite who had a good vineyard next to King Ahab's palace in Jezreel. Ahab told Naboth he wanted that land for a vegetable garden and he would pay him for it or give him another vineyard somewhere else.

Naboth said no. He had inherited that land from his father, and he wanted to keep it.

When Ahab told his wife, Jezebel, about the vineyard, she said, "I'll get it for you." She arranged to have some men accuse Naboth of cursing God and the king. Because of these charges, Naboth was stoned to death.

When Ahab went to claim the vineyard, he met the prophet Elijah, who told him God would judge him for what he had done to Naboth.

Where to find it: *1 Kings 21*

NADAB (see *Abihu*)

NAHUM *(NAY-hum)* was an Old Testament prophet who wrote a short book. Nothing else is known about the man except that he came from the town of Elkosh—the location of which is not known either.

His book is full of poetic, powerful word pictures about God's strength and goodness.

Nahum prophesied the defeat of Nineveh, the capital of Assyria. At this time in history (sometime between 663 and 612 B.C.) the Assyrians were threatening the Kingdom of Judah. The idea that Nineveh could ever be defeated seemed impossible.

But Nahum's prophecy came true in 612 B.C., when Nineveh was conquered by Babylon.

Where to find it

God has great power   *Nahum 1*
Nineveh will fall   *Nahum 3*

NAIN *(NAY-in)*, **WIDOW OF,** lived in the small village of Nain, about 25 miles southwest of the Sea of Galilee. The town is now called Nein. On the outskirts of the village, Jesus met a funeral procession on its way to bury a young man, this widow's only son. Jesus restored the young man to life.

Where to find it: *Luke 7:11-17*

NAIOTH *(NAY-oth)* was a place north of Jerusalem where Samuel was leader of a group of prophets. David went there to escape from Saul, who was trying to kill him. Saul followed him there, and Saul also began to prophesy. Meanwhile, David escaped.

Where to find it: *1 Samuel 19:18-24; 20:1*

NAKED or **NAKEDNESS** means several things in the Bible. Sometimes it means without any clothing. Other times it means without enough clothing, as when Jesus said, "I was naked and you clothed me."

Naked can also refer to a person being without a physical body after death. In a few places it is a word picture meaning that a person does not know God.

In the Old Testament, the words "uncover nakedness" refer to sexual acts between men and women.

Where to find it

Without any clothing   *Genesis 2:25*
Sexual acts   *Leviticus 20:17-21*
Without enough clothing   *Matthew 25:36*
Without a physical body   *2 Corinthians 5:3-4*
Does not know God   *Revelation 3:17; 16:15*

NAMES in the Bible meant more than names do today. The name of a person often told something about him. It might be:

1. A personal characteristic. *Esau* means "hairy." Even as a newborn baby, Esau had more hair than usual.

2. The parent's hopes for the child. *Obadiah* means "servant of God." His parents hoped he would become a servant of God—and he did.

3. The name of an ancestor—especially a grandfather. This was more common after 500 B.C. and throughout New Testament times.

Because people's names were so much a part of them, a person's name was often changed after something important happened to him. Jacob's name was changed to Israel after he had a special meeting with God. Abram's name was changed to Abraham after the Lord appeared to him.

In the Bible, the names of God and Jesus have special significance. When the Bible speaks of "the name of God," it really means God himself, and "the name of Jesus" means Jesus himself. To know "the name of God" means to know God himself and something about him. When the Bible says, "To all who believed in his name, he gave power to become children of God," it means "to all who believe in Jesus and commit themselves to him. . . ."

In the stories of the New Testament, miracles are often done "in the name of Jesus." This means by the power or authority of Jesus.

Where to find it

Esau named because of his hair *Genesis 25:25*
Jacob's name is changed to Israel *Genesis 32:27-28*
Believing in the name of Jesus *John 1:12; John 2:23*
Miracles done "in Jesus' name" *Mark 9:38-39; Luke 10:17; Acts 16:18*

NAOMI *(nay-OH-mee)* was the mother-in-law of Ruth. She and her family lived in Moab for a while. After Naomi's husband and Ruth's husband (Naomi's son) died there, Naomi and Ruth returned to Bethlehem, Naomi's former home. Naomi helped Ruth meet and marry Boaz and took care of Ruth and Boaz's baby boy.

Where to find it: *Book of Ruth*

NAPHTALI *(NAF-tuh-lie)* was the sixth son of Jacob, and the ancestor of the tribe of Naphtali. This tribe settled in good land west of the Sea of Galilee. That part of the Kingdom of Israel was conquered by the Syrians, and many of its people were sent into exile in 733 B.C.

Where to find it

Naphtali, son of Jacob *Genesis 30:7-8*
Tribe settles in Palestine *Joshua 19:32-39*
Conquered by Syrians *1 Kings 15:20*
Sent into exile *2 Kings 15:29*

NAPKIN was a piece of cloth usually used for wiping perspiration from the face, as we use a handkerchief or paper tissue. Sometimes a napkin was used to wrap things in. A napkin was also placed over the face of a person who had died.

Where to find it

Wraps something *Luke 19:20*
Over the face of the dead *John 20:7*

NARD (see *Plants*)

NATHAN *(NAY-thun)* was a prophet of God who was a counselor to King David. When David wanted to build a house of worship for God, he talked with Nathan. That night God spoke to Nathan. Nathan was to tell David that David's son was to build the Temple, not David. When Nathan delivered the message, David accepted it as God's will.

Several years later, King David wanted to marry Bathsheba. He arranged to have Bathsheba's husband killed in battle. Nathan then told him that God would judge him for his sin.

When David was an old man and soon to die, Nathan learned that Adonijah, one of David's sons, was plotting to become king instead of Solomon. Nathan told David, and then, following David's orders, Nathan and others quickly arranged for Solomon to be made king.

Nathan also wrote a history of the reigns of David and Solomon, but no copies of his work have been saved.

Where to find it

Tells David not to build Temple *2 Samuel 7*
Rebukes David for sin with Bathsheba *2 Samuel 12:1-25*
Helps make Solomon king *1 Kings 1:8-53*
Writes history of David and Solomon *1 Chronicles 29:29; 2 Chronicles 9:29*

NATHANAEL *(nuh-THAN-yul)* is listed in the Gospel of John as one of Jesus' disciples. He is mentioned only in the Gospel of John, but some scholars think he is the same as the person who is called Bartholomew in the other Gospels.

Nathanael was brought to Jesus by Philip. After Nathanael talked with Jesus, he was convinced that Jesus was the Son of God.

Where to find it: *John 1:43-51*

NATIONS *(NAY-shunz)* in the Bible often

means all people except the Jews. In the Old Testament, the Israelites were God's special people, in contrast to "the nations," who were Gentiles and pagans. Occasionally, however, *nation* refers to the Jews.

In the New Testament, *nations* sometimes means Gentiles and other times means all people, including Jews. When Jesus told his disciples to go into all the world and make disciples of all nations, he meant that the gospel was for all people—Jews and Gentiles. *Nation* is also used as a word picture to describe Christians. "You are a holy nation," Peter wrote.

Where to find it

Jews will be a nation   *Genesis 18:18*
Old Testament reference to Gentiles   *Psalms 9:15-20; 22:27; 2 Kings 18:33*
New Testament reference to Gentiles   *Luke 12:30*
New Testament reference to all people   *Matthew 28:19*
Christians are a nation   *1 Peter 2:9*

NATURAL *(NACH-er-ul)* **NATURE** *(NAY-chur)* has several meanings in the Bible.

1. It means in keeping with the physical universe. 1 Corinthians 15:44 (King James Version) says that when a person's body is buried after death, "it is sown a natural body."

2. Sometimes *natural* refers to the characteristics people inherit from their ancestors. James talks about someone "who observes his natural face in a mirror." Sometimes this kind of nature is contrasted with God's nature, or character. Peter says Christians can have some of the divine nature.

3. Sometimes *natural* means "unconverted" or "unspiritual." Paul says, "The natural man receiveth not the things of the Spirit of God" (King James Version). The Revised Standard Version uses "unspiritual" in this verse.

Where to find it

Unspiritual   *1 Corinthians 2:14*
Physical   *1 Corinthians 15:44*
Inherited characteristic   *James 1:23*
Character   *2 Peter 1:4*

NAZARENE *(NAZ-uh-reen)* was a person who lived in the town of Nazareth in Galilee. Jesus lived there as a child, so he was called a Nazarene. In New Testament times, Christians were sometimes called Nazarenes be-cause they were followers of Jesus.

Where to find it: *Matthew 2:23; Acts 24:5*

NAZARETH *(NAZ-uh-reth)* was the town in Galilee where Jesus lived during his childhood and youth.

Early in his ministry, he preached in the synagogue in Nazareth, but the people became so angry with him that they wanted to kill him. Jews who lived other places thought Nazareth was a city of low moral and religious standards.

The hills of Nazareth are filled with limestone caves; perhaps Joseph and Mary lived in one.

Today Nazareth is a large city, and most of the people who live there are Arabs.

Where to find it

Jesus' childhood   *Luke 2:39, 51*
Jesus preaches there   *Luke 4:16-30*
Bad reputation   *John 1:46*

NAZIRITE *(NAZ-uh-rite)* was a Hebrew man or woman who took a vow to commit himself to God in a special way for a certain length of time. The time could be anywhere from 30 days to a lifetime. While under the Nazirite vow, persons were not to eat anything made with grapes, they were not to cut their hair, and they were not to touch a dead body.

There are only two examples in the Bible of lifelong Nazirites: Samson and Samuel. Many scholars believe John the Baptist was also a Nazirite.

Some scholars think that Paul took a Nazirite vow for a short time and completed it in Cenchreae, where he cut his hair again.

Where to find it

Regulations for Nazirite vow *Numbers 6:1-21*
Samson a lifetime Nazirite *Judges 13:7; 16; 17*
Samuel a lifetime Nazirite *1 Samuel 1:11*
John the Baptist *Mark 1:6; Luke 1:15*
Paul's vow *Acts 18:18*

NEBO *(NEE-bo)* was the name of the mountain from which Moses saw the Promised Land. Nebo was also a town near Mount Nebo.

There was also a Babylonian god whose name was Nebo. He was supposed to be the god of science and learning.

Where to find it

Mount Nebo *Deuteronomy 34:1*
Town *Numbers 32:3; Isaiah 15:2*
Babylonian god *Isaiah 46:1*

NEBUCHADNEZZAR *(NEB-uh-kad-NEZ-er)* was the king of Babylon during its time of greatest glory. He ruled from 605 to 562 B.C. He made the city of Babylon beautiful; his hanging gardens became world-famous. He installed irrigation systems and built a strong defense system.

His armies invaded Judah three times—in 605, 597, and 586 B.C. In 597 the armies came

Nebuchadnezzar was furious when his wise men couldn't tell him what he had dreamed.

51

into the city of Jerusalem and took most of the furnishings of the Temple back to Babylon. Thousands of Israelites were forced to leave their country and go to Babylon to live. These included the leaders and educated people of Judah.

Among those forced to leave were the prophet Daniel and his three friends, Shadrach, Meshach, and Abednego. They were brought to the palace to be educated as advisers for the king. Twice Nebuchadnezzar had dreams that only Daniel was able to interpret. Nebuchadnezzar respected Daniel and his friends and gave them important jobs in his government.

In 586 B.C. Nebuchadnezzar's army again came to Jerusalem, this time destroying the city and the famous Temple Solomon had built. More Israelites were forced to leave Judah and go to Babylon to live.

Nebuchadnezzar was a proud, power-hungry king. He once set up a huge golden image and ordered everyone to worship it. When Shadrach, Meshach, and Abednego disobeyed the command, they were thrown into a furnace so hot that it killed the men who threw them in. But God kept the three safe, and they came out unharmed. Nebuchadnezzar then issued another order saying that no one could speak a word against the God of these Hebrews.

The second dream that Daniel interpreted foretold that Nebuchadnezzar would have a mental illness. He would be so sick that for seven months he would think and act like an ox instead of a human. All this came true.

When Nebuchadnezzar recovered from his illness, he worshiped the true God. He died in 562 B.C. after being king for 43 years.

Where to find it

Defeats Judah *2 Kings 24: 1–25: 21; 2 Chronicles 36: 6-21*
Daniel and friends taken to his court *Daniel 1: 1-21*
His dreams *Daniel 2: 1-3; 4: 1-37*
Throws men into furnace *Daniel 3*
Recovers from mental illness *Daniel 4: 34-37*

NEBUZARADAN *(NEB-oo-zar-AY-dan)* was the commander of Nebuchadnezzar's army that defeated Jerusalem in 586 B.C. He took captives back to Babylon as the king commanded. He also followed through on Nebuchadnez-

zar's order that the prophet Jeremiah be allowed to choose whether to go with the captives to Babylon or stay with the poor people left in the burned-out city. Jeremiah chose to stay in the ruins of Jerusalem.

Where to find it: *2 Kings 25: 8-12; Jeremiah 39: 9-14; 40: 1-6*

NECO or **NECHO** *(NECK-oh)* was the ruler of Egypt who killed Josiah, king of Judah, in a battle at Megiddo. Neco had gone to Megiddo to fight the king of Assyria and had warned Josiah not to become involved in the battle. But Josiah did not listen.

After Josiah died, Neco dethroned Jehoahaz, Josiah's son, and took him to Egypt. Neco chose another of Josiah's sons, Eliakim, to be the next king of Judah. Neco made the Jews pay a lot of money to Egypt.

Neco was finally defeated by Nebuchadnezzar, king of Babylon, at the battle of Carchemish in 605 B.C.

Where to find it: *2 Kings 23: 29-37; 2 Chronicles 35: 20-27; 36: 1-4*

NECK is sometimes part of several word pictures in the Bible. A conqueror often put his foot on the neck of the defeated king or general after he had won the battle.

A stiff neck is a picture of stubbornness or disobedience.

"To fall upon the neck" of someone means to hug that person with great emotion. Joseph "fell on the neck" of his father when meeting him for the first time after many years.

Where to find it

Fall on neck *Genesis 46: 29*
Stiff neck *Exodus 32: 9; Acts 7: 51*
Foot on neck *Joshua 10: 24*

NECROMANCY *(NEK-row-man-see)* was a form of witchcraft that usually involved trying to talk with the dead. God's Law forbade the practice.

Where to find it: *Deuteronomy 18: 10-11*

NEGEB *(NEG-eb)* was a dry hilly area south of Judea. Abraham went toward the Negeb when he first came to Canaan. This area was part of the Promised Land and was originally assigned to the tribe of Simeon.

The area is now known as the Negev in modern Israel. It has few inhabitants except

The Negeb is so dry that the people have to keep moving in search of water.

Bedouin (Arab) nomads, who use it to pasture their flocks. Water is scarce and the land is not good for farming.

Where to find it

Abraham goes toward Negeb   *Genesis 12: 9*
Belongs to the tribe of Simeon   *Joshua 19: 8*

NEHEMIAH *(NEE-huh-MY-uh)* was the governor who led the rebuilding of the walls of Jerusalem and much of the city. He also restored the worship of God among the people.

Nehemiah's work began in 445 B.C.—more than 100 years after Jerusalem had been destroyed by Nebuchadnezzar, king of Babylon. After Babylon conquered Jerusalem, Persia defeated Babylon. Nehemiah was a descendant of people who had been taken as exiles from Jerusalem.

Nehemiah held an important position in the court of Persia's King Artaxerxes. He was cupbearer—the one who served wine at the king's table. Nehemiah asked the king to let him return to Jerusalem to rebuild the walls of the city. The king not only gave him permission, but later appointed him governor of the area.

Nehemiah was a talented organizer. He ordered needed supplies and assigned various groups to build certain parts of the wall. The people trusted him and were willing to work hard for him. They rebuilt the walls in 52 days.

The work was hard, and it was even harder because some enemies of the Israelites tried to stop the work. This group was led by two men, Sanballat and Tobiah. They were afraid the country of Judah would become powerful again. Nehemiah ordered half the people to stand guard with swords and shields while the others worked on the wall.

When the wall was finished, Nehemiah gathered all the people together. Ezra the scribe read the Law of Moses to them. For many years, most of the people had not worshiped God. Nehemiah and Ezra taught them to observe the Sabbath and feast days and to restore other parts of their worship.

The Book of Nehemiah tells the last events of Jewish history recorded in the Old Testament.

Where to find it

Receives permission to go   *Nehemiah 2: 1-8*
Sanballat and Tobiah oppose him   *Nehemiah 4, 6*
People gather to hear the Law read   *Nehemiah 8*
Restores Sabbath observance   *Nehemiah 13: 15-22*

NEIGHBOR *(NAY-bur)* means anyone who is close to us. Both the Old and New Testaments say that we are to love our neighbors in the same way we love ourselves. The Bible also says we are to protect our neighbor's reputation ("you shall not bear false witness") and his property ("you shall not covet your neighbor's belongings").

Jesus told the story of the Good Samaritan to show that any person whom we can help is our neighbor.

Commandments about neighbors *Exodus 20:16-17; Leviticus 19:18; Matthew 19:19*
Story of Good Samaritan *Luke 10:29-37*

NEPHEW *(NEF-few)* is used in the King James Version four times to mean a grandchild or other descendant. In newer versions, more accurate terms are used in these passages.

Where to find it: *Judges 12:14; Job 18:19; Isaiah 14:22; 1 Timothy 5:4*

NEPHILIM *(NEF-ill-im)* were very large people mentioned in the early parts of the Old Testament. They lived in Canaan before the Israelites settled there.

Where to find it: *Genesis 6:4; Numbers 13:32-33; Deuteronomy 1:28*

NERO *(NEE-row)* was probably the empéror (Caesar) of Rome who had both Paul and Peter killed.

He began as a good ruler in A.D. 54. We know the apostle Paul appealed his case to the emperor and was taken to Rome in A.D. 60. It is possible that Paul appeared before Nero and was freed, perhaps in A.D. 62 or 63.

Nero's later rule of terror and cruelty began about A.D. 63. He had his own mother put to death, as well as some of his most trusted advisers. In A.D. 64 a large part of the city of Rome burned. Many thought that Nero had ordered the burning of the city. To draw suspicion away from himself, Nero accused the Christians of starting the fire. This became an excuse to begin a terrible persecution of Christians. Some were burned as torches in Nero's own gardens; others were crucified or thrown to wild beasts. Probably both Peter and Paul were included at this time.

The Roman Senate finally decreed that Nero should die. But before the decree could be carried out, Nero ordered the death of many senators and then, in A.D. 68, he killed himself.

Where to find it: *Acts 25:10-11*

NETHER WORLD (see *Dead, Abode of*)

NETHINIM *(NETH-in-im)* were Temple servants who helped the Levites. They may have been descendants of people captured in earlier wars. In the Revised Standard Version, *Nethinim* is translated "temple servants."

NETTLE (see *Plants*)

NEW BIRTH (see *Regeneration*)

NEW EARTH, NEW HEAVEN refer to the new creation that will come at the end of history as we know it. Heaven and earth will then be freed from all the effects of sin.

Where to find it: *2 Peter 3:13; Revelation 21:1; 22:5*

NEW JERUSALEM *(jeh-ROO-suh-lem)* is a word picture to describe both God's holy city and the people of God who will live there.

Where to find it: *Revelation 21:2-27*

NEW MAN is a term used in the Bible in two ways:

1. *New man* may mean a person who has become a follower of Christ and is therefore becoming more like Christ.

2. *New man* may mean the Church, "Christ's body," which is composed of both Jews and Gentiles who become Christians.

Where to find it

A follower of Christ *Ephesians 4:24; Colossians 3:10 (KJV)*
The Church *Ephesians 2:15*

Paul on trial before the emperor Nero.

NEW TESTAMENT *(TEST-tuh-ment)* is a collection of 27 books or documents written about the life of Christ, the early church, and the Christian faith. They were written between the years A.D. 50 and 90. *Testament* means "agreement" or "covenant," and these books are called the New Testament because they are about the new agreement or new covenant God made with people through the life, death, and resurrection of Christ. People can have a new life of fellowship with God by faith in Christ.

There are four kinds of books in the New Testament:

1. The Gospels. Each of these was written by a different author, Matthew, Mark, Luke, and John. Each one tells about Jesus Christ's life, teachings, death, and resurrection.

2. The Acts of the Apostles. This book tells about the early church, its leaders, and how it spread from Jerusalem around the then-known world within 30 years. Luke wrote the Book of Acts.

3. The Letters. These 21 letters were written mostly to specific churches, but some were written to Christians everywhere. They explain important truths of the Christian faith. Thirteen of the letters are believed to have been written by the apostle Paul. Others were written by James, John, Peter, and Jude. We do not know the writer of some letters, such as Hebrews.

4. The Book of Revelation. John wrote this book, which begins and ends like a letter and has seven short letters in chapters 2 and 3. However, most of the book is called an apocalypse—a writing that involves visions about the end of this world and about the next world. The apocalypse in Revelation tells how God is going to defeat sin, remove all evil, and live with his people forever. The visions include such things as living creatures, beasts, seals, trumpets, bowls of judgment, a dragon, and a beautiful city that will never be destroyed.

The books of the New Testament are not arranged in the order in which they were written or in the order of the events they describe. They are arranged by subject matter. To learn how they were gathered and chosen to appear in the Bible, see *Canon*.

NEW YEAR (see *Feasts*)

NIBHAZ (see *Ashima*)

NICODEMUS (*NICK-uh-DEE-mus*) was one of the Pharisees who belonged to the ruling Jewish council called the Sanhedrin. Nicodemus wanted to know what Jesus taught. Because the Pharisees were enemies of Jesus, Nicodemus had to come to see him secretly at night. Jesus told him that he must

Nicodemus first came to see Jesus at night.

become a whole new person—he had to be born again.

When the Sanhedrin wanted to condemn Jesus without a fair trial, Nicodemus objected. But he was afraid to be an open follower of Jesus until after Jesus died. Then Nicodemus boldly showed that he was a disciple by helping to bury Jesus' body.

Where to find it

Comes to Jesus at night   *John 3:1-5*
Defends Jesus in Sanhedrin   *John 7:45-52*
Helps to bury Jesus' body   *John 19:38-42*

NICOLAITANS *(NIK-uh-LAY-i-tunz)* were people whose actions were hated by Christ and by the church at Ephesus. The Bible does not say what they did that was so evil, but it seemed to involve immorality and eating food sacrificed to idols.

Where to find it: *Revelation 2:6, 14-15*

NIGHT means the period from sunset to sunrise. In the New Testament, *night* is often used as a word picture for evil. For example, 1 Thessalonians 5:5 says, "For you are all sons of light and sons of the day; we are not of the night or of darkness."

NIGHTHAWK (see *Birds*)

NILE RIVER is the third longest river in the world. Only the Amazon and the Mississippi are longer. It runs nearly 2,500 miles through the middle of Africa to Egypt and the Mediterranean Sea.

A very wide plain along the coast of Egypt is flooded each July by the Nile River. This flooding makes the land good for farming. Without the Nile River, the country of Egypt could not have survived. The seven years of famine in Joseph's time were probably caused when the Nile did not flood as usual.

NIMROD *(NIM-rod)* was the founder of the city of Nineveh and several other cities. He was also famous in his time as a mighty hunter. The Bible says, "He was the first on earth to be a mighty man. He was a mighty hunter before the Lord."

Where to find it: *Genesis 10:8-9*

NINEVEH *(NIN-uh-vuh)* was one of the oldest cities of the world. It was founded by Nimrod the famous hunter. Archaeological digging has shown that people lived there as early as 4500 B.C. When it was the capital of the empire of Assyria, it had beautiful palaces for its kings, temples for its pagan gods, and a canal 30 miles long that ran from a dam to the north.

In the Bible Nineveh is best known as the city to which Jonah went to preach. The people repented when Jonah warned them that God would destroy the city, and the city was spared. It was finally destroyed in 612 B.C. by the Babylonians, Medes, and Scythians.

Where to find it

Founded by Nimrod   *Genesis 10:11*
Capital of Assyria   *2 Kings 19:36-37*
Jonah preaches   *Jonah 1:2; 3:2-3; 4:11*

NISROCH *(NIS-rock)* was the name of the god worshiped by Sennacherib, the king of Assyria. Sennacherib went to his temple to worship Nisroch after his army had failed to conquer Jerusalem. God had sent an angel (probably with a disease) that killed 185,000 of his men.

While Sennacherib was worshiping Nisroch, his two sons killed him.

Where to find it: *2 Kings 19:32-37*

NO, or **NO-AMON** *(no-AM-un)*, was the capital city of Upper Egypt in the time of Joseph. It was known in other writings as Thebes.

NOAH *(NO-ah)* was a good man who continued to do right when everyone around him was doing wrong. The Bible says Noah "was blameless" and "walked with God." The other people were so evil that God sent the Flood to destroy everyone except Noah and his family. God told Noah the Flood was coming and instructed him to build a huge boat, or ark, so he and his family could be saved. Noah and his three sons spent many years building the ark. When it was completed, Noah's family went into the ark. Noah also brought into the ark a male and female of every known animal and bird.

Then the rains began. It rained for forty days—almost six weeks—until everything was flooded and the people and animals left outside were drowned. Noah and his family and the animals stayed in the ark almost a year. They had to wait until the land was dry enough

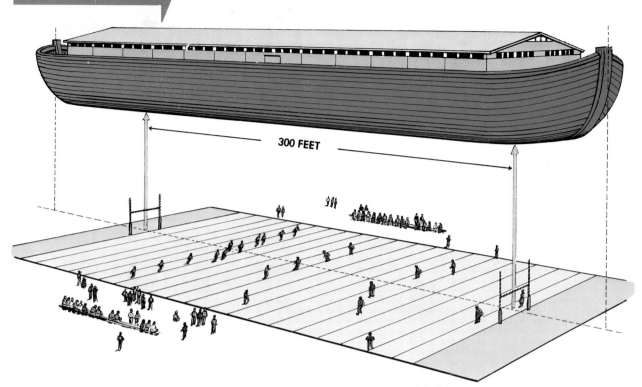

Noah's ark was longer than a football field.

so they could walk on the ground, build houses, and grow food again.

One of Noah's first acts when he got out was to build an altar to worship God.

After the Flood, God made a covenant, or agreement, with Noah. God promised he would never again send a flood to destroy all living things. As a proof of his promise, God sent a rainbow across the sky.

Noah lived for 350 years after the Flood; he died when he was 950 years old.

The New Testament says Noah was a preacher, or herald, of righteousness.

Where to find it

A righteous man   *Genesis 6: 9*
God tells Noah to build the ark   *Genesis 6: 13-22*
The Flood comes   *Genesis 7: 1–8: 19*
Noah builds an altar to God   *Genesis 8: 20*
God makes a new covenant   *Genesis 9: 9-17*
Noah, a hero of faith   *Hebrews 11: 7*

NOAH'S ARK is the boat God told Noah to build so he could escape the coming Flood. The Book of Genesis says the boat was to be 450 feet long (longer than a football field), 75 feet wide, and 45 feet high. It had three decks, or levels. It was to be made of gopher wood. (Bible scholars are not sure what kind of wood this was.) A model of the boat shows that it

was not made to be a sailing ship but more like a large barge. Its only purpose was to stay above the water during the Flood.

The Bible says it came to rest on the "mountains of Ararat." There is in present-day Turkey a range of mountains known as Ararat. These mountains might be the place mentioned in the Bible, but we do not know for sure. Some explorers have seen what they thought looked like a large boat under the ice on one of these mountains. Groups of explorers have tried to climb the mountains to find out for sure if a boat is there, but so far there is no final proof that what people have seen is Noah's ark.

Where to find it

Instructions for building the boat   *Genesis 6: 14-16*
Boat rests on mountains of Ararat   *Genesis 8: 4*

NOB was a town near Jerusalem where many priests lived. During the time Saul was king, the Tabernacle was at Nob.

King Saul was jealous of David and hated him so much he kept trying to kill him. So David and his small army ran from Saul. When they came to Nob, David asked the priest in charge of the Tabernacle to give them some food and a sword. The priest gave David bread and the sword with which David had killed Goliath.

One of Saul's followers, Doeg, saw the priest help David. When Doeg told Saul what had happened, Saul ordered that the whole city be destroyed and all the priests and people killed.

No one knows exactly where Nob was located.

Where to find it: *1 Samuel 21:1-10*

NOBLEMAN has two meanings in the New Testament.

1. An official in the king's army.

2. Someone related to a king or born into an important family.

Where to find it

Army officer   *John 4:46-53 (KJV)*
A prominent person   *Luke 19:12-27; 1 Corinthians 1:26*

NOMADS *(NO-mads)* are people who live in tents and who often move from place to place.

Many of the early stories in the Bible are about people who were nomads. Abraham was a nomad—he lived in tents, and moved whenever his cattle needed a new place to graze.

For many years Moses lived as a nomad in the wilderness, tending his father-in-law's sheep. The Israelites lived as nomads during the 40 years they wandered in the wilderness before they entered the Promised Land. Their place of worship, the Tabernacle, was a big tent so it could be moved from place to place with them.

Later, when the Israelites entered Canaan, most of them lived in permanent houses and earned their living as craftsmen or farmers.

Where to find it

Abraham   *Genesis 13:2-18*
Moses   *Exodus 3:1*
Israelites   *Deuteronomy 2–3*

NORTHERN KINGDOM refers to the northern tribes of Israel that separated from the tribes of Judah and Benjamin after the death of Solomon. The Northern and Southern Kingdoms had separate kings and sometimes fought each other. The Northern Kingdom was also known as Israel and as Ephraim (the name of one of the strongest tribes). Its capital was Samaria.

The Southern Kingdom was known as Judah. Its capital was Jerusalem.

The Northern Kingdom was defeated by Assyria in 722 B.C., and many of its people were sent as exiles into Assyria.

NUMBERS were very different in Bible times. Our use of numerals 1, 2, 3, 4, 5, 6, 7, 8, 9, and 10 did not begin until about A.D. 600. People in Bible times counted as we do, but as far as we know, they did not use numerals. In most of the Hebrew Old Testament, numbers were written out as words, such as "seventy-two" or "one hundred eighty-seven thousand."

The Greeks in New Testament times used the letters of the alphabet for their numbers. The first letter, *alpha*, meant "1"; the second letter, *beta*, meant "2," and so forth.

Some numbers had special meaning. From very early times, seven was a sacred number. God created the earth in seven days. The Feast of Unleavened Bread and the Feast of Tabernacles lasted seven days. The candlestick in the Tabernacle had seven branches; the

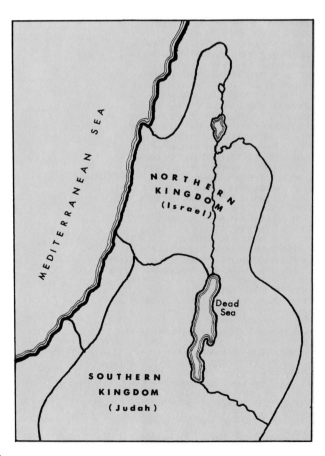

priests walked around Jericho seven times; John wrote to seven churches in Revelation. There are many such examples. Seven seems to mean something that is complete or whole.

Twelve is also a special number. There were 12 tribes of Israel; there were 12 apostles.

Forty seems to be a general figure meaning a long period of time. It rained for 40 days at the Flood of Noah; the Israelites were in the wilderness 40 years; Moses was on the mountain for 40 days; Christ was tempted for 40 days.

NUMBERS, BOOK OF, contains the story of the trials and victories of the Israelites from the time they escaped slavery in Egypt to the time, 40 years later, when they entered the Promised Land.

In the Hebrew Bible, this book is called "In the Wilderness," which describes what it is about. The name *Numbers* comes from the Greek translation of the Old Testament. The ancient translators called it *Numbers* because the beginning of the book and the end of the book tell the number of males over 20 years of age; there were about 600,000. They were counted to see how many men there were who could be in an army if the Israelites needed one. Therefore women, children, and priests (Levites) were not included in the count.

The Book of Numbers tells how 12 men were sent to spy out the Promised Land. Two of the spies, Caleb and Joshua, believed God would help the Israelites conquer the land. God was pleased by their faith. But ten of the men came back saying that the people were so big and strong the Israelites would never be able to conquer them. After they had heard what the spies said, most of the Israelites said they would rather go back to Egypt. Because of their lack of faith, God said they would have to live in the wilderness for 40 years. That would be long enough for the fighting men of that generation to die and a new group to grow up.

When the Israelites heard God's punishment, they insisted on going immediately to fight in Canaan even though Moses told them they must not. They fought one battle but were defeated.

Moses was the leader of the Israelites dur-

ing the time of the Book of Numbers. The book tells how God helped Moses and the people live in the wilderness. God let them know he was with them by putting a fire over the Tabernacle at night and a cloud by day. When the cloud moved, they were to move their camp to wherever the cloud led them. Numbers tells how the people were to camp in an orderly way. It tells how they were to divide the land when they arrived in Canaan.

Near the end of the book is the story of some of the battles the Israelites fought on the east side of the Jordan River—land not thought of as part of Canaan. The people of three tribes, Reuben, Gad, and Manasseh, had many cattle, and they asked for permission to build their homes on the east side of the Jordan. Moses said they could if they would promise to help the rest of the Israelites in their battles to win the land of Canaan.

Numbers also tells the strange story of the prophet Balaam and how God would not let him prophesy against the Israelites.

Numbers 6:24-26 is a beautiful prayer that is often used as a benediction in church services today.

The Book of Numbers shows how God took care of his people even when they disobeyed him. It shows how much he cared about all the details of their lives. It also shows how God punished sin.

Where to find it

Army men are counted   *Numbers 1:1-46; 26:1-62*
Famous benediction   *Numbers 6:24-26*
Cloud guides them   *Numbers 9:15-23*
Spies sent to Canaan   *Numbers 13*
God's punishment   *Numbers 14*
Story of Balaam   *Numbers 22–25*
Three tribes settle east of Jordan   *Numbers 32*

NURSE (see *Occupations*)

NUTS (see *Plants*)

God's people in the Old Testament both thanked the Lord and asked his forgiveness through offerings.

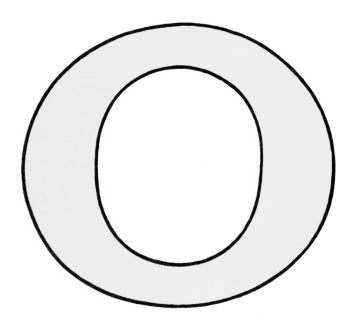

OAK OF THE PILLAR was a tree that was considered sacred. It grew beside a place of worship at Shechem, a town halfway between the Sea of Galilee and the Dead Sea. Next to this tree, Abimelech was crowned king of Shechem (see *Abimelech*). This was also probably the oak where Jacob hid the gods of his wives, and where Joshua placed a huge stone to remind the people that they had dedicated themselves to serve God.

Where to find it

Abimelech crowned king   *Judges 9:6*
Jacob hides wives' possessions   *Genesis 35:4*
Joshua places a huge stone   *Joshua 24:26*

OATHS are solemn vows that people make to promise that what they say is true. In Bible times, there were several methods of taking oaths. Sometimes a person said something like "as the Lord lives." They meant that their words were as dependable as the fact that God is alive. Other times a person made a signal, such as raising his hand toward heaven. In our country, we use oaths in court cases, where a person places his hand on the Bible and says, "I swear to tell the truth, the whole truth, and nothing but the truth, so help me God."

In Jesus' time, Jews had some oaths that were considered binding and others that were not. Jesus talked about these in Matthew 23:16-22. He also said that those who are his disciples should not need oaths—everything they say should be completely honest, without any special oath.

Where to find it: *Matthew 5:33-37*

OBADIAH *(OH-buh-DIE-uh)* was the prophet who wrote the shortest book in the Old Testament. We know nothing else about him; we are not even certain when the book was written.

The 21 verses in Obadiah are about the nation of Edom. These people were descendants of Esau, Jacob's brother. Their country was south of the Dead Sea. Even though the people of Edom and the people of Israel were distant relatives, they were usually enemies. The Edomites sometimes fought with the Philistines against the Israelites.

Obadiah said that the people of Edom would be punished by God for being proud and for joining other nations in trying to destroy God's people. He reminded the Edomites that all the earth belongs to God and that some day God would rule it.

OBED *(OH-bed)* was the son of Ruth and Boaz. He was the grandfather of King David.

Where to find it: *Ruth 4:17*

OBED-EDOM *(OH-bed-EE-dum)* was a Philistine man who lived near Jerusalem. After

Uzzah (see *Uzzah*) died when he touched the ark of God, King David left the ark in Obed-edom's house for three months. During that time the Lord blessed Obed-edom and all his family.

Where to find it: *2 Samuel 6:6-12; 1 Chronicles 13:9-14*

OBEDIENCE means doing what we're told to do. We are commanded to be obedient to God in every way. Romans 1:5 says part of faith is obedience. Children are told to obey their parents and to honor them.

Where to find it

Obeying God   *1 John 5:2*
Obeying parents   *Ephesians 6:1-2*

OBEISANCE *(oh-BAY-sense)* means bowing low to show respect to someone. In some societies, people put their faces to the ground to show respect or honor. In other places, bowing from the waist or simply bowing the head shows respect. The Israelites were not to bow before idols.

Where to find it: *Exodus 20:5*

OBLATION (see *Offerings*)

OCCUPATIONS *(ock-you-PAY-shuns)* are the jobs people do to earn a living. Jobs in Bible times centered mostly around farming, building and repairing homes, government, armies and defense, and religious life. Like today, a man or woman might earn money in two or three ways at the same time. There were very few big businesses, but many people ran small businesses from their own homes.

People were divided generally into two groups—those who were free and those who were slaves. The slaves usually worked side by side with their masters in the fields, or in the business of the master, but all the money went to the master. Slaves sometimes had important positions in the house—but they were still slaves.

The following list includes many of the ancient occupations. There were probably many other occupations that are not mentioned in the Bible.

Apothecary (see *Perfumer*)
Archer *(ARCH-ur)* was a soldier who used a bow and arrow as his weapons 1 Samuel 31:3

tells that King Saul was wounded by a Philistine archer. Egyptian archers wounded King Josiah so badly that he died, according to 2 Chronicles 35:23-24.

Armor-Bearer *(ARE-mur-BARE-ur)* was a personal servant of an army commander. Armor-bearers are mentioned only in the early part of the Old Testament—never in the New Testament. For a short time, David was the armor-bearer for King Saul, according to 1 Samuel 16:21.

Artificers (see *Craftsmen*)

Bakers were people who cooked bread. In ancient cities, bread dough was prepared at home and the loaves taken to large city ovens for baking. This saved fuel and kept individual homes from getting so hot.

Beggars asked others for food or money. Many people in Bible times never had jobs. They lived from what others gave them. Beggars were often crippled or blind, and thus could not work.

Brickmakers were important in Bible times. Building with sun-dried bricks was very common. Even though Palestine had many stones, bricks were often used to build city walls. In Bible times, bricks were made from wet clay mixed with straw or other vegetable materials. The clay mix was made into bricks either by hand or in a wooden mold. The Israelites in Egypt were forced to make bricks and to gather their own straw for them (Exodus 5:6-9).

Butler (see *Cupbearer*)

Centurion *(sen-TOUR-ee-un)* was a commander of 100 men in the Roman army.

Chamberlain *(CHAYM-bur-len)* had charge of a king's house. He made sure that everything was done properly and according to social custom.

Clerk usually refers to the town clerk. The town clerk mentioned in Acts 19:35 was a man of authority and influence, probably the chief officer of the town of Ephesus. Such a man would keep records, write down the laws passed by other groups, and be the go-between for the Roman government and the city council.

Coppersmiths made tools, cooking utensils, and other things. They used not only copper but also other metals.

Counselor *(KOWN-suh-lur)* usually refers to an important man in government, one who helped the king make decisions.

Craftsmen were skilled in certain trades—carpentry, wood carving, tent making, leatherwork.

Cupbearer was a palace official who served wine to the king. He was a loyal man whom the king trusted.

Custodian *(kuh-STOW-dee-un)* was a male slave who looked after the son of his owner. He walked to school with him and took care of him in other ways until the son was 16 years old.

Diviners *(dih-VINE-urs)* seemed to have some secret knowledge about what would happen in the future. Diviners were often involved in witchcraft or demon power.

Dyers *(DIE-urs)* colored woven cloth. They got their colors from natural sources—red came from worms, blue from the rind of pomegranates, purple from certain shellfish.

Elders *(ELL-durs)* were older men who usually ruled villages. This practice was common in the Old Testament and was carried over in some ways to the New Testament. The Sanhedrin that ruled Jerusalem was this type of government. When churches were formed, elders were appointed for each congregation (Acts 14:23).

Farmers grew crops for people to eat. More people were farmers than any other occupation. Many men who were soldiers or had some other occupation also worked as farmers (see *Agriculture*).

Farmers threshed wheat by driving oxen over it; then they used the wind to separate the chaff from the grain. What a contrast to modern machinery!

Fishers worked along every lake, river, or sea to catch fish. They fished mostly with large nets but also with hooks and spears. Fishing at night was common on the Sea of Galilee.

Fullers washed or bleached clothing. Both men and women were fullers. The soaps used by ancient people to clean and whiten cloth often smelled bad. So the fuller's shop was usually outside the city, where the smells wouldn't bother so many people.

Gatekeepers or **Porters** were in charge of gates to the city, or gates to the Temple, or even gates to a sheepfold. They served as guards, opening the gates only to those who had a right to come inside.

Herdsmen cared for oxen, sheep, goats, or camels. Usually a herdsman did not own the animals but was hired to look after them. He would protect them from wild beasts and make sure they had pasture for grazing.

Herald *(HAIR-uld)* was a town crier who went through the streets shouting the king's commands.

Hunters were common from earliest times, when people hunted to get food. Later, hunting became a recreation. Men hunted with bows and arrows. They also used nets and cages to catch ducks, quail, and partridges. For large animals such as wolves, bears, and lions, hunters often dug pits, covered the holes with brush, and waited for the animals to fall in.

Husbandman *(HUZ-bund-mun)* means the same as *farmer*.

Innkeepers rented overnight lodging to travelers. Their lodging places were more like campgrounds than hotels. Sometimes an inn was only a large courtyard with a fence, gate, and well. A few inns had buildings with rooms.

Judges performed several kinds of work. In the Book of Judges, a judge was the chief leader of the land—the military commander and the highest official.

Later in Israel, judges were those who decided court cases. These judges usually held court in the square inside the city gates, although Samuel traveled from city to city to hold court sessions.

Lawyers knew a great deal about the laws of the Old Testament.

Magicians practiced superstitious ceremonies to try to make things happen. They had many books about sorcery. Magic was condemned by the Old Testament and by the early church in Acts 19:19 (see *Magic*).

Magistrates *(MAJ-iss-traits)* were the highest ruling officials in each Roman colony.

Maids were usually female slaves. Fathers sometimes gave maids to their daughters as part of a marriage dowry.

Masons worked with stone. Their skill was important, since most buildings in Palestine were made of stone.

Merchants were men or women who bought things in one place and sold them in another. Sometimes they traveled to distant places to buy what people might want and then sold their goods from door to door. More often,

they set up a shop in the large city market and sold their goods there.

Midwives were women who helped whenever a baby was being born. Midwives are mentioned in Exodus 1:15-20.

Miners worked to get iron, copper, and other metals out of the ground. Mining was not common among the Hebrews.

Minstrels were musicians who played for special occasions. The prophet Elisha once called for minstrels to play for him (2 Kings 3:15). Minstrels were often hired to play at weddings or funerals.

Money Changers were Jews in New Testament times who sat in the Temple court and exchanged other kinds of money for Temple (Jewish) money. They sometimes charged unfair prices. Jesus drove them out of the Temple and said they had made the Lord's house into a "den of thieves" (Matthew 21:12-13; Mark 11:15).

Musicians included singers and those who played cymbals, harps, pipes, or trumpets (see *Musical Instruments*). Music played an important part in the life of Israel. Fifty-four psalms were written "to the chief musician" or choirmaster.

Nurses did more than care for the sick. They were often a kind of tutor and helped raise children.

Officers were people who held any official position. They usually had authority over others.

Overseers were people with some authority over others (see *Officers*).

Perfumers made perfumes, drugs, or healing oils. Most of their work involved making things with pleasant smells to overcome the many bad smells of the average village.

Physicians (fih-ZIH-shuns) treated the sick with salves, mineral baths, and medicines.

Plowman (see *Farmer*)

Porter (see *Gatekeeper*)

Potters made cooking and storage pots from clay (see *Pottery Making*). Many clay pots were needed in Bible times because they broke easily. Metal pots were very expensive. Pottery making was considered a low-class trade, and potters often lived in the poorest parts of the city. But the Bible sometimes uses *potter* as a word picture of God and his creative work (Isaiah 64:8; Romans 9:20-21).

Preachers announce news, usually messages about God. In 2 Peter 2:5, Noah is called a "preacher of righteousness." Paul said that he was appointed a preacher (1 Timothy 2:7). In Bible times, preachers had to have strong voices, since they often spoke outdoors.

Priests (preests) offered sacrifices and did religious duties. From the time of Moses to the New Testament, Hebrew priests were descendants of Aaron. Pagan religions also had their own priests.

Procurators (PRAH-cure-ay-turs) were governors of Roman provinces. They were appointed by the Roman emperor.

Prophets (PRAH-fits) and **Prophetesses** (PRAH-fih-tess-ez) were men and women who spoke for God to the people. They delivered God's message, calling people to repent and live a holy life. The message often included God's future blessing or judgment (see also *Prophecy*).

Publicans (PUB-lih-kunz) were Jewish men who worked as tax collectors for the Roman government. They often tried to collect as much money as they could. They were considered traitors by the Jewish people.

Rabbis (RAB-eyes) were Jewish teachers of the Old Testament Law and traditions.

Recorder (see *Clerk*)

Refiners (re-FINE-urs) were those who worked with metals. Sometimes they melted gold and silver to make it purer, and sometimes they extracted metals from iron and bronze ores.

Ruler of the Synagogue was responsible for making sure the synagogue was ready and prepared for services.

Sailors worked on the cargo ships that sailed the Mediterranean Sea.

Seller or **Salesperson** (see *Merchant*)

Schoolmaster (see *Custodian*)

Scribes wrote letters and kept accounts for someone else, somewhat like a secretary.

In the New Testament, scribes were men who studied the Old Testament Law and the Jewish traditions so they could tell others what was permitted and what was not permitted. They were men of great influence and were given the best seats at feasts and in the synagogue (see also *Scribes, Jewish*).

Seers were able to predict future events. Samuel called himself a seer in 1 Samuel 9:19.

Senators (see *Elders*)

Sergeants (*SAHR-jents*) worked with the chief Roman officers. They carried out the punishment the officers ordered.

Servants were under the authority of someone else. Sometimes servants were slaves; often they were not.

Sheepmasters were shepherds who *owned* their sheep. They did not take care of someone else's flocks.

Shepherds took care of sheep, either their own or someone else's. Since sheep are affectionate animals that never fight and need protection from wild animals, shepherds cared deeply about their sheep, knew them all by name, and saw that they were fed and brought safely to the fold at night.

Silversmiths made objects out of silver. They refined the ore and formed the finished objects. They made musical instruments, decorations, and furnishings for the Tabernacle and Temple. Pagan silversmiths made many idols. Acts 19:23-41 tells about one pagan silversmith who tried to stop Paul's preaching at Ephesus.

Singers were important in Jewish worship. Nehemiah 7:67 mentions a Temple choir of 245 men and women.

Slaves were persons owned by someone else. The owners completely controlled them. Sometimes Hebrews who could not pay their debts became slaves to the person to whom they owned money. Hebrew fathers might sell their own children as servants or slaves. Hebrews also got slaves through conquering other countries. And, in turn, Hebrews sometimes became slaves when other countries conquered them. Slavery led to evil in both Old and New Testament times. Eventually, the message of the gospel helped people see how wrong slavery was.

Smiths worked in stone, wood, or metal. They were so important to a nation that conquerors sometimes took the smiths as captives to weaken their defeated enemy.

Soldiers were those paid for defending their country. In the time of Moses and Joshua, every man above the age of 20 was a soldier and had to be prepared to fight whenever he was needed. Until the time of King David, all soldiers were foot soldiers. Later they began using chariots and horses.

Sorcerers (*SOR-sir-ers*) claimed they could foretell the future with the aid of evil spirits. God warned his people to stay away from sorcerers (Malachi 3:5).

Spinners made thread from flax, wool, or cotton. From their thread people wove cloth.

Stewards (*STEW-urds*) were managers of household business. Jesus told a parable about a steward who wasted his employer's belongings (Luke 16:1-3).

Stonecutters worked in quarries or cut stones for buildings such as the Temple in Jerusalem. 1 Kings 5:15 says Solomon had thousands of stonecutters working on the Temple.

Tanners made leather out of animal hides. This was considered by the Jews as an "unclean" occupation (see *Unclean*), so tanners usually lived outside of towns.

Taskmasters assigned work to those under them.

Tax Collectors (see *Publicans*)

Teachers in New Testament times were the rabbis in the synagogues. They conducted school to teach children to read and write. The rabbis also taught adults about the Old Testament Law.

In the Christian Church there were some traveling teachers, who went from church to church to help people learn more about the gospel.

Tentmakers made tents from hair, wool, or animal skins. In New Testament times, it was the custom for every Jewish boy to have some trade. Paul was a tentmaker. So were his Christian friends, Priscilla and Aquila (Acts 18:1-3).

Tetrarch *(TEH-trark)* was a ruler of a small section in the Roman Empire. He was often called king, even though he ruled for the emperor of Rome.

Tiller (see *Farmer*)
Town Clerk (see *Clerk*)

Treasurer was an important officer in ancient cities. He was in charge of the money that came in from taxes and the money that was paid out.

Tutor (see *Custodian*)

Wardrobe Keeper was a servant in the king's house who had charge of the king's robes. They were probably kept in a special room.

Watchman of the City patrolled the streets to protect people. His job was something like today's policeman, except that as he walked through the streets, the ancient watchman also called out the approximate hour of midnight (they had no clocks or watches) and the time called "cock-crow."

Weavers made cloth or rugs from the thread or string made by the spinners. Weavers were usually women, but some men were also weavers.

Witches and **Wizards** both practiced witchcraft and said they could communicate with demons and the spirits of the dead. Witches were women; men were wizards. Witchcraft is always condemned in the Bible.

ODED *(OH-dead)* was a prophet of God who reminded the Israelites of the Northern Kingdom that they must not make slaves of the Israelites in the Southern Kingdom.

King Pekah, who ruled Israel from 740 to 732 B.C., had defeated Judah in a battle and captured 200,000 men, women, and children. His soldiers brought all of them and most of their possessions to his capital city of Samaria. The prophet Oded met them there and told them that they had sinned against God in taking their own people as slaves.

The leaders of Israel then said the captives should be fed, clothed, and sent back to their own country.

Where to find it: *2 Chronicles 28:9-15*

ODOR *(OH-dur)* means a smell. In the Bible, *odor* nearly always refers to a *pleasant* smell. In the King James Version, the word always refers to a good smell; in the Revised Standard Version, *odor* refers to a pleasant smell except for two passages: Ecclesiastes 10:1 and John 11:39.

The usual way to get a pleasant smell in Bible times was by burning incense or by using perfumes.

OFFEND *(oh-FEND)* means to hurt or to dam-

In the wilderness, weavers and dyers made colorful curtains for the Tabernacle.

age a person. It might mean bodily hurt, or hurt feelings, or to make something difficult for another. In the New Testament, the word *offense* often refers to a "stumbling block"—doing something that causes someone else to sin.

Where to find it: *Matthew 15:22; Acts 25:8*

OFFERINGS *(OFF-ringz)* and **OBLATIONS** *(oh-BLAY-shunz)* are gifts to God. They show a person trusts God and wants to do what he commands. The Old Testament Law gave a long list of instructions about how offerings were to be made, when they should be given, and for what purpose.

Offerings were usually animals or other food, and most offerings were burned on an altar in the Tabernacle or Temple. Animal offerings always involved blood and were a symbol of sins being forgiven by death. Christians believe that Jesus Christ was the final, once-for-all sacrifice to bring forgiveness of sins to all who believe in him.

Some of the offerings mentioned in the Old Testament are these:

Burnt Offerings were burned upon the altar in the Temple or Tabernacle. These offerings might be bullocks, lambs, rams, or goats. The animal had to be in perfect condition. Blood was sprinkled around the altar, and the entire animal (except the skin) was burned up in the fire. Burnt offerings were always for sin.

Cereal Offerings (see *Meal Offerings*)

Drink Offerings were sometimes called libations. They were always given with other sacrifices—never alone. Most drink offerings were oil and wine, given separately or mixed together.

Evening Sacrifice refers to one of the daily sacrifices made to God in the Tabernacle or Temple. Every morning and every evening an animal was burned as a sacrifice to God. With it was offered a cereal offering and a drink offering. Details are given in Numbers 28:3-8.

Freewill Offering (see *Peace Offerings*)
Guilt Offering (see *Trespass Offering*)
Heave Offering (see *Wave Offering*)
Libations (see *Drink Offerings*)
Meal, Meat, or **Cereal Offerings** all refer to vegetable offerings. These were a mixture of fine flour, oil, and flavorings made into bread or cakes. Sometimes these offerings were

burnt at the altar. Other times, part was burned and the rest was given to the priest.

Peace Offerings were given to renew fellowship with God. There were three kinds of peace offerings:

1. **Thank offerings** for some unexpected blessing of God.

2. **Votive offerings** to go along with a vow made to God.

3. **Freewill offerings** given as an expression of love for God.

Peace offerings could be any animal normally used for sacrifices. No birds could be used. In peace offerings, the breast and shoulder of the animal were given to the priest. The blood was sprinkled on the altar and the fat was burned. The person who made the offerings and his friends ate the rest of the meat. They ate "before the Lord" in the Tabernacle or Temple. Eating it there showed that God was a guest at the meal.

Sin Offering could be a bullock, a male or female goat, a female lamb, a dove, or a pigeon. The sin offering was for sins that affected the life of the person who did them. A trespass offering was given for sins that hurt someone else (see *Trespass Offering*).

Trespass or **Guilt Offering** was a ram or a male lamb. This offering was given when a person had hurt someone else by his sin—as in stealing. In such cases, the person not only had to make a trespass offering to God but also had to pay back what he had stolen or make up in whatever way possible the wrong he had done.

Thank Offering (see *Peace Offering*)

Votive Offering (see *Peace Offering*)

Wave Offerings and **Heave Offerings** refer to the motions made by the priest when a peace offering was given (see *Peace Offering*). A wave offering meant that the breast of the animal was placed in the high priest's hands and "waved" before the Lord to show that it had been given to God's representative—the priest. In the heave offering, the right thigh of the animal (the choicest part) was treated in a similar way, and the offering was then eaten by the priests.

OFFERING FOR THE SAINTS (see *Contribution for the Saints*)

OFFICER *(OFF-uh-sur)* is a person who had some position of leadership, usually for a king or ruling group. In the Old Testament, those who gave orders to the Hebrew slaves in Egypt were called officers. There were officers in the army and in the palace of the king. In the New Testament, guards of prisons were called officers in Luke 12:58. Those who came from the chief priests and Pharisees to arrest Jesus in the Garden of Gethsemane were also called officers.

Where to find it: *Luke 12:58; John 18:3, 18, 22*

OFFSCOURING *(off-SCOW-ring)* refers to dirt that was swept off the floor of a house. Paul uses this word to explain how he and other Christians had sometimes been treated by the enemies of Christ.

Where to find it: *1 Corinthians 4:13*

OG *(ahg)* was a giant king of Bashan who ruled 60 cities east of the Jordan River. Moses led the Israelites to a stunning victory over Og and his army and captured all the cities Og ruled. Deuteronomy 3:11 says Og was the last of the "Rephaim"—a word meaning giants, or very large people. Og had an iron bed that was 13½ feet long (about 4 meters) and 6 feet wide (1.8 meters).

The victory of the Israelites over Og's armies is mentioned many times in the Old Testament.

Where to find it: *Deuteronomy 3:1-11*

OHOLAH AND OHOLIAB (see *Aholah and Aholiab*)

OIL is often mentioned in the Bible and usually refers to olive oil. Oil was important in cooking and in medicines. Oil was also used in very simple lamps to give light in homes and in the Tabernacle at night. Most lamps were small containers of clay with a wick lying in oil.

Oil was used as a soothing salve to help wounds heal; it was also a cleanser to wipe away the dust of the roads. People often poured oil on the heads of important visitors to make them feel better. The 23rd Psalm mentions this custom—"Thou anointest my head with oil."

Oil was often used in ceremonies to anoint men chosen for some special task or honor. Kings were anointed like this, and so were priests and prophets.

Where to find it

Used in cooking   *Exodus 29:2*
Used on faces   *Psalm 104:15*
To anoint kings or prophets   *1 Kings 19:15-16*
To anoint priests   *Exodus 29:1-9*

OINTMENT *(OINT-ment)* was a heavily perfumed salve. Many newer translations of the Bible use the word *perfume* for ointment. Palestine was often short of water, and people did not bathe often. In the hot climate, perfumes were needed to cover up other odors!

Once a woman came to Jesus with an alabaster flask of ointment—an expensive perfume—and put it on his feet.

Where to find it: *Luke 7:36-50; John 12:1-8*

OLD TESTAMENT is the first part of the Bible. It has 39 books or separate writings. These books tell some of the things that happened from the time God created the world until the time of Ezra and Nehemiah—about 400 B.C.

Except for the first 11 chapters of Genesis, the Old Testament tells mostly about the Hebrews, starting with Abraham, whose story begins in Genesis 12.

The books in the Old Testament are not arranged in the order of the events they describe. For instance, Ezra and Nehemiah were the last Old Testament books written, but they were placed about halfway through the Old Testament.

The Old Testament is arranged instead by subject matter and by the type of writing. Genesis, Exodus, Leviticus, Numbers, and Deuteronomy tell about the Hebrew nation from the beginning until the time the Israelites were ready to enter Canaan with Joshua as leader. These first five books are called the Law. They give the details of the Old Covenant—the agreement God had with Moses and the Hebrews telling what he expected of them. These books tell about the commandments, the sacrifices and feasts, the foods the people were to eat, how they were to treat each other, and how they were to live in the land God was giving them.

The next group of 12 books, sometimes called the books of history, tell what happened to the Hebrew people from the time they entered Canaan until about 400 B.C. The books of Joshua, Judges, 1 and 2 Samuel, and 1 and 2 Kings tell about the Israelites in their relationship with other countries; they especially point out whether the people obeyed God or turned from God to worship idols.

1 and 2 Chronicles tell about many of the same things that are recorded in 1 and 2 Kings.

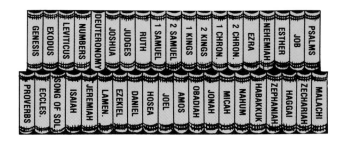

But Chronicles tells only about the happenings in the Southern Kingdom (Judah), while 1 and 2 Kings tell about both Judah and Israel, the Northern Kingdom.

Ruth, another historical book, shows us a good side of the people during one period of the judges.

Ezra and Nehemiah are historical books that tell about life in Jerusalem when some of the Hebrews returned from exile in Babylonia.

Esther, another historical book, tells about life in Persia for those who did not return to Israel after their Exile.

Five books of poetry appear next in the Old Testament. These are Job, Psalms, Proverbs, Ecclesiastes, and the Song of Solomon. However, there are several other books of prophecy that are all or nearly all poetry. These include Isaiah, Jeremiah, Joel, Lamentations, Amos, Obadiah, Micah, Nahum, Habakkuk, and Zephaniah.

After the poetry books come the books of the major prophets. These books are Isaiah, Jeremiah, Lamentations, Ezekiel, and Daniel. After these come 12 short books known as the minor prophets.

All the books of prophecy—major prophets and minor prophets—are writings of men whom God used to warn people of judgment if they did not worship God and obey his commands. While some of the prophets' messages were aimed at the nations around Israel, most of them were meant for the nation of Israel. Many of their writings, however, are about ideas and attitudes that apply to people of all times—including our own. Some of the writings of the prophets also apply in a special way to the coming of Jesus Christ—either the first time when he came to die for the sins of the world, or his future return when he will come again to rule the world.

The Old Testament laid the foundation for the time when Jesus would come and teach more about God. The Old Testament tells about God's concern for the Hebrew nation and his instructions on how they were to live and worship. The Old Testament shows how the people did not keep God's commands. Instead they often worshiped idols like the nations around them did. Even the kings often worshiped idols and punished the prophets God sent to warn the people of their sins. Finally God allowed pagan nations to defeat Israel and carry many of the people off to other countries as captives.

Eventually, about 536 B.C., some Jews came back to Jerusalem to rebuild the Temple. In 450 B.C., Nehemiah returned to lead the people in rebuilding the walls of the city.

The New Testament (or New Covenant) clearly completes the Old Testament (or Old Covenant). Jesus Christ came to give himself as the sacrifice for the sins of all men. He was what all the sacrifices of the Old Testament had been leading up to.

OLIVES (see *Plants*)

OLIVES, MOUNT OF, is sometimes called Olivet. It is not really a mountain but rather a rounded ridge east of Jerusalem that stands higher than other parts of the city. The valley of Kidron lies between the city walls and this mountainous ridge. The ridge is about a mile long with four small peaks on it.

Some say these olive trees outside Jerusalem are 2,000 years old—the original Garden of Gethsemane.

In New Testament times, the area was something like a park of Jerusalem. It was a wooded area where people came to get away from the heat and crowds of the city.

Many important Bible events took place on this ridge. Jesus often taught his disciples there. The Garden of Gethsemane, where Jesus prayed before his crucifixion, is somewhere on the hill. Jesus began his triumphal entry into Jerusalem from this place on the Sunday before his crucifixion.

The ridge was important in the defense of Jerusalem. When the Romans destroyed the city in A.D. 70, the soldiers camped on this hill, where they could get a good view of the city.

Today, the Mount of Olives is heavily populated with hotels, homes, businesses, and Hebrew University.

Where to find it

Jesus teaches his disciples   *Matthew 24:3–25:46*
Jesus prays in Gethsemane   *Matthew 26:30-46*
Jesus begins triumphal entry   *Matthew 21:1-3; Mark 11:1-9; Luke 19:29-40*

OMEGA (see *Alpha*)

OMEN *(OH-mun)* is a sign or warning of something that is going to happen.

The apostle Paul said in Philippians 1:28 that right living by Christians was an "omen of salvation" for believers but an "omen of destruction" for unbelievers. Christians' good lives are a sign that they are living in fellowship with God, and the contrast with the lives of non-Christians is a sign that others are not.

Where to find it: *Numbers 24:1; 1 Kings 20:33; Isaiah 44:25*

OMER (see *Measures*)

OMNIPOTENCE *(om-NIP-oh-tents)* refers to God's ability to do anything he chooses. Because God is good, he would never choose to do anything evil or foolish. The word *omnipotence* is not in the Bible, but the Bible does describe God's great power. Jesus said, "With God, all things are possible."

Where to find it: *1 Chronicles 29:12; Jeremiah 32:17; Matthew 19:26*

OMNIPRESENCE *(om-nih-PREH-zents)* means

being everywhere at the same time. Only God can do this. The Bible does not use the word *omnipresence,* but it does teach that God fills the whole universe with himself and that no one can ever hide from God.

Where to find it: *Psalm 139: 7-12; Jeremiah 23: 23-24; Acts 17: 27-28*

OMNISCIENCE *(om-NIH-shunts)* means knowing everything. God knows everything—past, present, and future. He knows the thoughts and actions of every person who has ever lived or who will ever live. He knows us far better than we know ourselves.

Where to find it: *Psalm 147: 5; Isaiah 46: 9-10*

OMRI *(OM-ree)* was the wicked sixth king of the Northern Kingdom, Israel. He reigned from about 885 to 874 B.C. He was the father of King Ahab, who married the evil woman, Jezebel.

Omri was made king by the soldiers he was commanding, after they heard that the previous king had been assassinated. Zimri, the man who had killed the previous king, had made himself king, but his reign lasted only seven days.

After Omri had been declared king by his army, the army marched on Tirzah, the city and palace where Zimri was staying. When Zimri saw that he would be defeated, he burned the palace and died in the fire.

Although Omri had been declared king by the army, many of the people of Israel did not want him as king. For a while, the two sides fought, but Omri's side finally won.

Omri reigned for 12 years. After six years, he moved his capital from Tirzah to Samaria, and Samaria remained the capital city of Israel until the nation was conquered by Assyria in 722 B.C.

The Bible says that Omri did more evil in the sight of the Lord than all who were before him.

Where to find it: *1 Kings 16: 8-28*

ONAN *(OH-nan)* was a grandson of Jacob. When his brother died, the early Old Testament custom said that he and his brother's widow should have a child. Then the child would inherit the dead brother's wealth.

Onan refused to follow this Old Testament custom. His refusal was displeasing to God, and Onan died.

Where to find it: *Genesis 38: 7-10*

ONESIMUS *(oh-NES-ih-mus)* was a slave of an early Christian named Philemon. Onesimus robbed his master and ran away to Rome. There he met the apostle Paul and became a Christian. Paul sent him back to his master Philemon with a letter, reminding Philemon that Onesimus was now a brother in Christ and must be treated as such. Paul asked Philemon to accept Onesimus in the same spirit that Philemon would welcome Paul! This beautiful personal letter is a part of the Bible—the book called Philemon.

ONESIPHORUS *(AH-nuh-SIF-uh-russ)* was a Christian friend of the apostle Paul. Onesiphorus lived in Ephesus, but when he went to Rome, he courageously searched until he found Paul in prison and offered his help.

Where to find it: *2 Timothy 1: 16-18; 4: 19*

ONION (see *Plants*)

ONLY BEGOTTEN *(be-GOT-tun)* is a term used in the King James Version to describe Jesus Christ. It means he is the only one who is truly equal with God. In a sense, every Christian is a son of God but not in the same way that Christ is. Jesus is the only begotten one-of-a-kind Son of God. Christ's relationship to God is based on his being part of God himself.

Where to find it: *John 1:14, 18; 3:16, 18; 1 John 4: 9*

ONYX *(ON-ix)* is a precious stone that has bands of white and black next to each other. It was one of the stones on the shoulder piece of Aaron, the high priest. Two onyx stones were engraved with the names of the 12 sons of Israel. Onyx stones were also used in the Temple that Solomon built. Onyx stones are mentioned as part of the wall foundations of the heavenly city.

Where to find it: *Exodus 28: 9-11; 39: 6; 1 Chronicles 29: 2; Revelation 21: 20*

OPHRAH *(OFF-ruh)* was a town in central Palestine where an angel of God appeared under an oak tree and told Gideon to lead his people to victory over the Midianites. Later, when Gideon died, he was buried at Ophrah.

Where to find it: *Judges 6:11, 24; 8:32*

ORACLE *(OR-uh-kul)* means a message or word from God. In the Old Testament, oracles were often predictions by a prophet of things that would happen, but the message came from God. In the New Testament, the word *oracle* may refer to the whole Christian message.

In the King James Version, *oracle* is sometimes used as the name of the place where God delivers his message, for example, the Holy of Holies in the Tabernacle.

Where to find it

Holy of Holies   *1 Kings 6:16; 8:6 (KJV)*
Whole Christian message   *1 Peter 4:11*

ORDAIN *(or-DANE)* has several meanings in the Bible. It can mean to decide or command. It is used this way in Esther 9:27 when it says the Jews "ordained" that their descendants should keep a feast to remember their deliverance from Haman.

It also may mean "to set apart for special work." The word *ordain* is used this way in Acts 10:42, where Jesus is said to be "ordained by God to be judge of the living and the dead."

We use *ordain* in a similar way when we speak of a person being "ordained" to the ministry. We mean he is set apart for a special work of God.

In the New Testament, such setting apart often involved fasting and praying by a group of people who "laid their hands" on the people set aside. This was done for Paul and Barnabas when they began their first missionary journey.

Where to find it: *Esther 9:27; Acts 10:42; 32:2-3*

ORDINATION *(or-din-AY-shun)* is the ceremony in which a person is ordained (see *Ordain*).

ORDINANCE *(OR-dih-nunce)* means a law or commandment. In the Bible, ordinances usually refer to laws or commandments of God.

Where to find it: *Leviticus 18:4; 2 Chronicles 33:8; Isaiah 58:2; Luke 1:6; Ephesians 2:15*

OREB *(OH-reb)* and **ZEEB** *(ZEE-eb)* were two princes of the Midianites, enemies of the Israelites. They were killed by Gideon's men as they tried to escape across the Jordan River after the Midianites were defeated.

Where to find it: *Judges 7:24-25*

ORGAN (see *Musical Instruments*)

ORION *(oh-RYE-un)* is a constellation of stars that is mentioned three times in the Old Testament. Orion was a warrior in myths, and his outline is supposed to be seen in this cluster of stars. The constellation is still called Orion today (see *Stars*).

Where to find it: *Job 9:9; Amos 5:8*

ORNAMENTS *(OR-nuh-muntz)* in the Bible were decorations on clothing, houses, temples, or tools. Ancient people were very artistic and often made beautiful carvings, jewelry, paintings, and other handwork.

Among the wealthy, clothing was beautifully embroidered. Those who could afford them wore gold necklaces, earrings, rings, bracelets, and buckles. Jewelry was also made of silver and other less expensive materials.

Even tools and weapons were often carved and decorated.

Both the Old and New Testaments warn against too much emphasis on jewels and fine clothing. Christians should work instead for inner beauty.

Where to find it: *Isaiah 3:18-23; 1 Timothy 2:9-10*

ORPAH *(OR-puh)* was the sister-in-law of Ruth. Both Ruth and Orpah were Moabite women who married sons of Naomi after

Naomi and her husband came to Moab. All the men in the family died, and Naomi decided to go back to Bethlehem, where she had lived before. Both Orpah and Ruth decided to go with her. Naomi told them to stay among their own people. Orpah followed her advice, but Ruth insisted on going with her mother-in-law to Bethlehem. Ruth later became the great-grandmother of King David.

Where to find it: *Ruth 1:1-14*

ORPHAN (see *Fatherless*)

OSEA, OSEE, OSEAS (see *Hosea*)

OSPREY (see *Birds*)

OSSIFRAGE (see *Birds–Vulture*)

OSTRICH (see *Birds*)

OTHNIEL *(OTH-nee-ul)* was the first of Israel's judges after the death of Joshua. The Israelites had stopped worshiping God and had been conquered by the king of Mesopotamia. After eight years, they cried to God for deliverance, and he sent Othniel as their leader. He was able to defeat Mesopotamia, and he later ruled Israel as judge for 40 years. He married Achsah, the daughter of Caleb, one of the two faithful spies in the time of Moses.

Where to find it: *Judges 1:11-15; 3:7-11*

OUTCAST *(OUT-cast)* in the Bible means a person who must leave his homeland and go to live somewhere else. When the Israelites were forced to go to Assyria or to Babylonia after their land had been conquered, they became outcasts. The word *outcast* in the Bible does *not* mean someone looked down on by people.

Where to find it: *Psalm 147:2; Isaiah 11:12; 16:3-4; Jeremiah 30:17*

OVENS in Palestinian homes were usually barrel-shaped, two or three feet across the middle, and made of baked clay. Fires were made with dry grass, bushes, or animal dung mixed with straw. Bread dough was pushed against the walls and baked very quickly. Large cities often had central ovens to which many women took their bread to be baked, so that their homes would not get so hot.

OVERSEERS *(OH-vur-see-urs)* were persons who directed the work of other people. Joseph was an overseer in the house of Potiphar in Egypt. In the New Testament, certain men were overseers of the church.

Where to find it

Joseph   *Genesis 39:4-6*
Church leaders   *Acts 20:28*

OWL (see *Birds*)

OX (see *Animals*)

OX-GOAD (see *Goad*)

PAGAN *(PAY-gun)* means a person who worships idols rather than the true God.

Where to find it: *1 Corinthians 5:1; 10:20*

PALACES *(PAL-uh-sez)* were the homes of kings or high government officials. In Bible times, some palaces were very large and fancy. Archaeologists have discovered that most palaces were built with similar plans. They had several open courtyards with rooms grouped around them. Some kings had two palaces—one for summertime and another for wintertime. Winter palaces were built to gather as much sun as possible for warmth. Summer palaces were built to shut out the hot summer sun.

The palace of King David at Jerusalem was made of cedar wood and stone. King Solomon, David's son, built a different palace—much larger and more decorated. It was 150 feet long, 75 feet wide, and 45 feet high. It took builders 13 years to finish. Other details about this palace are found in 1 Kings 7:1-51.

An even fancier palace was built by wicked King Ahab. His palace was about the size of a football field and lavishly decorated with expensive ivory. Many of its walls were covered

Paul often told crowds about the day God stopped him on his way to Damascus to arrest Christians.

with white marble. The remains of this palace have been found by archaeologists.

The most famous palace in the New Testament was the one used by King Herod the Great. It was described by the Jewish historian Josephus. Herod's palace and many other palaces had fortresses attached to them.

PALESTINE *(PAL-uh-stine)* is the area about 70 miles wide and 150 miles long between the Mediterranean Sea and the Jordan River. It is about the size of the state of Vermont. *Palestine* is a general name that applies to most of what is now Israel. In the Old Testament it was sometimes called Canaan.

The name *Palestine* actually means "land of the Philistines." The Philistines were people who occupied a *part* of Palestine.

People have lived in Palestine from the beginning of history as we know it. Archaeological excavations seem to indicate that people lived in the city of Jericho at least 8,000 years ago.

Although Palestine is small, it has great variations in climate. Along the northern coast, the climate is moderate—something like that of New York City.

Jerusalem, 34 miles inland, has a climate more like that of Tennessee or northern Georgia. Jericho is only 15 miles from Jerusalem, but it is 700 feet below sea level, and its climate is tropical—hotter than that of Florida!

Although all of Palestine is hilly, the northern part has the most rugged hills. The central part has the best farmland. Even though this area has many hills, there are fertile valleys between the hills, and the climate is good for farming. Much of southern Palestine has so little rainfall that it is barely usable for grazing sheep and camels. There is some land around wells that can be farmed.

In Bible times, fishing was an important part of life, especially around the Sea of Galilee. The Jordan River, although it was too shallow and had too many rapids for boats and shipping, was also important in the life of the people. It flows from the Sea of Galilee to the Dead Sea 65 miles away, but the river is so winding that it actually runs 200 miles. Along the river, there was fertile land on which the people grew good crops.

PALLET *(PAL-lut)* was a sleeping pad that could be carried. It was the usual bed of poor people. When Jesus told the crippled man to "take up your bed and walk," he was speaking of this kind of mattress or sleeping pad.

Where to find it: *Mark 2:1-12; John 5:2-13; Acts 5:15*

PALM TREE (see *Plants*)

PALSY (see *Diseases*)

PAMPHYLIA *(pam-FILL-ee-uh)* was a small Roman province along the Mediterranean Sea in what is now Turkey. It was only about 75 miles long and about 30 miles wide. Paul visited Pamphylia on his first missionary journey. In Perga, its chief city, John Mark got discouraged. He left Paul and Barnabas and returned home.

Paul went back to Perga on his way home and preached again. The New Testament does not tell about a church being formed there.

Where to find it: *Acts 13:13; 14:24*

PAPS means breasts. The word appears in the King James Version in Luke 11:27; 23:29 and Revelation 1:13.

PAPER (see *Writing*)

PAPHOS *(PAY-fus)* was a city on the west end of the island of Cyprus in the Mediterranean Sea. Paul visited Paphos, the capital city of the island, on his first missionary journey. At Paphos, a Roman official named Sergius Paulus became a Christian, and a false prophet was blinded for a while.

Where to find it: *Acts 13:4-12*

PAPYRUS *(puh-PIE-rus)* was a tall plant that grew in water and swampy places. It was made into sheets for writing. Although our word *paper* comes from *papyrus*, papyrus was not paper.

To make writing material from papyrus, ancient people took the inside of the papyrus stalk and cut it into thin strips. These strips were criss-crossed on top of each other with some kind of glue and then left under something heavy to make them stay together. When the sheets were dry, they were polished with stone and glued together to form rolls or scrolls for writing.

Papyrus was also used to make light boats or canoes. The little basket in which the baby Moses was placed in the Nile River was probably made of papyrus, although the word used in Exodus 2:3 is "bulrushes."

PARABLE (PAIR-uh-bul) is a story that teaches a lesson. Each parable usually points out *one* spiritual truth. Jesus often taught with parables. Usually his parables were easily understood by his listeners, but sometimes he had to explain what they meant.

Parables usually teach their lessons by comparing one situation with another. Jesus told many of his parables to show what the Kingdom of God (living under God's reign) was like. In one, Jesus said the Kingdom of Heaven is like a net thrown into the sea. The fishermen pull it to shore and sort the fish, throwing away some and keeping the good ones. Jesus compared this to the time when the angels of God will separate righteous people from evil people.

Perhaps Jesus' most famous parable is about the Samaritan who helped the man who was robbed and beaten. Jesus told this parable to show how persons ought to treat their neighbors.

Where to find it

Parable of the net *Matthew 13:47-50*
Parable of the Good Samaritan *Luke 10:29-37*

PARADISE (PAIR-uh-dice) means heaven. The word *Paradise* is used three times in the New Testament. During the crucifixion of Jesus, he said to one of the thieves dying next to him, "Today you will be with me in Paradise."

Where to find it: *Luke 23:43; 2 Corinthians 12:3; Revelation 2:7*

PARALLELISM (see *Poetry–Hebrew*)

PARALYTIC (see *Diseases*)

PARAN (PAY-ran) was a wilderness area in the central part of the Sinai Peninsula. Ishmael lived there when he was an adult. The Israelites camped there on their way to Canaan. They were at Paran when Moses sent the 12 spies to see the land of Canaan. The spies brought back a report that the people were too strong for Israel to conquer. Their lack of faith caused God to decide that they must wander 40 years in the wilderness.

A Mount Paran is mentioned twice, but scholars are not sure where that mountain was located.

Where to find it

Ishmael lives in Paran *Genesis 21:21*

Hebrews camp at Paran *Numbers 10:12; 12:16;
   13:3; 13:26*
Mount Paran *Deuteronomy 33:2; Habakkuk 3:3*

PARCHMENT *(PARCH-ment)* was an expensive writing material made from the skins of sheep or goats. It was made by removing the hair from the skins, soaking them in lime, and then stretching them on frames. The skins were finally rubbed smooth with chalk or pumice stone.

Parchment lasted much longer than papyrus (see *Papyrus*). For this reason, scribes often used parchment in making copies of Old Testament writings.

When Paul wrote his second letter to Timothy, he told him to "bring the parchments." He may have been asking for copies of the Old Testament writings.

Where to find it: *2 Timothy 4:13*

PARDON (see *Forgiveness*)

PARTHIANS *(PAR-thee-unz)* are mentioned among the people who were in Jerusalem at the Day of Pentecost. They came from Parthia, a country that is now part of Iran. It was once the center of a powerful empire that rivaled Rome.

Where to find it: *Acts 2:9*

PARTITION *(par-TISH-un)*, **MIDDLE WALL OF,** is a word picture used in Ephesians 2:14 in the King James Version. The apostle Paul was speaking of a wall that separated Jews and Gentiles into two groups who disliked each other. Paul said that Christ had broken down this wall, so everyone who believed in him now belonged to the same group.

The idea for this word picture may have come from the wall in the Temple that separated the Court of Gentiles from the rest of the Temple. No Gentile was permitted beyond that wall.

PARTRIDGE (see *Birds*)

PASCHAL *(PASS-kul)* **LAMB** means Passover lamb. Christ is called "our paschal lamb" who has been sacrificed. Paul compared the sacrifice of Christ on the cross to the death of the lamb at the first Passover. Its blood was sprinkled on the doorposts of Hebrew homes so that the angel of death would pass over those homes and the people would be saved. Christ died so that people could have their sins forgiven.

Where to find it

First Passover *Exodus 12:3-13*
Christ our Paschal lamb *1 Corinthians 5:7 (RSV)*

PASSION *(PASH-un)* **OF CHRIST** refers to the sufferings and death of Jesus Christ. "Passion Week" in our churches is the week before Easter, the last week of Jesus' life, including his last supper with his disciples, his prayers in Gethsemane, his arrest, trial, crucifixion, and burial. Although these events occurred in less than a week of Jesus' life, the four Gospels give about one-fourth of their space to Christ's "passion."

PASSOVER FEAST (see *Feasts*)

PASTORAL *(PASS-tor-ul)* **EPISTLES** refers to Paul's three letters known as 1 and 2 Timothy and Titus. They have been called pastoral epistles or letters because they gave Timothy and Titus some instructions for their work as leaders or missionaries to certain churches. Timothy and Titus were not pastors in exactly the same sense as we use the word today, but their work was somewhat similar.

These letters, in addition to their pastoral instructions, also have important teachings about salvation, the church, Christ, and Christ's Second Coming.

PATARA *(PAT-uh-ruh)* was a seaport in Lycia, on the southern coast of what is now Turkey. There is now a small village there named Gelemish.

On his third journey, Paul changed ships at Patara.

Where to find it: *Acts 21:1-2*

PATIENCE *(PAY-shunts)* means the ability to stay pleasant and helpful even when everything seems to go wrong. Christians must learn to be patient when they face trials.

Where to find it: *Galatians 5:22; James 1:3-4*

PATMOS *(PAT-mus)* is the small island where John was exiled about A.D. 95. The Roman emperor Domitian sent him there because of his Christian faith. While John was there, God sent him remarkable visions. John wrote these visions in a letter he sent to seven churches—the Book of Revelation, the last book in the Bible.

The island of Patmos is only about 16 square miles and is located about 35 miles off the coast of Asia Minor (now called Turkey). The island is now known as Patino.

Where to find it: *Revelation 1:9*

PATRIARCHS *(PAY-tree-arks)* were the men who founded the Hebrew nation. The word usually refers to Abraham, Isaac, and Jacob. Sometimes the sons of Jacob are included, and Acts 2:29 also calls David a patriarch.

Where to find it: *Acts 2:29; 7:8-9; Romans 9:5; 15:8; Hebrews 7:4*

PAUL is, next to Jesus Christ, the outstanding character in the New Testament. Although he was a devout Jew, he became the apostle to the Gentiles—the man God used more than anyone else to spread the Christian message around the then-known world. He was the author of 13 New Testament books.

Paul's Hebrew name was Saul, but after he became a believer in Christ, he began to be known as Paul.

Saul grew up in a strict Jewish home in Tarsus, a Roman city in what is now southeastern Turkey. Tarsus was strongly influenced by Greek culture and learning. There Saul learned to understand Gentile thought and culture. This helped him later when God called him to preach the gospel to Gentiles. He could speak and write fluently both in the Jewish language (Aramaic) and the Greek language of the Gentile world. In Tarsus, he also learned a trade—tent making.

When Saul was in his early teens, he was sent to Jerusalem, where he studied under a famous teacher, Gamaliel. He mastered the Old Testament and became devoted to his Jewish faith. When he was about 30 years old, he watched with approval as Jews stoned to death Stephen, the first Christian martyr.

Then Saul decided to try to stop Christianity. He headed for Damascus to persecute Christians. But on the way, Jesus appeared to him in a blinding vision, asking, "Saul, Saul,

why do you persecute me?" Saul realized he had been wrong, and he gave himself fully to Christ. After being blind for three days, Saul received his sight through Ananias, a Christian sent by God.

Saul began to preach in the Damascus synagogue that Jesus was the Son of God.

Then he went to Arabia for a time, perhaps to study, to meditate, and to let the Spirit of God teach him how Christ was the Messiah promised in the Old Testament that he knew so well.

He went back to Damascus and began preaching in the synagogue again. The Jews became so angry that they plotted to kill him, and he had to escape over the city wall in a large basket. He went to Jerusalem, but again his life was threatened. He finally went home to Tarsus for several years.

Eventually Barnabas, a Christian leader from Jerusalem, asked him to come to Antioch, where a new church was growing. The two men worked with the church there for more than a year.

About A.D. 48, the church at Antioch sent Saul, Barnabas, and John Mark (nephew of Barnabas) on a trip to Cyprus and parts of Asia Minor (now Turkey). (About this time, Saul's name was changed to Paul.) They often began in a city by preaching in Jewish synagogues. Often, after a few weeks they were forced to leave the synagogue and meet elsewhere. Opposition was so bad in Lystra that Paul was stoned and dragged out of the city, where he was left for dead. But God spared his life; he recovered, and the next day he went on to Derbe, another city.

Later Paul and Barnabas returned to Antioch, where they told how God was working among Gentiles and how new churches were beginning.

Paul brought money to the poor in Jerusalem.

While in Palestine, Paul met with other apostles at Jerusalem to try to decide how the new Gentile Christians should fit in with the Jewish Christians. The Jewish Christians believed that Gentile Christians must keep the Old Testament Jewish Law. After long discussion, the disciples agreed that Gentile Christians did not have to keep the Jewish Law, but they should not do some things that were particularly offensive to Jewish people.

When Paul and Barnabas were ready to make their second missionary journey, they had a serious disagreement. Barnabas wanted to take John Mark along again, but Paul said no because Mark had gone home halfway through the first trip. Finally, they decided that Barnabas and Mark should go back to Cyprus, and Paul should take Silas and go to cities in Asia Minor and Greece.

In his second missionary journey, Paul visited some of the churches he had started on his first journey and also went on to preach at Troas, Philippi, Thessalonica, Berea, Athens, Corinth, Ephesus, and Cenchreae. Then he returned to Antioch.

After a short time, he began his third journey, returning to many of the same cities again. In some he stayed for long periods of time. He lived at Ephesus for three years. He was eager to show that Gentile Christians and

PAUL'S MISSIONARY JOURNEYS

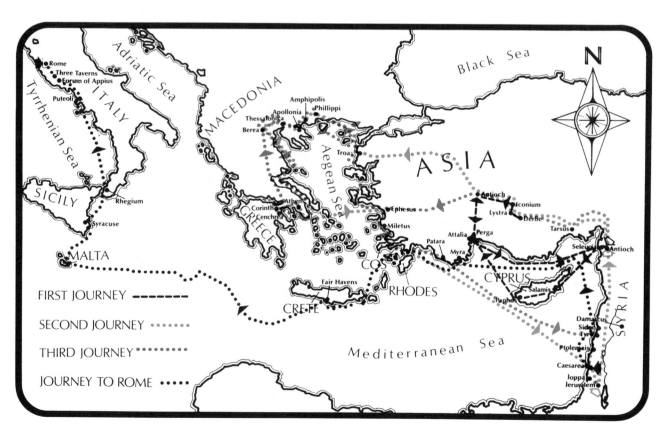

Jewish Christians were part of the same faith, so he encouraged the new churches to collect money for Christians in Jerusalem who were in need. He decided to take the offering to Jerusalem himself.

When he arrived, he was arrested on false charges of defiling the Temple by bringing a Gentile into it. A Jewish mob would have killed him if he had not been rescued by a Roman officer.

When the Roman officer learned that some Jews planned to kill Paul, he sent Paul to Caesarea, the city where the Roman ruler of the area lived. Paul was held in jail there for two years awaiting trial. During this time, he got to explain his faith to Felix and Festus, two Roman governors, and to Herod Agrippa, the Jewish puppet king of Galilee. When Paul saw that he could not receive a fair trial, he appealed to Caesar. This meant his case would be determined by Emperor Nero himself (see *Nero*). Paul could do this because he was a Roman citizen.

Paul was sent to Rome as a prisoner about A.D. 60. The ship was wrecked in a storm, but the group finally arrived in Rome. There Paul was treated well. He was allowed to live in his own rented house with a soldier guarding him. His friends could visit him. As a prisoner, he wrote several letters that are a part of our

New Testament: Colossians, Philemon, Ephesians, and Philippians.

The letters of Paul to Timothy and Titus show that Paul was released by Nero probably in the spring of A.D. 63. He returned to some of the churches he began. But by A.D. 64, Paul was again in prison in Rome. He was apparently executed in A.D. 66 or 67 as part of Nero's persecution of Christians.

Paul was one of the world's great thinkers, but he was also a man of practical common sense. He loved his own Jewish people very much, but he gave his life to bring the gospel to non-Jews. He had a physical ailment that he called his "thorn in the flesh." Scholars do not know what the ailment was, but it made him realize how dependent he was on God's help at all times.

Paul, more than any other person, helped the Christian church to understand the Christian message of salvation by faith in Jesus Christ. He also taught that God expected believers to live honestly and lovingly with all people.

Where to find it

Early life *Acts 22: 3; 26: 4-5*
Persecuted the early church *Acts 8: 1-3; 9: 1-2*
Converted on road to Damascus *Acts 9: 1-22*
Goes to Arabia *Galatians 1: 13-17*
Life threatened *Acts 9: 23-30*
Barnabas brings Paul to Antioch *Acts 11: 25-26*
First missionary journey *Acts 13: 1–14: 28*
Goes to council at Jerusalem *Acts 15: 1-35; Galatians 2: 1-10*
Second missionary journey *Acts 15: 36–18: 22*
Third missionary journey *Acts 18: 23–21: 26*
Arrest and imprisonment *Acts 21: 27–28: 30*
Preaches to Felix, Festus, and Agrippa *Acts 24: 1–26: 32*
Shipwrecked on way to Rome *Acts 27: 1–28: 10*
Held as house-prisoner in Rome *Acts 28: 30-31*

PAULUS, SERGIUS (PALL-us, SIR-jee-us) was the highest Roman official on the island of Cyprus when Paul and Barnabas visited there on their first missionary journey.

When they came to the capital city of Paphos *(PAY-fus),* Paulus asked the two men to come and explain their message. The court magician, a man named Elymas, tried to keep Paulus from listening. Through a miracle, Elymas was temporarily made blind.

Sergius Paulus was so amazed that he became a believer.

Where to find it: *Acts 13: 6-12*

PAVEMENT (PAVE-ment) was the courtyard outside the palace in Jerusalem where Pilate announced his decision at the end of Jesus' trial. It was probably an area paved with large blocks of stone or mosaic tile.

Where to find it: *John 19:13*

PAVILION (pa-VIL-yun) is used in the King James Version to mean a covered shelter where a person could hide. It usually referred to a thicket or shelter made of tree boughs. When the word *pavilion* is used in the Psalms, it means a place where God protects his people.

Where to find it: *Psalms 18:11; 27:5; 31:20*

PEACE in the Bible refers to being whole or complete. It means much more than being free from war or disorder. The Hebrew word for peace includes everything in a good life—health, prosperity, friends, loyal family, friendship with God, peace of mind, orderliness.

The Greek word for peace doesn't include as much as the Jewish word. But when Jewish writers used the Greek word, they meant the same as the Hebrew word. The apostle Paul probably was thinking of the richer Hebrew word when he started many of his letters with "Peace to you."

Where to find it: *Romans 8:6; 14:19; Ephesians 1:2; Philippians 1:2*

PEACE OFFERINGS (see *Offerings*)

PEACEMAKER is a person who helps to bring goodwill between persons or groups who dislike each other. Jesus said that peacemakers are blessed and would be called the sons of God.

Where to find it: *Matthew 5:9*

PEACOCK (see *Birds*)

PEARL was an expensive gem that may have been like today's pearls, which grow in oysters. The word *pearl* in the Bible may also mean crystal gems or corals.

It is usually used as a word picture of something precious or expensive.

Where to find it: *Job 28:18; Matthew 7:6; 13:46; 1 Timothy 2:9; Revelation 17:4; 18:12, 16; 21:21*

PEGS or **TENT PEGS** were used not only to stake a tent to the ground but also for digging and for hanging things on the clay walls of houses.

An Old Testament woman once killed an enemy commander by inviting him to rest in her tent. Then, while he was sleeping, she hammered a tent peg through his head.

A tent peg is sometimes used in the Old Testament as a word picture of the strength of the Lord.

Where to find it: *Judges 4:21-22; Isaiah 33:20*

PEKAH (PEE-kuh) was the wicked eighteenth king of Israel. He became king by murdering the king before him, Pekahiah. Pekah had been an officer in the army when he gathered a group of about 50 men to help him assassinate Pekahiah in about 734 B.C.

While Pekah was king, the neighboring Assyrians made trouble by demanding heavy payments of tribute (taxes). Pekah tried to strengthen his country by going with Syria to fight against Judah, the Southern Kingdom of the Israelites. He lost the battle, however, because the Assyrians went to help Judah! Isaiah the prophet had predicted this defeat.

Pekah's alliance with Syria did not help him to hold back the Assyrians. They conquered part of the land belonging to Israel and forced many people of Israel into exile in Assyria.

Pekah was later assassinated just as he had assassinated the king before him.

Where to find it

Kills Pekahiah   *2 Kings 15:23-25*
Tries to conquer Judah   *2 Kings 16:5-9; 2 Chronicles 28:5-21*
Isaiah prophesies against Pekah   *Isaiah 7–8*
Pekah is assassinated   *2 Kings 15:30*

PEKAHIAH (peck-uh-HI-uh) was Israel's seventeenth king. He ruled only two years before he was killed by Pekah, one of his military leaders (see *Pekah*). The Bible says Pekahiah did evil in the sight of the Lord.

Where to find it: *2 Kings 15:23-26*

PELETHITES (PELL-ee-thites) were a group of King David's bodyguards. They are usually mentioned with another group called the Cherethites.

Where to find it: *2 Samuel 8:18; 20:7, 23; 1 Chronicles 18:17*

81

PELICAN (see *Birds*)

PEN (see *Writing*)

PENIEL *(pee-NIE-el)*, **PENUEL** *(pee-NEW-el)* is the place where Jacob wrestled all night with the angel of God. Peniel means "the face of God."

In the time of Gideon, the people of the city of Peniel refused to give food to Gideon and his men when they were fighting the Midianites. Gideon destroyed the tower of the city and some of the men in the town. Its exact location is unknown, but it was east of the Jordan River and near Succoth.

Where to find it: *Genesis 32:24-32; Judges 8:8-9, 17*

PENCE (see *Money*)

PENINNAH *(pee-NINE-uh)* was one of the two wives of Elkanah, the father of Samuel. She had children, but Elkanah's other wife, Hannah, had none for many years. Peninnah ridiculed her for her lack of children.

Where to find it: *1 Samuel 1:2-7*

PENNY (see *Money*)

PENTATEUCH *(PEN-tuh-tuke)* is a name given to the first five books of the Old Testament: Genesis, Exodus, Leviticus, Numbers, and Deuteronomy. *Pentateuch* is a Greek word meaning "five volumes." The Hebrew word for these books is *torah,* meaning "the law" or "the teaching."

These books tell about the time from creation to the death of Moses. Most scholars believe that Moses played a large part in writing these books. The teachings and practices of the Jewish religion are based primarily on these five books.

PENTECOST *(PEN-tih-cost)* was originally a Jewish feast called "First Fruits" or "Feast of Weeks." It was celebrated 50 days after the Feast of Passover.

Pentecost is known among Christians as the time when the Holy Spirit was given in a special way to the Jerusalem disciples, who were celebrating the Jewish Feast of Pentecost. As the believers were together, they heard a sound like a strong wind and saw something that looked like tongues of fire on each person. Then they began to speak in languages they had never learned. Visitors attending the feast from distant places heard about the works of God in their own native languages. On that day, about 3,000 people became Christians.

Where to find it: *Exodus 34:22; Deuteronomy 16:9-11; Acts 2:1-42*

PENUEL (see *Peniel*)

PEOPLE OF GOD, or phrases like it, such as *people of the Lord,* in the Old Testament refer primarily to the Israelites, who had a special relationship with God. In the New Testament, believers in Christ are called "God's own people" or "people of his own."

Where to find it: *Titus 2:14; 1 Peter 2:9-10*

PEOR (see *Baal-Peor*)

PERDITION *(pur-DIH-shun)* means destruction. But it is often used in the New Testament to mean the same as hell or eternal punishment. Judas Iscariot, the disciple who betrayed Christ, is called "the son of perdition."

Where to find it: *John 17:12; 2 Thessalonians 2:3; Revelation 17:8, 11*

PERFECT in the Old Testament means "complete" or "fully developed." The Law of God is said to be "perfect."

When Jesus said, "You therefore must be perfect, as your heavenly Father is perfect," he meant primarily that we are to become complete and fully developed—the kind of persons God intended us to be.

Where to find it: *Psalm 19:7; Matthew 5:48; 1 Corinthians 13:9-10*

PERFUME was very important in a hot country where water was scarce and people could not take baths very often. Perfumes were made mainly from sweet-smelling spices and oils. People who made perfumes were called apothecaries.

Perfumes are mentioned often in the Bible. They were burned as incense during worship in the Tabernacle. They were used to embalm the dead, and also in oils with which kings were anointed.

Mostly, they were used to cover up bad odors and make life more enjoyable.

PERFUMER (see *Occupations—Perfumer*)

PERGA *(PUR-guh)* was a large city in Asia Minor (now called Turkey). Paul and Barnabas went through the city twice on their first missionary journey, going and returning. At that time, Perga had a huge temple to the Greek god Artemis. Today the city is known as Murtana.

Where to find it: *Acts 13:13; 14:25*

PERGAMUM *(PER-guh-mum)*, **PERGAMOS** *(PER-guh-muss)* was a city in what is now northeastern Turkey. John wrote one of his seven letters in Revelation to the church at Pergamum. He called it the city "where Satan dwells" and mentioned that some of the Christians there had died for Christ.

During the time when Greece was at its height (450 to 300 B.C.), Pergamum was a great cultural center with a magnificent library, outdoor arena, and civic center.

After it came under the power of Rome, it was the first place to have a temple erected to Caesar. It was also known for its worship of the Greek god Zeus.

Where to find it: *Revelation 2:12-17*

PERSECUTE *(PUR-see-cute)* means to try to harm or destroy, sometimes by injury or torture. Usually people are persecuted because of their beliefs. Prophets were sometimes persecuted in the Old Testament. Daniel, for example, refused to stop praying to God and was therefore thrown into a den of lions.

In the early church, Christians were often persecuted because they would not say, "Caesar is Lord." The New Testament teaches that Christians should be prepared for persecution.

Where to find it: *Luke 21:12; 2 Timothy 3:12*

PERSEVERANCE *(PUR-suh-VEER-unce)* means to keep going even under pressure without becoming discouraged. Christians are to persevere in their faith and in their prayers for each other.

Where to find it: *Ephesians 6:18; Hebrews 12:1; James 1:25*

PERSIA *(PUR-zhuh)* refers both to a specific country and to an empire that was very strong during one period of Old Testament history. The country was the part of the Middle East roughly similar to the present country of Iran.

The Persian ruler Cyrus began building the Persian Empire in 559 B.C. Persia defeated Nebuchadnezzar and the Babylonians and became the ruling empire from about 539 to 331 B.C. During this period, Persia controlled

not only Palestine but also Egypt and eastern Greece. In 539 B.C., Cyrus permitted many of the Jews who had been captured earlier to return to Israel and rebuild the Temple and the city of Jerusalem.

Persia was finally defeated by Alexander the Great of Greece.

The Book of Esther was written about the reign of one king of Persia, Ahasuerus.

Where to find it: *2 Chronicles 36:20-23; Ezra 1:1-8; 4:3-24; 6:1-12; Book of Esther*

PERVERSE *(pur-VERSE)* means crooked or bent, and it refers to someone who chooses the opposite of good and right. A perverse person is one who does the opposite of what God has commanded.

Where to find it: *Matthew 17:17; Luke 9:41; Philippians 2:15*

PESTILENCE (see *Diseases*)

PETER, THE APOSTLE, was the leader of the 12 disciples and later a leader in the early church. He is always named first in the lists of the 12 disciples. His original name was Simon. Jesus gave him the name *Cephas* or *Peter,* which means "rock." He was originally a fisherman who lived in Capernaum in Galilee. He was married, but we know nothing about his wife or whether they had children.

Peter first met Jesus along the shore of the Sea of Galilee. He and his brother, Andrew, both left their work of fishing to follow Christ.

Many stories in the Gospels show Peter to be full of energy, a man who often seemed to act before he thought. He sometimes bragged, as when he told Jesus that all others might turn away from him, but he never would. Within a few hours, Peter was denying that he even knew Jesus. Later, realizing what he had done, he wept.

During Jesus' trial, Peter turned against him.

Peter was the first of the disciples to recognize and say that Jesus really was the Messiah, the Son of God. But a few minutes later, Peter talked when he should have kept quiet. Jesus told his disciples that he would go to Jerusalem and die there, and Peter told Jesus to stop talking like that!

Peter's love for Jesus, however, was very deep. He tried to defend Jesus when the soldiers came to arrest him. He cut off the ear of one of the men, but Jesus healed it. Peter was one of two disciples who ran to the tomb on Easter morning and found that Jesus' body was gone.

When the Holy Spirit came at Pentecost, after Jesus had gone to heaven, Peter explained to the crowd what was happening. As the result of Peter's first sermon, 3,000 people became believers.

Peter was involved in many miracles after Pentecost. A lame man was healed at the Temple gate. When Peter explained that the miracle was done by the power of Christ, he was arrested and put in prison. This was the first of several times that Peter was imprisoned.

God sent a special vision to Peter to show him that the gospel was for the Gentiles as well as Jews. As a result, he went and preached to Cornelius and his family, who were among the earliest Gentile believers in Christ.

Peter is the major person in Acts 1 to 12. Beginning in Acts 13, more is told about Paul than about Peter. Because of this, little is known of Peter's later life, but he seems to have traveled widely preaching primarily to Jews.

Peter wrote two books in the New Testament. 1 and 2 Peter are letters to Christians in Asia Minor (now Turkey) to help them stand strong in Christ in spite of persecution.

Most scholars believe that Peter eventually went to Rome, where he was martyred in the persecutions ordered by the Emperor Nero.

Where to find it

Becomes a disciple *Luke 5:1-10*
Says that Jesus is the Son of God *Matthew 16:13-20*
Was married *Mark 1:30; 1 Corinthians 9:5*
Denies Jesus *Matthew 26:31-35, 69-75; Mark 14:27-31, 66-72; Luke 22:31-34, 54-62; John 18:15-18; 25-27*
Tries to defend Jesus *Luke 22:47-51; John 18:10-11*
Runs to tomb at Resurrection *John 20:1-10*
Preaches at Pentecost *Acts 2:14-42*
Heals lame man at Temple gate *Acts 3:1-26*
Raises Dorcas from dead *Acts 9:32-43*
Arrested for preaching *Acts 4:1-22; 5:12-41; 12:1-19*
Has vision and preaches to Cornelius *Acts 10:1–11:18*

PETER, FIRST LETTER OF, was written by the apostle Peter between A.D. 62 and 69 to Christians in northern Asia Minor (now Turkey). Peter may have visited some of these Christian groups earlier, but the apostle Paul had not.

Peter wrote this letter to encourage the Christians to have joy and trust God even though they would be facing persecution. Many scholars think Peter was in Rome when he wrote this letter and could see that Emperor Nero's persecution of the church would probably spread to other areas. He tells Christians to look forward to the time when Christ will return. However, since Christ suffered while he was on earth, Christians too must be prepared to suffer for him. Meanwhile, they should live for God, do what is right, show love to one another, and obey the laws of the land. Leaders of the church should be examples to others.

1 Peter 5:12 shows that Silvanus helped him with the letter, probably serving as his secretary.

PETER, SECOND LETTER OF, was written under the direction of the apostle Peter to warn about false teachers. Peter knew he would not live much longer, and he wanted the readers to beware of those who taught wrong things.

He warned that false teachers would say that Christ will not return a second time, but Christians should not believe such teachers. He also said that the person who really knows Christ in a true way will practice self-control and live a godly life.

PHARAOH (FAY-roh) was the title of the rulers in ancient Egypt, just as *president* is the name of the top official in the United States. Moses was raised in the home of the Pharaoh of his time. Later God sent terrible plagues upon Egypt because the Pharaoh would not let the Israelites leave his country, where they had become slaves (see *Exodus*).

Several other pharaohs are mentioned in the Old Testament. One of them, Pharaoh-Neco, killed Josiah, king of Judah, in a battle about 609 B.C.

Where to find it

Moses and the Pharaoh *Exodus 1–15*
Pharaoh-Neco and Josiah *2 Kings 23:29-35*

PHARISEES (FAIR-uh-seez) were the strictest and most influential group of Jews in the time of Jesus. They studied the Old Testament and were determined to keep every rule in it. Many traditions and interpretations of the Old Testament had grown through the centuries, and the Pharisees tried to follow these, too. They did not associate with others who did not share their ideas, and they often looked down on other Jews.

Pharisees often made a big show of their praying.

Because they put more emphasis on keeping rules than on loving people, they did not approve when Jesus made friends with those whom the Pharisees called "sinners."

Pharisees disliked Jesus especially because he did not follow their very strict laws of keeping the Sabbath. They objected when Jesus healed people on the Sabbath, because that was "work." Jesus often condemned their wrong attitudes. Some of the leaders of the New Testament church had once been Pharisees—men such as the apostle Paul, Nicodemus, and probably Joseph of Arimathea.

Where to find it

Jesus condemns the Pharisees *Matthew 9:10-13; 23:1-36*
Pharisees condemn Jesus *Matthew 12:1-14; Luke 5:21*
Paul a Pharisee *Acts 26:5; Philippians 3:4-6*
Nicodemus a Pharisee *John 3:1-15; 19:38-41*
Joseph of Arimathea a Pharisee *Mark 15:42-46; Luke 23:50*

PHEBE (see *(Phoebe)*

PHENICE (see *Phoenix*)

PHILADELPHIA *(fill-uh-DELL-fee-uh)* was a city in the western part of what is now Turkey. The name means "brotherly love." The church in Philadelphia was one of those to which John wrote the Book of Revelation. John praised this church: "Because you have kept my word of patient endurance, I will keep you from the hour of trial which is coming on the whole world."

Philadelphia was a city that had often been destroyed by earthquakes. It was a center of pagan worship.

Where to find it: *Revelation 3: 7-13*

PHILEMON *(fuh-LEE-mun)* was a Christian man in Colossae. The apostle Paul wrote him a short letter that is now a part of our New Testament.

Philemon had a slave named Onesimus who ran away and probably went to Rome, where he met Paul and became a Christian. Paul sent Onesimus back to Philemon with this letter. It is a loving letter, telling Philemon to receive Onesimus not as a slave but as a brother in the Lord. Paul told Philemon to charge anything Onesimus owed to Paul's account. Paul also told Philemon how helpful Onesimus had been to him in prison.

The letter was addressed not only to Philemon but to the "church in your house." Philemon, like many Christians of early times, opened his home as a place for Christian worship.

PHILETUS *(fuh-LEE-tus)* was a false teacher in Ephesus who taught that the resurrection of believers was already past. He probably taught that the "resurrection of the dead" referred to conversion or to some other spiritual experience. Paul said Philetus had upset the faith of some people.

Where to find it: *2 Timothy 2:17-18*

PHILIP *(FIL-up)* is the name of two important people in the New Testament:

1. Philip, the apostle or disciple of Jesus, grew up in Bethsaida, the hometown of Peter and Andrew. He was the disciple who brought Nathanael to Jesus. Later on, he also brought some Gentiles to meet Jesus.

Philip is not mentioned in the Bible after the time of Pentecost, but tradition says he did missionary work in Asia Minor (now Turkey).

2. Philip, the deacon and evangelist, was a Greek-speaking Jew who was one of the seven deacons appointed to help take care of food for widows in Jerusalem. After Stephen was stoned, the deacons became evangelists or missionaries. Philip went to the city of Samaria to preach. Many people believed in Christ, and God did some miracles of healing through Philip.

Then God called him to leave Samaria and go to a desert road, where he met an Ethiopian man who was reading the Book of Isaiah in his chariot. Philip sat in the chariot with him and

explained that Jesus was the Messiah about whom the prophet Isaiah had written. The Ethiopian believed in Christ, and Philip baptized him. Then "the Spirit of the Lord caught up Philip; and the eunuch saw him no more." Philip was soon found, however, preaching in other towns.

Philip later lived in Caesarea, where he was an evangelist. Paul often stayed with him when he traveled to Caesarea. Philip had four unmarried daughters who prophesied. The Bible tells nothing more of Philip's later life.

Where to find it

Philip the apostle   *Matthew 10: 2-3; John 1: 43-51;*
6: 5-6; 12: 20-23; 14: 8-14; Acts 1: 13
Philip the deacon   *Acts 6: 1-6; 8: 4-40; 21: 7-10*

PHILIPPI *(FIL-uh-pie or fuh-LIP-eye)* was a major city in northeastern Macedonia, an area that is now part of Greece. Philippi was a Roman colony. Many retired Roman soldiers lived there, and the people had all the legal rights of Roman citizens.

Philippi was a city of mixtures: the languages and culture were Greek; the government was Roman; the religions included the worship of Greek, Roman, and Egyptian gods plus emperor worship.

This city was the first place in Europe to hear the gospel. Paul went to Philippi on his second missionary journey after God sent him a vision of a Macedonian man saying, "Come over and help us."

When Paul arrived, he first preached to Lydia, a businesswoman, and a group of other Jewish women who had gathered at a riverbank to pray. Lydia and others of her household were the beginning of the church at Philippi. Paul was arrested in Philippi after he healed a young girl who was possessed by a demon. When Paul was miraculously freed from jail, his jailer became a Christian.

Philippi and other cities in Macedonia gave higher social status to women than many other areas in that day. This shows in Paul's letter to the Philippians, where he mentions two women who "labored side by side with me in the gospel."

Where to find it: *Acts 16: 1-40; Philippians 4: 2-3*

PHILIPPIANS *(fuh-LIP-ee-unz)*, **LETTER TO,** was written by the apostle Paul to the church at Philippi. He thanked the believers for sending one of their members, Epaphroditus, to visit Paul in prison and bring him a gift of money. It was the only church from which Paul ever accepted such a gift.

Epaphroditus became sick while he was with Paul and almost died. After he recovered, Paul sent him home to Philippi with this letter, telling the Philippians to receive Epaphroditus

PHILISTINES

with joy and to show honor to him, for he had risked his life in the service of Christ.

Paul had a closer relationship with this church than with any other. His love for the Philippians shows clearly in this letter. He wrote of his joy in remembering them and of their joy in the Lord. The idea of joy or rejoicing appears 16 times in this short letter—even though Paul was in prison when he wrote it.

He reminded the Philippians of how Christ gave up the joys of heaven to become a man and die on the cross. He reminded them how important it is for Christians to be content wherever God places them. And he said to think about things that are true, pure, lovely, and gracious.

Where to find it

Christ became a man   *Philippians 2: 5-11*
Paul commends Epaphroditus   *Philippians 2: 25-30*
Importance of right thinking   *Philippians 4: 8*
Paul thanks them for gifts   *Philippians 4: 10-20*

PHILISTINES *(FIL-uh-steenze or fuh-LIS-teenz)* lived along the coast of the Mediterranean Sea in southern Canaan during much of Old Testament times. The name *Palestine* means "land of the Philistines."

The Philistines were usually enemies of the Israelites and fought many battles with them during the time of the Book of Judges—about 1400 to 1050 B.C.

These people were the enemies in many famous Bible stories. A Philistine woman, Delilah, tricked Samson into telling the secret of his great strength. The giant that David killed with a sling and a stone was a Philistine. The Israelites never fully conquered the Philistines.

The Philistines apparently came to Canaan from islands in the Aegean Sea. By the time the Hebrews moved to Canaan, the Philistines were more wealthy than the Hebrews and were more advanced in using tools and crafts,

87

Delilah was the Philistine who trapped Samson.

particularly metals. Because of this, the Philistines knew how to build war chariots when the Hebrews did not.

When David was hiding from King Saul, he lived among the Philistines for a few years. He may have learned from them how to make iron. After David became king, the Israelites began using iron tools.

PHINEHAS *(FIN-ee-us)*, an Old Testament priest, was the son of Eli. He and his brother, Hophni, disobeyed the commands of the Lord. When the Hebrews brought their offerings to the Tabernacle, Phinehas and his brother took the best part for themselves.

They once carried the sacred ark of the Covenant into a battle with the Philistines because they thought it had some magical power to bring victory. Instead, God let the ark be captured by the Philistines, and Phinehas and his brother were killed in the battle.

Phinehas's wife was about to have a baby at this time, and the shock of the news about her husband's death sent her into childbirth. She died shortly after giving birth, but before her death she asked that her son be named Ichabod, which means "The glory has departed."

Where to find it: *1 Samuel 2:12-17; 4:1-22*

PHOEBE *(FEE-bee)* was a deacon and leader in the church at Cenchreae. She was praised by Paul, who asked her to carry his important letter to the church at Rome. Most translations say "deaconess," but the Greek word means "deacon."

Where to find it: *Romans 16:1-2*

PHOENICIA *(fuh-NISH-uh)* was a country along the eastern edge of the Mediterranean Sea. The Phoenicians were famous for their knowledge of sea travel, and they tried hard to keep this a secret from others. Their most famous cities were Tyre and Sidon. In fact, *Sidonians* became another word for *Phoenicians.* Jezebel, the wife of King Ahab, was a daughter of a Phoenician king. Jezebel brought the Phoenician religion—the worship of Baal—into Israel. She had 450 prophets of Baal live in her palace.

Phoenicia was later conquered by Babylon, Greece, and then Syria. In the time of Christ, the people from the area were called "Syrophoenicians," and the country was a part of Syria. Most of the land is now part of Lebanon.

Where to find it: *1 Kings 16:31*

PHOENIX *(FEE-nix)* or **PHENICE** *(fuh-NIE-see)* was a town and harbor on the island of Crete. The sailors on the ship that took Paul to Rome tried to reach this harbor but never made it. A terrible storm blew them out into the open sea instead.

Where to find it: *Acts 27:12-44*

PHRYGIA *(FRIDGE-ee-uh)* was an inland portion of Asia Minor that is now a part of southwestern Turkey. Its boundaries changed often in history.

Paul preached in the area on his second and third missionary journeys.

Where to find it: *Acts 16:6; 18:23*

PHYGELLUS *(fuh-JELL-us)* was a man in Asia Minor (now western Turkey) who turned away from Paul and his teachings.

Where to find it: *2 Timothy 1:15*

PHYLACTERIES (see *Frontlets*)

PHYSICIAN (see *Occupations*)

PIGEON (see *Birds*)

PILATE *(PIE-lut)*, **PONTIUS** *(PON-chus)*, was the governor of Judea during the time of Jesus' death. He was a Roman responsible for keeping peace among the Jews.

Pilate never got along well with the Jews. He

"I am innocent of this man's blood," Pontius Pilate said as he washed his hands during Jesus' trial.

did not understand them or their religion. The Jewish historian Josephus wrote that Pilate outraged the Jews by using Temple money to build an aqueduct. He also brought shields decorated with figures of Roman emperors into Jerusalem.

Although Pilate's headquarters were in Caesarea, he went to Jerusalem to help keep order among the crowds who came to the Passover feast. When Jesus was brought to him, he realized that Jesus was innocent of the charges against him. However, Pilate did not want to get into more trouble with the Jews, who had already complained to the emperor that he was not a good governor. So he allowed Jesus to be executed because he did not want to lose his job.

He was removed from his position about six years later. History does not record what happened to him after that, although Christian tradition says he later killed himself.

Where to find it: *Matthew 27:1-31; Mark 15:1-15; Luke 23:1-25; John 18:28–19:6*

PILGRIMS *(PILL-grimz)* were people who lived in a country other than their own—either because they wanted to, or because they were forced to leave their own land. *Pilgrim* is used as a word picture in the King James Version to show that Christians are not "in their own country" on earth; their true home is where Jesus is.

Some other versions use *exiles* instead of *pilgrims*.

Where to find it: *Hebrews 11:13-16; 1 Peter 2:11*

PILLAR *(PILL-er)* has several meanings in the Bible. It may mean a column that holds up a building, such as the pillars of Solomon's Temple.

It may also mean a stone that is set upright as a reminder of a special meeting with God.

89

At Bethel, Jacob took the stone he had slept on, poured oil on it, and set it up as a sign of his meeting with God. When Rachel died, Jacob set up another pillar (upright stone) to mark his wife's grave.

Standing stones were often used in idol worship. These are often called "images" in the King James Version and "pillars" in the Revised Standard Version. They were actually stones used as idols.

Where to find it

Bethel stone *Genesis 28:18-22*
Rachel's grave *Genesis 35:19-20*
Idols *Exodus 23:24; Deuteronomy 7:5; 1 Kings 14:23 (all RSV)*

PILLAR OF FIRE AND CLOUD was the sign God used to lead the Israelites through the wilderness. God showed this miraculous sign to the Israelites as they were fleeing from the army of the Pharaoh. It continued to guide them all during the 40 years before they entered Canaan. The cloud (in the daytime) and the fire (at night) were apparently shaped like a stone set upright (see *Pillar*).

Although the pillar normally went in front of the Israelites to show them when and where to travel, it moved in *back* of the Israelites when they were being pursued by the Pharaoh's army. As a result, the soldiers could not see the Israelites.

During the Hebrews' 40 years in the wilderness, God spoke to Moses many times from the cloud as it stood over the Tabernacle. Moses would go into the Tabernacle. Then the cloud would come down and stay at the door of the Tabernacle as God spoke to Moses from it.

At the end of the 40 years, when Joshua was ready to take over command from Moses, God spoke to both of them from the cloud in front of the Tabernacle.

The pillar is not mentioned after the death of Moses.

Where to find it

Helps escape from Egyptians *Exodus 13:21-22; 14:19-24*
Leads them through wilderness *Nehemiah 9:19*
God speaks to Moses from cloud *Exodus 33:8-11*
God speaks to Moses and Joshua *Deuteronomy 31:14-23*

PIN is a word used in the Bible for a tent peg, a nail, a stick with which to dig, a piece of wood used in weaving, or a peg on which to hang something. Crisping pins, mentioned in the King James Version of Isaiah 3:22, refer to a handbag or purse.

PINE TREE (see *Plants*)

PINNACLE *(PIN-uh-kul)* is the word used to describe the place in the Temple where Satan took Jesus to tempt him. It was apparently a high place, because Satan urged Jesus to

throw himself down to prove that the angels would care for him.

Where to find it: *Matthew 4:5-7; Luke 4:9-13*

PISGAH *(PIZ-guh)*, **MOUNT,** was the mountain from which Moses looked at the Promised Land just before he died. Mount Pisgah was on the east side of the Jordan River, near the Dead Sea, not far from Jericho.

In the story of the prophet Balaam, King Balak of Moab built seven altars to God on Mount Pisgah and offered a bull and a ram on each altar. God spoke with Balaam there—although Balaam did not like what God told him to say.

Where to find it

Balaam on Mount Pisgah *Numbers 23:14-30*
Moses sees the Promised Land *Deuteronomy 3:27; 34:1-4*

PISIDIA (*puh-SID-ee-uh*) was a small Roman province in what is now south central Turkey. The city of Antioch that Paul visited twice was on the northern edge of Pisidia (see *Antioch of Pisidia*).

Where to find it: *Acts 13:13-52; 14:21-24*

PIT refers to a hole in the ground, or a well, or a cistern. *Pit* is also sometimes used as a word picture for the grave or death.

Where to find it: *Job 33:18; Isaiah 14:15*

PITCH was a thick, sticky substance that ancient people used to make boats watertight. Moses' mother used pitch in the basket for her baby. Pitch burned easily.

Where to find it: *Exodus 2:3*

PITCHER was an earthenware jar normally used to carry or store water. A pitcher usually had one or two handles. The soldiers of Gideon carried torches in empty pitchers when they made a surprise attack on the Midianites. At Gideon's signal, the 300 men blew their trumpets and smashed their pitchers, suddenly showing the torches. The enemies were so frightened they ran away.

Where to find it: *Judges 7:19-21*

PITY in the Bible does not mean to feel sorry for someone. It means to show love, concern, and sympathy. The Bible says clearly that God has pity—meaning love, concern, and sympathy—for those who trust him. Psalm 103:13 compares it to the feeling that a father has for his children.

Where to find it: *Joel 2:18*

PLAGUE (see *Diseases*)

PLAGUES (*playgz*) **OF EGYPT** were disasters sent by God to convince the Pharaoh to let the Israelites leave Egypt. Although some of these plagues could be considered natural disasters, their timing was certainly arranged by God to fulfill his purpose for the Hebrews. There were ten plagues:

1. Water became blood. When the Nile River floods, as it does each year in Egypt, it sometimes becomes red in color from soil or little organisms. The water sometimes becomes too bad to drink. This may be why the Egyptian magicians were also able to make the water become like blood (Exodus 7:14-24).

2. Frogs swarmed throughout the land. When the waters of the flooded Nile began to dry up, frogs multiplied in the marshes and came up on the dry land. The Egyptian magi-

cians said they could also make this happen (Exodus 8:1-15).

3. Swarms of lice (or gnats, or sandflies, or fleas) came. Various translations use different words for this plague. The Egyptian magicians could not make the insects come, so they told the Pharaoh, "This is the finger of God" (Exodus 8:19).

4. Swarms of flies came in great numbers. They may have come to feed on the dead frogs. However, there were no swarms of flies in Goshen, the land where the Israelites lived. The Hebrews may have been more careful to bury the frogs in their area so the flies would not come, or God may simply have chosen not to let the flies come to Goshen (Exodus 8:20-32).

5. Cattle became diseased. The cattle of the Egyptians died, but none of the cattle of the Hebrews died (Exodus 9:1-7).

6. Boils or sores infected people and animals. A fine dust settled over the land, and all the Egyptians and their cattle broke out in boils (Exodus 9:8-12).

7. Hail destroyed animals and crops. Moses warned the people that hail was coming. The

Egyptians who believed him got their cattle into shelter. Then a terrible hail and thunderstorm came and destroyed all crops and animals not under shelter. But there was no hail in the land of Goshen, where the Israelites lived (Exodus 8:13-35).

8. Locusts came and ate up the crops that were just coming out of the ground and had not been destroyed by the hail (Exodus 10:1-20).

9. Darkness covered the land for three days. This may have been a terrible dust and sand storm that came when God sent the strong wind to drive away the locusts. However, it did not affect the land of Goshen (Exodus 10:21-29).

10. The oldest child in each family and the firstborn cattle all died. The Israelites were protected by God from this terrible plague by sprinkling the blood of the Passover lamb on their doorposts. This was the beginning of the Passover feast, which is still celebrated to the present time. This plague finally convinced the Pharaoh to let the Hebrews go (Exodus 11:1—12:32).

PLANE TREE (see *Plants*)

PLANTS AND TREES of many different types are mentioned in the Bible. Most of them can be identified as plants now growing around the Mediterranean or in other areas with similar climates. Some, however, are not known today by their biblical names, and scholars are not sure just what plants the Bible was referring to.

Acacia or **Shittah** trees still grow in the desert regions of Sinai and the Negev. Acacia wood is very hard and is orange-brown. The ark of the Covenant and many other objects in the Tabernacle were made of acacia or shittim wood, according to Exodus 25—27, 30, and 35—38.

Almond is a tree that blossoms earlier than most fruit trees. Moses used almond sticks to test who was called to be the spiritual leader. Only Aaron's rod budded overnight and bore ripe almonds (Numbers 17:1-11).

The design of the almond blossom was used to decorate the Israelites' golden candlesticks in the Tabernacle (Exodus 25:33-36).

Bulrushes

Almug (AL-mug) tree was used for the pillars of King Solomon's Temple. Its wood is strong, repels insects, and is a beautiful ruby-red color that can be highly polished (1 Kings 10:11-12). Most almug trees grow in India.

Aloes (AL-ohz) is a fragrant substance made from a tree and a plant. The tree was probably the eaglewood tree. The plant was a member of the lily family. Aloes made from the plant were used for embalming bodies as in John 19:38-40.

Anise (ANN-us) was probably similar to our dill weed. It is mentioned in Matthew 23:23.

Apples are mentioned several times in the Old Testament, especially in the Song of Solomon. However, they may not be the kind of apples we know today, since apples grow only in remote places in Israel and are of poor quality. Scholars suggest that the fruit might have been the apricot or quince instead.

Barley was the most common grain grown in Israel. Most of the poor people used it for bread and cereal because it cost less than wheat.

Beans, especially dried beans, were a regular part of the diet of poor people in Palestine. Dried beans were sometimes ground and mixed with grain to make bread (Ezekiel 4:9).

Box Tree is mentioned in the King James Version of Isaiah 41:19 and 60:13. It is translated "pine" by the Revised Standard Version. It was probably some form of evergreen. Our kind of box tree is not found in the Holy Land.

Bramble was probably something like our blackberry bush. It is mentioned in Judges 9:7-15 and Luke 6:44.

Briar was any of several thorny plants that were used as word pictures of enemies or something worthless (Isaiah 5:6; 7:23-25; 55:13; Ezekiel 28:24; Micah 7:4).

Broom Tree is a desert shrub or bush that grows large enough to give some shade. It grows freely in the desert areas of the Sinai Peninsula. Elijah once took refuge in its shade (1 Kings 19:4-5). Its roots and branches were used for fuel.

Bulrush is the papyrus plant, a tall slender plant that grows in swampy places. The boat for the baby Moses was made from this plant (Exodus 2:3). Bulrushes were also used to make writing material before the days of paper.

Camphire (see *Henna*)

Cassia *(KASH-ee-uh)* was a tree whose bark had a fragrant smell. Its small leaves were added to the oil used for anointing sacred things. It is described in Exodus 30:22-33.

Cedar *(SEE-dur)* **Trees** were often used in Bible times as building material. Cedar was also used to burn the sacrifices (Leviticus 14:4-6; Numbers 19:6).

One of the few remaining cedars of Lebanon.

Chestnut (see *Plane Tree*)

Cinnamon *(SIN-uh-mun)* is a tree that grows about 20 feet high. The spice cinnamon comes from its inner bark. Cinnamon was used in the holy anointing oil in the Old Testament (Exodus 30:23) and in perfume.

Cockle is the term used in the King James

Version of Job 31:40 to describe a foul weed that grew in wheat and barley fields. Its seeds were poisonous if ground with flour.

Coriander was a plant whose seeds were used for seasoning and medicines.

Corn is the word used in the King James Version for wheat (see *Wheat*).

Cucumbers were similar to our cucumbers.

Cummin was a plant whose seeds were used for seasoning food.

Cypress Tree in the Bible may or may not be the same as our cypress trees; authorities aren't sure. Some think the gopher wood Noah used to build the ark was cypress wood.

Dove's Dung was a flowering plant grown from bulbs. The bulbs could be used for food, as they were in 2 Kings 6:25.

Flag (see *Bulrush*)

Fig Tree is the first known tree mentioned in the Bible. Genesis 3:7 says that Adam and Eve made aprons from fig leaves.

Figs were an important food for the Israelites.

For a person to "sit under his fig tree" was a sign of peace and prosperity. It is also a picture of deep thought, as in John 1:50, where Jesus said he saw Nathanael sitting under a fig tree.

Fir Tree was an evergreen that grew in Palestine.

Frankincense *(FRANK-in-sense)* is a tree in northern India and Arabia. When a cut is made in its bark, a resin comes out that is used in incense. It was used in the Tabernacle and the Temple. The wise men brought a gift of frankincense to the baby Jesus (Matthew 2:11).

Gall, the juice of the opium poppy, makes a person so sleepy he cannot feel pain. When Jesus was dying on the cross, he was offered a drink made of vinegar and gall (Matthew 27:32-34).

Gourd is a large bush or tree with big leaves. Castor oil is made from its seeds. The King James Version says that Jonah sat under a gourd. This was not the kind of plant we call a gourd, which grows only in the warm part of the Americas.

Grape (see *Vine*)

Henna was a flowering shrub with fragrant blossoms that is also called camphire. It is mentioned in Song of Solomon 1:14; 4:13-14.

Herbs or **Bitter Herbs** were greens gathered fresh and eaten as a salad at the Passover. They may have included endive, chicory, lettuce, water cress, sorrell, and dandelions (Exodus 12:8; Numbers 9:11).

Hyssop *(HISS-up)* is an herb plant something like marjoram. Its stem is hairy and holds moisture well. In the story of the Passover feast in Exodus 12:21-22, the Hebrews were told to take a bunch of hyssop and use it as a brush to put blood on the lintel and doorposts. At the crucifixion of Jesus, John 19:29 says that Jesus was given vinegar on hyssop. This may have been the same kind of hyssop attached to a reed or stick, or it may have been a kind of sorghum cane stick that has a similar Latin name.

Hyssop

Juniper (see *Broom Tree)*

Leek was a plant in the lily family. Its small bulbs that grow above ground are used for seasoning. Parts of the leaves are edible (Numbers 11:5).

Lentils *(LEN-tulz)* were similar to today's lentils—a member of the pea family. The "pottage" that Jacob sold to Esau for his birthright was made of lentils (Genesis 25:34). Lentils are often mentioned as a food in the Old Testament.

Lilies that Jesus mentioned in Luke 12:27 may have meant any beautiful wild flowers, such as anemones or poppies, that grew freely along roadsides and fields in Palestine.

Lilies are mentioned in the Old Testament also. Whether they refer to the lilies we know or to flowers in general is not clear. The lotus water lily was common in Egypt.

Mandrakes *(MAN-drakes)* were plants something like potatoes with roots that are sometimes eaten. Although they can be eaten, they are slightly poisonous and make some people ill. They are called "love apples" because some people thought they increased sexual desire. They are mentioned in the story of

Rachel, Leah, and Jacob in Genesis 30:14-17.

Millet *(MILL-ut)* is a poor-quality grain that still grows in Palestine. People mixed it with other flours to make bread, or ate it as cereal. It is mentioned in Ezekiel 4:9.

Mulberry Tree is mentioned in the King James Version of 2 Samuel 5:23-24 and 1 Chronicles 14:14-15. However, many scholars think this was a balsam tree. The Revised Standard Version refers to it as balsam. The sycamine tree mentioned in Luke 17:6 was a black mulberry tree.

Mustard Plants are mentioned in one of Jesus' parables. The mustard seed is small and grows rapidly into a large plant. Jesus used the mustard seed as an example of how the Kingdom of God grows.

Where to find it: *Matthew 13:31-32; 17:20; Mark 4:30-32; Luke 13:18-19; 17:6*

Myrrh *(mer)* was a fragrant substance made from a plant. Used as part of perfume, it was among the gifts offered to the baby Jesus (Matthew 2:11). Myrrh was also used to embalm the body of Jesus (John 19:39).

Myrrh

Nard was a fragrant ointment made from the roots and stems of the spikenard plant. It was a favorite perfume of ancient people. It was very expensive because it had to be imported from India. This was the ointment Mary placed on the feet of Jesus, as told in John 12:3. Mark 14:3 tells of another time when nard was poured on the head of Jesus.

Nettles are weeds that grow in Palestine. They sting the skin when touched. They are mentioned several times in the Bible.

Nuts included both pistachio nuts and walnuts. Walnuts were eaten and also pressed to get oil.

Olive Trees were important to people in Palestine. Olives were eaten for food, and olive oil was used in cooking, lamps, medicines, and ointments. Olive wood was used in carpentry. Olive trees grow well in the rocky soil, require very little water, and produce fruit for hundreds of years.

Onions were a favorite food of the Hebrews in Egypt. They are mentioned in Numbers 11:5.

Palm Trees were date palms. They have grown in Palestine for at least 5,000 years. John 12:13 says that when Jesus rode into Jerusalem on the Sunday before his crucifixion, the crowds took branches of palm trees and went out to meet him. The Christian church calls the Sunday before Easter "Palm Sunday."

Pine Tree was probably a kind of fir tree, although scholars are not sure.

Plane Tree is mentioned in several Old Testament passages. Scholars are not sure what tree is meant. The King James Version sometimes calls it "chestnut," but this translation is questionable.

Pomegranate *(PAHM-uh-GRAN-ut)* **Tree** gives a delicious fruit about the size of an apple. The fruit has many seeds. Pomegranate trees grew in the famous hanging gardens of Babylon.

Pomegranate

Poplar Tree was probably the white poplar that grows in the hills of Palestine.

Pulse refers to a dish made from several different vegetables. Daniel and his friends ate pulse instead of the king's food. The word is used only in the King James Version. Other versions translate the word "vegetables" (Daniel 1:12, 16; also 2 Samuel 17:28).

Reed refers to the stalk of tall grasses that grew along the rivers of Palestine. Sometimes reeds grew as tall as 12 feet.

Rose of Sharon mentioned in Song of Solomon 2:1 was probably closer to a tulip than to our variety of roses.

Sycamine *(SICK-uh-min)* tree was a black mulberry tree.

Sycamore *(SICK-uh-more)* tree was not like the sycamore tree of our day, but rather was a kind of fig tree. Its wood was durable and was important to the economy in Bible times. This tree is still common in Israel. This is the kind of tree that Zacchaeus climbed because he was short (Luke 19:1-6).

Shittah, Shittim (see *Acacia Tree*)

Spikenard (see *Nard*)

Tamarisk *(TAM-uh-risk)* is a small tree or shrub with tiny leaves and feathery branches. Abraham planted a tamarisk tree in Beersheba (Genesis 21:33), and Saul was buried beneath a tamarisk tree (1 Samuel 31:13).

Tares probably refer to weeds called darnel that grow in wheat fields. Because they look so much like wheat, tares were usually left

Tares (above), wheat (below)

until harvesttime. Sometimes they were pulled out by hand; other times they were harvested with the wheat and then separated with a sieve. The seeds of tares were much smaller than wheat and would go through the sieve, leaving only the wheat. Jesus talked about tares in Matthew 13:25. The Revised Standard Version calls them "weeds."

Thistles are prickly plants. Many kinds grow in Palestine.

Thorns are plants with sharp points. They are common in Palestine and are mentioned several times in the Bible. The crown of thorns placed on Jesus before his crucifixion was probably made from a thorn bush now known as the Christ thorn.

Vine usually refers to a grapevine. The harvesting of grapes was always a time of festivals. Vineyards are mentioned often in the Bible.

Wheat was the most common cereal in Palestine. The King James Version often calls wheat "corn."

Willow trees of the Bible probably include poplars as well as willow trees. They grow freely along the banks of the Jordan River and other streams in Israel.

Wormwood is a plant something like sagebrush. It tastes bitter and is sometimes used in the Bible as a word picture of bad experiences.

PLASTER has been used since prehistoric times to cover walls and floors of rooms. Various materials were used for plaster, such as clay, straw, ashes, lime, and white sand.

PLEDGE was a piece of clothing or property. A person who owed a debt gave it as proof that he would pay the debt. In our time we call this "collateral." The Old Testament Law said that a person could not take a man's coat as a pledge and keep it overnight, because the person might then be cold. There were also other laws about what could be pledged.

Where to find it: *Exodus 22: 25-27; Deuteronomy 24: 10-13*

PLEIADES *(PLEE-uh-deez)* is a bright constellation of six stars.

Where to find it: *Job 38: 31*

PLOWMAN (see *Occupations–Farmer*)

PLOW in Bible times was a wooden or metal tool that farmers used to break up the ground. Oxen usually pulled plows, and farmers guided them as they walked in back of the plow. The earliest plows were only forked sticks that scratched the surface of the ground rather than turning it over.

PLOWSHARE *(PLOW-share)* refers to the blade of a plow. When the prophets spoke of beating swords into plowshares, it was a word

picture for a time of peace when weapons are not needed.

Where to find it: *Isaiah 2: 4; Micah 4: 3*

PLUMB *(plum)* **LINE** is a cord with a stone or weight (called a plummet) tied to one end. Builders use plumb lines to test whether a wall is straight up and down. In the Bible, *plumb*

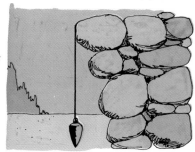

The prophet Amos once saw a vision of a plumb line.

line is sometimes used as a word picture for the way God tests the uprightness of his people.

Where to find it: *2 Kings 21: 13; Isaiah 28: 17; Amos 7: 7-9*

POETRY, HEBREW, is quite different from our poetry. Our poetry is usually based on a rhythm of *sound*. Hebrew poetry is based on a rhythm of *ideas*.

In most Hebrew poetry, an idea is expressed in the first line, and then that same idea is expressed in different words in the second line. This is called parallelism and is the most important characteristic of Hebrew poetry. Sometimes the idea in the first line is repeated two or three times in following lines.

Occasionally, the Hebrews wrote poetry in which the second line was a *contrast* to the first line. Proverbs 15: 1 says:

A soft answer turns away wrath,
but a harsh word stirs up anger.

Psalm 24 starts this way:

First idea	The earth is the Lord's and the fulness thereof,
repeated	the world and those who dwell therein;
Second idea	for he has founded it upon the seas,
repeated	and established it upon the rivers.
Third idea–question	Who shall ascend the hill of the Lord?
repeated	And who shall stand in his holy place?
Fourth idea–answer	He who has clean hands and a pure heart,
negative answer	who does not lift up his soul to what is false.

Much of the Old Testament is written in poetry. Some translations print the poetic parts so that they look like poetry. The Revised Standard Version and the New International Version do this. The King James Version and the Living Bible do not print the poetic parts to look like poetry.

The following Old Testament books are all, or nearly all, poetry:

Job	Joel
Psalms	Amos
Proverbs	Obadiah
Song of Solomon	Micah
Isaiah	Nahum
Jeremiah	Habakkuk
Lamentations	Zephaniah

The Old Testament poets were skillful writers. Not only did they say thoughtful and important things, but they used excellent word pictures, language, and rhythm. The poetry of the Bible is great literature as well as being part of God's message to us.

POLITARCH (see *Magistrate*)

POLLUTE *(puh-LOOT)* means to make impure or unfit for use. Usually, *pollute* is used in the Bible as a word picture of the results of sin. For example, Jeremiah 16:18 says, "They have polluted my land with the carcasses of their detestable idols." Idolatry had changed the Holy Land into "the unholy land."

Sometimes, as in Malachi 1:7-8, *polluted* refers to imperfect animals being offered as sacrifices. The Old Testament Law required that only perfect animals could be used as sacrifices in the Temple.

POLLUX *(PAH-lucks)* **AND CASTOR** *(KAS-tur)* were the Greek gods who were supposed to protect sailors. An image of them was used on the ship on which Paul sailed to Rome. The Revised Standard Version calls them "the Twin Brothers."

Where to find it: *Acts 28:11*

POLYGAMY *(puh-LIG-uh-me)* is having more than one husband or wife. A few cultures have polygamy today. During some periods of the Old Testament, some men had more than one wife. This was not common in New Testament times (see *Marriage*).

PONTIUS PILATE (see *Pilate*)

PONTUS *(PON-tuss)* was a province in what is now northern Turkey. During New Testament times, many Jews lived in Pontus. Aquila, a prominent man in the early church, came from Pontus. Paul did not go on to this province, but a group of Christians was there. Pontus is one of the places Peter sent his first letter. The New Testament does not tell who first preached or taught there.

Where to find it: *Acts 18:2; 1 Peter 1:1*

POMEGRANATE (see *Plants*)

POOL OF BETHESDA *(buh-THEZ-duh)* or **BETH-ZATHA** *(beth-ZAY-thuh)* was a spring-fed pool surrounded by five porches. When the spring flowed, the water in the pool bubbled. Many sick people gathered on the porches. They believed that the water could heal them when it was bubbling.

One Sabbath as Jesus walked beside the pool in Jerusalem, he healed a man who had been ill for 38 years. Some Jews were angry because Jesus healed him on the Sabbath.

We don't know for sure where the Pool of Bethesda was. However, in 1888 an old reservoir was found buried on the property of the Church of Saint Anne. The remains of five porches were also found around the pool. Many archaeologists think this was the Pool of Bethesda.

Where to find it: *John 5:1-16*

POOLS are mentioned often in the Bible. Some were natural pockets of water; others were built to collect water for drinking or irrigation. Because there was little rain in Palestine, people saved all the water possible and used it carefully.

POOR usually refers to those who don't have some of the necessities of life. Both the Old and New Testaments teach that those who have more than they need should share their possessions with those who don't have enough. Israel began as a nation of slaves, and the people were not to forget that. As they grew wealthier in Canaan, God sent prophets to keep telling them that he was displeased when they did not take care of the poor.

Jesus lived as a poor man among poor people. His acts showed that he understood the problems of the poor and had special concern for them.

One of the first acts of the early church in Jerusalem was to arrange to feed widows, who didn't have husbands to support them. Later most of the Christians in Jerusalem were poor because of a famine, and Paul spent more than two years collecting money from Gentile Christians for the poor Christians in Jerusalem. The Book of James reminds Christians that true faith shows itself in helping those in need.

Where to find it

Jesus was poor *Matthew 8:20*
Early church feeds widows *Acts 6:1*
Paul gathers collection *1 Corinthians 16:1-4; 2 Corinthians 8—9*
True faith shows in caring for others *James 2:14-17*

POPLAR (see *Plants*)

PORCH is usually an open area with a roof supported by pillars. Porches were around the pool of Bethesda. A certain part of the Temple was called "Solomon's porch."

Where to find it: *John 5:2; Acts 3:11*

PORTER (see *Occupations*)

POSSESSION, DEMON (see *Demons*)

POT was a container made of metal or clay. People used pots of many shapes and sizes to carry or store liquids, grain, and other materials (see *Pottery Making*).

POTIPHAR (*POT-uh-fur*) was one of the Pharaoh's officers. Potiphar bought Joseph as a slave. Potiphar soon recognized Joseph's keen mind and organizing ability and placed him in charge of running his household. When Potiphar's wife falsely accused Joseph of molesting her, Potiphar had Joseph put in prison.

Where to find it: *Genesis 39:1-20*

POTSHERD (*POT-shurd*) is a piece of broken pottery. Potsherds are sometimes mentioned as word pictures of something that is useless or worthless.

Where to find it: *Psalm 22:15; Proverbs 26:23*

POTTAGE (*POT-idge*) was a thick vegetable soup made with lentils, spices, and sometimes pieces of meat. Esau sold his birthright to Jacob for a bowl of pottage. Elisha and the sons of prophets ate pottage.

Where to find it: *Genesis 25:29-34; 2 Kings 4:38-39*

POTTER (see *Occupations*)

POTTER'S FIELD was a graveyard near Jerusalem where foreigners were buried. It was purchased with the money the chief priests paid Judas to betray Jesus. Before that, it had apparently been used by a potter as a place to weather his clay before he made it into pottery, or else it was a place where he got clay to make pots.

Where to find it: *Matthew 27:3-7*

POTTERY MAKING was important to people during Bible times. Almost all containers were made from pottery, because wood and metal were very expensive. Potters made bowls, cups, cooking pots, lamps, ovens, and storage jars for water, grain, and other supplies.

Almost all pottery made during Bible times was made on a potter's wheel. Potters' wheels began to be used in the ancient world before the Israelites left Egypt. In the Promised Land, every village had its potter.

The potter usually lived near the edge of town because he needed a field where he could weather his clay. He also needed a well or spring, because he used large amounts of water. He also had to have space for his kilns.

A good potter knew just what kind of clay was best for his work. Potters' clay in Israel was usually a red clay common in the land. After the clay had weathered, the potter mixed it with water to get the right softness. Then he walked around in the clay to tread out all the bubbles of air. If he was making only a small amount of clay, he would knead it with his hands.

Then a lump of clay was thrown on the potter's wheel. As the wheel turned, the potter formed it with his hands to the shape he desired. After it was partially hardened, he might put it on the wheel again to finish off any rough places. He also decorated the pot by painting it. Many times the potter would add a "slip"—a creamy clay with a mineral color added.

Finally the pot was fired in a kiln. This means it was baked a certain number of hours at very high temperatures. Firing was the most difficult job of the potter. The secrets of how to do it well were passed on from father to son.

Pottery was an important part of the culture of every period, and styles in pottery changed over the years. Because of this, the study of pottery is one way scientists can determine how old certain objects are. When archaeologists dig up ancient cities, the kinds of pottery they find are good clues to how long ago people lived in that place. They can tell the age of the pottery by the colors that were used, the shapes of the pottery, and the deco-rations and paintings on the pieces.

The potter is sometimes used in the Bible as a word picture of God creating or making people as he wants them to be.

Where to find it: *Jeremiah 18:1-6; Romans 9:20-21*

POUND (see *Measurements*)

PRAETORIAN *(pree-TORE-ee-un)* **GUARD** probably refers to the group of 9,000 soldiers who were the bodyguard of the Roman emperor. Most of them lived in the city of Rome, but some lived in other cities. They were also in charge of prisoners in custody of the emperor, such as Paul. He said once that it had become known throughout the praetorian guard that his imprisonment was for Christ.

Where to find it: *Philippians 1:13*

PRAETORIUM *(pre-TORE-ee-um)* in the New Testament usually refers to the headquarters of the Roman governor when he was in Jerusalem. The praetorium was either the Fortress of Antonio, next door to the Temple, or Herod's palace. Scholars are not sure which. This was the place where Jesus was tried before Pontius Pilate.

The governor usually lived in Caesarea, 60 miles away.

Where to find it: *Matthew 27:27; Mark 15:16; John 18:28, 33; Acts 23:35*

PRAISE refers to words or actions that give

honor to someone—usually God. The words or acts show the deep feelings and thoughts of the one giving praise. In the Old Testament, praise often involved singing, dancing, "glad shouts," sacrifices, or gifts of thanksgiving in the Temple or Tabernacle. Psalms 113 to 118 are called "The Praises."

In the New Testament, praise to God is equally important. Hebrews 13:15 says that Christians are to "continually offer up a sacrifice of praise to God."

PRAYER is conscious communication with God. The Bible does not discuss why Christians should pray. It assumes that anyone who is committed to Christ will pray.

Jesus, even though he was the Son of God, prayed often when he was on earth. He prayed when he was baptized, when he chose his 12 disciples, when he faced the crucifixion, and many other times. When his disciples asked Jesus to teach them to pray, he gave them a sample prayer. We call this "the Lord's Prayer."

Prayer is much more than asking God for things we want. Prayer includes praising God, giving thanks for his blessings, confessing our sins, asking God for help, and praying for other people.

The Bible teaches that when we pray we must have faith that God hears our prayers and will answer them. We are to pray in the name of Jesus Christ, seeking the will of God. The Holy Spirit will lead us in praying if we ask him to. And we must have a forgiving heart, if we want God to forgive us.

Where to find it

Jesus prays   *Mark 14:32-42; Luke 3:21; 6:12-13*
The Lord's Prayer   *Matthew 6:9-13*
Faith and prayer   *Mark 11:24*
Praying in Jesus' name   *John 14:13-14*
Christians must forgive   *Mark 11:25-26*

PREACHING in the Bible usually refers to telling the good news of Christ to people who had not heard it before. In our society, preaching includes not only telling the gospel to those who haven't heard it but also teaching Christians and others the truths taught in the Bible (see *Occupations*).

PREDESTINATION (see *Election*)

PREFECT *(PREE-feckt)* is a word used in the King James Version for governor.

PREPARATION, DAY OF, refers to the day before the Sabbath or the day before the Passover. The Day of Preparation for the Sabbath was a busy time, since all business matters had to be cared for and all food for the Sabbath prepared. (No business or cooking was permitted on the Sabbath.) There was also a great deal of preparation necessary for the Passover feast.

Jesus was crucified on the Day of Preparation for the Sabbath.

Where to find it: *Mark 15:42; Luke 23:54; John 19:31*

PRESIDENT is a term that appears only in the Book of Daniel. Daniel was one of three presidents or appointed chiefs in the Persian Kingdom. Their duties were similar to those of a governor or other high officials.

PRESS was a device to squeeze the juice or oil from fruit. Usually two large stones were used in a press. The fruit was placed between the stones, and the stones were turned by hand or by mules.

PRICK refers to a pointed stick or goad used to keep oxen or other animals moving along. A prick is used as a word picture in the conversion of Saul, when Jesus said to him, "It is hard for thee to kick against the pricks" (King James Version). This means Saul was hurting himself by going against God's ways.

Where to find it: *Acts 26:14*

PRIDE is a kind of selfish attitude. The Bible speaks of pride not as self-respect (which is good) but as a feeling of being better than others. It means giving ourselves honor that belongs to God.

Proverbs 16:18 says, "Pride goes before destruction and a haughty spirit before a fall."

Since people can't earn the friendship of God by anything they do, they have no right to be proud. All that we have comes from God.

PRIESTS in the Old Testament were the link between holy God and sinful people.

Priests among the Hebrews began in the wilderness after the Israelites escaped from

Caiaphas and the other priests put Jesus on trial illegally in the middle of the night.

Egypt. Three kinds of priests are described in the Old Testament Book of Numbers.

1. The high priest. Aaron was the first high priest. He was a member of the tribe of Levi. All priests were descendants of Aaron, but the high priest was supposed to be the oldest male descendant of Eleazar, Aaron's son.

The high priest wore beautiful robes (see *High Priest*). The high priest, like other priests, offered sacrifices in the Tabernacle and later in the Temple. His most important work, however, came once a year on the Day of Atonement. On that day he put aside his beautiful clothes and put on plain linen clothes. Then he entered the Holy of Holies to sprinkle blood on the mercy seat of the ark of the Covenant to atone for his sins and for the sins of the people.

2. The priests. The regular priests were all Levites, but they were also descendants of Aaron. The priests were divided into 24 groups. They took turns working in the Tabernacle and later in the Temple. They wore white linen robes. Only the priests could offer the sacrifices that the people brought to God. When King Saul and later King Uzziah offered sacrifices, they were punished by God.

The priests were supported primarily by the offerings people brought to the Tabernacle or the Temple. Part of these offerings went to the priests and their families. The Israelites were required to give one-tenth of their earnings or harvest to the tribe of Levi, and one-tenth of that was given to the priests.

During some periods of Old Testament history, the priests also taught the Law of Moses to the people, and some priests served as judges. The Book of Numbers tells many of the other responsibilities of the priests.

3. The Levites. They were the descendants of Levi, one of the sons of Jacob, so they were one of the 12 tribes of Israel. When the Israelites came out of Egypt, the Levites were assigned to help the priests care for the Tabernacle and later the Temple. Some were responsible for the furniture of the Tabernacle, others for all the screens, hangings, and coverings, and others for putting up the Tabernacle or taking it down. After the Temple was built, some Levites were singers and musicians, others were gatekeepers, porters, and assistants to the priests in offering sacrifices. During some periods Levites taught the Law of Moses and explained what it meant.

Levites were not given a particular part of the land of Israel as their own but were assigned instead to 48 cities where they could live and have some pastureland. The people

Priscilla, Aquila, and Paul made tents together for a while in Corinth.

of the other 11 tribes were told to give one-tenth of their income to the Levites for their service in the Tabernacle and the Temple. The Levites, in turn, were to give one-tenth of this to the priests.

Levites began their service when they were 25 years old and worked until age 50. When the first child was born in a Hebrew family, the family paid a tax to the priests to "redeem" their firstborn. This was a sign that the firstborn child in any family actually belonged to God. The Levites, who gave their lives to serve God, were the substitutes for the firstborn of the family.

In the New Testament, Christ is called the high priest who is superior to any high priest in the Old Testament. He is the final link between God and people. When he sacrificed himself for the sins of people, no further sacrifice by priests was needed.

In the New Testament all believers are called priests. We are called to be the links between God and people around us.

Where to find it

Saul punished   *1 Samuel 13:8-15*
Uzziah punished   *2 Chronicles 26:16-21*
Law of the firstborn   *Numbers 3:40-51*
Christ, the final high priest   *Hebrews 3–10*
Believers are priests   *1 Peter 2:5, 9; Revelation 5:9-10; 20:6*

PRINCE in the Bible does *not* mean the son of a king. It often means a man with high authority—clearly the leader in his group. A military commander, a king, and a governor may all be called "prince."

Sometimes *prince* means a person who deserves honor because of his noble birth or leadership ability.

PRINCESS refers to the daughter or wife of a chief or leader.

PRINCIPALITIES *(prin-suh-PAL-ih-teez)* refers to groups of angels or demons.

Where to find it

Angels   *Ephesians 3:10; Colossians 1:16*
Demons   *Romans 8:38; Ephesians 6:12; Colossians 2:15*

PRISCILLA *(pris-SILL-uh)* **AND AQUILA** *(uh-QUIL-uh)* were a Christian couple who were leaders in the early church. They were both tentmakers who moved from place to place around the Mediterranean Sea, teaching and preaching the gospel wherever they went.

They first met Paul in Corinth, and Paul lived with them. Later they lived in Ephesus, where they taught Apollos more about the gospel. They lived for some time in Rome, where they had a church meeting regularly in their home. Later they returned to Ephesus and again had a church in their home. Paul wrote of this couple as "my fellow workers in Christ Jesus, who risked their necks for my life, to whom not only I but also all the churches of the Gentiles give thanks."

Where to find it

Paul lives with them   *Acts 18:1-3*
They teach Apollos   *Acts 18:24-26*
Their church in Ephesus   *1 Corinthians 16:19*
Paul commends them   *Romans 16:3-5*

PRISON was a place where a person accused or convicted of a crime was held. Often the prisoners in Bible times were beaten and then placed in chains or stocks (Acts 16: 22-34). Often their food was only bread and water (2 Chronicles 18: 26). Sometimes a prisoner who had not been proven guilty but was awaiting trial would be permitted to stay in his own house with guards to watch him. This was true of Paul in Rome.

In ancient times, people were sometimes put in prison simply because they could not pay their debts. Jesus urged Christians to visit those in prison.

Where to find it

Bread and water   *2 Chronicles 18: 26*
Christians should visit prisoners   *Matthew 25:34-36*
Paul and Silas beaten   *Acts 16:22-34*
Paul imprisoned in a house   *Acts 28:16*

PROCONSUL *(PRO-kon-sul)* was the highest official in a smaller Roman province that was easy to control and did not need many Roman soldiers stationed there.

The proconsul was usually a former member of the Roman Senate and was responsible to the Senate rather than to the emperor. A proconsul usually served only a one-year term.

The New Testament mentions two proconsuls—Gallio in Achaia and Sergius Paulus in Cyprus (see *Province*).

Where to find it: *Acts 13: 7; 18:12*

PROCURATORS *(PRAH-kyur-ay-turz)* were Roman officials who served as governors of Roman provinces that were difficult to control. Procurators had full responsibility for the taxes and armies of Rome in their areas. Judea was governed by a procurator during the time of Christ and the early church. Procurators were usually appointed by the emperor. Pilate, Felix, and Festus were procurators mentioned in the New Testament. The Revised Standard Version calls these men "governors."

The Jewish historian Josephus tells more about Pilate, Felix, and Festus (see *Josephus*).

Where to find it: *Luke 3:1; Acts 23:26; 24:27*

PRODIGAL *(PRAH-dih-gul)* **SON** refers to the story Jesus told about a son who spent all of his inheritance on foolish things. (*Prodigal* means recklessly wasteful.) Then he returned to his father to ask forgiveness. The father forgave him freely and had a party to celebrate

his return. Jesus used the story to show that God freely and joyously forgives those who confess their sin and return to him.

Where to find it: *Luke 15:11-32*

PROFANE (pro-FANE) means to treat holy things or holy persons as if they were not holy. Among the Hebrews, it meant to use the Sabbath, other people, the name of God, or the furnishings of the Tabernacle and Temple in ways that were forbidden by the Law of God.

PROMISE (PROM-iss) in the Bible usually refers to God's sayings that he will bless and redeem his people.

The New Testament teaches that in Christ these promises are being fulfilled.

God made promises in both the Old and New Testaments. The complete fulfillment of these promises will come when there is no more sin or death. Then we will live with God in a new kind of life. The promises of the New Testament use word pictures of breathtaking grandeur.

Where to find it

Promises are being fulfilled in Christ *Romans 15:8; Ephesians 3:6*
Promises of future life *Revelation 21:1–22:5*

PROPHECY (PRAH-fuh-see) is a message of God delivered by a prophet—a man or woman chosen by God. Prophecies in the Old Testament were meant to tell the Israelites or other people something God wanted them to know. Prophecy reminded people to worship God by telling them what God had done in the past, what he was doing in the present, and what he would do in the future. Some Old Testament prophecies refer to the coming of Jesus Christ. They are only a small part of the Old Testament prophecies, but they are the best known.

In the New Testament, prophecies given by God to men and women helped to encourage the young church and to instruct believers in the ways of God.

Where to find it: *1 Corinthians 14:3*

PROPHETS were men and women in the Old and New Testaments whom God chose to deliver his messages to people. The prophets we remember best are Elijah, Isaiah, Jeremiah, and Ezekiel, but there were many others, including Deborah and Huldah.

Prophets received their messages from God in many ways. Sometimes God used dreams or night visions. Sometimes he used daytime

The prophet Jeremiah once smashed a clay vessel to illustrate how God was going to have to break the people for their sin.

visions, like the one Isaiah received in the Temple. And sometimes God spoke to his prophets directly, as he did when Isaiah was leaving King Hezekiah.

Prophets were often unpopular because they told of God's judgment. Jeremiah was imprisoned several times because he courageously spoke God's message to the people of his day.

Prophets such as Nathan, Isaiah, Jeremiah, and Ezekiel spoke to the kings of their time, often bringing messages of God's judgment for wrongdoing.

The kings of Israel and Judah often paid "court prophets" who, in turn, told the king the good things he wanted to hear. Often these prophets were not receiving their messages from God, but there are some examples in the Bible of court prophets who were true to God. King Ahab and King Jehoshaphat once called the court prophets. They all prophesied a military victory against the Syrians, except for Micaiah, who spoke the truth.

Some Old Testament prophets had additional roles. Deborah was a prophet, a judge, and a military leader. Samuel was both a judge and a prophet.

In the New Testament, many Christians are called prophets. The first mentioned is Anna, who recognized the baby Jesus as the one

who would redeem Jerusalem. Others include Agabus, the daughters of Philip, and Judas and Silas.

The apostle Paul explained how prophets were to conduct themselves in church services. "Let two or three prophets speak, and let the others weigh what is said. . . . For you can all prophesy one by one, so that all may learn and all be encouraged." These prophets were not predicting future things but were instructing, encouraging, and building up the believers to love and serve God and to turn from their sins.

Where to find it

Night visions *Numbers 12:6*
Deborah *Judges 4–5*
Micaiah *1 Kings 22*
God speaks directly to Isaiah *2 Kings 20:1-11*
Isaiah's Temple vision *Isaiah 6*
Anna *Luke 2:36*
Agabus *Acts 11:27-28*
Judas and Silas *Acts 15:32*
Philip's daughters *Acts 21:8-9*
Prophets in church *1 Corinthians 14:29-31*

PROPITIATION (see *Atonement*)

PROSELYTE *(PRAH-suh-lite)* was a Gentile per-

son who followed the Jewish religion. Proselytes were among the early Christians. One of them, Nicolaus, was chosen to be one of the early church leaders.

Where to find it: *Acts 6:5*

PROSTITUTE (see *Harlot*)

PROVENDER *(PRAH-ven-dur)* was grain or hay used to feed cattle, horses, and other animals.

Where to find it: *Genesis 24:25; 42:27*

PROVERB *(PRAH-vurb)* is a short wise saying (see *Proverbs, Book of*).

PROVERBS *(PRAH-vurbz)*, **BOOK OF,** is an Old Testament book of wise sayings. The book says that many proverbs came from King Solomon, the son of David. Some sections were apparently written by Agur (Proverbs 30) and Lemuel (Proverbs 31:1-9). There is no mention of these two men elsewhere in the Bible.

The main idea in this book is found in the words "The fear of the Lord is the beginning of knowledge; fools despise wisdom and instruction" (Proverbs 1:7).

Most of the proverbs tell what a wise person does and contrasts his acts with those of a foolish person. For example, "A soft answer turns away wrath, but a harsh word stirs up anger" (Proverbs 15:1). Most of the proverbs use contrasts. First a statement is made, such as, "A truthful witness saves life," followed by another statement beginning with *but:* "but one who utters lies is a betrayer" (Proverbs 14:25).

The proverbs show the difference between a person who tries to please God and a person who tries only to please himself.

Many of the newer translations print Proverbs in poetic form, showing that Proverbs is meant to be read and studied as poetry. Like most Hebrew poetry, Proverbs follows a He-

brew rhythm of ideas rather than a rhythm of sound (see *Poetry, Hebrew*).

PROVIDENCE *(PRAH-vuh-denss)* means providing for things to run smoothly. The word appears only once in the Bible—in Acts 24:2 in the King James Version.

Providence, when used in other writings about God, refers to God maintaining all that he has created. However, the natural world God created shows the effects of sin. We see this in famines, earthquakes, fires. God does not intend to keep a world spoiled by sin running smoothly.

PROVINCE *(PRAH-vinss)* was a section of a country with its own government, something like our states. The Roman Empire had two kinds of provinces—imperial provinces and senatorial provinces.

Imperial provinces were larger areas where part of the Roman army was stationed. These were sometimes areas that were difficult to govern, such as Judea. Governors of these provinces (sometimes called procurators) were appointed by the emperor.

A senatorial province, such as the island of Cyprus, was ruled by a proconsul appointed for a one-year term by the Roman Senate. The proconsul was responsible to the Senate (see *Proconsul* and *Procurator*).

PRUNING *(PROO-ning)* **HOOK** was a sharp blade attached to a handle. It was used for cutting back grapevines. It was such a common tool that it is mentioned in the Bible as a word picture for a time of peace—"They shall

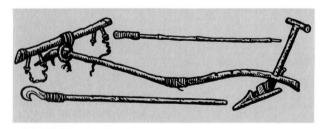

beat their swords into plowshares, and their spears into pruning hooks."

Where to find it: *Isaiah 2:4*

PSALMS *(salmz)* is an Old Testament book of 150 Hebrew poems of prayer and praise (see *Poetry, Hebrew*).

They were meant to be sung. Many psalms have an introduction that tells what tune was to be used. For example, Psalm 69 says, "To the choirmaster: according to Lilies." Apparently "Lilies" was the name of a tune for this psalm. Since the music was not written down, we don't know what those hymn tunes sounded like.

Other introductions, such as the one to Psalm 55, say, "To the choirmaster: with stringed instruments." Apparently these were to be sung with parts of an orchestra.

Most scholars believe that many of the Psalms came from David's time and later. The Psalms had their greatest use as a hymnbook when the Jewish people returned from exile in Babylon and rebuilt the Temple. Their new Temple was not as magnificent as Solomon's, but they had a great collection of psalms to sing. Some of the newer psalms, such as Psalm 137, told what it was like to be in Babylon.

The Psalms were divided into five "books." Most translations show these divisions.

Book I	Psalms 1—41
Book II	Psalms 42—72
Book III	Psalms 73—89
Book IV	Psalms 90—106
Book V	Psalms 107—150

Apparently these books were put together and used at different times, for some psalms appear in more than one book. For example, Psalm 14 is the same as Psalm 53.

Many scholars believe that King David wrote or collected the psalms in Book I and Book IV, while Solomon wrote or collected those in Book II. The psalms in Book III were written by other poets or musicians known as Korahites, who were the Temple musicians.

The Psalms are a favorite part of the Bible for most people. The language is beautiful and majestic, but it is also very personal. The poems describe how people feel in times of thanksgiving, joy, sorrow, distress, or when they feel a guilty conscience.

Some of the psalms are called Messianic psalms because they seem to describe the coming of the Messiah, Jesus Christ. Among the Messianic psalms are Psalms 2, 22, 72, and 110. When Jesus was dying on the cross, he quoted from Psalm 22:1.

Many psalms are songs of praise to God for

his majesty, love, and care. Many of our most beautiful choir anthems are psalms set to music.

PTOLEMAIS *(TAHL-uh-MAY-us)* is a city now called Acre *(AH-cur)* on the northern coast of Israel. Paul stopped for a day on his third missionary journey to visit Christians there.

Ptolemais was called Acco in the Old Testament. It was part of the land assigned to the tribe of Asher, but the Israelites never really conquered the city.

Where to find it: *Judges 1:31-32; Acts 21:7*

PUBLICANS *(PUB-luh-kunz)* were men who worked as tax collectors for the Roman government. They agreed to collect a certain amount for the government. Anything they could get above that amount became their salary. Publicans were considered traitors by the Jewish people.

One of these tax collectors, Matthew, became a disciple of Jesus.

Jesus once told a parable about a publican and a Pharisee who prayed. In the story, the publican turned out to be a better person in the eyes of God than the Pharisee.

Where to find it: *Matthew 9:9; Luke 18:9-14*

PUBLIUS *(PUB-lih-us)* was the leader of the island of Malta, where Paul was shipwrecked on his way to Rome. After Paul and the other men on the boat struggled to the island, Publius gave food and shelter to Paul and his friends for three days. While Paul was there, Publius's father became ill with fever and dysentery. After Paul prayed for him and put his hands on him, the man was healed.

Where to find it: *Acts 28:1-10*

PUL (see *Tiglath-pileser*)

PULSE (see *Plants*)

PUNISHMENT, EVERLASTING, refers to eternal separation from God. Those who reject God's love as shown by Christ Jesus will suffer the punishment of being separated forever from God.

Many word pictures are used to describe how awful this everlasting punishment will be. Among the word pictures are "lake of fire" and "blackness of darkness." Jesus told a parable about a wicked rich man and a good poor man who died. The rich man was "in torment" and "far off."

Those who go into everlasting punishment are those who do not believe in Christ as the light of the world. People refuse to believe because they "love darkness rather than light, because their deeds are evil." They want God out of their lives. Eternal punishment is what happens when God is gone from them.

Where to find it

Pictures of eternal punishment   *Matthew 25:41-46; Jude 13; Revelation 20:14-15*
Parable of rich man and poor man   *Luke 16:19-31*
Reason for eternal punishment   *John 3:16-21*

PURIM *(POOR-im)*, **PUR** *(POOR)* is a Jewish festival during February or March to celebrate the victory of the Jews over wicked Haman in the time of Queen Esther.

The feast is still celebrated today by Jews. Jewish families go to the synagogue to hear someone read the Book of Esther. People boo and shout whenever Haman's name is mentioned. Children often dress up in costumes to resemble the characters in the story. It is a time of joy.

Where to find it: *Esther 9:26-32*

PURITY *(PYOOR-ih-tee)*, **PURIFICATION** *(PYOOR-if-ih-KAY-shun)* has different meanings in the Old and New Testaments.

In the Old Testament, the Hebrew people had to obey certain laws to keep from being "impure" in God's sight. These included having all male babies circumcised, washing hands in a certain way, not touching a dead body, not eating forbidden foods, not cooking certain foods together, and many other things (see *Unclean*).

Some of these practices no doubt helped maintain good health as well as religious purity. The Old Testament prophets, however, said that people could keep all of these laws and still not have any real love for God. The prophets said that a loving attitude toward God was just as important as following all the rules.

In New Testament times, the Pharisees were very strict about keeping all of the Old Testament laws and the many traditions that grew up around the laws. When Jesus' disciples did not follow these traditions, the Pharisees became angry. Jesus said that a person's love for God and other people was far more important than keeping many rules.

The Gospels and the rest of the New Testament teach clearly that Christians are to treat their bodies as temples of the Holy Spirit. True purity comes when a person gives himself completely to God.

Where to find it

Some Old Testament purity laws   *Leviticus 17–18, 22*
Jesus' teachings about rules and inner purity   *Mark 7: 1-23*
Bodies are temples of the Holy Spirit   *1 Corinthians 6: 19-20*

PURPLE was a very expensive dye gotten from Mediterranean shellfish. The dye was made from the gland of a particular mollusk. Since different mollusks produced slightly different shades, the producing of purple dye became a highly skilled craft.

The dye was used to color cloth. Because the dye was so expensive, rich people wore purple clothing to show their wealth. Robes of kings and queens were often made of purple cloth.

When Jesus was crucified, the soldiers put a purple robe on him to make fun of him.

Lydia, the first convert in Europe, was a business woman who sold purple material.

Where to find it

Jesus' robe   *Mark 15: 17*
Lydia's business   *Acts 16: 14*

PURSES were small bags of leather or fabric with a drawstring at the top. They were used by men to carry money and other things.

Several versions use *purse* in Matthew 10: 9, but the word there really refers to a wide fabric used as a belt. Men often carried money in the folds of such a belt. The Revised Standard Version says, ''Take no gold, nor silver, nor copper in your belts.''

Where to find it: *Matthew 10: 9; Luke 10: 4; 12: 33*

PUTEOLI *(poo-tee-OH-lee)* was a seaport in Italy near Naples. Although more than 100 miles from Rome, Puteoli was the nearest harbor. Paul and the other prisoners landed there when they were being taken to Rome to prison. Some Christians at Puteoli invited Paul and Luke to stay with them. They stayed for seven days before going on to Rome.

The seaport is now called Pozzuoli.

Where to find it: *Acts 28: 13-14*

The queen of Sheba heard so many amazing things about King Solomon that she had to come visit him.

QUAIL (see *Birds*)

QUARRY *(KWOR-ee)* sometimes means a place from which stones are taken for building. Other times *quarry* refers to the process of cutting or removing stones.

Archaeologists have found quarries dating back to Bible times. In one quarry, the limestone was relatively soft until it was exposed to air for a long time; then it became hard and durable. The workers made slits in the soft stone and then inserted wedges of wood. Then they poured water over the wedges. When the wood swelled, the rock split into pieces that could be moved. Scholars think this may have been the way that huge stones were prepared for Solomon's Temple.

Where to find it: *1 Kings 6:7*

QUARTER, SECOND (see *Second Quarter*)

QUATERNION (kwah-TER-nee-un) means a squad of four soldiers. When Peter was in prison in Jerusalem, he was guarded by four squads of four soldiers each. They no doubt took turns on guard duty. Peter had two chains—probably each hand was chained to a different soldier, with the two other guards stationed outside the cell.

Where to find it: Acts 12:3-10

QUEEN is used three ways in the Bible.

1. A queen could be the ruler of a land, such as the queen of Sheba, or Candace, queen of Ethiopia. The Hebrews had one ruling queen, Athaliah, who ruled Judah for six years after the death of King Ahaziah, her son.

2. The wife of the king was also called queen. Queen Vashti and Queen Esther are both mentioned in the Book of Esther. The wife of a king had no official power, although some queens had great influence—either for good or for bad. Jezebel, wife of King Ahab, used her influence to put Naboth to death. Queen Esther used her influence to save the Jewish people.

3. The mother of the king was also called the queen or the queen mother. The queen mother usually had more power than the wife of the king. Asa, the king of Judah, removed Maacah, his mother, from being queen because she made an awful image to worship.

Many queen mothers are mentioned in the Bible.

Where to find it

Queen of Sheba *1 Kings 10:1*
Maacah *1 Kings 15:13*
Jezebel *1 Kings 21*
Athaliah *2 Chronicles 22:10–23:15*
Esther *Esther 8:1-17*
Candace *Acts 8:27*

QUEEN OF HEAVEN was a female goddess that many Jews worshiped during the time of Jeremiah the prophet. Many scholars believe the Queen of Heaven was Ashtoreth, the goddess of love and fertility, who is often mentioned in the Old Testament. Other scholars believe the Queen of Heaven refers to some other goddess or to a particular star that people worshiped. Jeremiah told the people that God would judge them severely because they worshiped this false Queen of Heaven.

Where to find it: Jeremiah 7:18; 44:17-25

QUEEN OF SHEBA (see *Sheba, Queen of*)

QUICKEN (KWIK-en) is used in the King James Version to mean "make alive." It refers to both physical life and spiritual life.

Where to find it: John 5:21; Romans 8:11; Ephesians 2:1

QUIRINIUS (kwih-RIN-ee-us) was the Roman governor of Syria when Jesus was born. He was appointed by the emperor of Rome and had been a military hero.

Where to find it: Luke 2:1-3

QUIVER (KWIV-er) was a leather container for arrows. It was usually carried over the shoulder.

Quiver is sometimes used in the Bible as a word picture. Psalm 127:5 compares sons with arrows and says, "Happy is the man who has his quiver full of them." In ancient times, having many sons made a man important.

In Isaiah 49:2, God is compared to a quiver in which a person could hide and be safe.

QUMRAN (see *Dead Sea Scrolls*)

RABBAH *(RAB-uh)*, **RABBATH** *(RAB-eth)* was a large Ammonite city in Old Testament times. It was located 20 miles east of the Jordan River near its southern end. During the days of King David, Israel captured this capital city and ruled it throughout the reign of King Solomon. Later Rabbah and the other Ammonite cities won their freedom. But they were condemned by the prophet Amos for their bloody warfare. He prophesied a "fire in the wall" of the city as a sign of its destruction. The prophet Jeremiah also foretold judgment on Rabbah because the Ammonites had conquered neighboring lands. Ezekiel said Rabbah would be conquered.

Rabbah was destroyed by Arab invaders about 580 B.C. Three hundred years later, Greek-speaking conquerors renamed it Philadelphia. Today it is Amman, capital of the country of Jordan (see *Ammonites*).

Where to find it: *Jeremiah 49: 2-3; Ezekiel 21: 20; Amos 1: 14*

RABBI *(RAB-eye)*, **RABBONI** *(ruh-BONE-eye)* were Jewish words meaning "my master" or "my lord." They were terms Jews used for teachers, especially teachers of the Old Testament Law. Jesus' followers and others often used this title of respect when addressing Jesus (see *Occupations*).

Where to find it: *Matthew 23: 7-8; John 1: 38, 49; 3: 2; 4: 31; 6: 25; 20: 16*

Only Jewish boys got to attend the classes taught by the rabbi in Bible times.

111

RACA *(RAH-cuh)* was an extremely insulting name used against people who were considered not very smart. It meant something like "stupid fool." Jesus strongly condemned such insults.

Where to find it: *Matthew 5: 22 (KJV)*

RACE was a highly competitive Greek game in which the athletes ran toward a goal at the end of a track. The winner's prize was a crown or laurel wreath. A race is also used by the apostle Paul as a word picture of the Christian life. In the end, the Christian will receive the crown of the Lord's approval if he or she runs well the race of life.

Where to find it: *1 Corinthians 9: 24-25; 2 Timothy 4: 7-8; Hebrews 12: 1*

RACHEL *(RAY-chul)*, the beautiful favorite wife of Jacob, was the mother of Joseph and Benjamin. She was also Jacob's cousin and the daughter of crafty Laban.

She met Jacob after he had to flee from his brother Esau's anger. He had come to stay with his mother's relatives. As he got to know Rachel, he wanted to marry her. Laban told Jacob he had to work seven years to earn Rachel for a wife.

But Laban tricked Jacob and, after the seven years' work, gave him Leah, his older daughter, instead. Then Jacob had to work another seven years to have Rachel as his second wife. After another dispute with Laban, Jacob and his wives and children fled.

Rachel stole some household gods from her father and hid them, although Jacob did not know this. The gods would have given Rachel the right to her father's property. Eventually Laban and Jacob made peace with each other, and Laban allowed the whole family to return to Jacob's home area, Canaan.

Rachel and her first son, Joseph, were Jacob's favorites. Even though Jacob loved Rachel more than Leah, Rachel was jealous of Leah because she had many children while Rachel had only one. Rachel later had another son, Benjamin, but she died in childbirth as he was born. She was buried near Ephrath. Her tomb is on the road between Jerusalem and Bethlehem, and many people visit it to honor her.

Where to find it: *Genesis 29–31; 35: 16-19*

RAHAB *(RAY-hab)*, one of the women mentioned in the genealogy of Jesus, was a prostitute who helped the Israelites in their battle for Jericho. She was a native of Jericho, but she let the Israelite spies stay in her home. Messengers from the king of the city told Rahab to turn the men over to them, but she hid them under stalks of flax on her roof. She sent the messengers away, saying the men had left already.

When she went back to the spies on the roof, she told them she knew they worshiped the one true God and that their God would help them conquer. She asked the spies to protect her and her family during the Israelite invasion.

They agreed, and she helped them escape by letting them down over the walls of the city using a scarlet rope. The spies told her to hang the rope from her window so the Israelite soldiers would know which house was hers.

She followed their orders, and Joshua had

Rahab and her family brought out of Jericho before the city was burned. Rahab is mentioned among the heroes of faith in Hebrews 11.

Where to find it: *Joshua 2, 6; Matthew 1:5; Hebrews 11:31; James 2:25*

RAIMENT *(RAY-ment)* is an old English word meaning "clothing." It is used in the King James Version of the Bible (see *Clothing*).

RAIN (see *Early Rain*)

RAINBOW is the arch of the seven colors of the prism often seen in the sky after or during rain. God gave the rainbow as his covenant to protect the earth from another huge flood. God gave this sign to Noah after the waters of the great Flood went down.

The prophet Ezekiel and the apostle John saw the rainbow as a sign of God's glory.

Where to find it: *Genesis 9:8-17; Ezekiel 1:28; Revelation 4:3*

RAISINS were grapes that had been soaked in water and oil and then spread to dry. People made raisin cakes by pressing these dried grapes together, sometimes with different kinds of grain. Such cakes kept a long time and were good food for travelers and soldiers.

People who worshiped idols sometimes offered raisin cakes to their gods.

Where to find it: *1 Samuel 25:18; 2 Samuel 6:19*

RAM (see *Animals*)

RAM'S HORN (see *Musical Instruments—Shofar*)

RANSOM *(RAN-sum)* was the price paid for a captive or slave to be set free. The price was sometimes 30 pieces of silver. The New Testament uses *ransom* as a word picture of Jesus' life and death. Jesus Christ paid the price for the salvation of us all by giving his life. He "ransomed" us from the powers of sin and death.

Where to find it: *Exodus 21:32; Zechariah 11:13; Matthew 20:28; Mark 10:45; 1 Timothy 2:6*

RAVEN (see *Birds*)

REAPING *(REEP-ing)* in the Bible means cutting grain with a curved sickle or else pulling it up by hand. Reapers often covered their fingers to prevent being hurt by the sharp spears of grain (see *Agriculture*).

Reaping is also used as a word picture of a person getting a reward or punishment for what he does. "Whatever a man sows, that he will also reap," says Galatians 6:7. Proverbs 22:8-9 says that a person who "sows injustice will reap calamity," but the person who shares what he has with the poor will be blessed.

REBEKAH *(reh-BECK-ah)* was the gracious bride of Isaac. However, she later became the scheming mother of Jacob and Esau.

When Abraham wanted a bride for his son Isaac, he sent his servant Eliezer back to his relatives at Haran to find a suitable woman. There he met Rebekah at a well and asked her for some water. She not only gave him water, but she watered all his camels. This was a big job, because camels that have been traveling drink many gallons of water.

When Eliezer learned that this beautiful young woman was a relative of Abraham, he praised the Lord. He gave gifts of jewelry to Rebekah. She quickly ran to show her brother Laban and her father Bethuel the gold ring and two gold bracelets.

RECONCILIATION

They invited Eliezer to their home to explain why he had come. He told them he was looking for a wife for his master's son. Laban and Bethuel asked Rebekah if she was willing to leave her home and marry someone she did not know. "I will go," she said.

The men replied, "Our sister, be the mother of thousands and tens of thousands."

So Rebekah traveled with Eliezer back to Abraham's home. There she became the bride of Isaac.

But they had no children for 20 years. Finally God answered their prayers, and twins were born. They were named Esau and Jacob. Although Esau was the firstborn, Rebekah loved Jacob much more and wanted him to get the birthright that belonged to the firstborn. She planned a scheme for Jacob to fool his aging, blind father. The scheme worked, and Jacob got the birthright and the blessing from his father that should have gone to Esau. But Esau was so angry that Rebekah had to send Jacob back to Haran to stay with her family to be safe (see *Jacob*).

After her death Rebekah was buried near her husband and his family in a field called Machpelah. The burial place is now a part of the modern city of Hebron.

Where to find it: *Genesis 24:1–27:5; 49:31*

RECONCILIATION (REK-un-sil-ee-AY-shun) means bringing together persons who have differences or disagreements and turning them into friends.

In the New Testament, reconciliation usually refers to bringing God and people together through Jesus Christ's life, death, and resurrection. People, because of sin, are hostile to God. Sin has destroyed their relationship. God himself took steps to heal this broken relationship by sending his Son, Jesus Christ, who gave his life to show God's love (see *Ransom*).

By coming to know and love Jesus, we learn to love God, and our hostility disappears. We are reconciled to God. One of the tasks of Christians is to tell others how to be reconciled to God.

Where to find it: *Romans 5:6-11; 2 Corinthians 5:17-21; Ephesians 2:12-16; Colossians 1:19-22*

RECORDER (see *Occupations–Clerk*)

REDEEMER (ree-DEEM-er) is one of the special names for Jesus. (In the Old Testament, a redeemer was a person, sometimes a relative, who paid the price to buy a slave his freedom.)

Jesus is called the Redeemer because he freed us from the slavery of sin. We all have been slaves to sin, but Jesus "redeemed" us by dying on the cross for us. That was the price he paid. Now we can live as free children of God.

Old Testament prophecies sometimes use the name *Redeemer* for the coming Messiah (see *Redemption*).

Where to find it: *Isaiah 59:20; Ephesians 1:7; Colossians 1:14*

REDEMPTION (ree-DEMP-shun) means paying the price for land or someone enslaved so that the land can be returned to its original owner, or the slave can be set free.

In ancient times, people could redeem a slave by paying the owner whatever the slave was worth, often 30 pieces of silver. Then the slave could be set free to live and behave like other persons. He had been redeemed by his friend or relative, who was willing to pay the price to buy him back.

In the New Testament, *redemption* is a word picture to show how Christ, by his death and resurrection, "bought us back" from our slavery to sin.

All people have been slaves to sin. On the cross, Jesus gave his life to set people free. He "bought them back" for his Father, God. Christ made possible a new life and new freedom to live as God's children. He sets us free from the slavery of sin in our daily lives, too. Because of Christ's redemption, we can live in friendship with God (see *Atonement* and *Ransom*).

Where to find it: *Romans 3:24; 1 Corinthians 6:20; Galatians 3:13; 4:5; Titus 2:14; Hebrews 9:12*

REDEMPTION OF LAND was a way to get back land that had been sold because of bad crops or because the owner couldn't pay his bills. His nearest relative could redeem—or buy back—that land from its new owner. Or if the first owner became prosperous again, he had the right to redeem it for himself.

If no one redeemed it, the land was supposed to be returned to its original owner in the Year of Jubilee (see *Jubilee, Year of*). Houses within a walled city had to be redeemed within a year; otherwise, they stayed with their new owners forever. Houses in small villages (no walls around the village) were to be treated like farm property.

However, no one knows whether the Israelites actually followed the rules in Leviticus about the Year of Jubilee.

Where to find it: *Leviticus 25:24-34*

RED HEIFER was the cow whose ashes were mixed in water for Old Testament ceremonial cleansing. This mixture was used by priests and others after they had been "defiled" by touching a dead body or a leper.

The heifer was burned with cedar wood, hyssop, and scarlet thread, and the ashes were stored outside the city to be used when needed.

Where to find it: *Numbers 19:1-11*

RED SEA is a large body of water 1,300 miles long, stretching from the Indian Ocean up to the Suez Canal. Although the Red Sea is salty, its waters are green and clear, and many fish and other forms of life thrive there.

A marshy area that may have once been a northern finger of the Red Sea between the Mediterranean and the Gulf of Suez was important in the Old Testament. This area, more

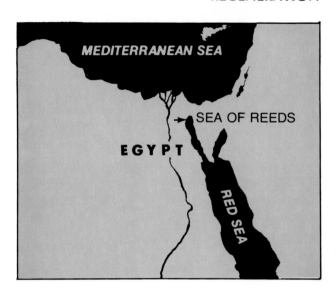

properly called the "Sea of Reeds," probably was the water God miraculously separated to let the people of Israel cross as they fled from the Egyptians (see *Exodus, Route of*).

Where to find it: *Exodus 13:17–14:30*

REED (see *Plants*)

REED is a Babylonian measure about three yards long (see *Measures*).

REFINE *(ree-FINE)* means to make pure. It originally meant changing metal to a purer stage by melting it and removing the impurities. It is much like smelting today. In Bible times, refining was done in pottery that could stand high heat. Good-quality gold, silver, iron, copper, and tin were produced this way.

Refining is also a word picture of being cleansed or made pure spiritually. God is the Refiner who—sometimes painfully—works out of us the impure qualities that keep us from living as we should for him.

Where to find it: *Isaiah 1:22-25; Zechariah 13:9; Malachi 3:2-3*

REFUGE, CITIES OF (see *Cities of Refuge*)

REGENERATION *(ree-jen-er-AY-shun)* means being "born again" or made new. It is the change that God brings into our lives when we accept Jesus Christ as Savior. The person who accepts Christ becomes new and different from the former self.

Every person has a sinful nature that is inherited from Adam and Eve. But we can be freed from our sinful natures, which cause us to hurt ourselves and others. We can be given Christlike natures through the work of the Holy Spirit and the Word of God.

Anyone who wants this new nature must admit to being a sinner, ask God through Jesus Christ for forgiveness for sin, and accept the salvation God offers. These steps lead to regeneration, and the person who takes them is "born again." God gives him or her new interests and a desire to live according to God's purposes.

Where to find it: *John 3: 3-16; Titus 3: 5; 1 Peter 1: 3, 23*

REHOBOAM *(ree-uh-BO-um)* was the foolish and luxury-loving son of King Solomon. He was king when the Israelites divided into two separate kingdoms—Judah and Israel.

When Rehoboam began to reign after the death of his father Solomon about 992 B.C., he was crowned king at Shechem. To pay for his many luxuries, he wanted to raise the people's taxes. The people, however, wanted lower taxes. They felt their taxes had been too high even under Solomon's rule. When Rehoboam consulted with his advisers about the people's complaints, the older advisers told him to reduce taxes. But the younger advisers told him to be firm and to threaten more taxes to let the people know he was boss.

Rehoboam took the advice of the younger men and raised the taxes. The people of the northern part of the kingdom rebelled. Jeroboam, a young official who had worked for Solomon, became the leader of the northern ten tribes. Only the tribes of Judah and Benjamin stayed with Rehoboam.

Rehoboam was not able to reunite the kingdom. When he prepared to wage war against the north, the Lord stopped him. "You shall not go up or fight against your brethren," God said. Therefore, Israel became two nations: the Northern Kingdom, called Israel, and the Southern Kingdom, called Judah.

In the Southern Kingdom, Rehoboam welcomed the priests and Levites who were forced out by Jeroboam after he set up pagan worship. However, the Southern Kingdom also turned to idols soon after the kingdoms separated, and "there was war between Rehoboam and Jeroboam all the days of his life," according to 1 Kings 15: 6.

Where to find it: *1 Kings 12: 1-24; 14: 21-31; 2 Chronicles 11–12*

REINS *(rains)* is the King James Version word for kidneys, or the innermost part of a person. Ancient peoples thought the kidneys were the place of the emotions (see *Kidneys*).

Where to find it: *Psalms 7: 9; 73: 21 (KJV)*

REJOICE means to be glad, or to express our joy. The Bible encourages us to rejoice—express our gladness—about the joy the Lord gives us because of his love and care for us. Sometimes we rejoice even when we are sad, because the Lord's presence is still with us. For example, Paul told the Philippians who were having hard times because of their faith in Christ to "rejoice in the Lord always; again I will say, Rejoice."

Where to find it: *Philippians 4: 4*

RELIGION *(ree-LIH-jun)* is a system of faith and worship.

The word *religion* is not used in the Old Testament. Belief was not separated from actions. Old Testament people knew that each person should respond to God with his or her whole self.

In New Testament times, some people had the mistaken idea they could "believe" certain truths without having their beliefs change their lives. James, especially, insisted that "beliefs" without a life of helping others was no belief at all. "What is true religion like?" he asked. "Religion that is pure and undefiled before God and the Father is this: to visit orphans and widows in their affliction, and to keep oneself unstained from the world."

Where to find it: *James 1: 27*

REMEMBRANCE *(ree-MEM-brunce)* is an action or thing that makes us remember a person or an event. The Lord often asked his people to do certain things to remind them of what he had done for them. The best-known remembrances are the Passover (a remembrance of delivery from Egypt), and the Lord's Supper (a remembrance of Christ's giving his life for us) (see *Memorial*). People who take part in these remembrances are acting out basic truths of their faith.

Where to find it: *Exodus 12: 14; 1 Corinthians 11: 24*

REMISSION *(ree-MISH-shun)* means pardoning or forgiveness. God remits our sins because of Jesus' death and resurrection.

Where to find it: *Romans 3: 25; Hebrews 9: 22 (both KJV)*

REMNANT *(REM-nunt)* means a small part that is left. In the Old Testament, *remnant* usually refers to the Jewish people who were faithful servants and worshipers of God after their time of exile in Babylon. Israel's prophets believed that through this faithful remnant of people God would build a new nation, and a new people to serve him.

This small group of people received God's mercy, while God judged the larger group that turned away. Many Old Testament prophets looked forward to a Messiah who would come through this remnant of faithful people.

Where to find it: *Ezra 9: 8; Isaiah 10: 20-23; 11: 16; 37: 31-32; Jeremiah 23: 3-6; Micah 2: 12; 5: 7; Zephaniah 3: 12-13*

RENDING OF GARMENTS was a sign of grief or mourning. Biblical people tore their clothes—rending their garments—when someone died or when misfortune came. They also tore their clothes as a sign of the sorrow they felt about their sins. This was one way they showed their grief for the way they had hurt God or other people (see *Mourning*).

Where to find it: *2 Samuel 3: 31*

REPENTANCE *(ree-PENT-unce)* means sorrow for sin, and turning away from that sin to serve God and do right. Repentance involves:

1. admitting before God that what we did was wrong,

2. feeling sorrow for that wrongdoing and the hurt it caused God or other people,

3. and most important, turning from wrong acts to right acts. As we turn away from sin, we turn back to God.

Repentance is necessary for salvation. To accept Jesus' gift of new life, we must deal with sin in our lives. The Holy Spirit brings us to repentance and then leads us to ask forgiveness. By faith we accept Jesus as our Savior. God gives the repentant sinner new attitudes and new power to resist sin.

Where to find it

Repentance is turning away from sin *Matthew 3: 8, 11; 27: 3-4; Luke 3: 3, 8*

Repentance is necessary for salvation *Matthew 3: 2; 4: 17; Acts 5: 31; 11: 18; 20: 21; 26: 20; 2 Peter 3: 9*

REPHIDIM *(REF-uh-dim)* is the place in the Sinai wilderness where Moses struck a rock to get water for the complaining Israelites (see *Massah, Meribah*). At Rephidim, the Israelites also fought and defeated the Amalekites. It was probably located somewhere in the southern tip of the Sinai Peninsula.

Where to find it: *Exodus 17: 1-16; 19: 2*

REPROBATE *(REP-row-bate)* is a word used in the King James Version to describe people who give themselves entirely to sin. They plan evil, do evil, and suffer the results of their evil deeds. Because of this, God gives them up. Such people are unfit for fellowship with God.

Where to find it: *Romans 1: 26-29 (KJV)*

RESPECT OF PERSONS means showing favor to some persons because they seem more important or have more money than others. It is the opposite of being fair. When the King James Version says, ''God is no respecter of persons,'' it means ''God does not play favorites.'' God expects us to be fair to all people.

Where to find it: *Acts 10: 34-35; James 2: 1*

REST is a word with some special meanings in the Bible.

God rests, but not because he is tired. Genesis 2: 2 says God ''rested'' after he created the world, meaning he had completed that task. God ''rested'' in his Temple, according to 1 Chronicles 28: 2, meaning he chose to dwell there.

The Bible tells people to rest so they can be refreshed. People are to follow God's example and complete their tasks so they can rest on the seventh day, according to Exodus 16: 23. In Matthew 11: 28 Jesus offered rest or refreshing of the soul to all who come to him. This rest includes freedom from anxiety.

Hebrews 4 speaks of an eternal rest or refreshing for God's people in the life to come.

RESURRECTION *(rez-ur-RECK-shun)* means coming to life again after being dead.

Two kinds of resurrection are mentioned in the Bible. One is the kind Jesus gave to

Lazarus when he brought him back from the grave after being dead four days. Jesus also raised from death the daughter of Jairus and the son of the widow of Nain. All of these people came back to the usual kind of physical life. And they all died again at the end of their earthly lives.

Another kind of resurrection will take place in the future—for all people who have ever lived on the earth. Our new bodies will not be like our old bodies. They will be "spiritual bodies" that will never die. (The Bible views the real person as including both body and soul.) In this final resurrection, God's people will live forever with him, while those who rejected him will be forever separated from God.

Where to find it

Jairus' daughter   *Mark 5: 35-43*
The widow's son   *Luke 7: 11-17*
Lazarus   *John 11: 1-44*
All people will be raised   *Daniel 12: 2; Acts 24: 15; Romans 6: 5; 8: 11; 1 Corinthians 15: 12-57*

RESURRECTION OF JESUS CHRIST is the very center of the Christian faith. Because Jesus became alive again after death, believers in Christ know they, too, will live after death.

Jesus had been put to death on a cross outside the city walls of Jerusalem. Many people had seen him die, and a Roman soldier even used a sword to pierce his side to be sure he was dead. His body was taken to a cavelike tomb in a garden belonging to a wealthy follower. Guards were posted to be sure no one interfered with the body. Because Jesus died near sundown on the day that would begin the Jews' Sabbath, the ancient burial customs were not completed that day nor the next day, for that was the Sabbath itself. So on the third day some of the women who were his friends returned to do what was required for dead bodies. But there was no body! Instead, they found angels, who told them, "He is risen; go and tell his disciples."

Soon after his resurrection, Jesus appeared several times to his disciples. They were surprised, but they recognized him. He was not a ghost. "See my hands and my feet, that it is I myself," he said to them. At least twice after his resurrection, Jesus ate with his disciples, showing that he was not just a spirit or a vision.

The resurrection of Jesus is a central theme of the New Testament. Paul wrote often about the power and purpose of the resurrection. Jesus Christ rescued us from the power of sin by dying on the cross; he showed his rule over the universe by rising from death. His resurrection was further proof that he was the Son of God.

Because of this glorious event, Christians know that they will receive new "spiritual" bodies like the one Christ had after his resurrection. Christians also have the power of the risen Christ (the same power necessary to raise him from death) available in their everyday lives and when they face death.

Where to find it

The resurrection   *Matthew 28; Mark 16; Luke 24; John 20*
The basis of our faith   *Acts 1: 15-22; 13: 26-27; Romans 8: 19-22; 1 Corinthians 15: 17-19*

REUBEN *(ROO-ben)* was the oldest of Jacob and Leah's sons. He saved the life of his younger brother Joseph when his other brothers wanted to kill Joseph. Reuben convinced them instead to sell Joseph into slavery in Egypt.

After Joseph became a powerful ruler in Egypt, Reuben and his brothers went to Egypt to get food because there was a famine in Palestine. As the oldest of the brothers, Reuben was the spokesman. Before Joseph let his brothers know who he was, he tested them to see if they were still cruel and uncar-

Mary Magdalene was the first person to see Jesus after he had come back from the dead.

ing. Reuben showed his concern for his brothers and his father during this testing time.

After Joseph and his brothers were reconciled, Reuben and his family moved to Egypt with all the other descendants of Jacob.

Reuben was the ancestor of the tribe of Reuben. When the Israelites left Egypt for the Promised Land 400 years later, the tribe had grown to more than 150,000. After the conquest of Canaan, the tribe of Reuben settled on the east side of the Jordan River. When the Northern Kingdom was defeated in 722 B.C., many of the tribe of Reuben were taken into exile in Assyria.

Where to find it

Reuben and Joseph   *Genesis 37:19-22; 42:22, 37; 46:9*
Tribe of Reuben   *Numbers 1:21; 2:16; 32:1-33; 1 Chronicles 5:25-26; 12:37*

REVELATION *(rev-ul-AY-shun)* is the way God explains himself or some truths about himself.

In the Old Testament, God revealed himself through his mighty acts and through his words to prophets and leaders such as Abraham, Moses, and David. Much of this revelation was passed down orally from parents to children and finally written down to become part of our Bible. In a similar way, Jesus' teachings were handed down orally at first. The four Gospels were probably written between A.D. 50 and 90. So God has revealed himself and his will in the Bible (see *Canon*).

But God revealed himself in a special way through his Son, Jesus Christ. In Jesus, God made himself known as one who could talk with people and respond to them. Jesus revealed God's self-giving love as well as his holiness and great power. In Jesus Christ we have the answer to the question "What is God like?" God's revelation through Jesus is superior to earlier revelations, but all are important in fulfilling God's purpose for the world.

Where to find it: *Hebrews 1:1-3*

REVELATION, BOOK OF, is the last book of the New Testament. John wrote it on the island of Patmos, where he had been exiled because of his faith in Christ. Revelation tells how God

gave John visions of the future church and the future earth. It is filled with strange word pictures using beasts, dragons, angels, thrones, scrolls, trumpets, and bowls. It is somewhat like the Old Testament prophecies of Daniel and Ezekiel.

John wrote specifically to the "seven churches that are in Asia," churches that were facing hard times around the close of the first century. He wrote to encourage them to stay true to their faith in Jesus Christ.

Revelation contains four great visions given "in the spirit" to John. The first vision shows Jesus Christ talking about the seven churches. He praises their good points and exposes their weaknesses.

The second vision talks about seals, trumpets, and bowls as word pictures of God's judgment upon the world, where evil seems to be winning.

The third vision shows the overthrow of this evil society and of the evil religion that governs it. It also talks of "Babylon," a wicked religious and political power that will be destroyed. The "beast"—forces of Satan and evil—is overcome in battle by Jesus Christ. In this vision, the discouraged seven churches could see the coming victory that Christians will win.

The fourth vision shows the glorious future for God and his people. After evil is overcome, a new heaven and a new earth are prepared, where God and his people enjoy each other. There is no night, no sadness, no evil. Those who have been faithful to God have only joy.

Then, as he closes the book, John commands Christians to be faithful to God and to be ready for the return of Christ.

Where to find it

First vision   *Revelation 1:9–3:22*
Second vision   *Revelation 4–16*
Third vision   *Revelation 17:1–21:8*
Fourth vision   *Revelation 21:9–22:5*

REVELING *(REV-ul-ing)* means noisy merrymaking with too much eating and drinking. In the New Testament it refers to people who let lust and drunkenness overcome all good sense. The King James Version sometimes uses *rioting* to express this idea.

Where to find it: *Romans 13:13; Galatians 5:21 (KJV); 1 Peter 4:3 (KJV); 2 Peter 2:13*

*Rhoda was so excited
she forgot to open the door.*

REVERENCE *(REV-er-unse)* is a feeling of deep respect mixed with wonder, fear, and love. Reverence is the idea behind the expression *fear of the Lord* that appears often in both the Old and New Testaments. Reverence should be our attitude and feeling about God and his holiness, power, and love.

REVILE *(ree-VILE)* means to call bad names or to abuse with words. Jesus was reviled as he was dying on the cross. Revilers have no part of the Kingdom of God says 1 Corinthians 6:10. Children are commanded not to revile their parents.

Where to find it

Children not to revile parents   *Exodus 21:17*
Jesus reviled   *Mark 15:32*
Revilers outside God's Kingdom   *1 Corinthians 6:10*

REWARD usually means something good that we receive for an achievement. In the Bible, however, the word *reward* is used for something given for either a good or bad act. The idea of sowing what you reap is important in the Bible. The ''reward'' of sin is punishment.

Where to find it: *Psalm 91:8; Jeremiah 32:19; Luke 23:41; Acts 1:18; 1 Corinthians 3:14*

RHODA *(ROAD-uh)* was a young servant girl in a house in Jerusalem where a group of Christians had gathered to pray for the release of the apostle Peter from prison. When she heard a knock at the gate of the house, she went to see who was there. When she heard Peter's voice, she was so surprised she forgot to open the gate! Instead, she ran inside to tell the others Peter had come. They insisted she must be imagining things. They did not believe her until they finally went to the gate, where Peter was still knocking.

Where to find it: *Acts 12:12-16*

RHODES *(roads)* was a Greek city on a large island in the Aegean Sea off the southwest corner of what is now Turkey. The island was also named Rhodes. Paul visited the city on his missionary journeys.

Rhodes was the center of a cult of sun worshipers, who once built a huge statue of their god. The statue was destroyed in an earthquake in 227 B.C. Although Rhodes had at one time been a great center of trade, by Paul's time it had become only a stop for travelers and a pleasant vacation place. It is now called Rodhos.

Where to find it: *Acts 21:1*

RIDDLES are found in both the Old and New Testaments. But they were more than a game. They were tests of wisdom. King Solomon's famous wisdom was often tested by riddles. When the queen of Sheba heard of Solomon's great wisdom, she traveled to Israel to ask him riddles, or "hard questions," to test his wisdom for herself.

Samson used a riddle to trip his enemies—and so angered them that they forced his wife to reveal the answer. His use of a riddle proved his mental strength.

Some prophecies are in the form of riddles. An example is the number 666 in the Book of Revelation (see *Six Hundred Sixty-six*).

Where to find it

Samson's riddle   *Judges 14*
King Solomon and the queen   *1 Kings 10:1-5; 2 Chronicles 9:1-4*
New Testament riddle   *Revelation 13:18*

RIGHTEOUSNESS *(RIE-chuss-ness)* means living according to God's will. In the Old Testament, God gave commands that he expected people to follow. The basis of these is the Ten Commandments and the command in Deuteronomy 6:5, "You shall love the Lord your God with all your heart, and with all your soul, and with all your might."

But no person except Jesus Christ has ever lived up to all of God's holy law. We all choose to sin at times. Even the good things we do, we often do for selfish reasons. That is why the Bible says, "All our righteous deeds are like a polluted garment."

Because only Jesus Christ is fully righteous, God has made it possible for us to share in his righteousness. Jesus Christ died for our sins; he atoned for our sins (see *Atonement*). When we accept this, he gives us his righteousness so we can have a loving relationship with God.

Christians seek Jesus' help to live righteously every day. We want to live up to our name *Christians* ("Christ's ones"). Christ's power and strength can help us live righteously.

Where to find it

God's standard of righteousness   *Exodus 20:1-17; Deuteronomy 6:5*
We are not righteous   *Isaiah 64:6; Romans 3:19-26; 5:12-21*
Christ's righteousness can be ours   *2 Corinthians 5:21; 1 John 1:7-9*

RIGHT HAND is a word picture in the Bible for either a "hand of strength and power" or a "favored place."

People fought or gave blessings with the right hand. The left hand was considered tricky or even deadly. "The right hand of God" became a word picture of God's power and care for his people. "My hand laid the foundation of the earth, and my right hand spead out the heavens," God said in Isaiah 48:13. When God withdraws his right hand, he allows judgment to come on his people, according to Psalm 74:11.

The right hand may also mean on the right side, which was the favored place in ancient societies. Psalm 110:1 says, "The Lord says to my lord: Sit at my right hand." New Testament believers understood that this was God the Father speaking to Christ, giving him the most honored place in the whole universe. From there he reigns with honor and power. This verse is quoted in Mark 12:36, Acts 2:34, and Hebrews 1:13.

RING was a piece of jewelry with special authority in ancient times. Important people used rings as their signatures. A ruler would have his own sign on a ring, and every important document would be stamped or sealed with that sign. If the ruler gave an assistant his ring to use, he was giving him his authority.

Later, each household had a ring that represented the authority of that household. When the father placed a ring on the hand of his prodigal son, it showed that the son was fully restored to his place of authority in the family.

Where to find it: *Luke 15:22*

RIOTING (see *Reveling*)

RISPAH or **RIZPAH** *(RIZ-pah)* was King Saul's concubine who became involved in a scandal. Saul's son Ishbosheth accused Saul's cousin Abner of having sexual intercourse with Rispah. Abner was so angry at being accused that he changed to David's side in the war between Saul and David. This was a great help for David.

Later Rispah's two sons were killed, along with the other sons of Saul. When David saw Rispah's grief, he arranged for the bodies to be properly buried in their grandfather's tomb.

Where to find it: *2 Samuel 3: 6-11; 21: 8, 10-14*

ROADS were especially important in ancient Israel, because it was a land bridge between the major countries of the ancient world. Many trade routes crossed Israel. One important road followed the coast of Israel; another cut across Galilee and led up to Damascus. Many others connected the important cities, such as Alexandria, Jerusalem, and Antioch.

Hittites, Babylonians, Assyrians, Persians, and Romans all built roads to increase trade and conquer other countries. A few Roman roads were paved with flat stones or bricks. Many, however, were only cleared paths for people and animals (see *Travel*).

ROBBERY was an everyday danger in ancient times. People often were afraid to travel because they feared robbers would take their goods and beat them. Deborah once sang about the fear that caravan leaders had of robbers. In the New Testament, the famous story of the Good Samaritan shows that robbery was common.

Houses were built with small, high windows to protect against robbers.

Robbery is strongly condemned by the Bible.

Where to find it

Commands against robbing *Exodus 20:15; Leviticus 19:13; Isaiah 61:8*
Deborah's song *Judges 5:6*
The Good Samaritan *Luke 10:30-37*

ROBES were a variety of outer garments worn in Bible times. Often a robe went all the way to the feet. The color of a robe often had meaning. Priests' robes had to be the color given in the Old Testament regulations. Kings' robes were purple. Many people believe the robe Jesus wore, for which the soldiers cast lots, was also purple (see *Clothing*).

ROD (see *Staff*)

ROE (see *Animals–Gazelle*)

ROMAN COLONY was a settlement of Roman citizens in territory the Romans had conquered from other countries. The town was authorized as a Roman colony by the government, and often retired Roman soldiers lived there. They had all the rights of the citizens of cities in Italy. They were exempted from poll and land taxes and governed themselves in local matters. Philippi was a Roman colony.

Where to find it: *Acts 16:12*

ROMAN CITIZENSHIP (see *Citizenship*)

ROMAN EMPIRE was the ruling government all around the Mediterranean from about 63 B.C. to A.D. 450.

It began as a small city-state in Italy and grew into an empire that controlled most of the then-known world. It reached from Britain, France, and Germany in the north to Morocco in Africa and east to what is now Turkey and Lebanon. As Rome conquered and controlled these areas, it brought some degree of peace that lasted about five centuries. This peace also permitted trade to flourish. Roman money became the common currency throughout the world.

In the time before Christ, the city-state had a form of democracy with a senate representing the citizens. Later the emperor became more and more powerful. By about A.D. 100,

The Roman Empire in the first century.

the emperor of Rome was even worshiped as a god in some places. The Romans insisted that everyone must say, "Caesar is Lord."

Because Christians would not do that, the huge Roman Empire persecuted the tiny early church, and many Christians were thrown to the lions. But this seemed to make the church even stronger.

The peace and the ease of travel that Rome established helped the church to grow and spread throughout the then-known world.

ROMANS *(ROW-munz)*, **LETTER TO THE,** is one of the most important books of the Bible. It was written about A.D. 58 by the apostle Paul to Christians he had never met in the city of Rome.

In this letter, Paul explained more fully than anywhere else what it means to be "justified by faith." He explained that Jews and Gentiles alike are sinners and cannot by themselves meet God's standards. "All have sinned and fall short of the glory of God," Paul wrote.

But after showing how impossible it is for anyone to keep God's laws, Paul showed that God has freely provided a way to become righteous in God's sight. That way is through faith in Jesus Christ, God's Son. It is the way of "grace"—God gives us something we don't deserve. Paul explained that even Old Testament saints such as Abraham *believed* God—and that was considered "righteousness."

Paul was very careful to point out that although salvation is a free gift of God, it does not mean that Christians may go on sinning freely because God forgives them. Not at all, he said. We are to use the power of God's Spirit to defeat sin.

The Letter to the Romans explains how God gives power, help, and happiness to believers. Chapter 8 ends with the promise, "For I am sure that neither death, nor life, nor angels, nor principalities, nor things present, nor things to come, nor powers, nor height, nor depth, nor anything else in all creation, will be able to separate us from the love of God in Christ Jesus our Lord."

In chapters 9, 10, and 11, Paul told how much he longed for his own people, the Jews, to recognize Jesus as Savior and Lord.

In the last five chapters, Paul gave advice on how to live as Christians. For example, "Bless those who persecute you . . . rejoice with those who rejoice, weep with those who weep. Live in harmony with one another . . . never be conceited."

ROME, CHURCH OF, was started before the year A.D. 50. Although Christians were often persecuted by the Roman government, the church survived and grew. Christians met in homes. By A.D. 95, Rome was a strong center of the Christian church.

After the Emperor Constantine became a Christian in the fourth century A.D., the leader of the church became more and more powerful.

In our day, the Roman Catholic Church is called the Church of Rome. Its leader, the pope, lives in a special part of Rome called Vatican City.

ROME, CITY OF, was the bustling capital of the Roman Empire. The city began about six centuries before Christ. Built on seven hills, Rome lies about ten miles up the Tiber River off the west coast of Italy. At the time of Christ, more than a million people lived there. By the third and fourth centuries A.D., the city had lost its glory and had less than half a million people.

Most Roman emperors lived in the city of Rome, and some of them were considered gods by the citizens.

Early Christians were severely persecuted in Rome. Many were killed. Christians sometimes hid and worshiped in tunnels called catacombs beneath the city. Most scholars believe that the wicked city John wrote about in Revelation 17 and 18 was the city of Rome.

Nevertheless, the gospel of Christ lived on, and Rome, the wicked city, became an important Christian center.

ROPE is a thick cord formed from twisting smaller cords or lines together. In Bible times,

leather, sinews, vines, or plants were used for making rope. Rope was used in farming and warfare as well as in the home.

Wearing rope, however, was a sign of poverty, as in Isaiah 3: 24, or a sign of humility, as in 1 Kings 20: 31.

ROSE OF SHARON (see *Plants*)

RUDDERS were two steering paddles or oars connected by a crossbar at the rear of a boat. They were operated by one man. Paul was once on a ship when the sailors loosened the rope that tied the rudders to try to avoid shipwreck.

Where to find it: *Acts 27: 40*

RUDIMENTS (*ROO-duh-munts*) is a word used in the King James Version of the Bible for man's mistaken ideas about the controlling forces of the universe. Christians know that God is the one who made the universe and controls it.

Where to find it: *Colossians 2: 8, 20*

RUE (see *Plants*)

RUFUS (*ROO-fus*) was a son of Simon of Cyrene, the man who carried the cross for Jesus on the way to Calvary. Paul greeted a man named Rufus in his letter to the Romans as ''chosen in the Lord'' (KJV). He may have been the same person.

Where to find it: *Mark 15: 21; Romans 16: 13*

RULER means one who has authority over others. It is used in the Bible of several kinds of officials. A ruler may be a king, captain, magistrate, or supervisor.

Ephesians 6: 12 speaks of ''the world rulers of this present darkness.'' It may mean the people who control the earth for their own selfish purposes, or it may refer to demonic powers.

RULER OF THE SYNAGOGUE was the person

who arranged for the synagogue services. He served as the leader or president of the congregation (see *Synagogue*).

Where to find it: *Mark 5: 35*

RUTH, BOOK OF, is an Old Testament book that tells the story of a romance between a foreign widow and her former husband's relative in the time of the judges. The story took place sometime between 1300 and 1010 B.C.

Naomi and her husband went to live in Moab during a famine in Israel. After the famine was over, Naomi's husband died, and she wanted to return home. Ruth, a Moabite woman, had married Naomi's son, but he had also died. Now Ruth and Naomi had only each other to love. So Ruth left her own country to return to Israel with her mother-in-law. As they started back to Bethlehem, Ruth showed her love to Naomi as she vowed, ''Where you go I will go, and where you lodge I will lodge; your people shall be my people, and your God my God.''

When the two widows arrived in Bethlehem, it was harvesttime. To get food, Ruth arranged to work as a gleaner—one who picked up what the threshers dropped or left in the fields. She worked for Boaz, a relative of Naomi. Boaz saw the young widow working hard in the field and began asking questions about her. Eventually Boaz and Ruth were married and had a son, Obed, whom Naomi helped care for.

Ruth stayed in Israel, accepting the country as her own. She was the great-grandmother of King David and is listed in Matthew 1: 5 as one of the ancestors of Jesus.

SABAOTH *(SAB-ee-oath)*, **LORD OF,** is a phrase used twice in the King James Version; other translations use "Lord of hosts." This term originally meant "Lord of the armies of Israel." Later it came to include the idea of Lord of the "hosts" of heaven—all that God has created in heaven or on earth.

Where to find it: *James 5: 4; Romans 9: 29*

SABBATH *(SAB-buth)* was and is the weekly day of rest and worship for the Jews and some Christians. It is observed on the seventh day of the week (Saturday).

The Hebrew word for *Sabbath* comes from a Hebrew word that means "cease" or "rest." This shows the purpose of the Sabbath.

After Christ rose from the dead on the first day of the week (Sunday), Christians began to gather on Sundays to celebrate Christ's resur-rection. In Jerusalem, where most of the Christians were Jewish, they also worshiped in the synagogue and rested on Saturday. However, as the Christian and Jewish faiths became more separate, most Christians kept Sunday as their holy day and gradually gave up observing Saturday as the Sabbath. Some Christians today, however, believe that Saturday is still the proper day for worship.

Stephen was not afraid to tell the Sanhedrin that they had often refused to listen to God.

The idea of the Sabbath goes all the way back to creation. The Bible says, "God blessed the seventh day and hallowed it, because on it God rested from all his work which he had done in creation."

The seventh day or Sabbath is not mentioned again as a day of rest and worship until the Israelites left Egypt and were on their way to the Promised Land of Canaan. Keeping the Sabbath was one of the Ten Commandments given by God to Moses. God meant for the Sabbath to be a day of rest, worship, and remembrance that he had brought them out of slavery in Egypt.

During the 500 years between the close of the Old Testament and the coming of Christ, Jewish scribes tried to clarify what could and could not be done on the Sabbath. This resulted in a very long list of rules to show what was work and what was not. For example, a Jew could tie a knot on the Sabbath if it could be untied with only one hand! Of course there could be no cooking, baking, sewing, plowing, or reaping. Not even a fire could be lit. A person could walk only a little more than half a mile.

Although Jesus regularly worshiped in the synagogue on the Sabbath, he sometimes ignored the long list of rules if they interfered with his helping people. He healed people on the Sabbath, although the strict Pharisees insisted this was "work" and against the Law. Jesus replied that the Sabbath was made to benefit people.

Where to find it

God rests on the seventh day   *Genesis 2:3*
Commandments about the Sabbath   *Exodus 20:8-11; 16:23-30; 34:21; Deuteronomy 5:12-15*
Jesus heals on the Sabbath   *Matthew 12:1-14; Mark 2:23–3:6; Luke 6:1-11; John 5:1-18*
Early Christians meet on Sunday   *Acts 20:7; 1 Corinthians 16:1-2*

SABBATH DAY'S JOURNEY was the distance the Jewish scribes said a Jew could travel on a Sabbath day without breaking their law about "working" on the Sabbath. This rule is not found in the Old Testament but was part of a long list of regulations drawn up over hundreds of years to say what could or could not be done on the Jewish Sabbath and still keep the day "holy."

The distance was set at about 3,000 feet—a little more than half a mile. This was the distance between Jerusalem and the Mount of Olives.

Where to find it: *Acts 1:12*

SABBATICAL *(suh-BAT-ih-kul)* **YEAR** was every seventh year. During that year in Old Testament times, the Israelites were not to plow their fields, plant any seed, prune any grapevines or fruit trees. The land was to have "rest." However, poor people and animals were permitted to eat whatever grew by itself.

God promised his people that if they would obey his Word, enough crops would grow in the sixth year to last through the seventh year and until harvesttime the year after that.

The Israelites believed their land was holy, a gift from God. The sabbatical year was a time to thank God for taking care of his people.

During the sabbatical year, Israelites were also supposed to set free their slaves and cancel any debts that people owed them.

Many times the Israelites ignored God's command about the sabbatical year. God warned them in Leviticus 26:32-35 that if they did not obey, he would send them off the land so it could be rested. He finally did; the people of Israel were later exiled into Assyria and Babylon.

Where to find it: *Exodus 23:10-11; Leviticus 25:1-7; 26:27-35*

SACKCLOTH *(SAK-kloth)* was clothing of a dark, coarse fabric made of goat's hair or camel's hair. People wore sackcloth when a loved one died, when people were taken captive, when a city had been defeated, when they were repenting, and at other times of sadness. Prophets sometimes wore sackcloth as a sign of the coming judgment of God.

Where to find it: *1 Kings 21:27; 2 Kings 19:1-4; Jonah 3:6; Revelation 11:3*

SACRAMENT *(SAK-ruh-ment)* is a word that does not appear in the Bible. However, it has been used for many centuries in the church. It means a special ceremony or outward sign ordained by Christ that brings inner spiritual blessing when we take part in the ceremony with the right attitude.

Baptism and the Lord's Supper are two ceremonies that many churches consider to

Just before his death, Jesus used food to dramatize for his followers what was going to happen.

be sacraments. The Roman Catholic Church has several other ceremonies or rites that it considers sacraments.

Martin Luther and other church Reformers believed that a New Testament sacrament had to be (1) something that Christ himself practiced, (2) something that he commanded believers to practice, and (3) a symbol or word picture of something that God does.

Baptism is a word picture or drama of faith showing the death and resurrection of Christ. It shows that the believer has died to sin, and God has given him new life in Christ.

The Lord's Supper is a word picture or drama of fellowship showing that Christ died for our sins, and that the believer shares Christ's new life (see *Baptism* and *Lord's Supper*).

SACRIFICE *(SAK-rih-fice)* in the Bible is an offering or gift of something valuable to God. Sacrifices have been a part of religions from the beginning of time. Cain and Abel, the first sons of Adam and Eve, brought sacrifices to God; so did Noah.

When Moses led the Israelites out of Egypt, he told the people what sacrifices God wanted. The sacrifices outlined in Exodus, Leviticus, Numbers, and Deuteronomy were followed by the Hebrews until the destruction of the Temple in A.D. 70 (see *Offerings*).

The Jews since then no longer offer sacrifices.

The Book of Hebrews says that after Christ's great sacrifice of himself for our sins, no further sacrifices for sin were necessary. However, the New Testament says we should offer to God a "sacrifice of praise." We should also offer ourselves as a "living sacrifice to God."

Where to find it

Cain and Abel   *Genesis 4: 3-5*
Noah   *Genesis 8: 20*
Ourselves as a "living sacrifice"   *Romans 12: 1*
Praise   *Hebrews 13: 15*

SADDUCEES *(SAD-you-seez)* were a group of Jewish priests who, during New Testament times, were loyal to the Roman government. The Sadducees were largely a political party made up of wealthy priests. Usually the high priest (who was appointed by the Romans) was a Sadducee. When the New Testament speaks of "chief priests," it refers to Sadducees. Although the Sadducees were small in number, they were very influential. Sadducees were a part of the Sanhedrin, the ruling council of Jerusalem.

Sadducees differed from other Jewish groups in the following ways:

1. They stressed the first five books of the Old Testament, but they did not observe many of the traditions that the Pharisees accepted.

2. They did not believe that bodies will be resurrected. It is not clear whether they believed in life after death.

3. The Sadducees did not believe in angels or spirits.

When Jesus began his ministry, the Sadducees ignored him. But when people began to think of Jesus as a teacher with authority, the Sadducees were angry. Later they joined the scribes and the Pharisees in trying to destroy Jesus.

After the death and resurrection of Jesus Christ, the Sadducees opposed the Christians. They put the apostles in prison, but God delivered them.

There is no record in the New Testament of any Sadducees becoming Christians.

Where to find it

Sadducees deny resurrection, angels, spirits *Matthew 22:23; Mark 12:18; Luke 20:27; Acts 4:2; 23:8*
Sadducees oppose Jesus *Matthew 21:23; Luke 19:47; 20:19, 27-40*

SAILOR (see *Occupations*)

SAINT means a person who has dedicated himself to God. However, in the New Testament, the word *saint* is used for all Christians and means "one of God's people."

The apostle Paul often addressed his letters to "all the saints" in a particular place such as Ephesus, Colossae, or Philippi. He spoke of taking a collection to help the "saints in Jerusalem," who were suffering from a famine.

Where to find it: *Psalms 16:3; 30:4; Romans 15:26; Ephesians 1:1; Philippians 1:1; Colossians 1:2*

SALAMIS *(SAL-uh-miss)* was a town on the east coast of the island of Cyprus where Paul and Barnabas preached on their first missionary journey. The Bible does not say that a church was started there, however.

Where to find it: *Acts 13:5*

SALEM *(SAY-lum)* means "peace." Salem was the name of the city of which Melchizedek was king. Its location is not known. Psalm 76:2 uses Salem as a name for the place where God dwells. Some scholars believe that Salem refers to Jerusalem, which means "city of peace."

Where to find it: *Genesis 14:18; Psalm 76:2; Hebrews 7:1-2*

SALOME *(suh-LO-mee)* was the name of two important women in the New Testament.

1. Salome was probably the mother of James and John, two of Jesus' disciples. She apparently traveled with the disciples when Jesus was in Galilee and Jerusalem. She was at the crucifixion and came with other women to the tomb on Easter morning to anoint the body of Jesus.

2. Salome was also the name of the daughter of wicked Herodias, and the stepdaughter of Herod, the ruler of Galilee. When Salome danced at one of Herod's banquets, Herod was so pleased he said she could have anything she wanted. At her mother's request, she asked for the head of John the Baptist. To keep his word, Herod ordered John killed.

Salome's name is not mentioned in the Gospels but was mentioned by the historian Josephus.

Where to find it

The mother of James and John *Matthew 27:56; Mark 15:40; 16:1*
Herod's stepdaughter *Matthew 14:3-11; Mark 6:17-28*

SALT is a seasoning that preserves food and improves its taste. To "eat salt" with a person meant sharing his food and was a sign of friendship. If a person ate in his friend's home, the friend was obliged to protect him from harm.

In a similar way, salt was a sign of people's loyalty to God and God's care for them. Salt was always required with the sacrifices to God in the Tabernacle and the Temple.

In the New Testament, salt is used as a word picture of a purifying influence. Jesus said his disciples were to be the "salt of the earth."

Where to find it

Salt necessary in offerings *Leviticus 2:13*
God's covenant of salt *Numbers 18:19*
Disciples are to be "salt of the earth" *Matthew 5:13; Mark 9:50*

SALT SEA (see *Dead Sea*)

SALUTE *(suh-LUTE)* means to greet someone. Jewish people saluted each other when they met with such words as "May you be blessed by the Lord" or "The Lord be with you" or "Peace be unto you."

Certain acts went with these words. Sometimes people embraced each other, kissed a hand, or knelt. The Pharisees were known to enjoy salutations in public places. Salutations were often long and involved. This may be why Jesus told his disciples not to salute anyone in the road when he sent them out to preach.

Paul began his letters to churches with the salutation "Grace to you and peace from God our Father and the Lord Jesus Christ."

Where to find it: *Matthew 23:6-7; Mark 12:38; Luke 10:4; Ephesians 1:2; Colossians 1:2*

SALVATION (sal-VAY-shun) has a broad meaning. The word comes from the idea of being saved from or delivered from some serious disease or some physical or spiritual danger. Today it usually refers to a person's being saved through Christ from the penalty and power of sin.

Often in the Old Testament, salvation referred to a person or a group being saved from physical danger. When the Israelites were crossing the Red Sea in their escape from Egypt, and the Pharaoh's army was close behind them, Moses said, "Fear not, stand firm, and see the salvation of the Lord, which he will work for you today; for the Egyptians whom you see today, you shall never see again."

The "salvation" in this case was the destruction of the Egyptian army in the Red Sea.

The Psalms often speak of salvation. Sometimes it refers to being saved from one's enemies; other times it refers to both physical and spiritual salvation. This seems to be true in Psalm 85: 9, "Surely his salvation is at hand for those who fear him."

The New Testament records only one time when Jesus used the word salvation. He said to Zacchaeus, the tax collector, "Today salvation has come to this house . . . for the Son of man came to seek and to save the lost." Jesus obviously meant a spiritual salvation, for Zacchaeus was not in any physical danger, nor was he physically lost.

The apostle Paul makes clear that spiritual salvation means being delivered from sin—both its power over our lives and the judgment it brings from God. This kind of salvation comes through faith in Jesus Christ, who gave his life so we could enter into the new life he made possible. Salvation begins when we give ourselves to Christ, but it is a process that continues throughout our lives. Paul wrote about "us who are being saved."

Although the believer experiences salvation day after day, we will understand it fully only when we meet God. Peter wrote of a "salvation ready to be revealed in the last time." All of creation will then be freed or saved from the penalty of sin.

Where to find it

Salvation from Pharaoh's forces   *Exodus 14: 13*
Salvation to the house of Zacchaeus   *Luke 19: 9*

Salvation through Christ   *Romans 1: 16*
Those who are "being saved"   *1 Corinthians 1: 18*
Salvation includes the future   *1 Peter 1: 5*

SAMARIA (suh-MAIR-ee-uh) is the name of both a city and an area in Palestine. It is not always clear in the Old Testament whether a verse refers to the area or to the city.

During most of the 210-year history of the Northern Kingdom (Israel), the city of Samaria was its capital. For this reason, the name *Samaria* often refers to the whole Northern Kingdom. King Omri made Samaria the capital city of Israel about 880 B.C. Later his son, King Ahab, built an elaborate palace there, decorated with so much ivory that it was called "the ivory house." Ahab and his wife, Jezebel, made it a place of luxury and idol worship.

The city was finally destroyed by the Assyrians in 722 B.C. after a three-year siege. Most of it was burned. It was later rebuilt.

In the New Testament, *Samaria* refers to an area about 40 miles wide and 35 miles long right in the middle of Palestine. Judea was south of it and Galilee was north. The people who lived in Samaria (see *Samaritans*) did not follow the same rules of Judaism as the people in Judea and Galilee. Terrible hatred existed between Samaritans and the other Jews of Palestine during the time of Christ. For this reason, most Jews would not travel through Samaria; they would take a much longer route so they wouldn't have to go through this province.

Jesus, however, traveled through Samaria, and on one such trip he had an important conversation with a woman at a well.

Where to find it

Omri moves capital to Samaria   *1 Kings 16: 24, 28*
Ahab builds an ivory house in Samaria   *1 Kings 22: 38-39*
Jesus goes through Samaria   *John 4: 3-6*

SAMARITANS (suh-MAIR-ih-tunz) were people who lived in Samaria, a province in Palestine between Judea and Galilee.

Although the Samaritans considered themselves Jews, the other Jews in Palestine did not think they were following the true Jewish religion. There was deep hatred between the Samaritans and the Jews, although scholars are not sure why. The hatred was present at least 400 years before Christ.

When the Northern Kingdom (Israel) was conquered by the Assyrians in 722 B.C., many of the people from the city of Samaria were sent into exile. The conquering country then sent people from Assyria or other areas to live in Samaria. This was the custom at that time. Eventually some of the new people married the Israelites who were left in Samaria.

About 125 years later, the Southern Kingdom (Judah) was conquered by the Babylonians, and many of its people were sent away to Babylon. About 80 years after that, some of their descendants were allowed to return to rebuild the Temple in Jerusalem. Their return brought conflict between the people in Judah and those in Samaria.

Eventually, the Samaritans built a temple of their own on Mount Gerizim. The Samaritans' religion differed from that of other Jews in a few points:

1. They accepted only Genesis, Exodus, Leviticus, Numbers, and Deuteronomy as the true law of God.

2. They felt that Mount Gerizim was the place God had chosen for worship instead of Jerusalem.

The hatred between Jews and Samaritans was so intense that Jews traveling between Judea and Galilee tried never to go through Samaria—even if it meant an extra day's journey to go around it.

However, Jesus chose to go through Samaria, and while on one such trip he had a remarkable conversation with a Samaritan woman about some of the Samaritan beliefs. The woman and many others in her village believed in Christ.

In the story of the Good Samaritan, Jesus made one of these hated people the hero.

Today, a few descendants of the Samaritans still live in a small town called Nablus in Israel.

Where to find it

Conflict between Samaritans and Jews about rebuilding the Temple   *Ezra 4:1-24; Nehemiah 4:1–6:18*
Jesus tells about Good Samaritan   *Luke 10:25-37*
Jesus talks with Samaritan woman   *John 4:1-42*

SAMSON *(SAM-sun)* was an Old Testament judge who had unusual God-given strength—but who was not very wise spiritually.

When the Philistines tried to capture Samson, he simply ripped loose the city gates.

An angel told Samson's mother that she and her husband would have a son who should become a Nazirite. (Nazirites spent their lives dedicated to God. They did not cut their hair, drink wine or anything with alcohol in it, or eat food God said was not clean.) The angel said Samson would help free Israel from its Philistine rulers.

When Samson was grown, he married a Philistine woman. At the week-long wedding feast, Samson gave a riddle to 30 men who were guests. If they could answer the riddle, he would provide each of them with two new outfits of clothing. If they could not, they would have to give him 60 new outfits.

When the men could not guess the riddle after several days, they told Samson's wife she would have to get the answer or they would burn down her father's house. She tricked Samson to get the answer.

Samson was so angry that he went out and killed 30 men to get their clothes to give to the guests. Then he went back to his parents' house.

When he later returned, he found that his wife had been given to another man. This made Samson even angrier. He caught 300 foxes, tied their tails together with flaming torches, and let the foxes loose in the Philistine grain fields. The grain harvest was destroyed.

In revenge, the Philistines burned Samson's wife and her father. Samson then killed more Philistines.

The Philistines came out to capture him, and Samson killed 1,000 of them with the jawbone of a donkey.

Later Samson met a woman named Delilah. The Philistines offered her much money to find out what made Samson so strong. Delilah coaxed and coaxed Samson until he finally told her he would lose his strength if his head were shaved. (He would then be breaking his Nazirite vow.)

While Samson slept, the Philistines shaved his head. His God-given strength left him. The Philistines then poked out his eyes and made him work in a prison.

During one of the feasts for their pagan god, Dagon, the Philistines brought Samson out of prison to make fun of him. By this time Samson's hair had grown and he was again fulfilling his Nazirite vow. Samson had someone help him find the two pillars that held up the building. Standing between the two pillars, Samson prayed to God for the strength to push them down. As the walls and ceiling fell, thousands of Philistines were killed—and so was Samson.

Where to find it

Angel comes to Samson's parents *Judges 13: 2-25*
The riddle and its results *Judges 14: 1–15: 20*
Delilah learns his secret *Judges 16: 1-22*
Samson pushes the pillars and kills the Philistines *Judges 16: 23-31*

SAMUEL (SAM-you-ull) was a prophet, a priest, and the last judge of Israel.

He was born in answer to the prayers of his mother, Hannah, who promised that if God would give her a son she would dedicate him to the Lord. To keep her promise, Hannah brought young Samuel to the Tabernacle, where he grew up under the care of the priest Eli.

Later, as a prophet, priest, and judge, Samuel told the Israelites they must stop worshiping false gods. He called all the people to a meeting at the city of Mizpah, where he offered a sacrifice to God and asked him to forgive the people.

The Philistines heard of the meeting and decided to attack the Israelites at Mizpah. Samuel prayed, and God sent such a severe thunderstorm that the Philistines got their orders mixed up. The Israelites went after them and defeated them.

For most of his life, Samuel was the spiritual and political leader of the Israelites. When he was an old man, the Israelites told Samuel they wanted a king to rule them. God told Samuel they could have a king, but they should know that a king would cause them a lot of trouble. At God's directions, Samuel anointed Saul as the first king of Israel.

When King Saul did not follow God's commands, Samuel warned him that God would make someone else king.

God told Samuel to anoint David as the new king. Later, when Saul was trying to kill David, David stayed at Samuel's home.

All Israel was sad when Samuel died.

Where to find it

Hannah prays for a son *1 Samuel 1: 9-20*
Samuel grows up in the Temple *1 Samuel 1: 21-28; 3: 1-21*
Teaches Israel to love only God *1 Samuel 7: 3-15*
Anoints Saul as king *1 Samuel 8: 4-22; 9: 15–10: 1*
Israel mourns his death *1 Samuel 25: 1*

SAMUEL, FIRST BOOK OF, is one of two books called Samuel in our modern Bibles. However, the two parts were one book until about 200 B.C., when the Bible was translated into Greek. The translators then divided it into two parts, and it is now known as 1 Samuel and 2 Samuel.

Although the books are named after Samuel, who was a judge, prophet, and priest, no one knows who wrote them.

1 Samuel tells the history of the Israelites from the birth of Samuel to the death of King Saul. Samuel had been dedicated to God by

Samuel grew up in the Tabernacle, helping Eli the priest. It was there that God spoke aloud to him one night.

his mother before his birth, and she took him as a young child to serve Eli, the priest, in the Tabernacle.

The sons of Eli carried the sacred ark of the Covenant into battle against the Philistines, and the ark was captured by the enemy. The ark brought such calamity to the Philistines that they sent it back to Israel.

Although Samuel was a good judge of the Israelites, the people wanted a king like the nations around them. God told Samuel to warn the people of the hardships they would have with a king, but the people still clamored for a king. So at God's command, Samuel anointed Saul to be the first king.

Saul started well. He was humble and a skilled military commander. He successfully fought one battle with the Philistines. However, he disobeyed God, and God told Samuel there must be a different king.

At God's command, Samuel secretly anointed David as king. David was a skilled musician, and Saul brought him to his palace as a musician and armor-bearer. Saul loved him. However, after David killed the giant

Philistine Goliath, David became so popular with the people that Saul was overcome with jealousy.

David also became good friends with Jonathan, Saul's son, and this made Saul even more jealous. After Saul tried to kill David, David fled to the wilderness. Saul and his army followed but were never able to capture him. Several times, David could have killed Saul, but he refused to do so.

Meanwhile, Saul and his army were also fighting the Philistines, and in one battle, Saul, Jonathan, and his two brothers were all killed. The story of Saul's death completes the book of 1 Samuel.

SAMUEL, SECOND BOOK OF, tells what happened during the reign of David as king. For seven years, David reigned from Hebron as his capital city. Later, he captured Jerusalem, which had previously belonged to the Jebusites. David then made Jerusalem his capital city. During David's early reign, Israel was often at war with the Ammonites and the Syrians.

During one battle, David plotted the death of Uriah, the husband of beautiful Bathsheba, because David wanted to marry Bathsheba. The child of David and Bathsheba died because of David's sin (see *Uriah*).

Later, David's son Absalom led a rebellion against his father. David and those faithful to him had to flee from Jerusalem. Eventually, Absalom was killed in battle. David returned to reign in Jerusalem, but with great sorrow because of Absalom's death.

David once wanted to count how many fighting men he had, so he ordered a census. This displeased God, and he sent a terrible disease that killed thousands of people. The disease was finally stopped at a place near Jerusalem, when David built an altar there to offer sacrifices to God. Later that became the place where Solomon's Temple was built. The book of 2 Samuel closes with the story of this disease and David's offering of sacrifices.

SANBALLAT *(san-BAL-lut)* was a leader of the Samaritans when Nehemiah was leading the Jews in rebuilding the walls of Jerusalem about 445 B.C. Sanballat tried to stop the building, probably because he did not want the Jews who were returning from Babylon to become a strong political force in the area. He was now an important leader and he wanted to stay important. Sanballat was either Jewish or part Jewish, for he gave his sons Jewish names.

To stop the building of the walls of Jerusalem, Sanballat gathered a group of men from Samaria to go to Jerusalem to fight. However, Nehemiah arranged to have half his men stand guard while the other men built.

When Sanballat saw that he could not defeat the builders by force, he tried to get Nehemiah to meet with him and others to discuss it. Nehemiah realized it was a plot to kill him, so he refused to meet with them.

Sanballat then hired a Jew to encourage Nehemiah to hide in the Temple at night, although that was against Jewish law. Nehemiah again refused. No matter what he tried, Sanballat could not stop the building of the wall.

Later, Sanballat's daughter married the son of Eliashib, the high priest in Jerusalem. However, because she was considered a "foreign wife," Nehemiah insisted that they leave Jerusalem.

Some historians believe that the conflict between Sanballat and Nehemiah was one cause of the hatred between Samaritans and Jews that lasted more than 400 years.

Where to find it: *Nehemiah 4:1–6:15; 13:28*

SANCTIFY *(SANK-tih-fie)* means to set apart, to consecrate, or to dedicate wholly to God. *Consecrate, dedicate, be made holy*—these all mean the same as *sanctify*.

In the Old Testament, many things were sanctified, including places, certain days, persons, or objects used in worship. They were given wholly to God.

In the New Testament, those who believe in Christ are sanctified through Christ's life and death. When a person becomes a Christian, he begins to be sanctified. The Holy Spirit continues the work of sanctification in the believer and helps the Christian to become more like Christ day after day.

Where to find it
Old Testament sanctifications
  Sabbath *Exodus 20:8*
  Tabernacle and priests *Exodus 29:44*
  Houses *Leviticus 27:14*
New Testament sanctifications
  Holy Spirit sanctifies *Romans 15:16*
  Sanctified through Christ *Hebrews 13:12*

SANCTUARY *(SANK-chew-air-ee)* means "holy place." In the Old Testament, it usually refers to the Tabernacle or the Temple. However, in Ezekiel 11:16 and Isaiah 8:14, God himself is said to be a sanctuary for his people—a holy place where they can find shelter.

In the Book of Hebrews, *sanctuary* is used as a word picture of God's heavenly dwelling place. Christ, as the high priest, has offered himself as a sacrifice so that no other sacrifices are necessary for Christians to enter the holy place where God is.

Where to find it: *Hebrews 9:24; 10:19; 13:11-12*

SANDALS AND SHOES have been worn since very early times. Sandals were the most common. Soles of sandals were made of wood, cane, or leather and held to the foot with leather straps tied around the ankles. Sandals were stronger than shoes, for shoes were made of soft leather.

Shoes and sandals were always removed at the door of a house so that dirt would not be brought inside.

SANHEDRIN *(san-HEE-drun)* was the highest Jewish council of men who governed the Jewish people in Palestine in New Testament times. They were subject to the Roman rulers, but they had the final say in religious matters, in collecting taxes, and in some criminal cases.

The current high priest served as president of the Sanhedrin. The 70 members included former high priests, heads of important families in Jerusalem, and leading scribes and Pharisees. Historical records do not show exactly how members were chosen or how long they served.

The Sanhedrin usually met in one of the Temple buildings or courts every day except the Sabbath or feast days.

The Sanhedrin could pass a death sentence on a prisoner but could not carry it out without permission of the Roman ruler. That is

why Jesus had to be brought before Pilate as well as the Sanhedrin. The Sanhedrin told Pilate a lie about Jesus—that he taught people that he was a king and they should not pay taxes to Rome (see *Trial of Jesus Christ*).

The power of the Sanhedrin ended after the destruction of Jerusalem in A.D. 70.

Where to find it: *Mark 14: 53-65; 15: 1-11; Luke 23: 1-12; Acts 23: 1-10*

SAPPHIRA (see *Ananias*)

SAPPHIRE *(SAF-fire)* is a blue precious stone. It was one of the gems on the breastplate of the high priest. It is usually mentioned as a word picture of something beautiful or valuable.

Where to find it: *Exodus 28: 18; 39: 11; Job 28: 16; Lamentations 4: 7; Ezekiel 1: 26; 10: 1; 28: 13; Revelation 9: 17; 21: 19*

SARAH *(SAIR-uh)* was the wife of Abram, later called Abraham. She became the mother of Isaac when she was 90 years old. In the New Testament she is called the mother of all believers.

At first her name was Sarai. God promised Abram, in Mesopotamia, that he and Sarai would be the parents of a nation of people. He told them to move south to Canaan, but they went instead to Egypt because there was a famine in Canaan.

Although Sarai was then about 70 years old, she was considered beautiful. Abram was afraid the Egyptians would kill him for his wife, so he pretended Sarai was his sister. The Pharaoh, or king, of Egypt did take Sarai to his palace to become one of his many wives, but God protected Sarai by sending a plague on the Pharaoh's household. When the Pharaoh learned she was already married, he returned her to Abram and sent them on their way.

Years went by, and still Sarai did not have a child. So she followed the land's custom and gave her servant, Hagar, to Abram as a second wife. Hagar had a son, Ishmael.

But God told Abram again that he and Sarai would have a child who would be the ancestor of a whole nation. God then changed Abram's name to Abraham, and Sarai's to Sarah, or "mother of a multitude."

One day, the Lord visited Abraham and Sarah's tent. While Sarah was inside preparing food for them, she heard the Lord tell her husband that she would have a son soon. Sarah laughed to think of having a child in their old age.

However, God kept his promise, and Sarah at age 90 gave birth to a boy. He was named Isaac, which means "laughter."

Sarah and her servant, Hagar, didn't always get along well. Sarah didn't want her son Isaac to play with Hagar's son, Ishmael, so she convinced Abraham to send Hagar and Ishmael away.

Sarah died when she was 127, and Abraham buried her in a cave in a field he bought. The field is now a part of the city of Hebron in Palestine.

Although Sarah had doubted that God could give them a child, she is called an example of faith in the Book of Hebrews (most translations).

Where to find it

Sarai's family on the move   *Genesis 11:29–12:20*
Sarai and Hagar   *Genesis 16:1-16; 21:1-14*
Name changed to Sarah   *Genesis 17:15-19*
Laughs at God's promise   *Genesis 18:1-15*
Isaac born   *Genesis 21:1-8*
Mother of all believers   *Galatians 4:21-31*
An example of faith   *Hebrews 11:11*

SARDIS (*SAR-diss*) was an ancient important city in the western part of what is now Turkey. It was famous for its woolen goods. It once had a huge stadium and theater built of concrete. Sardis also had a beautiful temple to a goddess. Archaeologists have uncovered the ruins of these buildings.

By A.D. 90 there was a Christian church in Sardis, and one of the messages in the New Testament Book of Revelation is addressed to this church. The message warns that many of the Sardis Christians were not living for God as they should.

Sardis was a prosperous city until at least A.D. 300. It was destroyed in a battle in A.D. 1403. Today there is only a small village called Sart where this great city once stood.

Where to find it: *Revelation 1:11; 3:1-6*

SATAN (*SAY-tun*) is the enemy who opposes God and man. He does not have a physical body. The Bible uses many names for him besides Satan. Among them are the devil, the evil one, the deceiver of the world, the father of lies, Beelzebub, the old serpent, and the prince of the power of the air.

The New Testament says much more about Satan than the Old Testament does. Christ often spoke about Satan as one who deceived people, who sometimes caused illness, and who fell from heaven.

Jesus himself was tempted by Satan in the wilderness following his baptism. Judas be-trayed Jesus after Satan entered into him.

The apostle Paul said that Satan sometimes disguises himself as an angel of light.

The Bible does not say directly where Satan came from, but he was already in the Garden of Eden when Adam and Eve were created. Although the serpent is not called Satan in the story of Adam and Eve, Satan apparently used that creature to tempt Eve. Many scholars believe that two prophecies in the Old Testament (Isaiah 14:12-14 and Ezekiel 28:12-15) describe the king of Babylon and the prince of Tyre in language that could also describe Satan—as one who rebelled against God and became his enemy.

Satan is the ruler of a kingdom made up of demons. He hates God and tries to destroy God's work. The Book of Revelation pictures Satan and his angels as finally being destroyed.

Where to find it

The serpent tempts Eve   *Genesis 3:1-15*
Satan tempts Jesus   *Matthew 4:1-11*
Jesus talks about Satan   *Matthew 12:22-32; Mark 4:1-20; Luke 10:18; 13:10-16*
Satan enters into Judas   *Luke 22:3; John 13:27*
Satan disguises himself as angel of light   *2 Corinthians 11:14*
God will finally crush Satan   *Matthew 25:41; Romans 16:20; Revelation 20:7-10*

SATRAP (*SAY-trap*) was the title for an official in the Persian Empire who ruled over a certain area. Darius appointed 120 satraps.

Where to find it: *Ezra 8:36; Esther 3:12; Daniel 3:2; 6:1*

SATYR (*SAY-ter*) seems to refer to a demon that had the appearance of a hairy goat. Isaiah mentioned satyrs that would dance in the ruins of Babylon. Satyrs are also mentioned as false gods to whom sacrifices were made.

Where to find it

False gods   *Leviticus 17:7; 2 Chronicles 11:15*
Creatures at Babylon   *Isaiah 13:21; 34:14*

SAUL was the first king of Israel. When the prophet Samuel anointed him king, Saul was a tall, handsome young man who knew how to work hard. He was humble and did not consider himself worthy to be king. God used him to win some battles against the Philistines, one of Israel's toughest enemies.

But although Saul was brave, he did not

King Saul could not stand to see the crowds praising David and decided to kill him.

become a good king. After David killed the Philistine giant Goliath, Saul became very jealous of David's popularity and tried to kill him, even though David was close friends with Saul's son Jonathan. Several times Saul and his army set out to find and kill David. But David, who now also had a small army of faithful followers, always escaped. Saul's mad jealousy of David kept him from doing the things he should have done as king.

Another fault also kept Saul from being a good king. He was impatient and did not always obey God's clear commands. Once he acted like a priest and made a sacrifice to God instead of waiting for the priest Samuel to come to make the sacrifice. Another time he disobeyed God and kept some of the good things he had found in the camp of the Amalekites after they were defeated. God had said he was to destroy everything.

Finally, in a battle with the Philistines, Saul and his three sons were killed. The Philistines, to show how they despised Saul, hung the bodies on the walls of one of their cities and placed Saul's armor in the temple of their heathen god. However, some brave Israelites, who came from a village Saul had helped earlier, risked their lives to rescue the bodies and give them a proper burial.

Where to find it

Is anointed king *1 Samuel 9:10*
Rescues people of Jabesh-gilead *1 Samuel 11:1-11*

Disobeys in offering sacrifice *1 Samuel 13:8-13*
Disobeys God in battle *1 Samuel 15:1-29*
Becomes jealous of David *1 Samuel 18:6-16*
Tries to kill David in battle *1 Samuel 19:11–20:34; 23:19–24:22; 26:1-25*
He and sons die in battle *1 Samuel 31*

SAUL (New Testament) (see *Paul*)

SAVIOR *(SAVE-yur)* is someone who saves or delivers others from evil or danger.

The Old Testament nearly always speaks of God as the Savior of his people. He saved his people from Egyptian slavery and delivered them from enemies in many other ways. The prophet Isaiah spoke of God as a spiritual Savior.

In a few instances, men were called "saviors" because they helped the people escape from some enemy.

In the New Testament, *Savior* usually refers to Christ saving us from sin. When the birth of Christ was announced to the shepherds, the angels said, "For to you is born this day in the city of David a Savior, who is Christ the Lord."

When the Samaritans had met Jesus, they said, "We know that this is indeed the Savior of the world."

God is our Savior, for he is the one who planned our salvation; Christ is our Savior, for he died for our sins.

Where to find it

God the Savior in the Old Testament *Isaiah 43:11; 45:21; 60:16*

God the Savior in the New Testament   *1 Timothy 1:1; 2:3; 4:10; Titus 1:3; 2:10; 3:4*
Christ the Savior in the New Testament   *Luke 2:11; John 4:42; Titus 1:4; 2:13; 3:6; 1 John 4:14*

SAVOR *(SAVE-er)* means a smell or taste. The King James Version often describes offerings brought to God as having a "sweet savor to God." Other translations usually use *odor* or *smell*. In the New Testament, sweet-smelling offerings are used as a word picture of a Christian's life that is pleasing to God.

Where to find it: *Genesis 8:21; Leviticus 23:18; Matthew 5:13; 2 Corinthians 2:15; Ephesians 5:2 (KJV)*

SCAPEGOAT *(SKAPE-goat)* (see *Azazel*)

SCARLET *(SCAR-let)* means bright red in color. The dye to make scarlet cloth was made from the eggs or bodies of certain insects that lived in one kind of oak tree in Palestine. Scarlet was considered a color of luxury or royalty. The Roman soldiers, just before the crucifixion of Jesus, made fun of him by putting a scarlet robe on him.

Scarlet cloth was used in the clothing of the high priests and for the heavy curtain that hung in the Tabernacle.

Where to find it: *Exodus 26:1, 31, 36; 28:5-8, 15, 33; Matthew 27:27-31*

SCEPTER *(SEP-ter)* was a rod or baton that symbolized the authority of a ruler. Some scepters were long and thin like a curtain rod; others were short and flat. King Ahasuerus

held out his scepter to Queen Esther to show that she had his permission to speak.

When the Psalms speak of a king as a word picture for God, they often speak of his scepter or authority.

Where to find it: *Esther 5:2; Psalm 45:6*

SCEVA *(SKEE-vuh)* was a Jewish chief priest who lived in Ephesus. His seven sons were not followers of Jesus, but they tried to cast out demons from people by using the name of Jesus. It didn't work, and they were publicly embarrassed for trying to use Jesus' name that way.

Where to find it: *Acts 19:13-17*

SCHISM *(SKIZ-um)* means a division or disagreement within a group of people. The apostle Paul reminded the church at Corinth that all Christians were part of the Body of Christ, and so there should be no schism among them. Instead, they should care for each other.

Where to find it: *1 Corinthians 12:25*

SCHOOLS are rarely mentioned in the Bible. What we know about education in Bible times comes mostly from other very old writings that have been found by archaeologists.

We do know that all learning among the Hebrew people centered around their belief in God. They did not think of arithmetic or history as separate from their understanding of God. In the Old Testament, parents were told to teach their children the stories about God's wonderful acts in bringing them out of slavery in Egypt and into their own land. They were expected to know history so they could understand the works of God. The same was true of all other learning.

So far as we can tell, the Jews who came back to Palestine from exile in Babylonia about 450 B.C. started synagogue schools, where boys were taught to read and write and to understand the writings of the Old Testament. (Girls did not go to school.) The Jewish scribes or rabbis (meaning "teachers") were in charge. If there were more than 25 boys in the school, an assistant helped. If anyone misbehaved, he was punished. Learning was mostly by memorizing.

If boys wanted more education than they received at the synagogue school, or if they wanted to become scribes themselves, they found a teacher they liked and studied with him. The apostle Paul studied with one such teacher—the famous Gamaliel.

Although Jesus never taught in any regular classroom, he was one of the world's greatest teachers. For three years he taught his 12 disciples and other men and women who traveled with him. He also taught thousands of other people who came occasionally to hear him teach as he walked among the villages of Galilee and Judea.

Where to find it: *Luke 8:1-2; Acts 22:3*

SCOFF *(skawf)* means to sneer at something or

to show scorn. The Bible speaks of the scoffer as a person who is foolish and proud. Psalm 1:1 says that a person is blessed who does not "sit in the seat of scoffers."

SCORPION *(SKOR-pee-un)* is a poisonous insect that looks like a tiny lobster. In its tail is a poisonous stinger that can kill small animals and be very painful to humans. Scorpions are

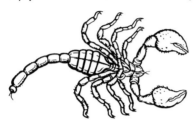

still found in Palestine. They are mentioned many times in the Bible, sometimes as word pictures of things unpleasant or to be feared.

Where to find it: *Deuteronomy 8:15; Ezekiel 2:6; Revelation 9:10*

SCOURGING *(SKUR-jing)* was a beating with a rod or a whip. Jews and Romans used scourgings as a punishment. Jewish Law said a man could not be hit more than 40 times, so the Jews usually stopped at 39 to be sure they did not go beyond the Law. The apostle Paul said, "Five times I have received at the hands of the Jews the forty lashes less one."

Roman government officials often used scourging to "examine" slaves and non-Romans who were accused of a crime so they would confess. This was forbidden, however, for Roman citizens. When Paul was arrested in Jerusalem, the Roman soldiers were going to "examine" him by scourging him. When he told them he was a Roman citizen, they stopped immediately.

Sometimes the scourging was with a whip that had tiny pieces of bone or metal attached to the ends to make it more painful. The victim was tied naked to a post and then whipped with this scourge across his back and chest. Victims sometimes died of the beating.

Jesus was scourged with this kind of whip before he was crucified.

Where to find it

Jesus is scourged   *Matthew 27:26; Mark 15:15*
Paul is beaten with rods   *Acts 16:35-38; 2 Corinthians 11:24*
Paul is saved from scourging   *Acts 22:24-29*

SCREENS are mentioned as part of the Tabernacle in the Old Testament. These screens were not metal; they were heavy pieces of linen cloth that divided the three sections of the Tabernacle. The screens were more like heavy drapes. They were beautifully colored and embroidered (see *Tabernacle*).

Where to find it: *Exodus 26:31, 36; 27:16; 35:12; 38:18; 40:21*

SCRIBES were important religious leaders of the Jews from the time of Ezra (about 450 B.C.) through the New Testament period.

Ezra was the most famous scribe of the Old Testament. He and other Jews who came to Palestine from exile in Babylonia taught the Law of Moses to the people. They also copied the Old Testament writings and handed them

down from one generation to another. Scribes came from the families of priests and Levites.

By New Testament times, the scribes were mostly Pharisees. They were known as the men who best understood the Law of Moses and could tell common people what they could and could not do as devout Jews. They taught children and adults in the synagogue schools. They often served as judges in Jewish courts because they knew so much about the Law of Moses. However, they were supposed to make their living some other way, so most of them had some trade.

Jesus accused them of greed, however, so they probably were getting fees for their teachings in some way. Jesus also accused them of pretending to be holy when they really were not.

The New Testament scribes were Jesus' worst enemies and played an important part in his death.

Ezra, the scribe   *Ezra 7: 6-11*
Jesus condemns the scribes   *Matthew 9: 3-7;
23: 2-31; Mark 2: 6-12; 3: 22-30; 7: 1-13; 12: 38-40;
Luke 20: 46*
Scribes help bring Jesus' death   *Matthew 20: 18;
26: 57; 27: 41; Mark 11: 18; 14: 1; 15: 1, 31; Luke
23: 10*

SCRIPTURES *(SKRIP-churz)* in the New Testament is a word that refers to scrolls of the Old Testament. When Jesus and Paul spoke of the Scriptures, they meant these scrolls. After the writings that form the New Testament were collected and recognized as having authority, Christians began speaking of both the Old and New Testaments as ''Scripture'' (see *Canon*).

Where to find it

Jesus refers to the Old Testament as Scripture   *Matthew 21: 42; Mark 14: 49; Luke 4: 16-21; John 5: 39; 13: 18*
Paul refers to Old Testament as Scripture   *Romans 4: 3; 1 Timothy 5: 18*

SCROLL was an ancient form of book. In Bible times, books were not made of pages but of papyrus or parchment (made from animal skins) glued together to form long rolls. Some were 20 to 35 feet long. Each end was fastened to a stick, and the scroll was rolled up so that the beginning of the scroll was on the right and the end on the left—because the Hebrew language reads from right to left. Jesus read from this kind of scroll in Nazareth.

Scrolls are still used today for reading the Old Testament in Jewish synagogues (see *Writing*).

Where to find it: *Luke 4: 16-20*

SCROLLS, DEAD SEA (see *Dead Sea Scrolls*)

SCYTHIANS *(SITH-ee-uns)* were an ancient group of nomads known for how cruelly they treated their enemies. They originally came from a part of what is now southern Russia and Bulgaria. Some migrated to Palestine and Egypt somewhere in the 700s and 600s B.C. They were eventually defeated by the Medes long before the time of Christ. When Paul spoke of Scythians, he used them as a word picture for warlike people of great cruelty.

Where to find it: *Colossians 3: 11*

SEA is used in the Bible of any body of water—large or small, salt or fresh. Because many ships sank in storms, the sea was looked upon as a place of terror. For this reason, heaven is pictured in Revelation as a place where ''the sea was no more.''

Where to find it: *Psalm 89: 9; Revelation 21: 1*

SEA, BRONZE or **MOLTEN** or **BRAZEN** was a huge bronze basin 18 feet across and 7½ feet high, holding about 12,000 gallons of water. It sat in the Temple on a base of 12 bronze statues of oxen. The priests washed in it.

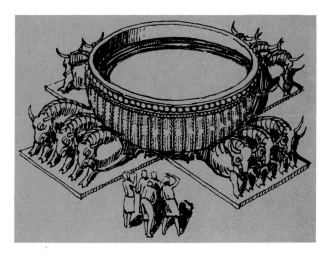

When the Babylonians conquered Jerusalem in 586 B.C., they broke the basin and took the pieces to Babylon.

Where to find it: *1 Kings 7: 23-26; 2 Kings 25: 13; 2 Chronicles 4: 6*

SEA OF GALILEE (see *Galilee, Sea of*)

SEA OF GLASS is mentioned in the Book of Revelation as part of a vision of heaven. In the vision, saints who had conquered the evil beast stood beside the sea with harps in their hands. This sea seems to be a word picture of the purity, power, and respect that people feel in the presence of God.

Where to find it: *Revelation 4: 6; 15: 2*

SEA GULL (see *Birds—Sea Gull*)

SEA MONSTER refers to any great fish or creature of the sea.

SEAL was a small beetle-shaped tool that had the engraved design of its owner on one side.

SECOND COMING OF CHRIST

Designs might be pictures of animals, birds, people, names, gods, or combinations. Seals were usually made into rings, but some were worn on a cord around the neck or even carried in a small box. Every person of importance had his own seal. The owner would press the seal into soft wax or clay. When hard, the wax or clay kept his impression in it.

A seal was in some ways like a person's signature. Seals were used to show who owned something; to show that an agreement had been made between two people; to give authority to letters or royal commands; or as a means of sealing doors, books, or documents so they would not be disturbed. A door or a tomb was sealed by stretching a cord across it and sealing the cord. This is probably the way Jesus' tomb was sealed.

A seal is sometimes used as a word picture. For example, Christians are "sealed with the promised Holy Spirit" to show that they belong to God. In the Book of Revelation, Christians are sealed to show they are protected by God.

Where to find it

Seal in a ring *Esther 8: 8*
Christ's tomb is sealed *Matthew 27: 66*
Christians are sealed with the Holy Spirit *Ephesians 1: 13*
Sealed for protection *Revelation 7: 2-8; 9: 4*

SECOND COMING OF CHRIST is referred to nearly 300 times in the New Testament. Early Christians sometimes spoke of the Second Coming as the "blessed hope."

The night before Jesus was crucified, he told his disciples he would return. When he ascended to heaven, two angels told the disciples that Jesus would come again in the same manner as they had seen him go.

Although sincere Christians differ about when and how the Second Coming will occur, most agree that Christ will return in a way that will be clearly visible to people, and that it will be an event of great joy to believers. The Second Coming will be the climax of all Christ's work on earth. He and his people will begin a new period in history. God and those who love him will finally live together in fellowship forever and ever.

Where to find it

Jesus' return is foretold *John 14: 3; Acts 1: 11*
Second Coming is the "blessed hope" *Titus 2: 13*

Jesus comes as conqueror *1 Thessalonians 4: 13-18; 2 Thessalonians 1: 6-12; Revelation 19: 11-21*

SEED has three meanings in the Bible. All of them refer to new life coming forth.

1. The seeds of plants used in farming. The farmer in Bible times planted his fields by taking seeds in his hand and scattering them as he walked.

2. *Seed* may mean children or descendants.

3. *Seed* may refer to the Holy Spirit or God's nature in believers. 1 John 3: 9 says that God's "seed" keeps the believer from sinning.

SEER (see *Prophet*)

SEIR *(SEE-er),* **LAND OF,** was an area southwest of the Dead Sea that was later called Edom. Esau and his descendants settled in this land. The Seir mountain range ran down the middle of the country.

Where to find it: *Genesis 32: 3*

SEIR *(SEE-er),* **MOUNT,** was a mountain about nine miles west of Jerusalem.

Mount Seir also sometimes refers to the mountains in the land of Edom (see *Seir*).

Where to find it: *Joshua 15: 10*

SELAH *(SEE-luh)* is a Hebrew word that appears 71 times in the Psalms and 3 times in Habakkuk. We are not sure what it means. Some scholars believe it was a term giving some musical directions for the singing of the psalms. It may have been a signal to sing some special doxology or benediction, or it may have been instructions for the singers to be silent while the musical instruments played.

SEMITES *(SEM-ites)* are the people who have descended from Shem, one of the sons of Noah. All Semites have related languages. Most of the people who lived in Palestine and surrounding areas during Old Testament times were Semites. In today's world, Jews and Arabs are Semites, as well as some Ethiopians.

SENNACHERIB *(sen-AK-er-ib)* was a famous king of Assyria between 705 and 681 B.C. He was a skillful army general who captured the city of Babylon in 689 B.C.

Sennacherib also captured most of the fortified cities of Judah except Jerusalem about 701 B.C. and forced King Hezekiah to pay heavy tribute to him. He then told Hezekiah that he would conquer Jerusalem, and the people should not be silly enough to think God would protect them.

But an angel of the Lord killed 185,000 Assyrian soldiers who were camped outside of Jerusalem one night. Sennacherib and the soldiers who were still alive went back to Assyria.

Sennacherib was assassinated in 681 B.C. by two of his sons as he was worshiping his pagan god, Nisroch.

Where to find it: *2 Kings 18:13–19:37; 2 Chronicles 32:1-22; Isaiah 36–37*

SEPTUAGINT *(SEP-too-uh-jint)* was the first and most important translation of the Old Testament from the Hebrew into the Greek language. It was completed sometime between 280 and 180 B.C. in Alexandria, Egypt.

Septuagint means "70," and the translation got that name because tradition says 70 men worked on it.

The translation was made because many Jews had moved away from Palestine and knew Greek better than Hebrew.

The Septuagint was the Bible of the early church everywhere except in Palestine. When Paul and other New Testament writers wrote to the early churches, they usually quoted the Old Testament from this Greek translation.

SEPULCHRE *(SEP-ul-ker)* is another word for tomb (see *Tomb*).

SERAPHIM (see *Angels*)

SERGIUS PAULUS (see *Paulus, Sergius*)

SERMON ON THE MOUNT is the name usually given to the teachings of Jesus recorded in Matthew 5—7.

According to Matthew, the teachings were given during the first year of Jesus' public ministry, outdoors, among the foothills of Galilee. The exact location is not known.

The teachings seem to be addressed mostly to the disciples, although a crowd was also present. The teachings explain the high ideals that followers of Christ should have.

Many of the sayings in this section are repeated in other parts of the Gospels. Since Jesus taught in many places, he no doubt repeated many of his teachings over and over. Some scholars believe this "sermon" is more a collection of Jesus' teachings than a sermon delivered at one time.

These chapters include some of the parts of the New Testament quoted most often, including the Lord's Prayer.

SERPENT *(SER-punt)* in the Bible seems to refer to a poisonous snake. *Serpent* is often used as a word picture for sin or for something evil. Revelation 20:2 speaks of "that ancient serpent, who is the Devil and Satan."

In the story of the temptation of Adam and Eve in the Garden of Eden, a serpent tempted Eve.

Where to find it: *Genesis 3:1-14; Psalm 58:4; 2 Corinthians 11:3; Revelation 20:2*

SERPENT, BRONZE (see *Fiery Serpent*)

SERVANT means one who works for the benefit of his master. In the Hebrew and Greek languages, it also means "slave."

A person could be a servant and still have a high position in the household. In the Old Testament, Joshua was a servant to Moses and later became the leader of the Israelites.

Jesus taught that Christians are to be servants of one another rather than trying to have authority over each other. Jesus even called himself a servant.

Where to find it

Joshua a servant to Moses *Exodus 33:11*
Christians are servants of each other *Matthew 20:26*
Jesus calls himself servant *Luke 22:27*

SERVANT OF THE LORD is a term that in the Old Testament referred primarily to the coming Messiah. However, it was also used of Moses, Joshua, David, the prophets, and others.

The most famous "servant" passages referring to the Messiah are Isaiah 42:1-9; 49:1-13; 50:4-11; and 52:13—53:12.

In the New Testament, these "servant" passages are quoted as being fulfilled in Christ. Some examples are Matthew 12:18-21; Luke 22:37; and John 12:38.

SETH was the third son of Adam and Eve, born after Cain killed Abel. Seth lived 912 years and had many sons and daughters.

Where to find it: *Genesis 4: 25-26; 5: 6-7*

SEVEN CHURCHES were the churches in Asia (now Turkey) to whom the Book of Revelation was written. These churches were in large cities—Ephesus, Smyrna, Pergamum, Thyatira, Sardis, Philadelphia, and Laodicea—

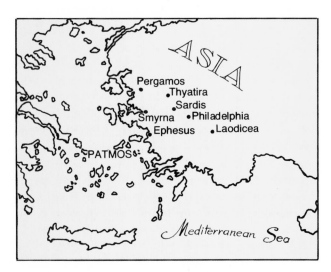

probably cities that the writer, John, had visited. Each of the seven churches was given a specific message in the Book of Revelation, but they were also told to read what the Spirit of God said to the other churches. The whole book was written to all of them.

Where to find it: *Revelation 1: 4–3: 22*

SEVEN LAST WORDS refers to the seven sentences Jesus spoke while he was dying on the cross. They are:

1. "Father, forgive them; for they know not what they do" (Luke 23: 34).

2. "Truly, I say to you, today you will be with me in Paradise" (Luke 23: 43). (Spoken to one of the thieves being crucified with him.)

3. "Woman, behold, your son! . . . Behold, your mother!" (John 19: 26-27). (Spoken to his mother and to the apostle John.)

4. "My God, my God, why hast thou forsaken me?" (Matthew 27: 46; Mark 15: 34). (Spoken by Jesus in his last agony.)

5. "I thirst" (John 19: 28).

6. "It is finished" (John 19: 30).

7. "Father, into thy hands I commit my spirit!" (Luke 23: 46).

SEVENTY, THE, refers to a larger group of Jesus' disciples than the 12. Jesus sent them out in pairs to the towns where he planned to go. They were told to say, "The kingdom of God has come near to you." This meant that what they did, through the power of God, showed the presence of God's Kingdom.

The Bible does not say how long the 70 were gone, but they came back excited about what had happened.

Where to find it: *Luke 10: 1-20*

SHADRACH *(SHAD-rak)*, **MESHACH** *(MEE-shack)*, and **ABEDNEGO** *(uh-BED-nee-go)* were the names of Daniel's three friends who were thrown into a furnace.

The three young men had been taken from Judah to Babylon when King Nebuchadnezzar invaded Palestine in 605 B.C. They were soon chosen, along with Daniel, to be trained for three years in the king's court.

They lived at the palace. But the food was too rich for them, and some of it was against the food laws of the Hebrews. So Daniel asked that they be given a trial period of ten days on "water and vegetables." They were healthier than ever on that diet, so they were allowed to keep on eating that way.

When Daniel was able to interpret one of the king's dreams, he was made ruler over the province of Babylon. However, Daniel asked that the position be given to his three friends instead—Shadrach, Meshach, and Abednego.

All went well until King Nebuchadnezzar made an image 90 feet high, which all his officers were to worship. When Shadrach, Meshach, and Abednego refused, the king had them thrown into a fiery furnace.

Then an amazing thing happened. As the king looked into the furnace, he said, "I see four men loose, walking in the midst of the fire, and they are not hurt; and the appearance of the fourth is like a son of the gods."

The king called the men—and they walked out unharmed. The king then ruled that no one was to speak a word against the God of Shadrach, Meshach, and Abednego, because "there is no other god who is able to deliver in this way."

The king then gave the three men even higher positions in his kingdom.

Where to find it: *Daniel 1–3*

SHALLUM *(SHALL-um)* was the name of 15 people in the Old Testament, including one king of Israel and one king of Judah.

1. The king of Israel ruled for only one month in 752 B.C. He became king by assassinating the king before him, Zechariah. Shallum, in turn, was soon killed by Menahem, who then became king.

2. The king of Judah was also called Jehoahaz, and he is better known by that name. He was the son of Josiah. He reigned only a few months and was then taken to Egypt, where he died (see *Jehoahaz*).

Where to find it

King of Israel   *2 Kings 15: 10-15*
King of Judah   *1 Chronicles 3: 15; 2 Kings 23: 30-34*

SHAMGAR *(SHAM-gar)* was one of the judges of Israel before there was a king. He was a mighty warrior who killed 600 Philistines with only an ox-goad—a sharp stick usually used to keep cattle going in the right direction.

Where to find it: *Judges 3: 31*

SHAPHAN *(SHAY-fun)* was an important secretary-officer during the reign of Josiah, who was king of Judah from 641 to 609 B.C. Josiah had Shaphan take charge of the money for repairing the Temple. When the high priest found the "book of the Law" in the Temple, Shaphan read it himself and then read it to the king.

Josiah then sent him with other men to the prophet Huldah to learn what should be done about the teachings they found in the book of the Law.

Where to find it: *2 Kings 22: 3-20*

SHARON *(SHARE-un)* was a plain along the Mediterranean Sea between the city of Joppa and Mount Carmel. The plain was famous for its beauty and its flowers, especially the "rose of Sharon."

SHAVING the face was not common among the Hebrews as it was among the Egyptians and the Romans. Hebrew men shaved only during rituals or as a sign of something terrible about to happen. Beads were considered a sign of dignity. Priests were not to shave, and Nazirites were prohibited from shaving during the period of their vow. Levites shaved only as part of a consecration ceremony.

When shaving is mentioned in the Bible, it usually involved the whole head of hair as well as the face.

Where to find it: *Numbers 6: 5; 8: 6-7; Ezekiel 44: 15, 20*

SHEAF *(sheef)* was a small bunch of grain left behind by the reaper. Usually women and children gathered such grain and tied it into small bundles. They were taken then by a cart or a donkey to a threshing floor.

Reapers were told to leave some sheaves behind for the poor to gather up and use for food.

Where to find it: *Deuteronomy 24: 19*

SHEATH (see *Weapons*)

SHEBA *(SHEE-buh)*, **QUEEN OF,** was the ruler of the Sabean kingdom in Arabia, about 1,500 miles from Palestine, during the time of Solomon.

She came to see Solomon, probably on a trading mission as well as to ask questions to test his wisdom. When she saw his great wealth and his wisdom, the Bible says "there was no more spirit in her." Solomon and the queen exchanged lavish gifts, probably made

trade agreements, and then she returned to her own country.

Where to find it: *1 Kings 10:1-13*

SHEBNA *(SHEB-nuh)* was an official in the court of Hezekiah, king of Judah. He was scolded by the prophet Isaiah for building a huge, ornate tomb for himself. Because of this, Isaiah predicted that God would remove him from his position.

Shebna was one of the men Hezekiah sent to reach an agreement with the Assyrians, who were trying to conquer Jerusalem. The Assyrians would not make peace, so Hezekiah sent Shebna and others to the prophet Isaiah for advice.

Where to find it: *Isaiah 22:15-21; 2 Kings 18:18–19:6*

SHECHEM *(SHEH-kem)*, an ancient city in central Palestine, is mentioned often in the Old Testament.

It was the first city where Abraham lived when he moved to Canaan. God appeared to Abraham at Shechem and promised that the land of Canaan would belong to his descendants someday. Abraham built an altar there. Jacob later lived at Shechem.

When the Hebrews came into Canaan from Egypt, Joshua made Shechem one of the cities of refuge.

In the period of the judges, Abimelech the son of Gideon made himself king of Shechem. When some of its people rebelled, Abimelech destroyed the city.

The city was later rebuilt and became the first capital of the Northern Kingdom. Later the capital was moved to Samaria.

Where to find it
Abraham goes to Shechem *Genesis 12:6-7*
Jacob lives at Shechem *Genesis 33:18-20*
Shechem becomes a city of refuge *Joshua 20:1-7*
Abimelech destroys Shechem *Judges 9:1-49*
Shechem becomes capital of Northern Kingdom *1 Kings 12:1-25*

SHEEP (see *Animals*)

SHEEPFOLD was a large pen to protect sheep and to keep them from getting lost at night. Sheepfolds were only walls made of stones. Often the top of the walls were covered with thorns to keep out robbers. There was no roof.

Several flocks would be kept in the same sheepfold at night, with one person guarding the door. Each shepherd knew his own sheep, and they knew him.

Where to find it: *John 10:1-16*

SHEM was the oldest son of Noah. His brothers were Ham and Japheth. He seems to have been the ancestor of all Semites, including the Hebrews. He helped to keep his father Noah from being disgraced when Noah became drunk.

Where to find it: *Genesis 9:18-23*

SHEOL *(SHEE-ohl)* is the Old Testament name for the place of the dead. In the New Testament this place is called Hades, but a great chasm separates the good people from the bad. Jesus told the dying thief, "Today you will be with me in Paradise." This shows that *Hades* refers only to the place where wicked people are kept from death to the final judgment.

Where to find it: *Genesis 37:35; Job 17:13-16; Luke 16:23-26; 23:43*

SHEPHERD (see *Occupations*)

SHESHBAZZAR *(shesh-BAY-zer)* was made governor of the Jews by Cyrus when the Jews went back to Jerusalem to rebuild the Temple in 538 B.C. Cyrus gave him all the sacred basins and bowls that had been taken from the Temple when it was destroyed by Nebuchadnezzar's men in 586 B.C. Sheshbazzar helped build the foundations for the new Temple.

Where to find it: *Ezra 1:8-11; 5:14-16*

SHEWBREAD (see *Showbread*)

SHIBBOLETH *(SHIB-uh-leth)* was a Hebrew word that meant "river" or "ear of grain." It was used as a test word by the soldiers of Gilead to find out whether men were from Ephraim or not. The people in Ephraim spoke a different dialect and could not say *sh* the way the people of Gilead did. By asking the men to pronounce "shibboleth," they could tell where they came from.

The word *shibboleth* is used in our society for any password or a test that people use to identify who belongs to their group.

Where to find it: *Judges 12: 5-6*

SHIELD (see *Weapons*)

SHILOH *(SHY-low)* was a city about 20 miles north of Jerusalem.

During the time of Joshua, the Tabernacle was set up at Shiloh. It stayed there during the approximately 400 years between the time the Israelites entered Canaan and the beginning of the United Kingdom of Israel about 1010 B.C.

During this time, Shiloh was something like the capital of the country. People came to Shiloh to worship, to offer sacrifice, and to observe the Hebrew feasts.

The ark of the Covenant was captured by the Philistines after it had been taken into battle from the Tabernacle at Shiloh by the sons of Eli. Later, the Philistines sent the ark back, and it was kept at Kiriath-jearim and never returned to Shiloh.

After the ark was removed, Shiloh became less important.

However, when Israel divided into Northern and Southern kingdoms in 930 B.C., one prophet, Ahijah, was at Shiloh representing God to the true believers in the Northern Kingdom. Later the city was destroyed.

Where to find it: *Joshua 18: 1; Judges 21: 19; 1 Samuel 1: 3; 4: 1-17; 1 Kings 14: 1-3*

SHIMEI *(SHIM-ee-eye)* was the name of 19 people in the Old Testament. The most important one was the Shimei who cursed King David and threw stones and dirt at him and his men when they fled from Jerusalem during the rebellion of Absalom, David's son. David's

men wanted to kill Shimei, but David would not let them.

Later, after David was restored to this throne, Shimei came and begged forgiveness. David pardoned him.

When Solomon became king, he ordered Shimei to stay within the city of Jerusalem. But he disobeyed, and so he was put to death.

Where to find it: *2 Samuel 16: 5-14; 19: 16-23; 1 Kings 2: 36-46*

SHIPMASTER was the pilot of a ship.

Where to find it: *Revelation 18: 17*

SHIPS AND SAILING were not a part of the life of most Hebrews in Old Testament times. The Israelites were farmers rather than sailors, because they had no harbors.

Most of the Mediterranean coast was usually controlled by their enemies, the Philistines and the Phoenicians, who were the main shipbuilders and sailors of the Mediterranean world.

But when Solomon became king, he bought many ships from the Phoenicians and had Phoenician men as crews. The ships were harbored at Ezion-geber on the tip of the Red Sea. After Solomon died, few ships were built for Israel until Jehoshaphat started building again and using Hebrews as sailors. However,

the ships were wrecked, perhaps because the Hebrew sailors were not experienced.

The New Testament mentions Galilean fishing boats and merchant ships. The Galilean boats had small sails and oars, and could carry about 12 men and a load of fish. Jesus sometimes preached from these boats.

Ships were important to Paul's journeys. There were no special ships for passengers, so Paul traveled on merchant ships that carried grain and other cargo.

Where to find it

The Phoenician ships Solomon built *1 Kings 9: 26-28; 2 Chronicles 8: 17-18*
The ships of Jehoshaphat *1 Kings 22: 48-50*
Jesus preaches from a boat *Luke 5: 3; Mark 4: 1*
Paul's journeys on ships *Acts 27; 2 Corinthians 11: 25*

SHISHAK *(SHY-shak)* was the king of Egypt from 940 to 915 B.C. After Solomon learned that the prophet Ahijah had said Jeroboam would become king instead of him, Solomon tried to kill Jeroboam. Jeroboam fled to Shishak and stayed there in Egypt until after the death of Solomon.

Later Jeroboam did become king of the Northern Kingdom of Israel. During his reign, Shishak made war against both the Northern and Southern kingdoms, capturing many cities. He took many of the treasures out of the Temple in Jerusalem.

Where to find it: *1 Kings 11: 40; 14: 25-26; 2 Chronicles 12: 1-9*

SHITTIM (see *Plants—Acacia*)

SHOFAR or **SHOPHAR** (see *Musical Instruments*)

SHOWBREAD were 12 loaves of bread, representing the 12 tribes of Israel. The loaves were placed on a special table in the Tabernacle (later the Temple) each Sabbath by the priests. This bread was also called the "Bread of the Presence," referring to the presence of God.

The 12 loaves were arranged in two rows on a table in the Holy Place (see *Tabernacle*). When fresh loaves were brought each Sabbath, the old loaves were removed and could be eaten only by the priests.

When David was fleeing from King Saul, he once stopped at the Tabernacle at Nob (where it was temporarily located) and asked the priest to give him the showbread that had been removed because he and his men were hungry.

Jesus referred to this incident when the Pharisees accused him of not obeying every small detail of the Law.

Where to find it

Regulations for its use *Exodus 25: 30; Leviticus 24: 5-9; 1 Chronicles 9: 32*
David and his men eat showbread *1 Samuel 21: 1-6; Matthew 12: 1-4; Mark 2: 23-25; Luke 6: 1-4*

SHRINE refers to a structure with an image of a god inside. Although usually a building, a shrine was sometimes only a corner or portion of a building. The apostle Paul said that God does not dwell in man-made shrines.

Where to find it: *Acts 17: 24; 19: 24*

SHROUD refers to a cloth or garment used to cover the dead.

SHUNAMMITE *(SHOO-num-ite)* refers to a person from the town of Shunem in northern Israel. A wealthy woman there built a special room for the prophet Elisha to use whenever he came to town. Later Elisha miraculously restored her son from death.

Elisha warned her of a coming famine so she took her family and left the city. When she returned seven years later, Elisha's servant helped her get back her land.

Where to find it: *2 Kings 4: 8-37; 8: 1-6*

SHUTTLE is a tool used by a weaver to carry thread rapidly back and forth from one side of a loom to the other. In Job 7: 6 *shuttle* is used as a word picture of how rapidly a person's life passes.

SICKLE was a farm tool for cutting grain. A sickle was often a series of sharp stones or flints inserted in a rounded wooden frame.

Sickle is sometimes a word picture of God cutting down evil people in judgment.

Where to find it: *Mark 4: 29; Revelation 14: 14-19*

SIDON *(SY-dun)* was a city now called Saida on the coast of what is now Lebanon.

It was a prosperous trading city known for its artistic metalwork and dyes. People in

Sidon were the first ones to discover how to blow glass into pleasing shapes. During Sidon's long history, it was conquered by Assyria, Babylon, Persia, Greece, and Rome.

In the Old Testament it was also known for its idolatry.

Jesus visited the area of Sidon and healed a girl there. The apostle Paul stopped to visit Christians in Sidon on his way to Rome and was kindly treated.

Where to find it

Old city known for its idolatry *Judges 1:31; Ezekiel 28:20-26*
Jesus heals a girl *Matthew 15:21-28*
Paul visits Sidon *Acts 27:3*

SIGNS AND WONDERS usually refer to things we can see or hear that show the presence of God.

The phrase *signs and wonders* appears 15 times in the Old Testament and 16 times in the New Testament.

Signs and wonders often involved miracles, but not always. The shepherds were told that the birth of Christ "will be a *sign* for you: you will find a babe wrapped in swaddling cloths and lying in a manger." The clothing and location were the "signs" of the Savior.

Acts 2:43 says, "Many wonders and signs were done through the apostles" of the early church. These were often miracles or other acts to show clearly the power of God.

Where to find it: *Deuteronomy 6:22; Luke 2:12*

SIGNET (see *Seal*)

SIHON (*SY-hahn*) was king of the Amorites when the Israelites came out of Egypt. His capital was the city of Heshbon, about ten miles northeast of the upper end of the Dead Sea. Sihon had won much of his territory in a war with the Moabites.

When Moses asked Sihon to allow the Israelites to march through his land on the way to Canaan, he refused. Instead, he fought the Israelites. However, the Israelites defeated Sihon and captured the land. This victory greatly encouraged them for the battles that were yet to come, and is often mentioned in other parts of the Old Testament to show how God had helped them.

Many years later, when Jephthah was a judge of Israel, the Moabites demanded that Israel return the land to them. The Israelites refused, saying that God had given it to them when they defeated Sihon.

Where to find it: *Numbers 21:21-35; Deuteronomy 3:1-8; Judges 11:12-28*

SILAS (*SY-luss*) was one of Paul's companions on his second missionary journey. He is sometimes called Silvanus. He was a Jew and a Roman citizen. The church in Jerusalem sent Silas with Paul and Barnabas to the Christians in Antioch to explain the decisions that had been made about Gentile Christians keeping the Jewish Law (see *Council of Jerusalem*).

Silas later returned to his home in Jerusalem while Paul and Barnabas stayed in Antioch. However, when Paul and Barnabas separated after their disagreement about taking Mark along on the second missionary journey, Paul chose Silas to go with him.

Silas was imprisoned and beaten with Paul in Philippi. They then went on to Thessalonica. After a three-week stay there that ended in a riot, they continued on to Berea. Silas and Timothy stayed in Berea for a short time, while Paul went on to Athens.

Silas and Timothy joined Paul again in Corinth and stayed there for some time. From Corinth, Paul wrote two letters back to the church at Thessalonica, and Silas is mentioned in both of them, although he is called Silvanus. Scholars believe Silas may have helped Paul in writing these letters.

A strange girl followed Silas and Paul in Philippi.

Silas is not mentioned again except in the Letter of 1 Peter, which says he helped Peter in writing his letter by serving as his secretary.

Where to find it

Goes to Antioch and joins Paul   *Acts 15: 22-41*
Is beaten at Philippi, flees Thessalonica, stays at
   Berea   *Acts 16: 19–17: 15*
Teaches at Corinth, helps with Paul's letters
   2 Corinthians 1: 19; 1 Thessalonians 1: 1; 2 Thessalonians 1: 1
Helps Peter with letter   *1 Peter 5: 12*

SILOAM *(sy-LOH-um)* is a pool or reservoir that still exists in Jerusalem. Jesus healed a man who was blind by putting clay on his eyes and telling him, "Go, wash in the pool of Siloam."

The pool was built in the time of Hezekiah, who was king of Judah from 716 to 687 B.C. The main source of water for Jerusalem was then the spring of Gihon, outside the city walls. In time of war, an enemy could cut off the city's water supply and make the city surrender. So Hezekiah built a tunnel 1,750 feet long that channeled the water from the spring into the city and into a pool or reservoir that was called the Pool of Siloam.

The tunnel still exists, and if you visit Jerusalem and don't mind getting very wet, you can walk in the water through that tunnel.

Where to find it: *2 Kings 20: 20; 2 Chronicles 32: 4, 30; Isaiah 22: 9-11; John 9: 1-12*

SILVANUS (see *Silas*)

SILVER has been known from very early times. It was used as money and also to make things: cups and crowns for kings and nobles, jewelry, idols, and the trumpets, bowls, and other furnishings in the Tabernacle and Temple.

Silver was refined in furnaces.

Where to find it: *Genesis 24: 53; 44: 2; Leviticus 27: 16; Numbers 10: 2; 7: 13, 19; Zechariah 6: 11; Acts 19: 24*

SILVERSMITH (see *Occupations*)

SIMEON *(SIM-ee-un)* was the name of three important people, one in the Old Testament and two in the New Testament. *Symeon* is another spelling of the name.

1. Simeon was the second son of Jacob by his first wife, Leah, and was the founder of one of the 12 tribes of Israel.

Simeon and his brother Levi massacred the men of Shechem because the prince of Shechem had raped their sister, Dinah.

Later Simeon was the hostage who stayed with Joseph in Egypt when his brothers returned home to get Benjamin.

When the Hebrews reached the Promised Land, the tribe of Simeon settled in the southern area of Palestine. Simeon's land had no clear boundaries. The tribe seemed to blend with the tribe of Judah and was eventually absorbed into Judah.

Where to find it

Simeon's birth   *Genesis 29: 33*
Massacre of Shechem   *Genesis 34*
Stays with Joseph   *Genesis 42: 24*
Tribe settles in Judah   *Joshua 19: 1-9*

2. Simeon in the New Testament was an aged, godly man who met the baby Jesus and his parents in the Temple. He said the Holy Spirit had promised him that before he died he would see the Messiah. When he saw

Jesus, he spoke the poem that begins, "Lord, now lettest thou thy servant depart in peace."

Where to find it: *Luke 2: 25-35*

3. Simeon, or Symeon, is another name for Simon Peter, Jesus' disciple (see *Peter*).

Where to find it: *Acts 15: 14*

SIMON *(SY-mun)* was a common name in New Testament times. It was the name of two of Jesus' 12 disciples. It was also the name of one of Jesus' brothers and of several other New Testament people.

1. One disciple was Simon Peter, the brother of Andrew. He was one of the best-known of the disciples (see *Peter*).

2. Another disciple was Simon the Cananaean, which means the Zealot. The Zealots were a Jewish political party who wanted to overthrow the Roman government. This Simon is not mentioned after the death and resurrection of Christ (Luke 6: 15; Mark 3: 18).

3. Simon, a half brother of Jesus, is mentioned in Matthew 13: 55 and Mark 6: 3.

4. Simon of Cyrene was the man who was forced to carry Jesus' cross on the way to the crucifixion, according to Matthew 27: 32; Mark 15: 21; Luke 23: 26.

5. Simon of Bethany was a man who had leprosy. Jesus visited his home, we are told in Matthew 26: 6-13 and Mark 14: 3-9.

6. Another Simon was a Pharisee who invited Jesus to have dinner in his home. He found fault with Jesus for permitting a woman to put expensive ointment on his feet. The story is in Luke 7: 35-50.

7. Simon Magus was a magician in Samaria. He became a believer in Christ through Philip, who came and preached the gospel. Then Peter and John came, laid their hands on the new believers, and they received the Holy Spirit. Simon was so impressed that he offered Peter and John money if they would give him that kind of power. Peter rebuked him for thinking he could buy the gift of God with money (Acts 8: 9-24).

8. Simon the tanner lived at Joppa, on the Mediterranean coast. Peter was staying with him when he had the vision of a sheet coming down from heaven. The story is told in Acts 9: 43—10: 23.

SIMON PETER (see *Peter*)

SIMPLE sometimes means someone who is easily influenced by others. Other times it means someone who is honest and straightforward.

Where to find it

Easily influenced   *Romans 16: 18*
Honest   *Romans 16: 19 (KJV)*

SIN is any act or thought that is contrary to God and his will. When we sin, we sin against God, who is perfect. "Against thee, thee only, have I sinned," wrote the psalmist in Psalm 51: 4.

Sin separates us from God. Every person who has ever lived, beginning with Adam and Eve, has sinned. We have all chosen to behave and think in ways that are contrary to God and his will. Our sin has separated us from the deep friendship with God that he meant for us to have. God has never turned away from us, but we have turned away from God. When we sin, we act as though God did not exist or as if we don't care if he exists. We do what we want to do. In this way, we place our own will above the will of God.

This attitude of ignoring God and his will causes us to do foolish and wrong things. We turn away from things that really matter— pleasing God and being helpful to our families and friends.

Sin makes us feel guilty because we know we are missing the mark of what God intended us to be. We feel like David in the Bible: "For I know my transgressions, and my sin is ever before me."

Some people try to ignore their feelings of guilt or to blame someone else. But that only increases the sense of loneliness and separation from God. The final penalty for sin is eternal separation from God.

A better way is for us to turn to God, asking him to forgive our sin.

God knew that we could never get rid of our sin or our guilt alone. But because he wants us to be free to love him and be friends with him, he sent his Son, Jesus Christ, to die for our sins so the penalty of our sin can be removed. This is the new agreement or Covenant he made with people when Christ came to die.

As we confess our sin to God and turn to him, God gives us new life and new power to overcome sin. We may never be perfect on this earth, but our new life in Christ makes us want to do right rather than wrong. We may not fully conquer sin, but sin will no longer fully conquer us.

Where to find it

Sin is against God   *Jeremiah 3: 25; 14: 7, 20*
Sin comes from the heart   *Isaiah 29: 13; Mark 7: 21-23*
Every person sins   *Isaiah 53: 6; Romans 3: 23; 5: 12*
Christ came to deliver us from sin   *Matthew 1: 21; John 1: 29*
Christ died for our sins   *1 Corinthians 15: 3; 2 Corinthians 5: 21; 1 Peter 2: 24; 3: 18*
We must confess our sins   *1 John 1: 7-9*
God makes us new persons   *Psalm 51: 10; Romans 6: 14*

SIN OFFERING (see *Offerings*)

SINAI *(SI-ni)*, **MOUNT,** also known as Mount Horeb, is the place where Moses went to receive the Ten Commandments from God. It is also the place to which Elijah fled to escape the anger of Jezebel. We are not sure of the exact location of this mountain, but most scholars believe it is one of the mountains in

Earthquakes shook Mount Sinai several times.

the southern part of the Sinai Peninsula.

Where to find it: *Exodus 19; 1 Kings 19: 1-8*

SINGLE EYE is used in the King James Version to refer to an eye that is healthy.

Where to find it: *Matthew 6: 22; Luke 11: 34 (both KJV)*

SINEW *(SIN-you)* refers to muscles or tendons that hold parts of the body together.

Where to find it: *Genesis 32: 32; Isaiah 48: 4*

SINGING was important to the Hebrews and to the early Christians. Moses and the people sang praises to God for their deliverance from Egypt.

Singing was important in Temple worship. Most of the psalms were songs of the people (see *Psalms*). In the time of King David and for several hundred years more, certain groups were designated as the chief singers in the Temple. Asaph and his sons are mentioned most often.

Singing was also important in the early church. Paul and Silas sang in the prison at Philippi. Christians are told to be "addressing one another in psalms and hymns and spiritual songs, singing and making melody to the Lord with all your heart."

Where to find it

Moses' song of praise   *Exodus 15: 1-18*
Deborah and Barak sing   *Judges 5: 1-31*
Singers in the Temple   *1 Chronicles 15: 16, 27; 16: 7; 2 Chronicles 5: 12-14; 35: 25*
Israelites commanded to sing   *Psalm 100: 2*
Paul and Silas sing in prison   *Acts 16: 25*
Christians sing   *Ephesians 5: 19; Colossians 3: 16*

SISERA *(SIS-er-uh)* was captain of an army of Canaanites who fought the Israelites over a 20-year period. The Canaanites were difficult to fight, for they had 900 chariots of iron, and the Israelites had none.

Deborah, one of the outstanding judges of Israel, sent for Barak, the commander of the Israelite forces, and told him to gather men from other tribes to fight Sisera's forces. The Israelites defeated Sisera's army. Sisera fled on foot, hiding in the tent of a woman named Jael. While he slept in her tent, she killed him.

Where to find it: *Judges 4: 1-22*

SIX HUNDRED SIXTY-SIX is the number in a riddle that appears in Revelation 13: 18. It represents "the number of the beast." Both Hebrew and Greek letters had numerical values; for example, the Greek letter *L* had a value of 30, while *N* represented 50. Using this system, the letters of the name *Jesus* added up to **888.**

Scholars think that the writer of Revelation was using the number 666 to stand for an evil ruler either in his own time or who was yet to come. No one has been able to make the numbers come out logically to any known name.

SKIRT in Bible times usually referred to men's clothing rather than women's. The skirt was the lower part of the outer robe that most men wore. David once cut off part of Saul's skirt while Saul slept.

Where to find it: *1 Samuel 24:1-12*

SKULL, PLACE OF (see *Golgotha*)

SLANDER *(SLAN-dur)* refers to spoken words that hurt the reputation of someone. Slander is a sin strongly condemned by the Old Testament, by Jesus, and by Peter and Paul.

Where to find it: *Proverbs 10:18; Matthew 15:19; Ephesians 4:31; 1 Peter 2:1*

SLAVERY was practiced in all of the Mediterranean area in Bible times. In the Old Testament period, Hebrews, like those in surrounding countries, had slaves and sometimes were slaves. However, most slaves were *temporary* rather than permanent slaves.

The most common form of slavery among Hebrews was debt-slavery. If a man could not pay his debts, he, his wife, and his children could be forced to become slaves of the person to whom he owed money. However, the Old Testament Law said they could be held as slaves for only six years, regardless of how much they owed.

The Law of Moses gave other specific rules about how slaves were to be treated.

Sometimes Hebrews were captured in war and carried away to other countries as slaves. Sometimes the Hebrews, when they won a war, used the captured soldiers as slaves. Most of such men were "state slaves"—they belonged to the king and had to build roads, erect fortresses, and work in royal industries. After the fall of the Northern and Southern kingdoms, this kind of slavery disappeared.

In New Testament times, slavery still existed but was not as common in Palestine as in surrounding countries.

None of Jesus' disciples were slaves or slaveholders. Jesus taught by word and example that we should freely serve each other and should treat every other person as we would like to be treated. This high ideal rules out every form of slavery, since most people don't want to be slaves.

Where to find it

Laws regarding slaves *Exodus 21:1-27; Leviticus 25:39-55; Deuteronomy 15:12-18*
Jesus' teachings about service *Matthew 7:12; 19:19; 20:25-28; Luke 6:31; 22:24-27*

The Jewish people have never forgotten their years of slavery in Egypt.

SLEEP usually means the same in the Bible as in our ordinary speech. In a few places, however, *sleep* is used as a word picture for physical death, such as, "We shall not all sleep, but we shall all be changed," in 1 Corinthians 15:51.

Occasionally, *sleep* is a word picture for spiritual indifference, as in Romans 13:11, "It is full time now for you to wake from sleep."

Where to find it

Refers to physical death *1 Thessalonians 4:14; 5:10*
Refers to spiritual dullness *1 Thessalonians 5:6*

SLING was a weapon carried by shepherds to throw stones or clay pebbles at animals that were attacking their flocks or cattle. Slings were sometimes used by soldiers.

The sling was made of two narrow strips of leather joined in the middle by a wider piece where the stone was held. The shepherd tied one end to his wrist. The other end was held in his hand. The sling was then skillfully swung around and the loose end released to make the stone fly.

David killed the giant Goliath with such a sling. Men with slings were a regular part of the armies of Israel. Seven hundred left-handed men in the tribe of Benjamin were once said to be so good with slings that they "could sling a stone at a hair, and not miss."

Where to find it

David kills Goliath with a sling   *1 Samuel 17: 40-50*
Left-handed Benjamites with slings   *Judges 20: 16*

SLOTHFUL means undependable and lazy. Such laziness is condemned in the Bible. Another word for *sloth* is *sluggard*.

Where to find it: *Proverbs 12: 24, 27; 13: 4; 15: 19; Matthew 25: 26*

SLUGGARD (see *Slothful)*

SMYRNA *(SMIR-nuh)* was a large, prosperous seaport city on the west coast of what is now Turkey. The city still exists and is now called Izmir.

One of the letters in the Book of Revelation was written to the church in Smyrna. The writer warned of the persecution that would come to the Christians there. He urged Christians to be faithful unto death.

There were many Jews in the city who be-

came very hostile to the Christians there. They are mentioned in the letter.

Later, Smyrna became known as a city that persecuted Christians. The 86-year-old church leader, Polycarp, was burned to death there for his faith in A.D. 156.

The city was one of the earliest to have a temple erected to the Roman emperor. It also had other temples for the worship of other gods.

Where to find it: *Revelation 2: 8-11*

SNARE is a trap used to catch birds or animals. It is often used in the Bible as a word picture of enemies or evils that God's people should avoid, such as idolatry and the love of riches.

Where to find it: *Deuteronomy 7: 16; Psalm 91: 3; 1 Timothy 6: 9*

SNOW is fairly common in Palestine, although it never becomes deep and rarely lasts more than a few days except in the mountains.

Snow is sometimes a word picture for purity and righteousness.

Where to find it: *Psalm 51: 7; Isaiah 1: 18*

SODOM *(SOD-um)* was the name of a city God destroyed for its wickedness during the time of Abraham. Scholars do not know where the city was located, for no genuine traces of it have been found. Many believe it is buried under the southern part of the Dead Sea. The southern part of the sea is much shallower than the northern part.

Lot and his family went to live in Sodom after he separated from Abraham. Later, God told Abraham he was going to destroy Sodom and Gomorrah because the people were so wicked. Abraham pleaded with God, and he agreed not to destroy Sodom if there were ten righteous people in it.

Lot and his family got out of Sodom just in time.

But ten could not be found. For the sake of Abraham, God warned Lot to take his family and flee without looking back. Then God destroyed the city "with brimstone and fire from the Lord out of heaven." Lot, his wife, and two daughters fled, but Lot's wife looked back—and turned into a pillar of salt.

Where to find it: *Genesis 18: 16–19: 29*

SOJOURNERS *(SO-jer-nerz)* were persons who moved from their own country or community to live in another for a long or short period of time. They were also called strangers or aliens.

In Bible times, people often moved from one place to another. Sometimes they moved to escape famine, as when Jacob and his family moved to Egypt. Sometimes they moved to escape military attack, or to find a new place because their own city or land had been destroyed by war.

The Law of Moses told Israelites how they were to treat sojourners or strangers. They were to be treated with kindness, and they were to have the Sabbath day for rest like the Israelites.

The sojourners, in return, were to observe the Sabbath and feast days, although they did not have to worship the God of the Hebrews.

The Old Testament laws reminded the Israelites that they were once sojourners in the land of Egypt, and God delivered them. Since God is the protector of the weak, Israel must also protect them.

Sojourner, pilgrim, exile, and *stranger* are used as word pictures of Christians in the New Testament. We are temporary sojourners or strangers on earth, because our real home is in heaven.

Where to find it

Rules for treatment of sojourners *Exodus 22: 21; 23: 9; Deuteronomy 5: 14-15; 16: 10-12; 24: 19; 26: 5-11*
Word picture of Christians *Hebrews 11: 13-16; 1 Peter 1: 17; 2: 11*

SOLDIER (see *Occupations*)

SOLEMN ASSEMBLY refers to the people of Israel gathered together for a serious occasion, such as fasting or a religious feast day. "Solemn assembly" is used to describe the

seventh day of Passover and the eighth day of the Feast of Booths.

Where to find it: *Leviticus 23: 36; Deuteronomy 16: 5-8; 2 Chronicles 7: 8-9*

SOLOMON *(SAHL-uh-mun)* was the third and last king of the United Kingdom of Israel, reigning from 970 to 930 B.C. He was the son of King David and Bathsheba.

He was known for his great wisdom and his ability as a leader and administrator. He developed a strong army, brought the Israelites into a unified nation instead of a group of 12 tribes, and built a nation larger and more prosperous than at any other time in its history. He was a skilled diplomat who maintained peace with the countries around him.

He is most remembered for the beautiful Temple to God that he erected, based on plans of his father, King David. It took seven years to build. It was the first Temple Israel had, and it replaced the simple Tabernacle, where the people had worshiped for about 400 years.

Solomon started his reign with great promise. He asked God to "give me now wisdom and knowledge to go out and come in before this people, for who can rule this thy people, that is so great?" God gave him his request, and he became famous for his wisdom.

He is thought to have written the books of Proverbs, Ecclesiastes, Song of Solomon, and Psalms 72 and 127.

However, as Solomon became richer, he turned away from God. He married many foreign wives. Eventually he also worshiped their gods and built temples for them. Because he built such ornate palaces for himself,

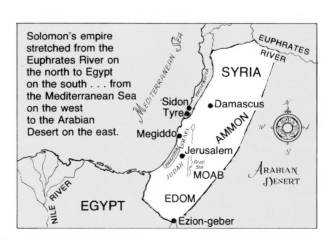

Solomon's empire stretched from the Euphrates River on the north to Egypt on the south . . . from the Mediterranean Sea on the west to the Arabian Desert on the east.

When the priests moved the ark into Solomon's new Temple, it was a day of great rejoicing.

he had to tax the people heavily, and they became dissatisfied. After his death, the unified kingdom fell apart and was never established again.

Where to find it

Solomon is crowned king   *1 Kings 1:11–2:12*
Asks God for wisdom   *1 Kings 3:3-28; 2 Chronicles 1:7-12*
Is visited by Queen of Sheba   *1 Kings 10:1-13; 2 Chronicles 9:1-12*
Is known for his wisdom   *1 Kings 3:15-28; 4:29-34; 10:23-24*
Builds Temple from David's plans   *1 Kings 6:1-38; 7:15-51; 1 Chronicles 28:11-19*
Dedicates Temple to God   *1 Kings 8*
Builds luxurious palace for himself   *1 Kings 7:1-8; 10:18-21*
Marries foreign wives and departs from worship of God   *1 Kings 3:1; 11:1-13*

SOLOMON'S PORCH or **PORTICO** *(PORT-ih-koh)* was a beautiful corridor in the outer court of Herod's Temple. Located on the east side of the court, it had magnificent columns supporting a roof over it. In this area, Jesus and the disciples sometimes taught.

Where to find it: *John 10:23; Acts 3:11; 5:12*

SON OF GOD is a term used in the New Testament to show that Jesus was the unique Son of God, equal to God, and God's revelation of himself on earth.

Although Jesus did not describe himself as the Son of God, he agreed that he was when others called him that. When the high priest asked, "Are you the Christ, the Son of the Blessed?" Christ answered, "I am."

At Jesus' baptism, and also on the Mount of Transfiguration, a voice from heaven said, "This is my beloved Son."

Jesus taught the disciples that his relationship to God was different from their relationship to God. He spoke of "my Father" rather than "our Father." Only when he was teaching the disciples to pray did he say, "Our Father."

Jesus stated clearly that "I and the Father are one" and that "I am in the Father and the Father in me." He also said, "He who has seen me has seen the Father."

The Gospel of John and the Letters of John often speak of Jesus as God's Son. The most well-known passage is John 3:16.

Paul spoke of Jesus as the Son of God in his preaching and his letters.

Where to find it

Voice from heaven   *Mark 1:11; 9:7*
Jesus before the high priest   *Mark 14:61-62*
Jesus preaches his oneness with Father   *John 5:18; 10:30; 14:9-11*
Paul teaches that Jesus is the Son of God   *Acts 9:20; Romans 1:2-4*

SON OF MAN was Jesus' favorite name for himself. It is used 78 times in the Gospels. With this term, Jesus identified himself as a true man as well as being the Son of God. He often spoke of himself this way when talking about the need to suffer and to give his life for the sins of all people.

Most scholars believe that Jesus also used the term to show that he was the fulfillment of the prophecy in Daniel 7:13, "There came one like a son of man. . . . And to him was given dominion and glory and kingdom."

Where to find it: *Mark 8:31; 9:31; 10:33; 14:41; Luke 18:31-33; 21:27-28; John 13:31*

SONG OF SOLOMON is a beautiful love poem in the Old Testament. It is sometimes called the Song of Songs, perhaps because it was such a favorite. In the past, some scholars thought it was really a word picture of God's love for Israel, or Christ's love for the Church.

Now, however, most scholars agree that it was meant to be a lovely poem showing the beauty of human love between a man and a woman.

SONGS (see *Singing*)

SONS OF GOD (see *Children of God*)

SONS OF THE PROPHETS does not refer to the physical children of prophets but rather to students or disciples taught by a particular prophet.

The prophets Elijah and Elisha were teachers or leaders of such groups of prophets.

Where to find it: *2 Kings 2:3, 5; 4:38; 6:1-7*

SOOTHSAYER (*SOOTH-say-er*) was a person who claimed to be able to foretell events or to interpret dreams. Both the Old and New Testaments condemn soothsaying.

Where to find it: *Deuteronomy 18:14; Micah 5:12; Acts 16:16-18*

SOP (*sahp*) is the word used in the King James Version for thin waferlike bread used to dip food from a dish. Dipping such pieces into a dish with other people was a sign of friendship.

Where to find it: *John 13:26-30 (KJV)*

SOPATER (*SOAP-uh-ter*) was a Christian man from Berea who went with Paul on his last journey from Corinth to Jerusalem. In Paul's Letter to the Romans, Sopater sent greetings to the Christians in Rome. In that letter he is called Sosipater.

Where to find it: *Acts 20:4; Romans 16:21*

SORCERER (*SORE-sir-er*) was a person who claimed to be able to work witchcraft, often by means of special herbs and magic potions. Sorcery is always condemned in the Bible.

Where to find it: *Malachi 3:5; Galatians 5:20*

SORES (see *Diseases*)

SOSIPATER (see *Sopater*)

SOSTHENES (*SAHS-thin-eez*) was the Jewish ruler of the synagogue at Corinth. The previous ruler, Crispus, had become a Christian after hearing Paul preach.

Sosthenes and a group of other Jews made legal charges against Paul, saying he was trying to persuade people to worship God in ways contrary to the law of the land.

However, the official, Gallio, refused to have anything to do with their case, saying it was only a Jewish religious matter. When the group was told to leave, some other people (probably Greeks) beat Sosthenes. But still Gallio paid no attention.

A man named Sosthenes is mentioned in 1 Corinthians as a companion of Paul. Some scholars believe he may have been the same man mentioned in Acts—showing that he later became a Christian.

Where to find it: *Acts 18:12-17; 1 Corinthians 1:1*

SOUL is often used in the Bible about the part of a person that is not physical. In Matthew 10:28 Jesus told his listeners not to fear those who are able to kill the body but cannot kill the soul. They were to fear God instead, who is able to destroy both body and soul in hell.

In other places in the New Testament, *soul* refers to the whole living part of a person. In most of the newer translations, Matthew 16: 26 says something like this: "What good is it for a person to gain the whole world at the price of his real life?"

Sometimes the Bible speaks of both soul and spirit, but they usually seem to mean much the same thing. For example, Proverbs 27: 9 says, "The soul is torn by trouble," while Proverbs 15: 4 says, "Perverseness breaks the spirit."

SOUTHERN KINGDOM refers to the Kingdom of Judah. After the death of Solomon, the Kingdom of Israel was divided into two parts: the Northern Kingdom (Israel), composed of ten tribes, and the Southern Kingdom (Judah), composed of two tribes—Judah and Simeon, plus a small part of Benjamin. The Southern Kingdom was less than half the size of the Northern Kingdom, and much of its land was desert. It had a population of only about 300,000.

At first Judah tried to force the Northern Kingdom to reunite with it, but could not.

The Northern Kingdom was defeated by Assyria in 722 B.C. The Southern Kingdom lasted until 586 B.C., when it was finally conquered by Babylon and many of its people carried away into exile (see *Judah, Kingdom of*, and *Israel, History of*).

SOWER was a person who planted seeds for crops during Bible times. He usually held a bag of grain or other seeds and threw them out on the soil with his hand. Sowing was used by Jesus as a word picture of how the Kingdom of God grows.

Paul used sowing as a word picture of the Christian giving to God and receiving good things from God as a result.

Where to find it: *Matthew 13: 1-43; Mark 4: 2-20; Luke 8: 5-15; 13: 18-19; 2 Corinthians 9: 6; Galatians 6: 7-8*

SPAIN in Bible times included what is now Spain and Portugal. In New Testament times, Spain was ruled by Rome. Paul said he hoped to go to Spain to preach the gospel. The New Testament does not record his going there, although Clement, an early church leader writing in A.D. 95, suggested that he did.

Where to find it: *Romans 15: 24, 28*

SPARROW (see *Birds*)

SPEAR (see *Weapons*)

SPICES usually refers to herbs having a sweet smell. Cinnamon is one of the spices mentioned in the Bible. Spices were used in seasoning and preserving food and in making perfume. Spices were mixed with oil as part of worship in the Temple and were used in preparing bodies for burial.

Where to find it: *Exodus 25: 1-6; 30: 22-38; John 19: 40*

SPIDER is an insect that spins a web. The spider's web is mentioned in the Bible as a word picture for something fragile.

Where to find it: *Job 8: 14; 27: 18; Isaiah 59: 5-6*

SPIES in Bible times went to enemy territories to find out about military strength or to spread rumors that would hurt the enemy.

Moses sent spies into Canaan. The chief priests sent spies to find some charges against Jesus.

Where to find it: *Numbers 13: 1-33; Joshua 2: 1-24; Luke 20: 19-20*

SPIKENARD (see *Plants–Nard*)

SPINNING (see *Occupations*)

SPIRIT refers to the inner part of a person rather than his physical body. Jesus said, "God is spirit," showing that God does not have a physical body as we have. Sometimes *spirit* is used in the New Testament as that part of a person that is able to have fellowship with God. Paul wrote that God's Spirit confirms with our spirit that we are children of God.

Where to find it: *John 4: 24; Romans 8: 15-16*

SPIRIT, HOLY (see *Holy Spirit*)

SPIRITS IN PRISON is a phrase used in 1 Peter 3: 19. We are not sure exactly who these "spirits in prison" were, to whom Christ preached after his death. Some scholars think they were those who had refused to listen to Noah's message. Others think they were the angels who fell from heaven because of sin. The term appears nowhere else in the Bible.

SPIRITUAL GIFTS refer to callings, talents, or abilities that God gives to his people for two purposes:

1. To help other Christians develop in their faith. The Bible term is "edifying the church."

2. To help win others to belief in Christ as Savior (see 1 Corinthians 14: 21-25).

Paul wrote about spiritual gifts four times in his letters. Each time he mentioned some of the gifts, but the lists are never the same, showing that there were many gifts, probably including some that Paul never mentioned. Among the gifts he did mention are prophecy, teaching, helping, speaking in tongues, hospitality, working miracles, healing, and being a pastor, evangelist, administrator, or apostle.

The New Testament teaches that we Christians are responsible to God for the gifts he gives us, and we are to use them to benefit each other. Paul teaches that many gifts are needed if "the body" (the church) is to grow in a balanced way.

Where to find it: *Romans 12: 6-8; 1 Corinthians 12, 14; Ephesians 4: 7-13*

SPITTING on a person was a terrible insult in Bible times, just as it is today. At Jesus' trial before his crucifixion, his enemies spat on his face.

However, during Bible times spittle was considered by some to have special power to heal diseases. Three times Jesus used his spittle, sometimes mixed with clay, while he was healing someone. Not only was this in keeping with the local customs, but it also helped him to communicate with those who were blind or deaf by touching them.

Where to find it

Jesus used spittle in healing *Mark 7: 32-36; 8: 22-26; John 9: 6-12*
Jesus was spat upon *Mark 14: 65; Matthew 26: 67*

SPOILS were the goods taken from an enemy after a battle. In Old Testament times, the conquering army regularly took away all it could carry from a city that had been defeated—jewelry, goods of all kinds, cattle,

After the Lord worked a miracle victory for Jehoshaphat and his people, it took them three days to carry away the spoils.

men, women, and children. The captives usually became slaves; the goods were divided up among the conquerors and those who stayed home.

Israel and the nations around it all followed this practice. In Israel, part of the spoils were usually offered to God.

Where to find it: *Numbers 31: 26-27; Joshua 22: 7-8; 2 Kings 14: 14*

SPRING RAIN and **LATTER RAIN** mean the same thing. They are showers in April and May, at the end of the rainy season. What the Bible calls "early rain" comes in autumn.

Where to find it: *Jeremiah 3: 3; 5: 24; Hosea 6: 3; Zechariah 10: 1*

SQUAD (see *Quaternion*)

STABLE (see *Stall*)

STAFF and **ROD** mean the same thing. It was a shaft of wood used for support in walking or climbing. The staffs or rods of Moses and Aaron were used by God to work miracles. A staff was often a sign of authority. A shepherd used his rod or staff to beat off attacking animals or to rescue lost sheep. He also used his staff to count the sheep every day.

Rod and *staff* were often used as word pictures of the judgment of God. But Psalm 23: 4 ("Thy rod and thy staff, they comfort me") is a word picture of God's care and protection.

Where to find it: *Exodus 7: 9-20; 8: 16-17*

STAIRS were necessary in almost every house in Bible times. Houses had flat roofs, and the rooftops were the place for many family activities. Steps usually led up the outside of the house to the roof.

Cities were often built on steep hills, so stairs were needed to get from one level of streets to the next. Water had to be carried from wells, and often there were many steps down to the well. Women climbed down and back up the many steps with heavy jugs of water on their heads.

STALL was a tent or enclosure where animals were fed and cared for. In the average home, animals were kept in the yard or in a cave stable under the house or nearby (see *Manger*).

King Solomon built special stables for his thousands of horses. Archaeologists have found the remains of some of Solomon's stables at a place called Megiddo, where there were places for 450 horses.

Where to find it: *1 Kings 4:26*

STARS are often mentioned in the Bible. Early people knew there were many more stars than their eyes could see. God told Abraham, "I will multiply your descendants as the stars of heaven and as the sand which is on the seashore." Abraham knew he could never begin to count either the grains of sand on the seashore or the stars in the sky.

Throughout the Bible, God is recognized as the Creator of the stars and the one who keeps the universe in order. Psalm 147:4 says God knows how many stars there are and has given each one a name!

Ancient people probably developed the calendar and the concept of weeks by studying the movement of the stars. Because the stars and the sun were so important in their lives, it is not surprising that many people worshiped them. The Israelites were told not to do this, but sometimes they built altars to the sun anyway.

Two constellations' names that we still use—Orion and Pleiades—are mentioned in the Bible in Job 9:9; 38:31; and Amos 5:8.

Some descriptions in the Bible fit an eclipse of the sun. Amos 8:9 says, "I will make the sun go down at noon, and darken the earth in broad daylight." Amos had probably seen such an eclipse.

The most famous star in the Bible is the Star of Bethlehem (see *Star of the East*).

In Revelation 22:16, the "bright and morning star" is a word picture of Christ.

Where to find it

Promise to Abraham *Genesis 22:17*
Israelites not to worship stars *Deuteronomy 4:19*

STAR OF THE EAST is mentioned in Matthew 2:2 as the light that guided the wise men to Bethlehem.

Many astronomers have tried to figure out what could have caused this star to shine at that time in such a distinctive way, since the movement of most stars is so exact that their

What was the bright star that the wise men followed? Astronomers still don't know for sure.

positions can be determined for centuries ahead or centuries past.

One idea is that it was the result of a conjunction of the planets Jupiter and Saturn that is known to have occurred about 7 B.C.

It could also have been a supernova—a faint star that suddenly becomes brighter and then fades slowly for no known reason.

Whatever the star was, God, who controls the universe, planned whatever was necessary to make it shine at the right time.

Where to find it: *Matthew 2:1-12*

STATURE *(STAT-chur)* refers to size. When the Bible says, "Jesus increased in wisdom and in stature," it means he grew normally.

Where to find it: *Luke 2: 52; 19: 3*

STEADFAST *(STED-fast)* means to be reliable and patient even when life is very difficult. Christians are urged to be steadfast even in persecution and trouble. James said, "The testing of your faith produces steadfastness."

Where to find it: *Romans 15: 4-5; 2 Thessalonians 3: 5; James 1: 3-4*

STEPHANAS *(STEF-uh-nuss)* was one of the few Christians to be baptized personally by the apostle Paul. He and his family were the first to become Christians in Corinth. They served the church there in valuable ways. Stephanas himself went with two other men to see Paul at Ephesus and to report about the church at Corinth.

They perhaps brought a letter from the church, which Paul answered. Paul's answer is our New Testament Book of 1 Corinthians.

Where to find it: *1 Corinthians 1: 16; 7: 1; 16: 15-17*

STEPHEN *(STEE-vun)* was the first Christian known to die for his faith. He was a member of the early church in Jerusalem and one of

seven men chosen to be in charge of giving food and money to poor widows.

Stephen did miracles and spoke about the power of Christ. Some Jews became angry and debated with him, but Stephen let the Holy Spirit speak through him, and he won the arguments.

That made the Jews even more angry. They found men who would agree to lie about what Stephen had said. They took Stephen before the Jewish council, the Sanhedrin, and accused him of speaking disrespectfully about the Law of Moses and the Temple.

In Stephen's answer, he showed how often in the history of Israel the Jews had closed their eyes to God's truth.

The listeners became so angry they took him outside the city and stoned him to death. Saul, who later became the apostle Paul, watched and agreed to his death.

After Stephen's death, all Christians were persecuted. Many had to leave their homes in Jerusalem, but they carried the gospel wherever they went, and the church began to spread through other parts of Palestine.

Where to find it: *Acts 6: 1–8: 4*

STEWARD (see *Occupations*)

STIFF-NECKED means to be rebellious and unwilling to be taught. When the Israelites refused to listen to God's message brought by the prophets, they were called stiff-necked.

Where to find it: *Exodus 33: 3-5; 2 Chronicles 30: 8; Acts 7: 51*

STOCKS were a way of punishing people. It was a wooden frame in which a prisoner's hands and feet were locked, often in a painful position with legs stretched apart.

The prophet Jeremiah was locked in stocks, and so were Paul and Silas in the prison in Philippi.

Where to find it: *Jeremiah 20: 2-3; Acts 16: 23-34*

STONECUTTER (see *Occupations*)

STONES were an important part of the economic and religious life of the Israelites. Israel was and still is a country covered with stones. The first job of every farmer was to clear the stones from the fields and build fences with them.

Stones were used for doors of caves, for coverings over wells, for altars and memorials, for weapons, for boundaries. During times when the Hebrews forgot God, they even worshiped stones.

Stones are often used as word pictures. Jesus is called the chief cornerstone. Believers are called living stones in God's temple.

Where to find it

Stone worship   *Isaiah 57:6*
Jesus the chief cornerstone   *Ephesians 2:20*
Believers   *1 Peter 2:5-8*

STONING was the usual Hebrew method of killing someone who had disobeyed certain parts of the Jewish Law, such as offering human sacrifices or idolatry.

The Roman method of executing criminals was crucifixion.

Where to find it

Stoning for offering human sacrifices
   Leviticus 20:2
Stoning for idolatry   *Deuteronomy 13:6-10*

STORE CITIES were cities where food, weapons, and other supplies were stored for the government. The Israelites were forced to help build Egyptian store cities at Pithom and Ra-amses. The remains of these have been found by archaeologists.

King Solomon also built store cities.

Where to find it: *Exodus 1:11; 1 Kings 9:17-19; 2 Chronicles 8:4-6*

STORK (see *Birds*)

STOVES in Palestine were usually made of clay. They were round and wide enough at the bottom to put in the dry grass, sticks, and sometimes charcoal that were used for fuels. The stove was shaped smaller at the top—just large enough to hold a pan or pot. Air vents at the bottom kept the fire going.

Wealthy people had stoves that were small metal containers in which charcoal was burned (see *Ovens* and *Cooking*).

STRANGER (see *Sojourner*)

STRAW in the Bible was wheat or barley stalks that had been cut to about two-inch lengths. This was used in making bricks in Egypt, for bedding for animals, and for animal food

when mixed with grains (see *Stubble*).

Where to find it: *Exodus 5:6-18; Isaiah 11:7*

STRIPES (see *Scourging*)

STRONG DRINK refers to any alcoholic beverage made from either grain or fruit. Priests and Nazirites were forbidden to drink any wine or strong drink. Most of the references to strong drink in the Bible are warnings against using too much of it.

Where to find it: *Deuteronomy 29:6; Proverbs 20:1; 31:4, 6; Isaiah 5:11, 22; 28:7; Micah 2:11*

STRONGHOLD means a fortress or a place of refuge. Psalm 9:9 says, "The Lord is a stronghold for the oppressed, a stronghold in times of trouble." Here *stronghold* is a word picture of God's protection of his people.

STUBBLE is the dry stalks of grain left in a field after reaping. *Stubble* sometimes refers also to the refuse from threshing. It burns easily and is worthless.

When the Pharaoh wanted to make the Hebrews work harder in Egypt, he stopped supplying them with straw to make bricks. He insisted that they go to the fields or threshing floors and find their own stubble.

Elsewhere in the Bible, *stubble* is usually used as a word picture of something easily burned up. The works of some teachers were said to be built on foundations of gold, silver, precious stones, wood, hay, or stubble. The

In the Middle East today, bread is sometimes baked on small, flat stoves on the ground.

fire of God's judgment will burn up all that is worthless.

Where to find it: *1 Corinthians 3:12*

SUFFERING refers to physical, mental, or emotional pain.

Many Israelites in the Old Testament thought that suffering and pain were signs of God's punishment for sin. In the Book of Job, Job's friends kept insisting that Job must confess his sin, because they thought all his troubles and suffering were caused by his sin. However, at the end of the book, Job stated that he knew God had his divine purpose in all things.

In New Testament times, many Jews still believed that sickness and other suffering were always caused by sin. The disciples once asked Jesus about a man who had been born blind. "Who sinned, this man or his parents?" Jesus answered, "Neither."

Jesus taught that suffering is part of the life of every person, even of every person who is his follower. He explained that he was going to suffer for the sins of the world. He told his followers, "In the world you have tribulation; but be of good cheer, I have overcome the world."

Jesus also taught that when others cause us to suffer, we are to respond as he did—in love and care for them.

The apostle Paul often wrote about the suffering he had experienced. He was beaten, imprisoned, sick, and persecuted. He wrote, "I consider the sufferings of this present time are not worth comparing with the glory that is to be revealed to us." He also wrote, "In all these things we are more than conquerors through him who loved us." He reminded Christians that if they followed Christ, they would also suffer for his sake.

Where to find it

Jesus said suffering was not always caused by a person's sin *John 9:2-3; Luke 13:1-5*
Jesus suffered for the sins of the world *Matthew 16:21; Mark 8:31*
Paul's teachings about suffering *Romans 8:18; 35-39; Philippians 1:29-30; 2 Timothy 1:8, 12*
We are to respond in love to suffering *Matthew 5:38-45; Luke 6:27-30; Romans 12:14-20; 1 Peter 2:19-24*

SUN (see *Stars*)

SUNDAY (see *Lord's Day*)

SUPERSCRIPTION *(SOO-pur-SKRIP-shun)* means a writing or marking on the outside of something. The King James Version uses "superscription" for the markings on Roman coins and for the sign placed above the cross at the crucifixion of Jesus.

Most newer translations use "inscription" or "mark."

Where to find it: *Matthew 22:20; Mark 12:16; 15:26; Luke 20:24; 23:38 (all KJV)*

SUPERSTITION *(SOO-pur-STIH-shun)* is a word whose original meaning in the New Testament is not easy to define.

In the Greek language, *superstition* could mean proper respect or reverence for a god, or it could mean exaggerated fear of gods, or it could mean religious devotion.

Paul told the Athenians that he could see they were very "superstitious." Since Paul would not try to insult his listeners, he probably meant "very religious" because he could see so many images of gods around them. Later, when the Roman governor Festus explained the charges against Paul, he said Paul's accusers had their own superstitions. Here he may have meant "religions" or "exaggerated religious beliefs," depending on his attitude toward Paul.

Where to find it: *Acts 17:22; 25:19*

SUPPER, LORD'S (see *Lord's Supper*)

SUPPLICATION (see *Prayer*)

SURETY *(SHUR-tee)* means a person has promised that he will pay or do something if another person fails to do so. Judah was surety for Benjamin when they went to Egypt. He said he would be personally responsible if anything happened to Benjamin.

The Book of Proverbs often warns people not to be surety for anyone, because it will usually bring them to grief.

Jesus is said to be the surety or guarantee for believers—he personally took the responsibility and penalty for our sins before God, as our high priest.

Where to find it: *Genesis 43:9; Proverbs 11:15; 17:18; 22:26; Hebrews 7:22*

SURNAME (SIR-name) for us means our last name or family name. However, in Bible times it meant "an added name." Simon was given the surname Peter by Jesus. Peter was not a family name but rather an added name. Jesus gave James and John the surname Boanerges, which means "sons of thunder." Barnabas, which means "son of consolation," was the surname given by the apostles to a Christian named Joseph. He is known by the name Barnabas in the rest of the Book of Acts.

Where to find it: Mark 3:16-17; Acts 4:36

SUSANNA (SOO-zan-uh) was one of the women who traveled with Jesus and the 12 disciples. She and other women provided financial help.

Where to find it: Luke 8:1-3

SWADDLING (SWAD-ling) **CLOTHS** describes the usual ancient way of wrapping a newborn infant. The baby was placed diagonally on a square piece of cloth. Then the bottom of the cloth was folded over the feet and body. The baby was then wrapped with wide strips of cloth called swaddling bands to keep him warm.

Where to find it: Luke 2:7, 12

SWALLOW (see Birds)

SWORD (see Weapons)

SYCAMINE (see Plants)

SYCAMORE (see Plants)

SYCHAR (SIE-kar) was a small village in Samaria on the road from Jerusalem to Galilee. Near the village was Jacob's well. At the well, Jesus met a Samaritan woman drawing water. In his conversation with her, he stated for the first time that he was the Messiah. She was so excited that she ran to her village and encouraged many others to come out and see Jesus. As a result, many Samaritans from the village of Sychar believed in Jesus.

Where to find it: John 4:3-43

SYMBOL (SIM-bul) is an object or idea or action that stands for something else. Symbols are used often in literature. Hundreds of symbols appear in the Bible. In the Bible, as in other literature, the symbols are usually taken from the daily life of the people, and we must understand the symbol if we are to understand what the writer is saying.

For example, the loving care of a shepherd is used in Psalm 23 as a symbol for the loving care of God for his people. Sheep who go astray from their shepherd are a symbol or word picture of people who wander away from God.

The same symbol sometimes has different meanings. The lion is used as a symbol for the strength and power of Christ in Revelation 5:5, where he is spoken of as the "Lion of the tribe of Judah." But in 1 Peter 5:8, the lion is used as a symbol of Satan, who prowls around looking for people to devour.

In the Old Testament, prophets often used symbolic dramas to deliver God's message.

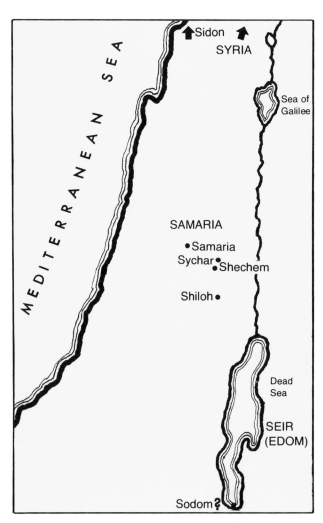

Jeremiah once bought a new linen sash and buried it. After a long time, he dug it up and found it rotted and useless. He said it was a symbol of how God had rejected Israel. He said Israel was as useless as the sash that was now falling apart.

Numbers and colors in the Bible are often symbols. The number seven seems to be a symbol for completeness; the color red or purple is a symbol for royalty.

Jesus used much symbolic language in his teaching. He spoke of himself as the "bread of life" and "the door" and "the light of the world."

Often the Bible states clearly the meanings of its symbols. In Revelation 5: 8, the bowls of incense are clearly said to represent the prayers of the saints.

When the meaning for symbols is not clearly stated, we must try hard to understand the culture of the times and the message the writer was trying to give. This helps us understand what the first readers or hearers understood the symbol to mean. If we don't do this, we can misunderstand what the Bible writers were trying to say in their use of symbols.

Where to find it

Jeremiah's sash *Jeremiah 13: 1-11*
Jesus, the bread of life *John 6: 35-58*
Jesus, the light of the world *John 8: 12*
Jesus, the door *John 10: 7-9*

SYMEON (see *Simeon*)

SYNAGOGUE (*SIN-uh-gog*) is a place where Jews meet together to read the Old Testament and to worship God. Many historians believe that synagogues began after the Jewish

people were taken into exile in Babylonia in 597 B.C. They had no Temple there, but they began to gather together on the Sabbath to read the Old Testament and to worship God. These gatherings developed into synagogues. *Synagogue* can refer both to the building in which they met and to the people who met there.

By the time of the New Testament, synagogues were common throughout the Mediterranean area wherever there were ten or more Jewish families in a city.

Old records show that a fairly large synagogue had at least two officials.

1. The ruler of the synagogue was responsible for the building and property. He also appointed persons to read the Scriptures and pray. He invited qualified visiting teachers to give a short sermon.

2. The attendant of the synagogue took care of the sacred scrolls of the Old Testament. He brought the proper scroll from the chest to the person who would read it on the Sabbath and replaced it afterward in the chest. He announced the beginning and end of the Sabbath (sunset to sunset) by blowing three blasts on a trumpet from the roof of the synagogue. He also taught in the synagogue school, where Jewish boys learned to read and write.

Most synagogues were simple buildings, unlike the Temple in Jerusalem. Each synagogue had a wooden chest in which the scrolls of the Old Testament were kept wrapped in a linen cloth. The persons who read from the scrolls stood on some kind of platform.

The people usually sat on benches along the sides of walls. Sometimes there was a gallery or balcony where the women sat. Some scholars think that in some synagogues women were seated on one side and men on the other, or women were seated in a separate room. In some areas, women may not have been permitted in the synagogue at all.

The usual synagogue service had the following parts:

1. Everyone repeated the *Shema:* "Hear, O Israel: the Lord our God is one Lord, and you shall love the Lord your God with all your heart, and with all your soul, and with all your might" (Deuteronomy 6: 4).

2. A prayer by some man in the congrega-

tion who was chosen by the ruler of the synagogue.

3. Reading from the Pentateuch (the first five books of the Old Testament). This could be read by any male member of the congregation appointed by the ruler of the synagogue. Sections were so arranged that all of the books were read during a period of three years.

4. Reading from the Old Testament Prophets. (Everything except the first five books was called "the Prophets.") Luke 4:16-21 tells that when Jesus went into the synagogue in Nazareth, he read a passage from Isaiah as a part of the synagogue service.

5. Sometimes a short sermon followed the reading from the Prophets. A visiting teacher was often called on to give this short sermon.

6. A closing prayer by a priest or some member of the congregation.

Because ordinary Jewish men were able to take part in the services, the apostle Paul usually began his teaching in a synagogue as he went from place to place.

The basic pattern of the synagogue service was followed by the early Christian church and is an important part of the heritage of Christians today.

SYNOPTIC *(sin-OP-tik)* **GOSPELS** refers to the Gospels of Matthew, Mark, and Luke. Synoptic means "seeing the whole together," and these three Gospels are called synoptic because they give a very similar picture of the life of Jesus Christ.

The Gospel of John is not included because John's Gospel gives different information from that of Matthew, Mark, and Luke. John tells about the crucifixion and resurrection of Jesus, and also about the feeding of the 5,000, just as do Matthew, Mark, and Luke. But the rest of the material in John is different from that in the synoptic Gospels.

SYNTYCHE (see *Euodia*)

SYRIA *(SEER-ee-uh)* in Bible times was an area north of Palestine. It covered most of the land south of modern Turkey, north of the Sea of Galilee, west of the Arabian Desert, and east of the Mediterranean Sea. The modern nation of Syria covers some of the same territory.

Damascus was Syria's most active city in Bible times, and it is the capital of modern Syria. The Bible cities of Antioch, Tyre, and Sidon were also in Syria. In early Old Testament times, Syria was part of the land known as Aram. The people were called Aramaeans. The Aramaean, or Aramaic, language that Jesus spoke is still used in some churches in Syria today. The Arabic language is the common language used in Syria now.

Syria was usually richer, larger, and more powerful than Israel, with abundant fruits, farms, and flocks of sheep and goats. It has been famous for silk, wool, and metal.

Ahab, the wicked king of Israel, fought against Syrian armies three times.

Naaman, the leprous soldier who went to Elisha to be healed, was a Syrian army commander.

The apostle Paul was converted in Syria near Damascus.

Where to find it

Israel under Ahab battles Syria   *1 Kings 20–22*
Naaman seeks healing   *2 Kings 5*
Paul is converted near Damascus   *Acts 9*

SYROPHOENICIAN *(SY-row-fih-NISH-un)* refers to a person who lived in the Roman province of Syria in the part that had previously been called Phoenicia. This included the cities of Tyre and Sidon. This area is now a part of modern Lebanon.

When Jesus visited the area, he healed the daughter of a Syrophoenician woman.

Where to find it: *Matthew 15:21-28; Mark 7:24-30*

TABERNACLE *(TAB-er-nack-ul)* was the Israelites' sacred tent for worship. They used it during their wanderings in the wilderness on their Exodus from Egypt and for many years after they conquered Canaan. Moses and the Israelites built it as "God's house"—where God revealed himself and lived among his people. It was used for worship and sacrifice until it was replaced by King Solomon's Temple.

Tabernacle means "tent," and that's exactly

what it was. It is also mentioned in the Bible as "tent of meeting," "sanctuary," "sacred tent," and "tabernacle of the testimony."

God said the Tabernacle was to be built from materials that people gave. The Israelites brought gold, silver, and bronze metals; blue, purple, and scarlet fabrics; fine linen; goat's hair, goatskins, rams' skins; acacia wood; oil for the lamps; spices and incense; onyx stones and other valuable gems. They brought their gifts to Moses so he could supervise the building of a place of worship worthy of the God who had brought them out of slavery.

The Tabernacle stood in an enclosure or court about 150 feet long and 75 feet wide. The walls of the court were made of linen draperies, fastened to posts of bronze. In this courtyard the people worshiped God. They never entered the Tabernacle itself. Near the center of the courtyard stood the altar of burnt offerings, where priests offered the sacrifices the people brought.

The Tabernacle itself was about 45 feet long and 15 feet wide—no bigger than an average classroom, only longer and narrower. It was made from cloth drapes and animal skins held up by acacia wood supports. Only the priests entered the Tabernacle. A heavy curtain embroidered with red, purple, and blue cherubim divided the Tabernacle into two smaller rooms.

The room nearest the entrance was called the Holy Place. It had an altar for incense. It also had golden candlesticks with seven branches and a table for special bread called showbread. The table was acacia wood overlaid with gold. Twelve loaves of bread were placed in two heaps on the table. Fresh bread was placed there every week. This was also called "the table of the Presence," because it reminded Israel of God's daily care in providing their food.

The room beyond the Holy Place was called the Holy of Holies. Only the high priest could enter this room, and he went in only once a year on the Day of Atonement. On that day he offered a sacrifice for the sins of the people and of himself.

The Holy of Holies contained the ark of the Covenant, a small box made of wood covered with gold. Inside the ark were three things:

the tablets of the Law given to Moses on Mount Sinai, a sample of the manna that Israel ate in the wilderness, and Aaron's rod that had budded with flowers. The ark was very sacred. Only certain Levites could carry it when the Tabernacle was moved.

When the Tabernacle was taken apart for moving, the ark and the two altars were carried by Levites. The rest of the Tabernacle was folded up and placed in six covered wagons, each drawn by two oxen. For 35 years during the wilderness wanderings, the Tabernacle stayed in one place, at Kadesh. In Joshua's time the Tabernacle was settled in Shiloh.

The Tabernacle was a symbol to the people of God's presence with them. The ark represented God's presence and forgiving love. The 12 loaves of showbread stood for the 12 tribes of Israel. The candlestick pictured the light of God's Word and will. The incense reminded the people of prayer rising toward God.

Where to find it: *Exodus 25–27, 35–40*

TABITHA (see *Dorcas*)

TABLE most often means a piece of furniture where people eat, but in the Bible it also has several other meanings.

Table sometimes means "tablet"—for example, the two slabs of stone on which the Ten Commandments were carved. Stone slabs like this were often used for official documents in Egypt (see *Tables of the Law* and *Writing Materials*).

Tables also were pieces of furniture used for sacrificial offerings. Some were used for pagan sacrifices, but tables were also used for worship of the true God. The table of showbread was an important part of the Tabernacle (see *Table of Showbread* or *Tabernacle*). "The table of the Lord" in the Old Testament means the altar of burnt offerings. In the New Testament, this phrase refers to the Lord's Supper.

Tables were also used for money changing, as we know from the story of Jesus in the Temple.

Where to find it

Tables of stone   *Exodus 24:12*
Pagan tables for sacrifice   *Isaiah 65:11; 1 Corinthians 10:21*
Tables for money changing   *Matthew 21:12*

TABLE OF SHOWBREAD, a gold-covered table in the Holy Place of the Tabernacle, held 12 loaves of bread that were changed weekly. It was also called "the table of the bread of the Presence" and reminded the 12 tribes of ancient Israel of God's daily care for them.

Where to find it: *Leviticus 24: 5-9*

TABLES OF THE LAW were stone slabs or tablets on which Moses received the Ten Commandments from God. When Moses brought them down from his meeting with God on Mount Sinai, he found the Israelites worshiping a gold calf they had made in the 40 days while he had been gone. In anger, Moses threw down the tablets, breaking them.

God called Moses to cut two new slabs of stone and take them up the mountain to receive the Law again. This time Moses put the tables of the Law into the ark of the Covenant. The ark was placed in the Tabernacle and later in King Solomon's Temple.

The tables were finally lost forever when the Temple was ruined by the Babylonians in 586 B.C.

Where to find it: *Exodus 24: 12-18; 32: 15-20; 34: 1-35*

TABOR *(TAY-bur)*, **MOUNT,** a hill about six miles east and southeast of Nazareth, may have been the Mount of Transfiguration (see *Transfiguration*). Early Christians established a memorial to the Transfiguration there.

Mount Tabor is also the place Barak chose as a base from which to attack the army of Sisera. Although the mount is only 1,843 feet high, you can see the entire Jezreel valley from its summit. Its steep sides and domed top make it an inspiring sight, so it is often mentioned with higher mountains—Mount Carmel or Mount Hermon—in poems.

Where to find it

Barak's staging area	*Judges 4: 6-14*
Mentioned in poetry	*Psalm 89: 12*
Jesus' transfiguration	*Mark 9: 2-8*

TACKLE and **TACKLING** refer to pulleys, ropes, and other gear used in handling cargo. In the story in Acts 27: 13-44, sailors threw the tackle overboard to try to keep the ship from sinking.

TALEBEARING is the King James Version word for gossiping and saying damaging things about a person. This is strongly condemned in the Bible.

Where to find it: *Leviticus 19: 16; Proverbs 11: 13; 20: 19*

TALITHA CUMI *(tuh-LEE-thuh COO-me)* were the Aramaic words Jesus spoke when he raised Jairus's 12-year-old daughter from the dead. They are warm, loving words meaning, "Little girl, stand up."

Where to find it: *Mark 5: 41*

TALMUD *(TAHL-mud)* is a collection of Jewish stories, teachings, traditions, comments about and interpretations of the Old Testament that were gathered and written down between A.D. 250 and 550.

At first the Talmud was oral teachings to help the Jewish people interpret the Old Testament Law. Later it included teachings to interpret the rest of the Old Testament. As the collection of teachings grew over the centuries, it became necessary to write them down.

Through the centuries the Talmud has had a great influence on Jewish people, and they rank it second in importance to the Old Testament itself.

In Jewish education, the Talmud became the most important book studied in both elementary and secondary schools. Its study helped preserve the Jewish way of life and instill a loyalty to Jewish ideas and traditions.

It is still studied by devout Jews today.

TAMAR *(TAY-mar)* is the name of several Old Testament women.

1. Tamar was the widowed daughter-in-law of Judah who pretended to be a prostitute in order to bear children by her father-in-law. Her children were Perez and Zerah. She is listed in Matthew 1: 3 as an ancestor of Jesus.

2. Tamar was King David's daughter. Her half brother Amnon raped her, then got angry at her and drove her out of the house. Her brother Absalom had Amnon murdered to get revenge.

Where to find it

Judah's daughter-in-law   *Genesis 38: 6-30*
David's daughter   *2 Samuel 13: 2-29*

TAMARISK (see *Plants*)

TANNER (see *Occupations*)

TARES (see *Plants*)

TARSHISH *(TAR-shish)* was a place somewhere along the western Mediterranean Sea to which Jonah tried to flee instead of going to Nineveh, where God had told him to go. Tarshish may have been in Spain. The Bible mentions "ships of Tarshish," large seagoing vessels, that brought silver, iron, lead, and even monkeys to Israel in King Solomon's day.

Where to find it: *Jonah 1: 3; 1 Kings 10: 22; Ezekiel 27: 12*

TARSUS *(TAR-sus)*, a city ten miles from the northeast coast of the Mediterranean Sea, was the birthplace and early home of the apostle Paul. Although it was located in what is now Turkey, it was then the capital of the Roman province of Cilicia. During Paul's time the city had a famous university, and the people were greatly influenced by Greek thought. Tarsus was also famous for its goat's hair cloth. People from Tarsus were very proud of their city, as we can see in Paul's boast in Acts 21: 39.

TASKMASTER (see *Occupations*)

TAUNT (see *Scoffer*)

TAVERNS, THREE (see *Three Taverns*)

TAX means money paid by citizens to support their rulers. Taxes were collected both by the government and by the religious authorities in Bible times. Early Old Testament taxes included a half shekel yearly for the support of the Tabernacle. Both rich and poor paid the same tax. After the Israelites demanded a king, the people had to pay heavy taxes, just as Samuel had warned. King Solomon put such heavy taxes on the people that after he died the northern tribes revolted, and the kingdom was divided.

During New Testament times the Roman rulers of Israel used local Jewish people to collect taxes for them. These men agreed to collect a certain amount for the government. Anything additional became their salary. That way tax collectors could make big profits for themselves. A census for taxation brought Mary and Joseph to Bethlehem at the time of the birth of Christ. Jews paid taxes on personal property, produce grown in the field, items bought and sold, customs at seaports and city gates, and, in Jerusalem, on houses. During this time the Jews also continued to pay the annual half shekel Temple tax.

Where to find it

Half shekel   *Exodus 30: 13-15*
Samuel's warning about taxes   *1 Samuel 8: 11-18*

TEACHER is a name used often as a title of respect for Jesus in the New Testament. Jesus was considered a leader of his group, and his teaching was recognized as having authority. Even those who opposed him called him "Rabbi" (teacher).

Some leaders of the early church were also called teachers. Teachers proclaimed the gospel, repeated Jesus' teachings so Christians could hear them, and taught about Jesus and the Old Testament.

Where to find it

Jesus called "Rabbi"   *Mark 12: 14*
Teachers in the Antioch church   *Acts 13: 1*

TELL is a mound of earth or heap of ruins that marks the site of an ancient city. Over a period of centuries, some cities were destroyed and rebuilt many times because of wars, earthquakes, fire, and neglect. New buildings were erected on top of old ruins. Today archaeologists, when they find a tell, sometimes uncover many layers of the same city. They can study many different periods of history from just one tell.

TEMPERANCE *(TEM-pur-unce)* means self-control in all matters.

TEMPLE *(TEM-pul)* was the permanent place of Jewish worship through much of the Old Testament and New Testament period. Between 950 B.C. and A.D. 70, three different temples were built on the same hill in Jerusalem—Mount Moriah, the place where Abraham was going to sacrifice Isaac.

The idea of building a Temple was David's, but his son Solomon carried out the plans.

King Solomon ordered the building of the first Temple in 950 B.C. to replace the Tabernacle. Its basic floor plan resembled that of the Tabernacle. It took 7 years to build the Temple itself, and 13 more to finish the other buildings that were part of the complex. Babylonians destroyed this Temple in 586 B.C. when they burned Jerusalem. Nothing remains of King Solomon's Temple, so we don't know exactly what it was like. The Old Testament, however, does have many details about the Temple.

It had three parts inside a large court. People entered the Temple through a porch.

To reach the porch, they climbed ten steps, because the whole Temple was on a nine-foot platform above the huge open courtyard surrounding the building.

Inside the porch was the Holy Place, which was 60 feet long, 30 feet wide, and 45 feet high. Its walls were made of cedar with gold inlay. In the Holy Place were 10 golden lampstands, 10 tables of showbread ("bread of the Presence"), and an altar to burn incense.

Beyond this Holy Place was the Holy of Holies. It was a 30-foot cube-shaped room paneled with gold. Two cherubim figures carved of olive wood and covered with gold were placed over the ark of the Covenant, the wooden chest covered with gold that contained the Ten Commandments. (Aaron's rod and the samples of manna had apparently been destroyed; see *Ark of the Covenant*). The lid of the ark of the Covenant was called the mercy seat. On the mercy seat the high priest sprinkled blood on the Day of Atonement, the only day of the year he entered the Holy of Holies. No one else ever entered there.

In the courtyard in front of the Temple, worshipers saw the sacrificial altar and a 7½-foot-tall bowl, or "laver of molten sea." The altar, made of bronze, was the central part of sacrificial ceremonies. In addition to the huge laver, ten smaller lavers held water for ceremonial cleansing. Ordinary worshipers never went beyond this courtyard. Only priests could enter the Temple itself—and then only for special purposes, such as offering sacrifices on feast days.

The whole Temple complex was beautiful. Many of the furnishings were made of gold or bronze. The nation of Israel was very proud of this great Temple. Unfortunately, between 950 and 586 B.C. some of the wicked kings allowed pagan worship inside this Temple that had been dedicated to God. Other kings took treasures from the Temple to pay off foreign attackers. King Josiah removed the pagan altars, cleaned up and repaired the Temple, and restored it to its proper use. But the Temple was finally plundered and destroyed by the Babylonians in 586 B.C.

The Restoration Temple was built by Zerubbabel, the governor of the Jews return-

169

The New Testament Temple, built by Herod the Great.

ing from Babylon, and Jeshua, the high priest. It was completed in 515 B.C. No description of this Temple exists, but it probably followed the same general pattern as Solomon's. Although it was beautiful, it was much simpler and less expensive than Solomon's. Some Jews wept because it was so modest compared to Solomon's Temple. The returning Jews had little money for the building. The Holy Place of the new Temple had a curtain at the door. It had one lampstand, a golden altar of incense, and one table of showbread.

Another curtain formed the door to the Holy of Holies. A slab of stone marked the place where the ark of the Covenant should be. (The ark had been destroyed in 586 when Solomon's Temple was ruined.)

In 168 B.C. the Syrians robbed this Temple of all its furnishings. The Syrian king forced the high priest to sacrifice a pig upon the altar. This caused a revolt in which a group of Jews called the Maccabees recaptured and rededicated the Temple. These events are remembered in the Jewish festival of Hanukkah (see *Maccabees* and *Hanukkah).*

In 63 B.C., Roman soldiers captured Jerusalem, and a few years later a Roman consul took all the gold in the Temple.

The third Temple, Herod's Temple, was begun about 20 B.C. It was a rebuilding of the old structure, piece by piece, without disturbing Temple worship. It took more than 46 years to build. This was the Temple in which Jesus worshiped.

When worshipers entered the Temple area in Jesus' day, they came first into the Court of the Gentiles. Non-Jews were permitted there. Sacrificial birds and animals were sold in this area. Once Jesus angrily chased out the money changers from this part of the Temple.

Within the Court of the Gentiles was a platform 22 feet high on which stood the smaller Temple building. Stone walls surrounded this area, with signs forbidding non-Jews to enter. The first section, the Women's Court, was for both men and women. The next part, the Court of Israel, was only for Jewish males. The interior Priest's Court was only for priests.

Inside these elaborate courts was the sanctuary itself, 12 steps above the rest of the building. This sanctuary also had a porch, a Holy Place, and a Holy of Holies. A curtain served as the door to the Holy Place; two curtains, one in front of the other, veiled the Holy of Holies. These two curtains were the veil that mysteriously split at the time of Jesus' crucifixion.

Herod's Temple was burned and destroyed along with the rest of Jerusalem in A.D. 70 by Roman armies. But the foundation of one wall remains today; it is called the Western Wall, or "Wailing Wall," at which Jews in Jerusalem often worship and pray.

The writer of Hebrews says that Christ fulfilled all the requirements of the Old Testament sacrifice and worship needed in the Temple. Christ brings a better way to approach God, and each believer becomes a "temple" where Christ dwells.

Where to find it

Solomon's Temple *2 Samuel 7; 1 Kings 6–8; 2 Chronicles 2–7*

TEMPT has both a negative and a positive meaning in the Bible.

The negative meaning is to try to make a person do something wrong. The positive meaning is to test a person to improve his spiritual strength.

Satan tempts us to do evil, sometimes working through our own desires. Satan first appeared in the form of a serpent. He appealed to Eve's taste, sight, and pride. Eve believed Satan rather than God and yielded to temptation.

Satan used these same ideas to tempt Jesus in the wilderness (see *Temptation of Jesus*). But unlike us, Jesus resisted all temptation.

Although we often fail, God offers help when we are tempted. 1 Corinthians 10: 13 says, "No temptation has overtaken you that is not common to man. God is faithful, and he will not let you be tempted beyond your strength, but with the temptation will also provide the way of escape, that you may be able to endure it."

This verse may also involve another meaning of temptation—a positive one we might call testing. God wants us to be strong in faith. To produce that strength, he sometimes allows obstacles in our paths to build up our "spiritual muscle." He tested Abraham by asking him to be willing to give up his son, and he tested Job by taking away everything he owned (see *Abraham* and *Job*). "Blessed is the man who endures trial," says James 1: 12, "for when he has stood the test he will receive the crown of life which God has promised to those who love him."

Although testing may seem unpleasant, the results are good. We have a closer relationship with God, and we know we have passed the test.

TEMPTATION OF JESUS is the 40-day period Jesus spent in the wilderness just after his baptism. At the end of this time, Satan tried to tempt him to do wrong.

Jesus had been fasting—eating little or nothing. Naturally, he was hungry. Satan first suggested to Jesus that he turn stones into bread so he could eat. Satan was really saying, "Since you are God's Son in a special way, there is no reason for you to be hungry. Use your power to live the way you deserve."

Jesus showed that obeying what God says is more important than eating. He answered, by quoting part of Deuteronomy 8: 3, "It is written, 'Man shall not live by bread alone, but by every word that proceeds from the mouth of God.' "

Then Satan took Jesus to a very high mountain and pointed out the magnificent kingdoms of the world. "All these I will give you," he said, "if you will fall down and worship me." Satan was telling Jesus that he could control all of the world without having to suffer on the cross—*if* he would only show respect to Satan.

But Jesus answered, "Begone, Satan! for it is written, 'You shall worship the Lord your God and him only shall you serve' " (a quotation from Deuteronomy 6: 13).

In another temptation, Satan took Jesus to the highest part of the Temple. He suggested that Jesus jump off to prove that the angels would catch him in time to escape injury. By this, Satan was saying, "Why spend all that time teaching, preaching, healing, and helping people? Just jump off the Temple. After the angels rescue you, everyone will know God sent you. Do what you want to do. Get what you want the easy way."

Jesus again answered by quoting the Old

Testament, this time Deuteronomy 6:16. "It is written, 'You shall not tempt the Lord your God.' " He knew people must not tempt God to see whether he will rescue them from their own foolishness.

Jesus resisted all of Satan's temptations, setting a pattern for us in overcoming similar temptations. His resistance also showed that he was the Son of God.

Where to find it: *Matthew 4:1-11; Mark 1:12-13; Luke 4:1-13; Hebrews 2:18; 4:15*

TEN COMMANDMENTS, a list of rules of conduct given by God through Moses, showed God's people how he wanted them to live. The first four commandments discuss how people should live in relationship to God. The last six discuss how people should live with each other.

God called Moses to the top of Mount Sinai early in the Israelites' journey from Egypt. On two tablets of stone, God wrote these rules as a covenant or agreement between himself and the people he had chosen as his own. These Ten Commandments have become the standard of behavior for much of the world.

The first commandment, "You shall have no other gods before me," guarantees the worship of the one true God.

The second, "You shall not make for yourself a graven image," guards against worshiping idols.

The third, "You shall not take the name of the Lord your God in vain," protects against dishonoring God's name or using it in a meaningless or disrespectful way.

The fourth, "Remember the sabbath day, to keep it holy," provides a special day each week for worship.

The fifth, "Honor your father and your mother," shows God's desire for close, loving families where members respect each other.

The sixth, "You shall not kill," the seventh, "You shall not commit adultery," the eighth, "You shall not steal," and the ninth, "You shall not bear false witness against your neighbor," all involve a person's relationships with other people.

The tenth, "You shall not covet," warns against wrong desire for things that don't belong to us. If we envy other people's money, clothes, popularity, or skills, this desire can lead to breaking other commandments and can cause pain both to ourselves and others.

When we live by these commands, we enjoy a happier, healthier relationship with God and other people. However, no one has ever kept all these commandments all his life. That's why God offers salvation freely by believing in Jesus Christ, his Son. Jesus is the only person who has ever lived up to God's high standards. By faith, we can share some of his power to carry out what we know God wants us to do.

Where to find it: *Exodus 20:2-20; Deuteronomy 5*

TENT, a movable shelter made of cloth or skins supported by poles, was the regular living place of many Old Testament people and of shepherds and soldiers in the New Testament. Most tents in Bible times were made of strong goat's hair cloth. Often the covering appeared striped because of the addition of patches over worn or torn places. People slept inside on coarse straw mats and cooked on stoves that were only a group of stones at the tent entrance, or a hole in the ground.

The Tabernacle used by Israel in the wilderness was a kind of tent (see *Tabernacle*).

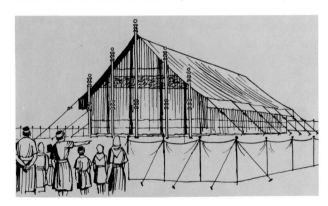

TENT OF MEETING (see *Tabernacle*)

TENTMAKER (see *Occupations*)

TERAPHIM *(TEAR-a-fim)* were household idols that many ancient people worshiped. Such idol worship was condemned in the Bible.

Where to find it: *2 Kings 23:24; Zechariah 10:2*

TERRESTRIAL *(tuh-RES-tree-ul)* **BODIES** refer to our bodies that exist here on earth. The apostle Paul contrasted these earthly bodies with "celestial" or heavenly bodies, which will not die.

Where to find it: *1 Corinthians 15:40*

TERTIUS *(TUR-she-us)* was the man who wrote down Paul's Letter to the Romans as Paul dictated it. He added his own greeting to the greetings Paul sent to his friends in Rome.

Where to find it: *Romans 16:22*

TERTULLUS *(ter-TUL-us)* was a lawyer for the high priests in Jerusalem. He prosecuted Paul before the Roman governor of Judea. He began his case by flattering the governor, Felix; then he charged Paul with being a disturber of the peace, a public nuisance, and a leader of an unapproved group.

Where to find it: *Acts 24:2-8*

TEST (see *Temptation*)

TESTAMENT *(TESS-tuh-ment)* in the Bible usually refers to an unbreakable agreement or covenant between God and his people.

The two parts of the Bible—the Old Testament and the New Testament—are named for the two Covenants God made with his people. In the Old Testament, God made a Covenant with the Israelites (stated at Sinai and repeated later) that if they would obey him and follow his commands, they would be his people in a special way. In the New Testament, God put into operation a new Covenant with his people that he had first revealed to Jeremiah. In the New Covenant, salvation is by faith in Jesus Christ, God's Son. Through Christ our sins are forgiven, and every person, whether Jew or Gentile, can by faith become a member of God's family. God's Law is written in our hearts; we obey it because we want to, not because we have to.

The word *testament* in our day and among the Greeks in New Testament times refers to the unbreakable written instructions a person gives about who should have his property when he dies. We call this a "will." The apostle Paul compared God's Covenant with Israel with a will, which cannot be changed after the person dies. Paul showed that Christ's coming does not destroy the Old Testament Covenant but rather fulfills it.

When Christ ate the Last Supper with his disciples, he took a cup of wine and said, "This cup is the new covenant [testament] in my blood." Christ's coming was the beginning of a new spiritual inheritance for those who accept him.

Where to find it

First mention of the New Covenant *Jeremiah 31:31-34*
The New Covenant in Communion *1 Corinthians 11:25*
God's Covenant like a will *Galatians 3:15-16*

TESTIMONY *(TEST-ih-MOAN-ee)* has several meanings in the Bible. In the Old Testament it often refers to the Law of God or to all the teachings of the Old Testament. Other times it refers to the actual tablets of stone on which God wrote the Ten Commandments for Moses. These were later stored in the ark of the Covenant. For this reason the ark was often called "the ark of the testimony," and the Tabernacle was sometimes called the "tabernacle of the testimony."

In the New Testament, *testimony* usually refers to giving proof or evidence that something is true. This is our usual meaning when we speak of giving a testimony for Christ.

Where to find it

Law, teaching *Psalm 119:14, 22, 24, 31, 36*
Ark of the testimony *Exodus 30:6*
Tabernacle of the testimony *Numbers 1:50, 53*
Evidence *John 3:32-33; 21:24; Acts 22:18*

TETRARCH *(TET-trark)* was originally the title for a ruler of one-fourth of a country. Later it came to mean any prince whose rank and authority was lower than that of a king. In the New Testament, Herod Antipas is sometimes called a tetrarch and sometimes a king. He was ruler of Galilee during the life of Jesus.

Where to find it: *Matthew 14:1; Mark 6:14, 26; Luke 3:1, 19; 9:7*

TEXT has two basic meanings in reference to the Bible.

1. It may mean a passage of the Bible being used in a sermon or lesson.

2. It may mean the original words of the authors of the Bible. One important work of Bible scholars is to try to determine what the exact words were in the original writings of the Bible. This study is called textual criticism.

There are no known copies of any of the original writings of any of the books of the Bible. The Old Testament books were written roughly between 1500 and 500 B.C.; the New

Testament between A.D. 50 and 100. And all of the originals have been lost.

The originals were written by hand on sheets of papyrus (see *Writing*) or parchment (animal skins). Since there were no printing presses at that time, persons very carefully copied the original writings or other copies. When many copies were made like this, some mistakes naturally crept in.

Textual scholars compare all the known copies that have been handed down and try to determine what the original writer said. For the New Testament, scholars feel sure they know exactly what the original writer wrote about 95 percent of the time. The Old Testament, because it had to be handed down and copied through so many more years, has more difficult "unsure" places. However, none of the unsure passages involve any important matters of faith. Most deal with trivia.

We can be very sure that our good translations of the Bible are made from a text that has been restored so as to be very similar to the original. Thus, these good translations carry the message that God intended the Bible to bring us.

THADDAEUS *(THAD-ee-us)* was one of Jesus' 12 disciples. In some lists he is called Judas the son of James. The writer of the Gospel of John was careful not to get him mixed up with Judas Iscariot, who betrayed Jesus. In the lists of the disciples, the names are always given in the same basic order. Thaddaeus, or Judas the son of James, comes just before Judas Iscariot.

Little is known about Thaddaeus except that he traveled with the other disciples.

Where to find it: *Matthew 10:3; Mark 3:18; Luke 6:16; John 14:22; Acts 1:13*

THANKSGIVING means giving thanks to God and recognizing God as the one who creates all that is good. All the letters in the New Testament except Galatians include thanks to God near the opening of the letter.

THEATERS did not exist in ancient Israel, but theaters were a part of Greek culture as early as 400 B.C. To the Greeks, drama was part of their religious tradition. Greek culture had so influenced the world by New Testament times that theaters were found in many lands.

Herod the Great built theaters in Caesarea and in Jerusalem. These were built outdoors in natural land formations. Spectators sat in a semicircle on stone steps on the side of a hill. They watched actors—and sometimes sports participants—perform on a raised stage or track in front of them.

Theaters were often used for public meetings like the one mentioned in Acts 19:29.

THEBES *(theebz)* was the capital city of Egypt in about 2000 B.C. Located in the southern part of Egypt on the Nile River, it was also the center for the worship of the Egyptian god Amon.

THEOCRACY *(thee-AHK-ruh-see)* means government in which God himself is the ruler. Ancient Israel was apparently meant to be a theocracy, in that God was the ruler, and all judges and other officials were under him. However, during the time of Samuel, the Israelites wanted a king like the nations around them, so God permitted it.

When Saul became king, the people were under the king. This made it very easy to forget God and become idol worshipers like other people.

Where to find it: *1 Samuel 8:1-22*

THEOPHANY *(thee-AH-fun-ee)* is a visible appearance of God in the Bible. God usually appeared as a human being or an angel. Before sin came, God visited often with Adam and Eve. Once Abraham had a theophany in his tent in the desert. God also appeared as an angel to Hagar, Sarah's maid, in the wilderness.

Where to find it

God appears to Adam and Eve *Genesis 3:8*
God visits Hagar *Genesis 16:7-13*
God visits Abraham *Genesis 18*

THEOPHILUS *(thee-OFF-uh-lus)* was the man for whom Luke wrote his Gospel of Luke and the Acts of the Apostles. Luke addressed him at the beginning of both books. Because Luke referred to him as "most excellent," Theophilus probably was an important official who would be able to share the letters with many people. Scholars believe he was a Gentile who took the name Theophilus when he became a Christian.

Where to find it: *Luke 1:3; Acts 1:1*

THESSALONIANS *(thess-uh-LOW-nee-uns),*
FIRST LETTER TO THE, is the thirteenth book of
the New Testament. Paul wrote it to the
church he had started in Thessalonica during
a stay of only three weeks (see *Thessalonica*).
His coworkers Silas (Silvanus) and Timothy
had been with him. Paul had been forced to
leave Thessalonica because of opposition
from Jewish leaders. He went on to Berea,
then Athens, and finally Corinth, but he sent
Timothy back to Thessalonica from Athens.
After Timothy returned to Paul in Corinth with
a good report of the new church in Thessalonica, Paul wrote this letter to the Thessalonians.

Paul began by saying how thankful he was
for these new Christians. He loved them and
admired the love they had for each other. But
he needed to correct some of their ideas. The
people of Thessalonica were so excited about
the promise of the Second Coming of the Lord
Jesus that some had even given up their jobs.
Paul wrote to tell them that no one knows for
sure when Christ will come again. Some
people will die before that day, but all Christians will share in the glory of Christ's return,
for God will raise them up when he comes.
Meanwhile, each person must live each day in
a way pleasing to the Lord. That's the best way
to prepare for his coming.

First Thessalonians is probably the earliest
letter from Paul that we have in the New Testament. It was written about A.D. 51.

Where to find it

The unexpectedness of the Lord's return   *1 Thessalonians 4: 13–5: 8*

THESSALONIANS, SECOND LETTER TO THE,
was the second letter to the new Christians at
Thessalonica from Paul and his coworkers Silvanus and Timothy. It was written a few
months after the first letter. Paul wrote to encourage these new Christians to remain faith-

ful to Christ. They were suffering harsh persecution. To keep them true, Paul said, "To this
end we always pray for you, that our God may
make you worthy of his call."

Then Paul told them more about the Second
Coming of Christ. This added to what he had
said in his first letter (see *Thessalonians, First
Letter to the*). He said that when Christ comes,
Christians will receive rest, and their perse-
cutors will be punished. Jesus will be glorified
in his saints, and all believers will be filled with
wonder.

He reminded them that no one knows when
Christ will return. Before he comes, there will
be even worse persecution. Someone who is
anti-Christ will bring lawlessness to the world.
Christians will suffer, but they must make a
habit of living as directed by God's Spirit.
That's how they will remain true both now and
in the last days.

For that reason the people at Thessalonica
were to encourage each other to live godly
lives. They were not to allow idleness. People
must work for a living. Those who didn't obey
this were to be gently shown their error.

Where to find it

Comfort in persecution   *2 Thessalonians 1: 5-11*
Understanding the Second Coming   *2 Thessalonians 2: 1-12*
Living the Christian life   *2 Thessalonians 2: 13–
3: 18*

THESSALONICA *(thess-uh-low-NYE-kuh)* was
the chief seaport of Macedonia. Sometimes
called Salonika, it is now the second largest
city in modern Greece.

In New Testament times it was an important
trade city. Paul visited there on a missionary
journey but had to leave after three weeks
because of persecution. However, the church
he started there grew vigorously. He later sent
Timothy to help the new Christians. A few
months after his visit, Paul wrote 1 and 2 Thessalonians to encourage the people and to explain to them some of the things that would
occur before Christ came again.

Where to find it: *Acts 17: 1-10*

THIEF is any person who takes what belongs
to another person. The Bible condemns stealing. The Old Testament Law required that captured thieves repay twice what they had sto-

len. If the thief could not pay, he could be sold into slavery.

In the New Testament stealing is also condemned. The most famous thieves in the Bible were those who were crucified with Jesus.

Where to find it: *Luke 23: 39-43*

THIGH *(thye)* in the Bible may refer to the upper part of the leg or the lowest part of the trunk of the body. Sometimes *thigh* is used as a word picture for the life-power of a person. Because the reproductive organs are located there, it was a sacred part to ancient people. When swearing to an oath, a person who was taking the oath would put his hand under the other person's thigh. This was saying, "Your life and your children's lives are involved in this oath." Abraham's servant made this kind of oath when he promised to look for the right wife for Abraham's son.

Where to find it: *Genesis 24: 9*

THISTLE, THORN (see *Plants*)

THOMAS *(TOM-us)* was one of Jesus' 12 disciples. He was also called Didymus, which probably meant he was a twin. Although he is most remembered for his doubting, the Gospels show he was deeply devoted to Jesus.

When Jesus went to Bethany to heal Lazarus, most of the disciples hesitated because they were afraid. They knew that Jewish leaders wanted to get rid of Jesus. Yet Thomas

"Put your finger here, and see my hands," Jesus said to convince Thomas that he really was alive.

said, "Let us also go, that we may die with him."

Later, Thomas showed his honesty and sincerity in the question he asked after Jesus foretold his coming crucifixion. Thomas asked, "Lord, we do not know where you are going; how can we know the way?"

Thomas was not with the other disciples when Jesus appeared after his resurrection. When Thomas heard about it, he said he would not believe unless he could see and feel Jesus' body himself. Yet as soon as Jesus appeared, Thomas was convinced. "My Lord and my God!" he said.

Where to find it

Ready to die with Jesus *John 11: 16*
Honest about not understanding *John 14: 5*
Doubting, then believing *John 20: 24-29*

THORN (see *Plants*)

THORN IN THE FLESH was the apostle Paul's description of a problem he asked God to remove. We are not sure what the trouble was, but most scholars feel it was some physical ailment, probably involving his eyesight. Paul dictated most of his letters and wrote only a postscript in his own handwriting.

Whatever it was, God did not take it away. Paul achieved great things for God in spite of this "thorn in the flesh."

Where to find it: *2 Corinthians 12: 7*

THORNS, CROWN OF (see *Crown of Thorns*)

THOUSAND YEARS (see *Millennium*)

THREE TAVERNS, or "Three Inns," was a village 33 miles from Rome. On Paul's journey to prison in Rome, he was met there by Roman Christians who came to greet him. He felt encouraged that they would come that distance to greet him.

Where to find it: *Acts 28: 15*

THRESHING separates ripe grains from their stems and husks.

If the farmer was threshing only a small amount of grain, he beat the sheaves of grain with a rod or flail. For a larger quantity, he spread the sheaves on a large outdoor floor of stone or clay that was packed hard and

Two rows of carved lions led up to Solomon's majestic throne.

smooth. Oxen pulled heavy wooden sleds over the grain. The pressure rubbed the kernels out of the husks. Then the farmer winnowed the grain by throwing it into the air so the wind would blow away the lighter chaff. The heavier grain fell back to the floor. If possible, farmers built their threshing floors on hilltops to catch the most wind.

In some countries, people still thresh grain this way.

THRESHOLD is the plank or stone that lies under the door of a building. Because crossing this threshold was a symbol of the power to enter, people often regarded the threshold as a sacred place.

THRONES are special chairs for kings or other heads of state on official occasions. Because rulers sit on thrones, *throne* is often used as a word picture for authority and power.

Thrones were often beautifully decorated. Solomon's throne was made of ivory and gold.

Old Testament worshipers thought of the ark of the Covenant as "God's throne." In visions, Isaiah, Ezekiel, Daniel, and John all saw God on his throne reigning over the earth. The New Testament also speaks of Jesus sitting on a throne to judge and rule the world, and believers reigning with him with justice and fairness.

Where to find it

Solomon's throne   *1 Kings 10:18-20*
God on his throne   *Isaiah 6:1-3; Ezekiel 1:4-28; Daniel 7:9-10; Revelation 4*
Jesus and believers reign   *Revelation 2:26-28; 3:21; 20:4-6*

THUMMIN (see *Urim and Thummin*)

THUNDER, SONS OF, is a nickname Jesus gave to two of his disciples, the brothers James and John. Perhaps it described their bold and sometimes reckless personalities.

Where to find it: *Mark 3:17; Luke 9:54; Matthew 20:20-23*

THUNDER AND LIGHTNING are common during spring and autumn in Israel but rare during summer. An electrical storm is vividly described in Psalms 29:7-8; 144:6; Matthew 24:27. When thunder and lightning appeared out of season, people thought they were signs of God's displeasure. Thunder and lightning reminded people of God's power, and thunder reminded them of his voice. Lightning was seen as his sword or spear.

THYATIRA

Where to find it

Sign of displeasure   *1 Samuel 12:17*
Voice of God   *Psalm 29:3-4; John 12:28-29*
God's spear   *Habakkuk 3:11*

THYATIRA *(THY-uh-TIE-ruh)* was a city in what is now western Turkey. It had one of the seven churches to which John wrote the New Testament Book of Revelation. He accused the church of permitting some of its people to eat meat offered to idols and to practice immorality. There were many pagan shrines in Thyatira, and some converts had not fully stopped their pagan practices. The Lord insisted that they worship him alone.

Where to find it: *Revelation 1:11; 2:18-29*

TIBERIAS *(tie-BEER-ee-us)* was a city on the southwest shore of the Sea of Galilee. Israel's puppet king, Herod Antipas, built it in about A.D. 20 to honor the Roman emperor Tiberius. Jesus apparently never visited it; in early years, mostly Gentiles lived there. However, after the fall of Jerusalem, it became a center for Jewish study.

Where to find it: *John 6:23*

TIBERIAS, SEA OF (see *Galilee, Sea of*)

TIBERIUS *(tie-BEER-ee-us)* was the Roman emperor during Jesus' adult life. He was the second emperor of the Roman Empire, reigning from A.D. 14 to 37. He was the stepson of Emperor Caesar Augustus. Because Tiberius was not directly related to Augustus, he was never very sure about his power. He constantly feared that others were trying to dethrone him.

He was also suspicious of non-Roman religions. He would not let Jewish people practice their religion in Italy. Many Jews were deported from Rome. Most of the references to "Caesar" in the Gospels mean Tiberius. He was probably the Caesar whose picture was stamped on the coin Jesus once told his questioners to look at.

Where to find it: *Luke 20:22-25*

TIGLATH-PILESER *(TIG-lath puh-LEE-zer)* was the name for several Assyrian kings. The most famous was Tiglath-pileser III, who became king in 745 B.C. and reigned until 727. He was a strong leader who made Assyria powerful. He was especially interested in capturing Syria and its capital, Damascus.

Ahaz, king of Judah, asked Tiglath-pileser for help in his war against Syria and the Northern Kingdom of Israel. Tiglath-pileser agreed to help. He captured several Israelite cities and took some Israelites captive back to cities in Assyria. He extended Assyrian rule into much of Israel.

Then, Damascus fell to him in 732. Civil war had made Babylon divided and weak. Tiglath-pileser conquered it and made himself king of Babylon in 729. He thus ruled over a great part of the then-known world.

Where to find it: *2 Kings 16:5-8; 15:29; 1 Chronicles 5:26*

TIGRIS *(TIE-griss)* **RIVER** is an important river about 1,150 miles long. It begins in mountains in Turkey, flows through modern-day Iraq, and empties into the Persian Gulf. The area between the Tigris and the Euphrates rivers is considered by many to be where civilization started.

TILES mentioned in the Bible were made of clay and baked in a furnace. Some kinds were used for writing. After the messages were written in soft clay tiles, they were baked in a furnace to make the writing permanent.

Tiles were also used on roofing, floors, and wall decorations of expensive homes and palaces.

Where to find it: *Luke 5:19*

TIMBREL (see *Musical Instruments*)

TIME was not the same to ancient people as it is to us. They did not have clocks to tick off exact minutes. Instead, they noticed changes in nature: the sun determined night and day; the moon measured months; the movement in the sun's pattern determined years. The hottest part of the day was noon. For many, many centuries, years were dated only in relationship to some great event, such as "two years before the earthquake" (Amos 1:1). This is one reason it is hard to know exact dates for the events recorded in the Bible.

Each country numbered its years from important dates in its own history. Some countries started their years in autumn, others in spring. Historians must match events in the Bible to events outside the Bible to figure out when something happened.

Although the Roman day began at midnight and was 12 hours long, the Hebrew day began at sunset and lasted 24 hours. In the New Testament, nighttime was divided into four "watches," according to the shifts when army guards and others had to stay awake for protection. That meant the length of each watch varied during the seasons, according to how long it was dark. Midnight was always in the second watch. Dawn was in the fourth. For example, Matthew 14:25 tells us of Jesus coming to the disciples at the "fourth watch." That is, he came just before or at dawn.

TIMOTHY (TIM-uh-thee) was a close friend and helper to the apostle Paul. He became the person Paul depended on the most to help churches that had problems. When Paul was in prison or faced other hardships, Timothy was the person he wanted most to see.

During the closing years of Paul's life, Timothy was in Ephesus, serving as pastor and leader of the churches there. Two books of the New Testament—1 and 2 Timothy—are letters that Paul wrote to Timothy at Ephesus.

The letters Timothy received from Paul are now part of our New Testament.

Things Paul wrote show that Timothy was naturally timid. But he apparently was so dependable and earnest in his work for God that he developed into an important leader in the early church.

Timothy was the son of a Gentile father and a Jewish mother, Lois. Paul called Timothy his "spiritual son." This probably meant that Paul helped Timothy become Christian.

Timothy joined Paul in Lystra on Paul's second missionary journey. After they were driven out of Thessalonica by Jewish persecution, Paul sent Timothy back to help the Christians there. Several times, Paul sent Timothy to churches as his representative.

Timothy was with Paul during much of his third missionary journey, too. The second letter of Paul to Timothy was probably written while Paul was in prison in Rome, shortly before his death. In it he wrote, "Do your best to come before winter."

Paul clearly expressed his opinion of Timothy in Philippians 2:19-24. "I have no one like him, who will be genuinely anxious for your welfare. . . . Timothy's worth you know, how as a son with a father he has served with me in the gospel."

Where to find it

Timothy's family   Acts 16:1-3; 2 Timothy 1:3-5
Timothy's strengths   Philippians 2:19-22; 1 Timothy 4:12-15

TIMOTHY, 1 and 2, are personal letters from the apostle Paul to Timothy, who was serving as pastor or overseer of the church (or churches) at Ephesus. Paul and Timothy had a deep friendship, and these letters are full of personal encouragement and advice from Paul to Timothy.

1 Timothy was probably written about A.D. 63, while Paul was in Philippi between his first and second imprisonments in Rome. He gave Timothy practical advice about qualifications for church officials, how to conduct worship, and how to deal with false teachings that come into the church. Paul also told Timothy what to do about some of the social problems in the church, such as the care of widows and children.

Paul explained again how God wants all people to be saved, and that Jesus is the mediator between God and people. He reminded him that Christ, the King of Kings, will come again.

2 Timothy is the last known letter of Paul before he was executed in Rome. Writing from prison about A.D. 64, Paul knew he was near the end of his life. He wrote about Christ as the conqueror of death, and the joy he was going to have in being with Christ.

He urged Timothy to come to see him if possible, but he also urged him to study the Scriptures, to be faithful in his work in Ephesus, and to live in a way that would glorify Christ. He warned Timothy that he probably would suffer persecution as Paul had.

TIN is a soft, silvery metal that does not corrode easily. It was first mixed with copper in late Old Testament times to make bronze.

TIRZAH *(TUR-zuh)* was a beautiful Canaanite town six miles east of Samaria. Joshua captured it when the Israelites conquered Canaan. Later it was the capital for the Northern Kingdom of Israel during the reigns of Jeroboam I, Baasha, Elah, and Zimri—about 40 years—until Omri moved the capital to Samaria.

Where to find it

Joshua conquers *Joshua 12:24*
Capital of Northern Kingdom *1 Kings 14:17; 15:21, 33; 16:6-18*
The beauty of Tirzah *Song of Solomon 6:4*

TITHE *(tieth)* means a tenth of one's income set aside for special use. Early in Bible times, people who worshiped God gave a tithe of their income as part of their worship. Abraham gave his tithe to Melchizedek, a priest of the Most High God. After the Law of Moses was established, Israelites were expected to give a tenth to support the priests, Levites, and needy people. The tithe was sometimes crops and animals, sometimes money. People who gave food as a tithe sometimes ate it with

the Levites in the place of worship after it had been offered to God.

In Jesus' time, the rule of tithing was strictly enforced for practicing Jews. In fact, the Pharisees insisted on tithing even the herbs they used to season their food. But they were not always fair in everyday dealing with others. For this, Jesus condemned them.

Christians are told to give regularly to God's work and to help others, because we love God and know he will supply our needs.

Where to find it

Abraham tithes *Genesis 14:17-20*
The law requires tithing *Deuteronomy 14:22-27; Malachi 3:8-10*
Pharisees strictly enforce tithing *Matthew 23:23; Luke 11:42*
Christians should give cheerfully *2 Corinthians 9:6-15*

TITTLE (see *Iota*)

TITUS *(TIE-tus)* was a friend and helper of the apostle Paul. He was a son of Greek parents, and he probably became a Christian after listening to Paul preach. Later, he went with Paul to Jerusalem to meet with Jewish Christians there. These Jewish Christians did not realize that a Gentile could become a Christian without becoming a Jew first. They wanted Titus to be circumcised as a sign that he accepted the Jewish religion. Paul said, "No, Titus does not have to be circumcised. He does not have to become a Jew first." This helped the new Christians realize that Christianity was larger than Judaism. In time, Titus became so well accepted that he was given many responsibilities among the early churches.

Later, Titus became a Christian leader or pastor of the church on the island of Crete. The church had many problems. Paul wrote a letter to him there. This letter, the Epistle to Titus, is a part of the New Testament.

Where to find it

A new Christian *Galatians 2:1-10*
A helpful worker *2 Corinthians 2:13; 7:5-16*
Christian leader *Titus 1–3*

TITUS *(TIE-tus)*, **LETTER TO,** is a letter from the apostle Paul to his friend Titus. Titus was a Christian leader or pastor on the island of Crete, where the church had many problems. Paul reminded Titus that pastors and leaders in a church must be holy people. They must be able to live happily with their own families if they are going to work happily with the larger church family. They must be honest in all they do and not be lazy. In chapter 1, verse 16, Paul warned Titus to watch out for hypocrites, who "profess to know God, but they deny him by their deeds."

The letter says Christ "gave himself for us to redeem us from all iniquity" and that the Holy Spirit has been given to us through Christ.

TITUS *(TIE-tus)*, **FLAVIUS VESPASIANUS,** was the son of the Roman emperor Vespasian, the next emperor after Nero. Titus led the army that destroyed Jerusalem in A.D. 70 and stopped the four-year revolt of the Jews. Nine years later he became emperor, although he reigned only two years. When he died in A.D. 81 at the age of 42, the Roman Senate declared him to be a god.

TOBIAH *(toe-BY-uh)* was the name of several men in the Old Testament. The most famous was the Tobiah who tried to stop Nehemiah from rebuilding the walls of Jerusalem.

Although he was called "the Ammonite," this Tobiah was probably part Jewish. His family married into important Jewish families. At one time, unknown to Nehemiah, the priest fixed up a room so Tobiah could live in the Temple.

The Bible does not say why Tobiah was against rebuilding the city, but he probably knew his influence would be less as the Jews became more faithful to God.

First Tobiah tried to stop the rebuilding by making fun of the work. He said the new wall was so flimsy that "if a fox goes up on it he will break down their stone wall."

Tobiah and his friend Sanballat also tried to arrange to have Nehemiah killed, but Nehemiah foiled their plans.

When Nehemiah found out Tobiah was liv-

ing in the Temple, he threw out all of Tobiah's belongings and ordered the Temple cleansed. Nehemiah rebuilt the city walls in spite of the efforts of Tobiah and Sanballat.

Where to find it: *Nehemiah 2: 10-20; 6: 10-19; 13: 4-9*

TOMB refers to a burial place, usually a natural or artificial cave. Early tombs were often natural caves in the rocky hills.

Lazarus may have been buried in this tomb.

Many of the heathen nations around Israel built fancy burial places. Although Hebrew burial places were simple, they were very important to them. Abraham paid 400 shekels of silver for the field and cave that became the family burial place. That would equal thousands of dollars in our money. Old Testament people often were buried in vaults or caves with their ancestors.

In New Testament times, Jews were buried in caves in stone cliffs. Several bodies might be in each tomb. Each body was wrapped in graveclothes and prepared with spices. One opening was the entrance to all the ledges prepared for the bodies.

Tombs in Rome were called catacombs.

181

These were large underground networks of caves and corridors. Niches in the walls served as ledges for bodies. Each niche could be sealed with bricks or a marble slab. When persecution was bad, early Christians hid in the catacombs.

TONGS were part of the Temple equipment. Priests used gold tongs to snuff out the candles burning in the Temple. In Isaiah's vision of God, he saw an angel using a tong to bring him a coal from the altar as he worshiped in the Temple.

Where to find it: *1 Kings 7:49; 2 Chronicles 4:21; Isaiah 6:6*

TONGUE in the Bible usually refers to the tongues in our mouths. Sometimes, however, it refers to a language, or the people who speak a certain language. In Isaiah 66:18, God talks of gathering together all nations and "tongues," meaning people of every language.

Tongue is sometimes a word picture for the acts of the whole person, especially what we say. Our words reveal our ideas and desires.

In James 3:1-12, the tongue is pictured as directing the whole person. It can do good or evil. We are told we must control our tongues (what we say) if we are to please God.

TONGUES OF FIRE were among the signs of the Holy Spirit's coming on the Day of Pentecost. All of the disciples, the brothers of Jesus, and some of the women followers of Jesus had gathered together in Jerusalem. Suddenly a sound like a mighty wind filled the house. Something like a tiny tongue of flame seemed to rest on each person in the room as they were all filled with the Holy Spirit (see *Pentecost*).

Where to find it: *Acts 1:14; 2:1-3*

TONGUES, GIFT OF, was one of the signs of the coming of the Holy Spirit on the Day of Pentecost. This miracle allowed the disciples and other believers to speak in languages they did not know. Visitors were amazed when they heard the Christians praising God, not in Greek or Aramaic, but in the visitors' own foreign languages.

They were so impressed that they listened carefully as the apostle Peter told how Old Testament prophecy was being fulfilled (see *Pentecost*).

Later another gift of tongues was given to Christians at Corinth and elsewhere. The speakers did not understand what they were saying themselves, but God knew how they felt and whether they were praying, praising him, or repeating some promise or truth.

Because this gift sometimes got out of order, Paul wrote that no one was to speak in a church service with this gift of tongues unless someone else was given a gift by God to tell what the sounds meant. Otherwise persons were to pray or praise God this way only when they were alone.

Where to find it

Pentecost *Acts 2:1-11*
Gift of tongues at Cornelius's house   *Acts 10:44-48*
Gift of tongues in church at Corinth   *1 Corinthians 14:1-33*

TORAH *(TOR-uh)* is the Hebrew word for the Law of God, and it refers to the first five books of the Old Testament. Other parts of the Old Testament Law were later also considered part of the Torah by the Jews. Taking care of the Torah was the responsibility of the Old Testament priests. Learning and reading the Torah is still important for Jewish people.

TOUCH was an important part of Jesus' healing ministry. It was a sign of his care and concern for the suffering. The Greek word does not mean a quick touch. It involves a firm contact like that in a long, friendly handshake.

Where to find it

Jesus touches a leper   *Matthew 8:3; Mark 1:41; Luke 5:13*
Jesus touches Peter's mother-in-law   *Matthew 8:15*
Jesus touches and blesses   *Mark 10:13; Luke 18:15*
Jesus touches a dumb tongue   *Mark 7:33*
Jesus touches blind eyes   *Matthew 9:29; 20:34*
Jesus touches a severed ear   *Luke 22:51*

TOWERS were common in ancient times as places of refuge or defense. Often they were at the corner or gate of a city. Some were large enough to hold all the people of a village. Others were large enough for only one soldier on lookout.

Tower is also a word picture for God's protective care.

Where to find it: *Psalm 61:3*

TOWER OF BABEL (see *Babel*)

TOWN CLERK (see *Occupations–Clerk*)

TRADE was important as early as Abraham's time. People traded food and furs for goods such as pottery and cloth at the local marketplace. Usually this was at a city gate. Sometimes each gate of a city was for one kind of item. Grains might be traded at one, livestock

at another. In ancient Jerusalem, potters had their workshops near the southern part of the city. Bakers had their own street.

In earliest times, all trade was done through barter. Later, metal pieces and jewelry began to be exchanged for products (see *Money*).

Gradually, trade with other countries and regions became important. Trade routes grew up between large cities, and small cities were born along these roads. As tradesmen made better products, their markets increased. They had more and more need for raw materials.

Ancient Israel exported mainly agricultural products. Olive oil, grains, resin, honey, dried nuts, wine, figs, raisins, and dates went at first to Egypt and Syria. Later Italy, Spain, and Asia Minor traded tin, lead, silver, and iron for Israel's goods. Israel produced some textiles but imported finer cloth from Egypt, Syria, and Phoenicia. When Solomon built the Temple, he traded widely to get the best materials. Much trade was carried on by sea, especially with the Phoenicians, but caravans across long land routes were also common.

By New Testament times, trade was regulated by Rome. Roman coins could buy products anywhere in the known world. Roman traders may have reached even India and Scandinavia. Israel was no longer an important trading country, except for the trade routes that crossed it.

Many cities in Asia Minor mentioned in the New Testament were important trade centers. Paul followed the usual trade routes on his missionary journeys, for they were the highways of his day. Many churches began in cities such as Thyatira and Laodicea that were famous for their trade.

Where to find it: *Revelation 18:11-19*

TRADE GUILDS really began in Roman times, when tradesmen of the same occupation began to band together for social and political purposes.

There were guilds of bakers, doctors, fishermen, bankers, embalmers, silversmiths, and more. It was usually necessary for persons in these trades to belong to the guilds—just as plumbers in our day, for example, usually must belong to a union.

Christians who belonged to the trade guilds sometimes had hard problems. At meetings where food was served, they might be expected to eat meat offered to idols—perhaps to the special god of that business. This may have been the case with people in the church at Thyatira, mentioned in the Book of Revelation.

Silversmiths in Ephesus who made pagan silver shrines opposed Paul. They started a riot because they were afraid of losing customers as people became Christians.

Where to find it: *Acts 19:23-41; Revelation 2:18-20*

TRADITION *(truh-DISH-un)* includes ideas

and customs passed from one generation to another by word of mouth, writing, or example. Traditions preserve the culture as well as the good and bad beliefs of people.

Jesus said the Pharisees sometimes paid more attention to man-made tradition than to obeying the principles of the Scriptures. Paul warned against false teachers who put their traditions higher than God's revelation in Christ.

Paul also said Christians should hold to the traditions he taught them.

Where to find it: *Matthew 15: 2-6; Mark 7: 3-8; Colossians 2: 8; 2 Thessalonians 2: 15*

TRAIN meant a group of followers who went with a ruler or commander and carried what was needed. When the queen of Sheba came to see Solomon, she had a train, or retinue, that included servants, camels, and probably soldiers to protect them. She brought gold, jewels, spices, and other things to trade with Solomon.

Where to find it: *1 Kings 10: 1-13*

TRANCE is mentioned in the Bible as a deep mental state in which a person received a message from God. The person in a trance may not have been conscious of where he was. Both Peter and Paul had trances in which God revealed messages directly to them.

Where to find it: *Acts 10: 9-16; 11: 5-10; 22: 17-21*

TRANSFIGURATION *(tranz-fig-yur-AY-shun)* means a change in form or appearance. The word is used to describe the time when a dramatic change took place in Jesus' physical appearance as three of his disciples watched.

Shortly before his last trip to Jerusalem, Jesus took Peter, James, and John to a high mountain. As Jesus was praying, his face began to shine like the sun. His clothes became dazzling white. Moses and Elijah appeared and talked with Jesus about his coming death.

Peter became so excited he said, "Master, it is well that we are here; let us make three booths, one for you and one for Moses and one for Elijah." But as Peter was speaking, a bright cloud surrounded them. A voice came from the cloud: "This is my beloved Son, with whom I am well pleased; listen to him."

The three disciples were overwhelmed. They kneeled with their faces touching the ground. But then Jesus came and touched them. "Rise, and have no fear," he said. When they opened their eyes, they saw Jesus—all alone. Jesus told them they were not to tell anyone what they had seen until after his resurrection.

Where to find it: *Matthew 17: 1-8; Mark 9: 2-8; Luke 9: 28-36*

TRANSGRESSION (see *Sin*)

TRANSLATE *(trans-LATE)* usually means to take an idea from one language and express it accurately in another. However, the King James Version uses *translated* in Colossians 1: 13 to mean "transferred" or "moved" from the kingdom of Satan to the Kingdom of Christ.

TRAVAIL *(TRAH-vail)* means very hard work. It is often used of the intense effort involved in giving birth to a baby. Sometimes it is used as a word picture of other hard work or agony of soul.

Where to find it: *Isaiah 53: 11; Galatians 4: 19*

TRAVEL in ancient times usually meant walking. As people and animals made the same trips over and over, they wore paths. As more and more walked, these paths became roads. When people traveled on foot or rode camels or donkeys, it didn't matter much if roads had rocks and pebbles or were overgrown with weeds. But by the time of King Solomon, horses and chariots were used in travel, and roads became trade routes. They had to be cleared and straightened. Good roads brought business to people along the way.

Caravans passed along the "king's highway," a road that ran south from Damascus and through Israel east of the Jordan River. Another road, "the way of the sea," passed the west coast of Lake Galilee on its way to the sea. It followed the Mediterranean shore south to Egypt. All this time, of course, the common people traveled by foot.

In Israel, all religious Jews made at least one trip every year to Jerusalem, usually at Passover time. From Galilee, it took several days to walk to Jerusalem. Thieves hid along the way to rob travelers.

By New Testament times the Romans had improved roads throughout the empire. Although the roads were safer, robbers still threatened. Jesus' story of the Good Samaritan shows how common robbery was.

When Jesus was born, the 75-mile trip from Nazareth to Bethlehem took five days' travel time. Mary and Joseph were required by Jewish Law to take the baby Jesus from Bethlehem to the Temple in Jerusalem—five miles away—before he was 40 days old. The trip they later took to Egypt was more than 200 miles each way. Although they probably had a donkey, they no doubt walked most of the way.

As Jesus grew, he made many trips from Nazareth to Jerusalem. His parents were devout Jews. They would go to the Temple several times a year. To avoid robbers and to make the trip more pleasant, many people walked together, singing and talking with each other. This is why Jesus' parents did not miss him on the trip back from Jerusalem when he was 12 years old.

There were many sailing ships on the seas. Their main purpose was to carry goods, but sometimes they carried passengers. When Jonah in the Old Testament and Paul in the New Testament wanted to take a ship, they looked for a cargo ship. They paid the captain to take them along. But the captain was always more interested in his cargo than in his passengers.

Paul is the best-known traveler in the Bible. His missionary journeys—by foot and by boat—are recorded in the Book of Acts (see *Missionary Journeys*). But other early Christians—Philip, Peter, Priscilla and Aquila—also moved around the known

Israelites used tree limbs to build small shelters for the Feast of Tabernacles each year.

world. Travel was not easy or pleasant for any of them.

Where to find it: *Luke 2:1-5, 22, 41-51; Matthew 2:13-15*

TREASURER (see *Occupations*)

TREASURE *(TREH-zhure)* means something of great value. In the Bible, Temple treasures included basins of silver and gold, garments of priests, altars, and all furnishings that had special meaning or were valuable to those seeking wealth.

Royal treasures of kings included gold, silver, jewels, and cattle. Conquering armies tried to take all the treasures they could.

Treasure is also a word picture of anything precious. Wisdom is called a treasure. We are told to store up "treasures" in heaven, where no thieves can steal them. Paul spoke of the gospel as a treasure.

Where to find it

Wisdom   *Proverbs 2:4*
Treasures in heaven   *Matthew 6:20-21*
The gospel   *2 Corinthians 4:7*

TREASURY is a place where valuable things are kept or placed. In the Temple where Jesus worshiped, tithes and taxes were paid at the treasury, or collection box. Jesus once sat near the treasury as he watched a poor widow bring her offering.

Treasury is also a word picture of God's grace. God opens his treasury and pours out good things for us.

Where to find it: *Deuteronomy 28:12; Mark 12:41*

TREASURE CITIES (see *Store Cities*)

TREES were plentiful in some parts of ancient Palestine and scarce in others. There are more than 300 references to trees in the Bible. Scholars have identified more than 25 kinds of trees that grew there. Israelites used tree limbs to build booths or small shelters for the Feast of Tabernacles each year.

The people often waved branches of palm trees, willows, and leafy trees as a sign of rejoicing.

Some groves of trees were used as places of pagan worship. During the years between A.D. 70 and 1900, most trees in Palestine were cut down. Thousands of new trees have been planted in Israel since 1948. (For names of specific trees, see *Plants.*)

TREE OF KNOWLEDGE was a special tree that grew in the middle of the Garden of Eden. God commanded Adam and Eve not to eat its fruit, because they would then know good and evil—they would know what sin was. But Adam and Eve did eat some of the tree's fruit. Then they knew that sin was disobeying God's command. After they ate, they were ashamed both of what they did and of who they were. Their sin led to death for themselves and all people since then.

Where to find it: *Genesis 2:8–3:7*

TREE OF LIFE is a special tree mentioned at the very beginning and the very end of the Bible. In the Garden of Eden, the tree was a symbol of everlasting life for Adam and Eve. The fruit of another tree in the garden, the Tree of Knowledge, was forbidden to Adam and Eve. But they disobeyed God and ate the fruit of the Tree of Knowledge. They were then put out of the garden so they could not eat the fruit of the Tree of Life.

The Tree of Life and its fruit stand for a life free from sin, from sorrow, and from death. Adam and Eve (and all of us) lost that kind of life because of sin.

The Book of Revelation tells about the Tree of Life growing close to God's throne in the new heaven and new earth. Its fruit brings healing, wholeness, and everlasting fellowship with God.

Where to find it: *Genesis 2: 9; 3: 22-25; Revelation 22: 1-2*

TRESPASS *(TRES-pass)* means to go against the rights of someone else. We may trespass against our neighbors by breaking laws. We may trespass against God by breaking God's Law.

In Jewish law, trespassers had to pay the value of what they had stolen or damaged plus one-fifth to the person whose property was stolen or damaged. The trespasser also had to bring to the Temple a special trespass offering (see *Offerings*).

When we trespass against God's law, we sin against God and suffer the penalty of sin—separation from God. Christ came to pay the penalty for our sin so that we can have fellowship with God.

Where to find it: *Leviticus 6: 1-7; Romans 5: 15-17; Galatians 6: 1*

TRESPASS OFFERING (see *Offerings*)

TRIAL OF JESUS was in two parts—first before the Jewish leaders, then before the Roman authorities.

After his arrest in the Garden of Gethsemane, Jesus was immediately brought to Jerusalem, to the court of the religious authorities called the Sanhedrin. Caiaphas, the high priest, was in charge of the trial. Caiaphas and his followers were jealous of Jesus and his popularity with the people. They feared an uprising against the Romans that would destroy their influence. They found people who would tell lies about Jesus so they could have an excuse to get rid of him. As people accused him, Jesus remained silent.

Finally the high priest said to Jesus: "Are you the Christ, the Son of the Blessed?"

Jesus answered, "I am." By saying this, Jesus affirmed that he was the Son of God. The Jews considered this blasphemy, and for blasphemy a man should be put to death.

Caiaphas tore his robe as he said to the Sanhedrin, "You have heard his blasphemy. What is your decision?"

"He deserves death!" they answered. They and the guards spit at Jesus, hit him, and made fun of him.

But the Jewish government had only limited power under Rome. These leaders could not execute Jesus. So the Sanhedrin sent him to Pilate, the Roman governor. There they accused Jesus of treason—of saying he was a king.

To the Romans this would be a serious crime, for it could mean Jesus was trying to stir up a rebellion.

Roman soldiers were ordered to crucify Jesus.

187

"Are you the King of the Jews?" Pilate asked Jesus.

"You have said so," Jesus answered. Jesus stayed silent during the rest of the questioning. Pilate didn't think Jesus was a threat to the emperor, but Pilate did not want the Jewish leaders to be angry at him. So he thought of a way to sidestep the problem. Jesus was from Galilee—an area under the rule of a half-Jewish puppet king named Herod Antipas. Herod happened to be in Jerusalem right then, so Pilate sent Jesus to him.

But Herod only sent him back. Then Pilate had another idea. During the Passover feast, the custom was to release a Jewish prisoner. If the Jews chose Jesus for release, it would solve his problem.

But the crowd was stirred up by the Jewish leaders. The people shouted, "Release to us Barabbas." Barabbas was a murderer and a revolutionary.

"Then what shall I do with Jesus who is called Christ?" asked Pilate.

"Crucify, crucify him," screamed the mob. Pilate tried whipping Jesus. He hoped this cruelty would be enough for the crowd. But even when the people saw Jesus beaten and bleeding, they ranted on. They wanted him dead.

Pilate washed his hands to try to show the guilt was not his. Then he delivered Jesus to be crucified.

Where to find it: *Matthew 26: 57–27: 26; Mark 14: 53–15: 15; Luke 22: 54–23: 25; John 19: 1-15*

TRIBE, in ancient times, referred to all the people who descended from the same ancestor. The smallest unit of people was a household, or the immediate family. A clan was a group of closely related families—uncles, aunts, cousins—and a tribe was all the clans that traced their families back to that one ancestor. When tribes grouped together, they became a nation.

Each of the 12 tribes of Israel descended from one of the 12 sons of Israel (formerly called Jacob), Abraham's grandson. During the time of David and Solomon, these tribes joined together to form a great nation. At other times they argued and were divided. After the fall of Samaria in 722 B.C. and the exile of many Israelites to Assyria, the tribal distinctions became less important.

TRIBULATION *(trib-u-LAY-shun)* is another word for misery, oppression, sorrow, or trouble. Jesus said Christians would have tribulation because of their faith. Paul said that "through many tribulations we must enter the Kingdom of God" (see *Tribulation, Great*).

Where to find it: *John 16: 33; Acts 14: 22*

TRIBULATION, GREAT, has occurred whenever anyone is put to death for Christ. There will be a final great tribulation when Satan and many people will be intensely angry at God's people and will persecute and kill many of them, blaspheming God as they do. But throughout this time of terrible trouble, God's plans for the earth will be accomplished. Many will stay true to God, and God will finally destroy Satan and his angels.

Where to find it: *Revelation 13; 14: 12-13*

TRIBUTE *(TRIB-yoot)* was usually money or service paid by a weaker nation to a stronger nation. In return, the stronger nation agreed not to invade and sometimes provided some protection and peace. Throughout their history Israel and Judah either paid or received tribute from each other or other surrounding nations, depending on which nations were stronger or weaker.

TRINITY *(TRIN-uh-tee)* is a word to show that God is a unique Being. He shows himself as Father, Son, and Holy Spirit. While the word *trinity* is not found in the Bible, the idea is there.

In the Great Commission, Jesus told his disciples to baptize people so that in their baptism they declare their loyalty to the triune God—"in the name of the Father, and of the Son, and of the Holy Spirit."

These three persons in the Godhead are one in power and glory. They differ only in their functions during different times in history. With our human minds we cannot understand God in all his greatness, and so we do not clearly understand the Trinity.

Where to find it

Old Testament glimpses of the Trinity *Psalms 51: 11; 110: 1; Isaiah 63: 10-11; Jeremiah 33: 15-16*
New Testament glimpses of the Trinity *Matthew 28: 19; John 1: 1-8; 1 Corinthians 12: 4-6; 2 Corinthians 13: 14; Hebrews 1: 2-3*

TRIUMPH (*TRY-umff*) in ancient times was a parade in honor of a victorious general. He entered the city in a magnificent procession, riding in a chariot, leading captives in chains. When the Bible talks of God's triumph, it means all the true glory that goes with his victory over evil.

Where to find it: *2 Corinthians 2:14; Colossians 2:15*

TRIUMPHAL ENTRY was Jesus' kingly entrance into Jerusalem on the Sunday before his crucifixion. He came riding a colt, a sign that he was on a mission of peace, not war. Conquering generals rode on a horse or in a chariot.

Earlier on the day of Christ's entry, the disciples had found the colt just as Jesus had predicted. They had said to its owners, "The Lord has need of it," and the owners had given it to them without question.

As Jesus entered the city from the Mount of Olives, his followers shouted and sang, "Blessed is the King who comes in the name of the Lord!" Some cut palm branches and laid

When you stand on the Mount of Olives today, this is how the city of Jerusalem looks.

them as a carpet for the colt to walk on. Some even spread their clothes in the road. Their enthusiasm filled the city. Each Palm Sunday we remember that day.

Where to find it: *Matthew 21:1-11; Mark 11:1-11; Luke 19:28-44; John 12:12-19*

TROAS (*TROW-as*) was an important city in New Testament times located near the Aegean Sea in what is now Turkey. Paul visited this Roman colony at least three times but never stayed long. Here Paul received a vision calling him to Macedonia. This vision caused him to take the gospel into Europe.

Later Paul came again to Troas and preached so late into the night that a young man sitting on a windowsill fell asleep and fell out of the third-floor window to the ground! (See *Eutychus*.)

On a later visit he left a cloak and some books in Troas, which he asked Timothy to bring to him in his prison in Rome.

Where to find it: *Acts 16:8-9; 20:5-12; 2 Timothy 4:13*

TROPHIMUS (*TROF-uh-mus*) was a Gentile Christian from Ephesus who traveled with Paul from Troas to Jerusalem. They carried the offering the churches in Greece and Asia (now Turkey) had collected for the needy Christians in Jerusalem.

When some Jews saw a Gentile in Jerusalem with Paul, they became very upset. They assumed that Paul had brought Trophimus into the part of the Temple where no Gentiles were allowed. The Jews became so angry they tried to kill Paul, but soldiers arrived in time to save him.

Trophimus apparently traveled more with Paul. When Paul was in prison in Rome, he wrote to Timothy that he had left Trophimus sick at Miletus.

Where to find it: *Acts 20:3-6; 21:29-40; 2 Timothy 4:20*

TRUMPET (see *Musical Instruments*)

TRUMPETS, FEAST OF (see *Feast of New Moon*)

TRUTH in the Old Testament usually means firm, consistent reliability and righteousness. Truth is a quality of God. Because he is reliable and righteous, people can depend on him. The Greek word for truth in the New Testament sometimes has this same meaning.

Sometimes *truth* in the New Testament means that which is genuine and complete in contrast to that which is false or incomplete. The gospel is called "the word of truth." Jesus called himself "the truth."

A few times, *truth* means something authentic or real in contrast to something that is only a copy. Jesus said he is the "true" bread. He also spoke of "true" (genuine or real) worshipers.

Where to find it

True worshipers   *John 4:23*
Jesus is the truth   *John 6:32, 35; 14:6*
Reliability and righteousness   *Romans 15:8; Ephesians 5:9*
The gospel   *Galatians 2:5; Ephesians 2:5*

TUMORS (see *Diseases*)

TUNIC *(TOO-nik)* was a loose body garment, with or without sleeves, reaching to the knees. Usually it was worn as an undergarment (see *Clothing*).

TURBAN *(TER-bun)* was a man's ornamental head covering, made by twisting a long piece of fine linen around the head several times. Priests and kings wore turbans in Bible times. They removed the turbans during periods of mourning.

TURTLEDOVE (see *Birds*)

TUTOR is the King James Version word for "guardian" in Galatians 4:2.

TYCHICUS *(TICK-uh-cuss)* was a close friend and helper of Paul. He traveled with Paul to Jerusalem to carry the gift of money from the other churches to the poor Christians there. He was probably the man who delivered the letters Paul wrote to the churches at Colossae and Ephesus.

Tychicus was with Paul during his first and second imprisonments in Rome. When Paul asked Timothy to come to Rome, he sent Tychicus to Ephesus as a replacement.

Paul also sent Tychicus or another man to Crete to take the place of Titus for a while.

Where to find it: *Ephesians 6:21; Colossians 4:7-9; 2 Timothy 4:12; Titus 3:12*

TYRANNUS *(tuh-RAN-us)* was a teacher in Ephesus for whom a school hall was named. Paul preached in this hall for two years, probably in the afternoons when regular school was not in session. Scholars do not know whether Tyrannus was alive at the time or whether he was a former teacher for whom the building was named.

Where to find it: *Acts 19:9*

TYRE *(tire)* was an island city along the coast of what is now Lebanon. About 50 miles north of Nazareth, Tyre was a center of trade in ancient times and was famous for the purple dyes produced there.

Ships from Tyre sailed all around the Mediterranean.

During some of the Old Testament period, Tyre was a kingdom by itself and threatened Israel. Later Tyre fell to Assyria, then Egypt, Babylonia, and Persia. Three chapters of the Book of Ezekiel prophesy the fall of Tyre.

When Alexander the Great conquered Tyre in 333 B.C., he built a long breakwater that connected the island city to the mainland. Tyre was still a center of trade in Roman times. Modern Tyre is on the mainland of Lebanon, across from the ancient island city.

Jesus once visited the area of Tyre and healed the daughter of a Greek woman.

Paul once stayed there for seven days with Christians. When he left, he and the Christians from Tyre, including children, had a prayer meeting together on the beach.

Where to find it: *Ezekiel 26–28; Mark 7:24-31; Acts 21:3-7*

Ur of the Chaldees, where Abraham grew up, was famous for its worship of the moon-god.

U

UNCIRCUMCISED (see *Circumcision*)

UNCLEAN refers to thoughts, acts, people, places, and foods that are displeasing to God. Either they are contrary to God's specific commands, or they involve moral wrongdoing.

In the Old Testament, *unclean* usually referred to certain meat that the Israelites were forbidden to eat, or to people who were "unclean" because they had touched a dead body, had bodily discharges, or had leprosy.

Unclean foods in the Old Testament were certain meats. Animals were considered good for food and therefore "clean" if they both chewed the cud and had parted hoofs. These included oxen, sheep, goats, and deer. Animals or birds that fed on dead animals were not to be eaten. Such unclean birds of prey included the vulture, sea gull, hawk, ostrich, and bat.

Only fish with fins and scales could be eaten; crabs, eels, and clams were forbidden.

Insects that had two legs for leaping as well as four regular legs were considered clean. This meant most insects such as grasshoppers could be eaten, but no others. All lizards were considered unfit to eat as well as rodents and other animals with four paws.

Even clean animals could become unclean. The Hebrews could not eat any animal that died of natural causes or had been killed by another animal.

A person could become unclean for several reasons. Anyone who touched a dead person was unclean for seven days and had to have special washings on the third and seventh days to become clean again. A woman who had a baby was unclean for a week or two weeks, depending on the sex of the baby. Then she had to offer a young pigeon or a turtledove as a sacrifice.

Bodily discharges in men or women made them unclean. Special bathing and clothes washing was necessary to be considered clean once more.

Persons with leprosy were called unclean and were separated from all other people. They had to wear torn clothes and cry, "Unclean, unclean," whenever someone without leprosy came near them. If the person was cured of leprosy, he or she offered certain sacrifices in order to be clean again.

After Christ died and rose again, these regulations about uncleanness faded away. God sent a special vision to Peter to show him that all foods were now "clean." In Acts 15: 28-29, only four restrictions were given to new Christians: eat no food offered to idols, eat no blood, eat no animal that has been strangled, and keep away from sexual immorality (see *Council of Jerusalem*).

The prophets also sometimes spoke about unclean thoughts. Isaiah said he lived among people with "unclean lips," referring to thoughts and words that were contrary to the holiness of God.

In the New Testament, *uncleanness* refers either to such things as eating wrong foods or to moral sins. Jesus cast out unclean spirits (demons), who caused people to do evil.

Where to find it
Clean and unclean foods *Leviticus 11*
What made people unclean *Leviticus 12, 15; Numbers 9: 1-13*
Leprosy and skin diseases *Leviticus 13–14*
Moral uncleanness *Isaiah 6: 5; Galatians 5: 19-21; Ephesians 5: 5*
Unclean spirits of demons *Matthew 10: 1; Mark 3: 11*

UNFORGIVABLE SIN is mentioned several times in the New Testament. Jesus said, "Whoever speaks against the Holy Spirit will not be forgiven, either in this age or in the age to come."

The work of the Holy Spirit is to make people aware of who Christ is and how our sins can be forgiven through him. If a person throughout his life "speaks against" the Holy Spirit, he is saying he does not want Christ's remedy for his sin. For this reason, his sin is unforgivable, because he is refusing the cure or the forgiveness that Christ came to make possible.

John 3: 16, 18 says that a person who believes in Jesus has eternal life, and "he who believes in him is not condemned; he who does not believe is condemned already."

Where to find it: *Matthew 12: 32; Mark 3: 29; Luke 12: 10; Hebrews 10: 26-29; 1 John 5: 16*

UNITY *(YOU-nit-ee)* refers to people having a feeling of oneness with each other. Psalm 133: 1 says, "How good and pleasant it is when brothers dwell in unity!"

Christians are told to "maintain the unity of the Spirit in the bond of peace." This does not mean that everyone has to think alike in everything or be alike. Ephesians 4: 2-4 explains that unity comes when we are humble instead of proud, show consideration to each other, and are loving and patient with each other's faults.

To develop "unity of the faith and of the knowledge of the Son of God" is a part of our becoming mature, like Christ. We develop unity as we learn all we can about our faith and try to live in day-by-day fellowship with Christ.

Where to find it: *Psalm 133: 1-3; Romans 15: 5-6; Ephesians 4: 2-13; Philippians 2: 1-5; 1 Peter 3: 8*

UNKNOWN GOD were the words the apostle Paul found on an altar in Athens, Greece. Among the many altars in the city, he saw this one built "To an Unknown God." Paul told the people their unknown God was the one who had raised Jesus from the dead.

Where to find it: *Acts 17: 23*

UNLEARNED *(un-LERND)* is what Jewish religious leaders called Peter and John because they had not been trained as priests, scribes, or rabbis.

In other parts of the New Testament, *unlearned* refers to people who knew little or nothing about the gospel of Christ or who didn't care to know what it really teaches.

Where to find it: *Acts 4: 13; 1 Corinthians 14: 16, 23; 2 Peter 3: 16 (all KJV)*

UNLEAVENED *(un-LEV-und)* **BREAD** is bread made without yeast. Unleavened bread does not rise. On the night of the Passover, the Hebrews prepared a quick meal of roasted lamb and unleavened bread. They took some of the unleavened dough with them in their packs. At the Passover feast, which is still observed today by Jews, they eat unleavened bread to remind them of how God delivered his people out of Egypt.

Where to find it: *Exodus 12: 1-28*

expected it. Because he was first a persecutor of the Christians, he felt he did not deserve to be born into God's family at all, except by God's mercy.

Where to find it: *1 Corinthians 15: 8*

UPPER ROOM is the place where Jesus had his last supper with the disciples before his crucifixion. It may have been the same upper

After a special meal and a long talk, Jesus and his disciples left the upper room.

room where the disciples met together to pray after Jesus ascended into heaven.

It probably was a second-floor room built on the flat roof of the home of a friend of Jesus. Such rooms were commonly used as guest rooms and often had outside stairways.

Where to find it: *Mark 14: 12-25; Luke 22: 7-13; Acts 1: 12-14*

UPRIGHT (see *Righteousness*)

UNPARDONABLE SIN (see *Unforgivable Sin*)

UNTIMELY BIRTH means a miscarriage or premature birth of a baby.

The apostle Paul used *untimely birth* as a word picture to describe how he was born spiritually into the family of God when no one

UR was the city where Abraham was born and grew up. It was near the north end of the Persian Gulf in what is now Iraq.

Ur was a center of advanced learning in Abraham's day; it had libraries, schools, and many temples to pagan gods. The people

193

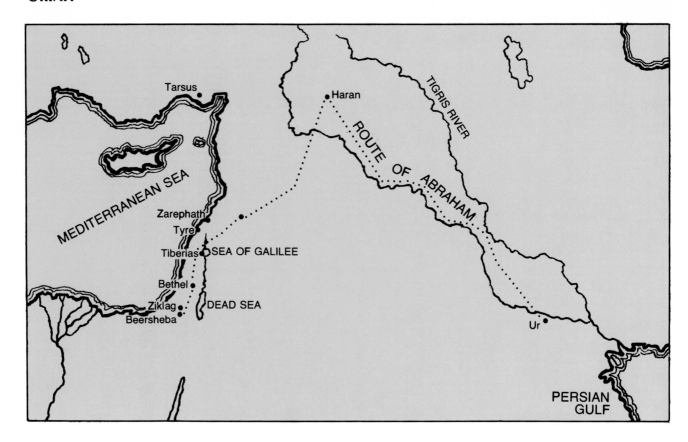

worshiped the moon-god Nanna. They built a large temple and tower (called a ziggurat) to their god. People also kept small idols in their homes. These things are not mentioned in the Bible, but archaeologists discovered them as they dug up the ruins of the old city.

Ur was also a trading center. Ships carried alabaster, copper ore, ivory, gold, and hard woods to trade at Ur.

God called Abraham out of Ur and sent him to the land of Canaan.

Where to find it: *Genesis 11:28, 31; 15:7; Nehemiah 9:7*

URIAH *(your-EYE-uh)* the Hittite was the husband of Bathsheba and a loyal soldier in King David's army. When King David committed adultery with Bathsheba, she became pregnant. David used several tricks to try to make it look as though Bathsheba's baby was Uriah's baby. But the tricks didn't work.

Finally, David told the commander of his army to put Uriah in the front lines, where he would be likely to be killed. Uriah was killed, and David later married Bathsheba, but he was punished by God for his sin.

Where to find it: *2 Samuel 11:1–12:15*

URIJAH *(you-RYE-juh)* is the name of two Old Testament men:

1. A prophet who said the nation of Judah would be punished for its sins. King Jehoiakim became so angry he tried to kill him. Urijah fled to Egypt, but the king's men found him, brought him back, and killed him.

2. A priest during the reign of King Ahaz. King Ahaz had Urijah build an altar patterned after one Ahaz had seen in Damascus.

Where to find it

The prophet *Jeremiah 26:20-23*
Ahaz's priest *2 Kings 16:10-16*

URIM AND THUMMIM *(YOU-rim and THUM-im)* were objects—perhaps stones—that were carried in the breastplate of the chief priest. They were used in some unknown way to find the will of the Lord concerning the nation, as in military battles.

Where to find it: *Exodus 28:30; Leviticus 8:8; Numbers 27:21; 1 Samuel 14:41; Ezra 2:63*

USURY *(USE-your-ee)* means charging for the use of money. We call it interest charges on loans or charge accounts.

In the Old Testament, the Hebrews were told not to charge interest to other Hebrews, because those who borrowed were usually poor. Hebrews were supposed to share what they had with their poor. However, they could charge interest to non-Hebrews.

When the Jews were in exile in Babylon, they ignored God's commands about helping the poor and not charging interest. When they returned with Nehemiah to rebuild the walls of Jerusalem, they kept on charging interest on loans. Nehemiah urged them to stop.

In the New Testament, most businesses charged interest. Jesus did not condemn this practice in his parable of the owner who gave his servants money to invest.

Where to find it

Commands against charging interest *Exodus 22:25; Deuteronomy 23:19*
Jews are condemned for charging interest *Nehemiah 5:10-11; Ezekiel 18:5-13*
Jesus' story about investing money *Matthew 25:14-30*

UZZAH *(UZZ-uh)* was a Hebrew who died suddenly after he touched the ark of the Covenant. (The Old Testament Law in Numbers 4:15 said no one was to touch it.)

The ark had been kept in Kiriath-jearim, in the house of Abinadab, Uzzah's father. King David wanted to bring it to Jerusalem, the capital of Israel, so he and many Israelites went to Kiriath-jearim to get it. They put the ark on a new cart pulled by oxen. Uzzah and his brother, Ahio, drove the cart.

During the journey, the oxen stumbled, and Uzzah reached out to steady the ark. He died immediately.

David and the other Israelites were too frightened to take the ark on to Jerusalem. They left it at another man's house for three months before they came back to get it.

Where to find it: *2 Samuel 6:1-7; 1 Chronicles 13:1-14*

UZZIAH *(uh-ZIE-uh)* was the eleventh king of Judah. He is called Azariah in 2 Kings. After his father, Amaziah, was assassinated, the people of Judah chose Uzziah as king. He began to reign when he was 16 and ruled for 52 years.

He developed a strong army that defeated the Philistines and other enemies. He had helmets, shields, spears, and bows made especially for his soldiers. He ordered skillful men to invent machines that could shoot arrows and stones from the towers of his cities.

He also built wells and improved the land.

One of several prophets named Zechariah instructed King Uzziah in the ways of God, and for a while Uzziah followed the Lord. But later he became proud. Once he entered the Temple to offer incense like a priest. The high priest and 80 other priests tried to stop him.

Uzziah became angry at the priests and picked up the censer in front of the altar of incense. At that moment, Uzziah broke out with leprosy on his forehead. After that, he had to live in a separate house away from other people until he died.

Where to find it: *2 Kings 14:17-22; 15:1-5; 2 Chronicles 25:25–26:23*

King Ahab could not keep his eyes off Naboth's vineyard next door and finally had him killed in order to get it.

V

VAIN sometimes means conceited. Galatians 5:26 tells Christians not to boast—"Let us not be desirous of vainglory" (King James Version).

In other places *vain* may mean empty or worthless. Matthew 6:7 says the heathen pray "vain repetitions." Their prayers are meaningless sounds.

Exodus 20:7 forbids taking the Lord's name in vain. Here *vain* means in an empty way, or not meaning what we say.

VANITY *(VAN-it-ee)* means emptiness and worthlessness. The word *vanity* is used many times in the Book of Ecclesiastes. A common phrase in this book is "Vanity of vanities; all is vanity." The writer is saying that life seems empty and worthless to him.

Christians are told not to live like unbelievers, whose minds are filled with worthless thoughts, "in the vanity of their mind" Ephesians 4:17 (King James Version).

VASHTI *(VASH-tee)* was the beautiful wife of Ahasuerus (also called Xerxes I), the pagan king of Persia from about 485 to 465 B.C.

196

During the third year of Ahasuerus's reign, he held a huge banquet for the princes and army chiefs in his kingdom. There was much drinking and merriment. On the seventh day of the feast, when the king and many of the guests were quite drunk, the king ordered Queen Vashti to come and show off her beauty to the men.

Queen Vashti was having a separate banquet for the women, and she refused.

The king and his counselors were very angry. They said Vashti was setting a bad example for other wives, who might think they, too, could disobey their husbands. (In that time, wives were thought of as part of their husband's possessions.)

They advised King Ahasuerus to remove Vashti from being queen and look for a new queen to take her place. The king followed their advice and chose Esther as the new queen (see *Esther*).

Where to find it: *Esther 1: 5-20*

VEILS *(vales)* in the Old Testament were thin scarves or shawls covering the face. They were usually worn by women. Rebekah covered herself with a veil before she met Isaac. Tamar tricked Judah, her father-in-law, by disguising herself with a veil.

Moses' face shone brightly after he received the Ten Commandments on Mount Sinai, and he hid his face behind a veil. The apostle Paul used the idea of Moses' veil as a word picture of something that hides the truth.

The Revised Standard Version and some other translations speak of veils in 1 Corinthians 11: 2-10, where Paul gave instructions about how men and women were to pray and prophesy in public meetings. The Greek word for *veil* is not used, however; instead, there are phrases such as "down from the head" and "authority upon the head." So we are not sure whether Paul was referring to some sort of head covering or perhaps a particular long hairstyle.

Where to find it: *Genesis 24: 65; 38: 14; Exodus 34: 33-35; 1 Corinthians 11: 2-10; 2 Corinthians 3: 12-16*

VEIL OF THE TEMPLE was a pair of thick curtains about 18 inches apart that hung at the entrance of the Holy of Holies in the Temple.

The veil hid the ark of the Covenant and the mercy seat from the view of the people (also see *Temple*).

The curtains were woven with blue, purple, and scarlet thread with pictures of cherubim worked into them.

In the early days, no one could go behind the veil except the Levitical priests. Later, only the high priest could enter behind the veil, and even he could go only once a year—on the Day of Atonement.

At Jesus' death, the veil in the Temple was ripped by a miracle from top to bottom. This act showed that because of Christ's death, all people could now come into God's presence by faith in Jesus Christ.

Where to find it

Construction of the veil   *Exodus 26: 31-33; 36: 35*
Priests only   *Numbers 18: 7; Leviticus 16: 2-28*
The veil rips   *Matthew 27: 51; Mark 15: 38*
We have access   *Hebrews 10: 20*

VENGEANCE *(VEN-jens)* means punishment for wrongdoing. In Old Testament times, a relative of a murdered person was supposed to kill the murderer.

But the New Testament tells Christians not to try and punish those who have wronged them. They are to trust the Lord instead. "Vengeance is mine, I will repay, says the Lord." God is the only one who can punish justly.

Where to find it: *Genesis 9: 5-6; Deuteronomy 32: 35; Romans 12: 19; 2 Thessalonians 1: 8*

VERSIONS OF THE BIBLE refers to translations of the Bible from its original languages (Hebrew, Aramaic, Greek) to languages of today.

New versions of the Bible are written to help make the meaning clear. Through the last five centuries, people have translated the Bible into many languages.

The Old Testament was first written in Hebrew. The Septuagint version of the Old Testament was used in Jesus' day. It was a translation into Greek from the Hebrew (see *Septuagint*).

The New Testament was written first in Greek. By A.D. 250, both Old and New Testaments had been translated into Latin. But it was a poor translation. In A.D. 382, a scholar named Jerome began work on a revision. His work became known as the Latin Vulgate Bible. This was the translation used by the Roman Catholic Church for more than 1,500 years.

After Latin began to die as a language, some Christians believed the Bible was needed in the languages that people spoke. John Wycliffe translated the first English version of the Bible in A.D. 1382. He wanted the average person to be able to read and understand the Bible. His version was based on Jerome's Latin Vulgate.

After the printing press was invented, William Tyndale made a translation of the Bible that was printed in 1525. Many religious leaders did not believe common people should be able to read the Bible in their own language. They tried to stop Tyndale, but he paid no attention. He made another translation of the Bible, this time based on the Hebrew and Greek copies of the Bible.

In 1604, King James of England ordered that a new translation be made of the whole Bible, working from the original Greek and Hebrew as much as possible. He appointed 54 scholars to do the work. The King James Version was completed in 1611 and is still read widely today.

Since that time, many other versions of the Bible have been written. Some of the best known are the Revised Standard Version, the Good News Bible, the Living Bible, and the New International Version.

In 1947 the Dead Sea Scrolls were found. These included some Old Testament writings dated 200 B.C. to A.D. 100. These have been a great help in bringing modern translations closer to the original writings of the Bible.

VESSELS are containers made to hold liquids or dry materials. In Bible times, vessels were made from pottery, straw, metals, leather, cloth, and wood.

Pottery was the most common. Baskets, metal containers, leather buckets and pouches, and cloth, wooden, and stone containers were also common. Vessels made of alabaster often held perfume.

Leather was used for buckets to draw water from the wells. Leather vessels were used for wine.

In the New Testament, the word *vessel* is sometimes used as a word picture of people. 2 Timothy 2:21 speaks of a purified person as "a vessel for noble use." 1 Peter 3:7 in the King James Version uses "weaker vessel" to mean woman.

VESTMENTS *(VEST-ments)* means clothing.

VICTUALS *(VIT-uls)* is a word used often in the King James Version to mean food (see *Food*).

VILLAGES were usually located near larger cities. The villagers fled to the city in times of war. A village had no walls around it; it was only a cluster of small, one-room houses, often made of mud or grass.

Villages in Palestine today sometimes look a lot like they did in earlier times.

In the New Testament, a village was sometimes defined as a place without a synagogue.

VINDICATE *(VIN-di-kate)* means to justify or to defend the actions of a person. Jesus told the parable of a widow who begged a judge to protect her rights from an enemy. In vindicating her, the judge would punish her enemy and protect her rights, thus showing that she was in the right.

Writers of the psalms often cried to God to vindicate them.

Where to find it: *Psalm 54:1; Luke 18:3-8*

VINES grow grapes in **VINEYARDS** *(VIN-yerds)*. Grapes were grown in ancient Egypt

198

and Canaan even before Abraham's time. The hilly areas of Judea and Samaria were good for growing grapes.

A vineyard was usually surrounded by a wall of stones or thorny hedges to keep out wild animals.

Most vineyards had a tower for a watchman, a winepress hollowed out of rock, and a vat, which held the wine. Jesus once told a parable that described the planting of a vineyard.

Grapevines needed much care. Each spring they had to be pruned and the dead branches burned. Jesus used this as a word picture of how God helps each Christian become a better person.

During the harvest, sometimes the whole family guarded the vineyard against thieves.

The time of stamping out the juice was one of great happiness. The people sang as they crushed the grapes with their feet. The wine was kept in new goatskin bags.

Jesus called himself the "true vine" and his disciples "the branches."

Where to find it: *Matthew 21: 33-41; John 15: 1-8*

VINEDRESSER *(VINE-DRESS-er)* was a person who grew grapes.

Jesus told a parable about a vineyard owner who hired vinedressers to take care of his vineyard, but they could not be trusted.

Where to find it: *Matthew 21: 33-41*

VINEGAR was sour wine or wine vinegar. It was a cheap wine often drunk by Roman soldiers.

In the New Testament, vinegar is mentioned only at Christ's crucifixion, when a soldier offered Jesus a drink of vinegar.

Where to find it: *Matthew 27: 48*

VIPER (see *Animals*)

VIRGIN *(VIR-jin)* is a person who has had no sexual intercourse. Usually it refers to a woman, but Revelation 14: 4 speaks of men virgins also.

In the Old Testament, girls wore certain clothes to show that they were virgins. David's daughter Tamar wore a long robe with sleeves, to show she was a virgin.

Jesus told a parable about ten young virgins who went to a wedding feast.

Virgin is often used as a word picture of dedication to God. The term "virgin daughter" is used in 2 Kings 19: 21 to apply to Jerusalem. Paul called the church a virgin in 2 Corinthians 11: 2 (King James Version).

Where to find it: *2 Samuel 13: 18; Matthew 25: 1-13*

VIRGIN BIRTH refers to the miracle of Jesus being born by the virgin Mary and the Holy Spirit (see *Virgin*).

An angel told her that the Holy Spirit would come upon her so that "the child to be born

will be called holy, the Son of God." Jesus was not conceived as the result of sexual intercourse.

Where to find it: *Matthew 1: 18-25; Luke 1: 26–2: 7*

VIRTUE *(VERT-choo)* means strength, ability, excellence, and moral worth.

Proverbs 12: 4 says that "a virtuous woman is a crown to her husband." Proverbs 31: 10-31 describes a virtuous woman who skillfully and lovingly helps provide for her family.

When the woman with internal bleeding touched Jesus, the King James Version of Mark 5: 30 says he knew "that virtue had gone out of him." In this verse, *virtue* means power.

VISIONS *(VIH-zhunz)* were the most common way God revealed truth to his prophets. A vision is something like a dream, except that it is given by God and reveals truth in pictures. Most prophets were awake and very alert when they received visions from God. Daniel was with others when he saw the vision God gave him. His companions did not see it, but they felt great fear and ran away.

The apostle Paul saw Ananias in a vision coming to renew his sight. The Lord spoke in a vision to Ananias, telling him to go.

Cornelius, a godly Gentile man, had a vision instructing him to send for Peter.

At the same time, Peter received a puzzling vision in which a huge sheet came down from heaven with animals that Jews were forbidden to eat. God told Peter to "kill and eat." Peter did not understand the vision until Cornelius and his family and friends received the Holy Spirit. Then Peter realized that his vision showed that God would accept all people by faith in Jesus Christ.

The Bible mentions many other godly people and prophets who received visions. The prophet Isaiah had a remarkable vision of God.

False prophets also claimed to have visions.

Jeremiah and Ezekiel said God would punish the false prophets with their lying visions.

Where to find it

Isaiah's vision   *Isaiah 6: 1-13*
Visions of false prophets   *Jeremiah 14: 14; Ezekiel 13: 2-9*
Daniel's vision   *Daniel 10: 4-8*
Ananias's and Paul's visions   *Acts 9: 1-19*
Peter's and Cornelius' visions   *Acts 10: 1–11: 18*

VISITATION *(vis-ih-TAY-shun)* refers to God coming to earth to punish or reward people for their deeds.

Jesus wept for Jerusalem because the Jews had not recognized that when Jesus was on earth, God had visited them.

1 Peter 2: 12 speaks of "the day of visitation," perhaps meaning the judgment day. On this day, a Christian's good deeds will glorify God.

Where to find it: *Isaiah 10: 3; Jeremiah 8: 12 (KJV); Luke 19: 41-44; 1 Peter 2: 12*

VOWS were a voluntary promise to God, made in hope of certain benefits. Jacob vowed to give a tenth of all he had to God, if God would be with him, provide for him, and bring him back home safely.

Once a vow was made, it had to be kept or else it was sin. A vow had to be spoken out loud to be binding.

Fathers could cancel vows made by their wives or daughters, but only at the time they were spoken. If a husband did not cancel his wife's vow when she made it and then later wanted her to break it, the sin was his, not hers.

In the New Testament, Jesus said everything his followers said should be just as binding as a vow. A simple yes or no should be enough. But if people did make vows, they must keep them faithfully.

Where to find it: *Genesis 28: 20-22; Numbers 30: 1-16; Deuteronomy 23: 21-23; Matthew 5: 34-36; 23: 16-22; Mark 7: 10-13*

VULTURE (see *Birds*)

When farmers threw their crushed grain into the air so the wind would blow away the chaff, it was called winnowing.

W

WAFERS were very thin, crisp crackers made of flour, water, and sometimes honey. Jewish people often ate them as part of their every-day meals. The people also spread wafers with oil and used them as offerings to God. Wafers were different from unleavened cakes, which were made of flour mixed with oil and were thicker.

The word *cake* sometimes means wafer and sometimes means a portion or small loaf of something. The Bible speaks of "cakes of bread" and "cakes of raisins."

Where to find it: *Exodus 16:31; 29:2; Leviticus 2:4; 7:12; 8:26; Numbers 6:15, 19*

WAGES are the pay a person earns by working for someone else. Wages in the Bible are sometimes called "reward" or "hire."

Wages were not common in the Old Testament, because most work was done by family members. But Old Testament laws said that fair wages (such as food, clothing, or money) should be paid to hired workers such as farm helpers, shepherds, and fishing crews. The Pharaoh's daughter promised wages to Moses' mother for taking care of him.

In the New Testament, wages were commonly paid to workers. An employer would go to the marketplace in the morning and look for workers. At the end of the day, he would pay wages (usually very little) for their work. Jesus told a parable about this.

Wages is often used as a word picture of getting what we deserve, especially for the bad things we do. The New Testament says that the "wages of sin is death, but the free gift of God is eternal life in Christ Jesus our Lord." Every person earns or deserves death, but eternal life is a gift (not a reward or wages) from God.

Where to find it

Laban and Jacob talk about wages   *Genesis 29:15*
Rules about wages   *Leviticus 19:13*
Jesus' parable about wages   *Matthew 20:1-16*
Wages of sin is death   *Romans 6:23*
Wages for preachers of the gospel   *1 Corinthians 9:14*

WAILING is loud crying at a funeral. During Bible times people would cry, tear their clothes, and even beat their chests at funerals to show their sorrow. If they wailed loudly, it showed that the dead person had been greatly loved.

Sometimes people were hired to wail at funerals. Before Jesus raised the daughter of Jairus from the dead, there had been this kind of wailing (also see *Mourning).

Where to find it: *Jeremiah 9:17; Amos 5:16; Mark 5:35-42*

WAISTCLOTH is a piece of clothing made of leather or linen and worn underneath the outer clothes. This garment is also called a "girdle." Both men and women wore waistcloths. Some waistcloths had shoulder straps and pockets.

Elijah in the Old Testament and John the Baptist in the New Testament wore waistcloths made of leather.

Where to find it: *2 Kings 1:8; Job 12:18; Matthew 3:4; Ephesians 6:14*

WALK means many different things in the Bible. It often has our usual meaning, for in Bible times people traveled great distances by walking.

Walk also means to do something. Ephesians 2:10 says God has prepared good works that we might "walk" in them (do them).

Walk in the New Testament usually means the way a person lives. Christians are no longer to walk or to live in "darkness" (the way Satan wants). We are to walk or live "by the Spirit," the way Christ walked, being loving and helpful to others.

Where to find it: *Romans 6:4; Ephesians 2:2, 10; 1 John 2:6*

WALLS in Bible times were the major way of defending cities against attack. Every ancient city had huge walls made of mud, stones, or brick. Some of those walls are still standing today.

Famous city walls in the Old Testament include Jericho's walls, which were wide enough to have houses built on top of them, and the walls of Jerusalem, which were built and rebuilt many times. Nehemiah had a group of Jews repair the walls of Jerusalem after the Exile.

New Testament cities also had walls. Paul escaped over the Damascus wall.

Where to find it

The Canaanite walls scare the Israelites   *Deuteronomy 1:28*
The walls of Jericho fall down   *Joshua 6*
Solomon builds Jerusalem's walls   *1 Kings 3:1*
Paul goes over Damascus wall   *Acts 9:23-24*

WAR was very common in ancient Palestine, and the Israelites were often in battles against other people. They saw war as God's way of giving them the Promised Land. Sometimes God did miracles to allow Israel to win battles, such as the time the sun stood still for Joshua.

The Old Testament also states that God used wars to punish the Israelites for their idolatry and disobedience. The wars of Old Testament times were often vicious and cruel. Sometimes whole cities, including men, women, and children, were destroyed or taken into slavery by the armies that won the battles.

The Israelites had experienced the cruelties of war. Isaiah said the promised Messiah would be a "Prince of Peace," not war.

During the New Testament, the Roman Empire had established more peaceful times in

202

Palestine. But Jesus said there would be wars and rumors of wars until he returned to rule. In his Sermon on the Mount, Jesus said, "Blessed are the peacemakers, for they shall be called sons of God."

One of the important promises of the Old Testament is that God will make wars cease to the ends of the earth. However, the Book of Revelation states that when Christ returns, he will himself use war to bring an end of war, defeating the forces of evil. Then the Old Testament promise "Neither shall they learn war any more" will be fulfilled.

In our present sinful world, soldiers and policemen seem to be necessary to keep order. Misuse of their power, however, brings terrible results.

Paul used *war* and *weapons* as word pictures of the battles Christians must fight against evil spiritual forces. He said Christians should "put on the whole armor of God" to defeat Satan (also see *Weapons*).

Where to find it

Sun stands still for Joshua's battle   *Joshua 10: 12-14*

God punishes Israel through war   *2 Chronicles 36: 15-21*

Peacemakers are blessed   *Matthew 5: 9*

Christ will use war to destroy war   *Revelation 19: 11-21*

God will make wars cease   *Psalm 46: 9; Isaiah 2: 4; Micah 4: 3*

Soldier's armor is word picture   *Ephesians 6: 10-17*

WASHING in the hot, dry, dusty land of Palestine was important. The people usually washed their feet when they came into a house, and also their hands and faces before they ate. Because water was scarce, few people could take baths; instead, they washed in streams and small fountains.

In Old Testament times, washing was an important part of worship. A huge basin of water in the Tabernacle reminded the people that God wanted them to be "clean," or free from sin. Priests washed themselves with great care before taking part in sacrifices. If things or persons were "unclean" in the Old Testament, they had to be washed before becoming "clean" again.

The idea of washing and being clean is also found in the New Testament. Jesus washed the disciples' feet at the Last Supper. In a spiritual sense, baptism is a sign that our sins have been "washed" away—or forgiven—by Jesus.

Where to find it: *Exodus 30: 17-21; Isaiah 1: 16; John 13: 1-11; Titus 3: 5; Hebrews 10: 22*

WATCHES OF THE NIGHT was a name for the hours of nighttime. In Bible times most people started their day at sunrise and ended it with sunset.

In the Old Testament the Jews divided their night into three watches: the beginning of the night ("evening"), darkness ("twilight"), and the end of the night ("dawn").

By the time of Jesus, the Roman way of counting watches was more common. Mark 13: 35 lists them as (1) evening, (2) midnight, (3) the cockcrowing, and (4) morning.

Where to find it: *Exodus 14: 24; Psalm 90: 4; Luke 12: 38*

WATCHMAN was a guard. In the Old Testament, watchmen were used to guard the city walls and gates at night, and also fields and vineyards during harvest. The watchmen would be alert for any signs of approaching danger and would notify the king or the owner of the field if enemies appeared. Nehemiah set out watchmen when he was rebuilding the walls of Jerusalem. Roman soldiers were watchmen at the tomb of Jesus.

Prophets of God in the Old Testament were called "watchmen" because they warned Israel about coming spiritual dangers.

Where to find it: *2 Samuel 18: 24-27; Nehemiah 4: 9; Isaiah 21: 6-12; Hosea 9: 8; Matthew 27: 62-66*

WATCHTOWER was a small tower built in a field or on a city wall for guards. Watchtowers were round, built of stone, and usually about ten feet tall. Those built into the large city walls were sometimes used as small houses for the watchmen to live in. During harvest season someone was on duty in watchtowers in fields day and night.

Where to find it: *Isaiah 21:8; 27:3; Habakkuk 2:1*

WATER is mentioned many times in the Bible. Because Palestine had little rainfall, water was precious. Drinking water carried in goatskins was sold in the marketplace. Wherever wells, fountains, and springs were found, people built towns. When rain fell, it was considered a blessing from God. One of the plagues God sent upon Egypt was bad water.

Water was recognized by Old Testament writers as one of the essentials of life. The Levitical priests used water in their worship ceremonies.

Water is used in many word pictures in the Bible. It stands for the source of all life and for eternal life. Jesus talked to the woman at the well about the "living water" of eternal life.

Another word picture is found in Matthew 10:42, where it says we should offer "a cup of cold water" to people in need, meaning we should care for them and help them.

Where to find it

Water is essential for life *Genesis 21:14*
Water is bought, sold *Deuteronomy 2:28*
Water in worship *Exodus 30:17-21*
God's blessing *Psalm 23:2*
Word picture of eternal life *John 4:14*

WATER FOR IMPURITY or **WATER FOR SEPARATION** was what an Israelite who had touched a dead person, a human bone, or a grave needed to be "clean" again.

To create the water for separation, running water was mixed with the ashes of a reddish-brown cow that had been sacrificed and burned under very strict rules. On the third and seventh days after the person had touched the dead body, he was sprinkled with the water for separation by the high priest. After this ceremony, and after the person had thoroughly washed himself and his clothes, he was again considered "clean."

If the person did not go through this cleansing with the water for separation, he was not allowed to continue as a member of the Jewish community.

Where to find it: *Numbers 19*

WATER HEN (see *Birds*)

WATERPOTS were clay pitchers used in ancient times by people who had to haul water from wells or springs to their houses or to troughs for their animals. Each clay pot held several gallons of water. At the wedding in Cana, Jesus performed his first miracle by turning the water in large waterpots (20-30 gallons) into wine.

Where to find it: *Genesis 24:15-20; Luke 22:10; John 2:6-10*

WATERS OF MEROM (see *Merom, Waters of*)

WAVE OFFERING (see *Offerings*)

WAY has many different meanings. Many times the word *way* simply means the path or road that people travel.

But *way* also describes how a person lives, whether it is good or evil. "Blessed is the man" who does not stand "in the way of sinners," says Psalm 1, because "the way of the wicked will perish." People can choose the way they will follow, either good or evil. God knows the ways of all people.

Way sometimes describes God's conduct. His ways are pure and good, and they are different from the ways of people, said Isaiah the prophet.

The way also describes how a person can know God. Jesus said, "I am the way, the truth, and the life; no one comes to the Father, but by me."

The Way was the first name that followers of Jesus used for themselves, before they were eventually called Christians. It referred to following the way or teachings of Jesus.

Where to find it

A path, or route *Genesis 18:16*
The ways of the wicked *Psalm 1:1*
God's ways are good *Isaiah 2:3*
The two ways open to people *Matthew 7:13-14*
"I am the way" *John 14:6*
The early name for Christians *Acts 9:2*

WAYFARERS *(WAY-fair-ers)* were usually merchants, musicians, metalworkers, or beggars who walked the roads of ancient Palestine with no home of their own.

During times of war, wayfarers disappeared from the roads because traveling alone was too dangerous.

Where to find it: *Judges 19:17; 2 Samuel 12:4; Job 31:32; Jeremiah 9:2*

WEALTH in ancient times was associated with many servants, large herds of camels, sheep, or other animals, silver, gold, and other precious metals. Job, Abraham, Lot, Isaac, and Jacob were wealthy men. Wealth was considered a blessing from God.

God teaches that he is the giver of wealth. But he also teaches that wealth is to be shared with the poor and those in need.

Jesus told a parable about a wealthy man who trusted only in his riches. He did not realize that his death would occur that very night. Through this parable, Jesus taught that a person should aim to please God rather than to pile up riches. The rich young ruler was an example of a person enslaved by his wealth.

James denounced rich men who cheated the people who worked for them.

Paul wrote Timothy that the love of money is the root of evil. It is better, Paul said, to be content with what God gives.

Where to find it

Abraham and Job were wealthy *Genesis 13:2; Job 1:3*
God gives the power to become wealthy *Deuteronomy 8:17-18*
Danger of trusting in riches *Psalm 52:7; Mark 10:17-27; Luke 12:13-21*
Rich men who cheat employees *James 5:1-6*
Contentment is better than desiring riches *1 Timothy 6:6-10*

WEAPONS were used in Bible times to protect people from wild animals and robbers and also to fight wars. The Israelites were often involved in small- and large-scale wars. Sometimes one tribe fought another, or the Southern Kingdom fought the Northern Kingdom, or all the people fought other enemies such as the Assyrians and Babylonians.

Cities were usually walled and often built on hilltops so guards on the walls could see any approaching enemy.

The following list includes common weapons used in Bible times.

Armor for soldiers was usually made of leather coated with a thin layer of metal for added protection. Strips of the leather were fastened together to form a kind of sleeveless coat that was tied together at the back with leather strings. Sometimes soldiers wore a square of bronze over the chest under this armor as a kind of heart guard. Kings often had armor made with more metal.

When the word *armor* is used in Ephesians 6:11, it refers to all the weapons a soldier used rather than just the leather covering for his body.

Bows and Arrows were used for hunting animals for food, and also for war. Bows were made of wood; bowstrings were made of ox-gut. Arrows were light wood or reeds tipped with metal. When bows and arrows were used as weapons of war, the bows were sometimes as long as five feet. Israelites from the tribes of Reuben, Gad, and Benjamin were famous for their skill with bows and arrows in warfare (1 Chronicles 5:18; 12:2).

Buckler (see *Shield*, below).

Clubs are mentioned as part of the weapons carried by the Temple guard who came to arrest Jesus in the Garden of Gethsemane. The clubs were probably something like the nightsticks carried by our police officers.

Coat of Mail (see *Armor*, above)

Dagger (see *Sword*, below)

Helmets for soldiers, during most of the Old Testament period, were made of leather; those for kings were of bronze. In New Testament times, soldiers' helmets were made of bronze.

Javelin, Spear, and **Lance** were roughly the same—long, slender pieces of wood with heads of stone or metal. They were used in war either to thrust or throw at the enemy.

Sheath was the case or covering for a sword as it hung at the left side of a soldier.

Shields (sometimes called bucklers) were large or small objects that soldiers carried to protect themselves from the spears and swords of enemies. Shields were usually either wickerwork (thin, flexible twigs woven together) or leather stretched over a wooden frame. The leather was oiled before battle to preserve it or to make it glisten (Isaiah 21: 5).

Spear (see *Javelin,* above)

Sling was a common weapon in early times for hunting animals and for war. It was not like our slingshots. Instead it was a band of leather that was wide in the middle to hold a stone. The soldier held both ends together in his hands, swung it around his head to get thrust, then let one end go to release the stone.

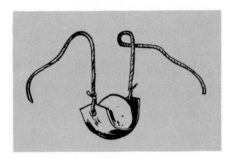

Seven hundred left-handed men from the tribe of Benjamin were so skilled that they could "sling a stone at a hair and not miss."

This is the weapon David used to kill Goliath, the giant.

Where to find it: *Judges 20: 16; 1 Samuel 17: 40-50*

Swords are the weapons most frequently mentioned in the Bible. Normally they were long, broad knives with a handle. Some swords had two sharp edges, some only one. They were usually carried by the soldier in a sheath on his left side. A dagger is a smaller sword. *Sword* is often used in the Bible as a word picture for the judgment of God or for violence of any kind. Jesus said, "All who take the sword will perish by the sword."

Sword is also used as a word picture of the power of the Word of God.

Where to find it: *Matthew 26: 52; Ephesians 6: 17; Hebrews 4: 12*

WEASEL (see *Animals*)

WEAVING (see *Occupations*)

WEEDS (see *Plants*)

WEEKS, FEAST OF (see *Feasts*)

WEIGHTS (see *Measures*)

WELL is a hole dug in the ground to find water. Since water was very scarce in dry Palestine, wells were important for people and animals. Often people fought over wells.

When a well was dug, rocks were placed around it and a cover over it to keep animals or people from falling in. Some wells were shallow, others were very deep. Sometimes dry wells or cisterns were used for hiding places. Joseph's brothers threw him in an old dry well.

Among the famous wells in the Bible are the well where Jacob met Rachel, the well of Bethlehem, and the well at Sychar, where Jesus met a Samaritan woman.

Where to find it

Eliezer and Rebekah *Genesis 24: 10-21*

Jacob and Rachel *Genesis 29:1-10*
Two men hide in a well *2 Samuel 17:18-21*
David's favorite well *1 Chronicles 11:16-19*
Jesus at Sychar *John 4:5-15*

WEEPING (see *Mourning*)

WHALE (see *Animals*)

WHEAT (see *Plants*)

WHIRLWIND is a violent storm with strong, gusting winds, sometimes like a tornado. Whirlwinds sometimes occur on the Sea of Galilee suddenly and without warning. Jesus once calmed such a storm. Elijah was carried to heaven by a whirlwind. It was also called a "tempest" in the Bible.

Whirlwind is sometimes a word picture for the judgment of God.

Where to find it: *2 Kings 2:11; Job 38:1; Hosea 8:7; Zechariah 7:14; Luke 8:23-24*

WHORE (see *Harlot*)

WIDOW (WID-oh) is a woman whose husband has died. In ancient times, widows were usually poor because most women did not inherit anything from their husbands—all property was inherited by sons.

In Old Testament times, a widow wore special clothes to show she was a widow. The Old Testament Law said the Israelites were to use some of the Levites' tithes to feed widows. Hebrews also were to include widows at feasts and other happy occasions. God would punish any who cheated widows or harmed them.

In the New Testament, the early church in Jerusalem appointed seven men to see that widows had enough food. The Book of James says that visiting widows and orphans is part of true religion.

The apostle Paul wrote to Timothy that the church should make special provision for widows who were over 60 years old and had lived a good life, if they had no relatives to care for them. He advised younger widows to marry again.

Where to find it

Israelites were to treat widows fairly *Exodus 22:22-24; Deuteronomy 14:28-29; 24:17*
Early church helped feed widows *Acts 6:1-6*
Instructions about helping widows *1 Timothy 5:3-16; James 1:27*

WIFE (see *Marriage*)

WILDERNESS (WILL-der-ness) was land where few people lived. Depending on the amount of rainfall, the wilderness might be barren, riverless desert, or it might be grassy land where nomads grazed their flocks and cattle.

Moses led the Israelites through a large wilderness area to Canaan. Many Israelites died there because of their lack of faith in God. Their children became shepherds in the wilderness until every adult who had left Egypt had died.

Many years later, the prophet Isaiah said that God would someday make the desert wilderness like a garden.

Jesus was tempted by the devil in a wilderness area.

Where to find it

Israelites would die in wilderness *Numbers 14:32-33*
Wilderness would be like a garden *Isaiah 43:19-20; 51:3*
Jesus tempted in wilderness *Matthew 4:1*

WILL (see *Testament*)

WINE is fermented grape juice. In Bible times, it was used as a drink, a medicine, and a disinfectant.

Wine was also poured out as a special drink-offering to God, a symbol of thanksgiving or repentance.

In the Bible, wine is spoken of both as a blessing and as a curse. Isaac blessed his son, wishing him plenty in grain and wine. But the prophet Hosea said wine takes away understanding. Proverbs calls wine "a mocker . . . a brawler; and whoever is led astray by it is not wise." The writer of Proverbs also gave a colorful description of a person who gets drunk on wine.

Jewish priests were commanded not to drink wine when they were on duty, and Nazirites were never to drink wine.

In Old Testament times, wine was not diluted, but during the time of Jesus wine was usually mixed with water. The Pharisees complained because Jesus ate and drank with sinners. He once turned water into wine at a wedding in Cana. At the Last Supper, Jesus said the wine symbolized his blood, which was to be poured out for sinners.

Wine is sometimes used as a word picture for the wrath of God. It is also pictured as part of times of joy and love.

The apostle Paul told Christians not to be drunk with wine but to be filled with the Spirit.

Where to find it

Wine as a disinfectant   *Luke 10:34*
As a drink offering to God   *Leviticus 23:13; Numbers 15:5*
As a blessing   *Genesis 27:28*
As a curse   *Proverbs 20:1; 23:29-35; Hosea 4:11*
Priests could not drink on duty   *Leviticus 10:9*
Nazirites could not drink wine   *Numbers 6:1-4, 20*
Pharisees complain that Jesus drank   *Luke 7:33-34*
Jesus turns water into wine   *John 2:2-11*
Wine the symbol of Jesus' blood   *Matthew 26:27-29*
Word picture of wrath of God   *Jeremiah 25:15; Revelation 14:10*
Picture of joy and love   *Song of Solomon 5:1; Isaiah 55:1*

WINEPRESS was a large square pit or trough, often lined with cement. Workers put grapes into the winepress and then walked and stamped on the grapes to press out the juice. The grape juice flowed through a hole near the bottom of the winepress into a smaller vat.

Then the juice was made into wine. Archaeologists have found some ancient winepresses in Palestine.

The workers sang and shouted as they stamped on the grapes. It was a time of joy.

Winepress is sometimes a word picture for God's anger.

Where to find it: *Isaiah 16:10; 63:2-3; Jeremiah 25:30; Revelation 14:19-20; 19:15*

WINESKIN was a leather bag for storing wine, water, or milk. Wineskins were usually made from goatskin.

Since fermenting wine creates gases, wineskins had to stretch enough to get larger. Jesus said that if you put new wine into old wineskins, the bags would burst. New wine must be put into newer, more elastic wineskins.

Where to find it: *Genesis 21:14-19; Matthew 9:17*

WINNOWING *(WIN-oh-wing)* was the way farmers separated the good parts of grain (the kernels) from the waste parts (the chaff). Using wooden pitchforks or shovels, the farmers threw the grain into the air when there was a strong breeze. The wind would blow away the chaff, and the heavier kernels would fall to the ground.

Winnowing is mentioned many times in the Old Testament. In Psalm 1 evil people are compared to worthless chaff.

Where to find it: *Ruth 3:2; Psalm 1:4; Isaiah 30:24*

WINTER in Israel is the cold, rainy season of the year. Although Israel's winter is mild, it is much cooler than the hot, dry summer. Snow falls occasionally in Jerusalem because of its higher altitude.

Sometimes rains don't come during the winter, and then Israel has a drought.

Where to find it: *Matthew 24:20; Acts 28:2*

WISDOM *(WIZ-dum)* in the Bible means not only learning but also skills, common sense, and good judgment.

A skill such as weaving or building was considered wisdom.

The Old Testament Book of Proverbs applies wisdom to daily life situations such as rearing children, handling money, telling the truth, and controlling anger. In Proverbs 8, wisdom is described as a woman who invites people to listen to her wisdom and live by it.

Some parts of the Old Testament are called Wisdom Literature. They include Proverbs, Ecclesiastes, Job, and Psalms 19, 37, 104, 107, 147, 148.

In the beginning of his reign, King Solomon asked God for wisdom, and God gave it to him. Solomon became known as the wisest king on earth.

God is the source of wisdom. Job told some examples of the wisdom of God. Fearing or honoring the Lord is the starting point of wisdom for people. Following God's commands is a sign of wisdom.

In the New Testament, Christians are told that if they lack wisdom, they may ask God, and he will give it generously. Paul wrote that Jesus is both "the power of God and the wisdom of God." He said that all wisdom and knowledge are found in Jesus Christ.

Where to find it

Weaving is called wisdom *Exodus 28: 3 (KJV)*
King Solomon and wisdom *1 Kings 3: 9-14; 10: 23-24*
God's wisdom *Job 28: 20-28*
Honoring and obeying God is wisdom *Deuteronomy 4: 6; Psalm 111: 10*
God gives wisdom to those who ask *James 1: 5*
All wisdom is in Christ Jesus *1 Corinthians 1: 24, 30; Colossians 2: 3*

WITCHES are persons who do supernatural things by the power of the devil. Witches use evil spells, potions, and curses. The Bible forbids witchcraft. Witches, sorcerers, soothsayers, wizards, magicians, enchanters, and diviners are very much alike.

Witchcraft was common in ancient Palestine, Egypt, Assyria, and Babylon. Queen Jezebel was involved in witchcraft.

In the New Testament, Simon Magus (or "magician") practiced witchcraft, and so did Elymas on the island of Cyprus. Paul called Elymas a "son of the devil."

Where to find it

Witchcraft and sorcery forbidden *Leviticus 19: 26; Deuteronomy 18: 9-14*
Jezebel involved with witchcraft *2 Kings 9: 22*
Witchcraft in the New Testament *Acts 8: 9-24; 13: 6-12*

WITNESS *(WIT-nuss)* in the Bible usually means a person who tells the truth no matter what it costs. The word *martyr* comes from the Greek word meaning "witness."

In the Old Testament, the Law of God was called a witness to God's holiness and the people's sins. The Tabernacle was called a witness to God's presence.

The Ten Commandments include a rule that "you shall not bear false witness against your neighbor." False witnesses were severely punished.

The men who told lies at Jesus' trial were false witnesses.

God calls his people to be his witnesses—to tell his truth no matter what it costs. The disciples were witnesses to the death and resurrection of Christ, and they told about it. When Jesus was taken into heaven, he told the disciples that they were to be his witnesses to the end of the earth.

The Holy Spirit is a witness to Christians (see *Witness of the Spirit*).

Where to find it

Law and Tabernacle are witnesses *Numbers 17: 7-8; Deuteronomy 31: 26*
False witnessing forbidden *Exodus 20: 16; Deuteronomy 19: 16-18*
False witnesses at Jesus' trial *Matthew 26: 60*
Disciples were witnesses of Jesus' resurrection *Luke 24: 46-48; Acts 2: 32*
Disciples were to be witnesses to ends of the earth *Acts 1: 8*

WITNESS OF THE SPIRIT refers to the Holy Spirit as a true witness—someone who tells the truth (see *Witness*).

Jesus told his disciples that the Spirit would be a witness to the world about sin, righteousness, and coming judgment. The Spirit would remind Christians of Jesus' words and what he did.

The apostle Paul wrote that the Spirit tells believers they are the children of God. He also helps believers understand God's thoughts.

John told Christians that the Spirit of God witnesses that Jesus Christ, the Son of God, became a man with a human body.

The writer of Hebrews illustrates that the Spirit sometimes tells believers truths about God through writings in the Bible—in this case through something written in Jeremiah.

Sometimes the Spirit witnesses about something very specific. Paul said the Spirit told him he would face imprisonment and suffering.

Where to find it

Witnesses to world about sin and judgment *John 16: 7-11*
Reminds Christians of Jesus' teachings *John 14: 16-17, 26; 16: 12-15*
Witnesses that we are children of God *Romans 8: 15-17*
Helps us understand God's thoughts *1 Corinthians 2: 11-13*
Witnesses that Jesus had human body *1 John 4: 2*
Witnesses through Scripture *Hebrews 10: 15-18*
Tells Paul what will happen *Acts 20: 22-23*

WIZARD (see *Sorcerer*)

WOLF (see *Animals*)

WOMAN, according to the Bible, is half of humanity, or mankind. God created the first man and the first woman, both in the image of God. He gave to them—man and woman together—dominion over his creation. He told them to multiply and to subdue the earth. They were to be "one flesh."

Sin destroyed the relationship God had meant for men and women. In the Old Testament, the Israelites, like some of the pagan people around them, often treated women as possessions of men rather than as equal partners. In spite of this, many women in the Old Testament showed outstanding leadership ability and were used by God. Deborah was a skilled Old Testament judge. Miriam, Deborah, and Huldah were called by God to be prophets. The picture of a good woman in Proverbs 31:10-31 shows a woman who is a capable leader both in her home and in the community.

When Jesus came to earth, he showed clearly by his actions that he believed in the dignity and equality of women. He commended Mary for her desire to sit at his feet like the disciples and listen to his teaching. He made his first announcement that he was the Messiah to the woman at the well; he included women in the group of those who traveled with him. Women were the first to receive the news of the resurrection and were told to make it known. Women prayed and prophesied publicly in the early church. Phoebe was an early leader in the church at Cenchreae.

Where to find it

Creation of woman *Genesis 1:27-28*
Sin destroys relationships *Genesis 3:1-19*
Women leaders in Old Testament *Exodus 15:20-21; Judges 4:4–5:31; 2 Kings 22:14-20*
Jesus includes women *Luke 8:1-3*
Jesus commends Mary *Luke 10:38-42*
Women at resurrection *Matthew 28:1-10; Mark 16:1-8; Luke 24:1-11; John 20:1-18*
Women pray and prophesy *1 Corinthians 11:5*
Phoebe in church at Cenchreae *Romans 16:1*

WORD in the Bible sometimes has special meanings different from our usual use of it.

Here are some of its special meanings:

1. *Word* sometimes means God's truth as it is now found in Old Testament writings. "Thy word is a lamp to my feet and a light to my path" (Psalm 119:105).

2. It sometimes means the gospel, or the Christian message, as in "Be doers of the word, and not hearers only" (James 1:22).

3. *Word* (with a capital letter) is sometimes a name for Christ, as in John 1:1, "In the beginning was the Word, and the Word was with God, and the Word was God." Using Word as a name for Christ shows that Christ was revealing God and his truth to people, just as we use words to show others our thoughts.

WORD OF THE LORD or **WORD OF GOD** is a phrase that appears nearly 400 times in the Old Testament. It was used when God gave his prophets or other leaders a message that they were to give to other people. *The Word of the Lord* meant that this was truth from God that was absolutely sure, and the people could depend on it.

Many of the Old Testament books of prophecy, including Jeremiah, Hosea, Joel, Jonah, Zephaniah, Haggai, and Zechariah have in the first verse something like "The word of the Lord came to . . ." to show that the message was from God.

The Word of the Lord involves not only a message but also power to do the thing mentioned. "By the word of the Lord the heavens were made" is the way the psalmist described creation.

Where to find it

The Word of the Lord involves power *Psalm 33:6; Hebrews 11:3*
The Word of the Lord is sure *Isaiah 40:8; 1 Thessalonians 4:15*
Prophets spoke the Word of the Lord *Jeremiah 1:1; Hosea 1:1; Joel 1:1; Jonah 1:1; Zephaniah 1:1; Haggai 1:1; Zechariah 1:1*

WORKS OF GOD refers to what God has done and is doing. His works include creating the universe, keeping it going, working miracles, and providing for the needs of people. Among his works, the greatest was sending his Son, Jesus Christ, so that those who believe in him can be freed from the power and penalty of sin.

The Bible describes the works of God as great, wonderful, and faithful. The works of God come from his love and wisdom.

In the New Testament, spreading the gospel is called the work of God, or the work of Christ. Believing in Christ is also called the work of God. Once some men asked Christ, "What must we do, to be doing the works of God?"

He answered, "This is the work of God, that you believe in him whom he has sent."

Where to find it

Descriptions of God's works *Psalm 92: 5; 104: 24; 105: 1-2; 107: 15; 139: 14*
Believing in Christ is a work of God *John 6: 28-29*
Spreading the gospel is a work of God *Romans 14: 20; 1 Corinthians 15: 58; 16: 10; Philippians 2: 30*

WORLD has several meanings in the Bible:

1. The planet earth. Genesis 1 and 2 tell about the creation of the world, or earth.

2. Wherever people live. Jesus told his disciples to go into all the world and preach the gospel.

3. The Roman Empire. At the time of the birth of Jesus, Caesar Augustus wanted "all the world" to be taxed.

4. Greek culture. When Paul preached in Ephesus, a silversmith said that "the whole world" worshiped the goddess Artemis.

5. The world to come. This involves not only a new physical place but also a new way of life.

6. The people who live on the earth. This is the meaning in John 3: 16, "For God so loved the world that he gave his only Son, that whoever believes in him should not perish but have eternal life." Jesus told his disciples that the "world" hated him because he pointed out their sins.

7. The world system ruled by Satan, who wants disobedience and rebellion against God. Jesus told the Pharisees that they were "of this world" but he was not. Paul said he had died to this world's ideas of doing whatever pleases self. True holiness is to keep oneself unstained from the world's basic idea of "me first."

Where to find it

The earth *1 Samuel 2: 8*
Wherever people live *Mark 16: 15*
The Roman Empire *Luke 2: 1*
Greek culture *Acts 19: 27*

The world to come *Hebrews 2: 3-9; 6: 5; Revelation 11: 15*
People who live on earth *John 3: 16; 7: 7*
Satan's system *John 8: 23; Galatians 6: 14; Ephesians 2: 2; James 1: 27*

WORSHIP means to honor, praise, and adore someone who is worthy of such high honor. The English word was originally *worthship* to show that the one being honored was worthy of praise.

True worship involves not only things we do but also our thoughts and feelings as we do them. The Old Testament prophets said that acts of worship meant nothing unless the thoughts, feelings, and lives of the worshipers were controlled by God.

Only God fully deserves our worship. When Jesus was tempted by Satan, he said, "You shall worship the Lord your God and him only shall you serve."

The Book of Revelation says that John once began to worship an angel. However, the angel cried out, "You must not do that! I am a fellow servant. . . . Worship God."

People can and should worship God both publicly and privately. After the Hebrew people came out of Egypt, they worshiped God publicly at the Tabernacle set up in the wilderness (see *Tabernacle*). Later, when the Temple was built in Jerusalem, the Israelites worshiped together in a more highly organized way. The people sang many of the Psalms as part of their worship in the Temple.

Scholars believe that during the Exile in Babylon, the Jews began to meet in synagogues for worship and instruction. Eventually, synagogues were built wherever Jewish people lived. The Temple sacrifices were not carried on in the synagogues, however.

The early Christians met in homes to worship God. Their worship included preaching, reading the Scriptures, praying, singing, celebrating the Lord's Supper, and using other gifts the Holy Spirit gave them.

Today, Christians meet in church buildings and other places to worship God publicly.

Where to find it
Jesus tells Satan only God should be worshiped *Matthew 4: 10*
John tries to worship an angel *Revelation 19: 10*
A psalm of worship *Psalm 135: 1-6*
Early Christian worship *Acts 2: 42; 1 Corinthians 14: 26; Ephesians 5: 19-20*

WRATH OF GOD means God's anger with sin. The Old Testament prophets talked often about the wrath of God and the judgment that would come upon his people if they turned away from him.

The Bible makes it clear that God's anger or wrath is caused by his people forgetting him, turning away from him and his commands, and despising his love and care for them. When God's people acted this way, they began treating each other unfairly, they trusted in their own strength instead of in God, and they began to worship other gods. God's judgment followed, and that included the destruction of Israel as a nation. The people were sent into exile in Assyria and Babylonia.

Because God is holy and because he loves us, he is angry when we turn away from him and fail to become all he meant us to be. If God did not care about us, he would not be angry when we follow the destructive path of sin.

Jesus Christ came to die for our sins and to free us from the punishment of God's wrath. Those who do not trust and obey Christ cannot have the reconciliation with God that Christ made possible, because they have not obeyed the gospel.

In the final judgment, all people who refuse Christ's way of salvation must face the wrath of God.

Where to find it

Israelites' murmuring brings God's wrath *Numbers 11: 1; Deuteronomy 1: 26-28*
Christ delivers us from God's wrath *1 Thessalonians 5: 9; Revelation 5: 9*
Wrath of God in judgment *Psalm 110: 5-6; Isaiah 2: 20-21; Romans 1: 18; John 3: 36; 2 Thessalonians 1: 8-9; Revelation 14: 9-10*

WRESTLING was a popular game during New Testament times. Paul may have watched wrestling matches in Corinth. He used *wrestling* as a word picture of the way Christians must struggle against Satan.

The most famous wrestling match in the Bible was between Jacob and God's angel.

Where to find it: *Genesis 32: 24-30; Ephesians 6: 12*

WRITING probably began in Bible lands about 3500 B.C. Early writing was something like very simple pictures or lines. Gradually, over a period of many hundreds of years, these pictures developed into other symbols that were more like an alphabet.

So far as we know, the Hebrew language always had an alphabet. Many Hebrews knew how to read and write before 1000 B.C.

Hebrew (the original language of the Old Testament) is written from right to left and from the "back" of the book to the "front"— just the opposite of our kind of writing. The Hebrew alphabet had no vowels—only consonants. The vowels had to be supplied by the reader (see *Hebrew Language*).

The Greek language (of the New Testament) had both vowels and consonants and reads from left to right, like English. However, Greek and Hebrew were both written at first in all capital letters, with no spaces between words and no punctuation marks. John 14: 1 would look something like this:

LETNOTYOURHEARTSBETROUBLED
BELIEVEINGODBELIEVEALSOINME

So Hebrews and early Christians had a harder time than we do learning to read!

There was no such thing as paper in Bible times. *What did ancient people write on?*

1. Stones were used for permanent records. When Moses received the Ten Commandments from God, they were written on stone tablets. Sometimes people covered stones with plaster and then wrote in the plaster while it was still soft.

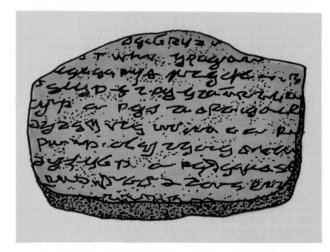

2. Metal was used for writing. Engraving on gold is mentioned in Exodus 28: 36.

3. Wood was sometimes coated with wax or clay and then used as a writing tablet. This is

probably the kind of tablet Zechariah used to tell that his son should be named John.

4. Potsherds, or pieces of broken pottery, were used for ordinary writing purposes. People could write on them with ink and then wash the writing off and use the pieces again.

5. Clay tablets were commonly used throughout the Middle East. If people wanted to make the writing permanent, they baked the clay in the sun or in an oven.

6. Papyrus was used very often for important letters or documents. Papyrus was a tall plant that grew in water and swampy places. Ancient people took the inside of the papyrus stalks and cut them into thin strips. They glued these strips on top of each other crisscross and left them under something heavy to make them stick together. When the sheets were dry, they were polished with stone and glued together to form long strips (scrolls) for writing. People could use pen and ink to write on papyrus. Probably Jeremiah's scroll that King Jehoiakim burned was made of papyrus.

7. Parchment was an excellent but expensive writing material. It was made from the skins of sheep or goats. People removed the hair from the animal skins, soaked them in lime, and then stretched them on frames. When the skins dried, they were rubbed smooth with chalk or pumice stones.

Parchment lasted much longer than papyrus. Scribes often used parchment to make copies of the Old Testament writings.

What did ancient people write with?

1. Chisels were used to engrave stones or metal.

2. Styluses—pointed pieces of bone, wood, or metal—were used for writing on clay or wax. The Old Testament mentions "iron pens" that were probably metal styluses.

3. Pens were made from the stiff stems of plants. They were cut diagonally on the end, and the ends were then frayed to feel like a brush. These pens were used to write on potsherds, papyrus, and parchment.

4. Ink was made in two colors—black and red. Black ink was made by mixing soot with a thin solution of sticky resin from trees. This was dried and formed into cakes. When a person wanted to write, he moistened the cake of ink with water and dipped his stylus or pen into it.

Red ink was made like black ink, but with red iron oxide instead of soot.

How were books formed?

Early books were written on long scrolls. These were formed from sheets of papyrus or parchment glued together. Most scrolls were about 9 to 11 inches high and about 30 feet long. Sometimes the scroll was written on

both sides. Scrolls were usually stored in pottery jars.

Where to find it

Early Hebrews know how to read and write *Judges 8:14*

Writing on stones *Exodus 24:12; Deuteronomy 27:2-8*

Wood tablets *Ezekiel 37:16-17; Luke 1:63*

Jeremiah's scroll is burned *Jeremiah 36:23*

"Iron pens" *Job 19:24; Jeremiah 17:1*

Scrolls written on both sides *Ezekiel 2:10; Revelation 5:1*

Scrolls stored in pottery jars *Jeremiah 32:14*

XERXES I *(ZERK-zees)* was the king of Persia from 485 to 465 B.C. Most scholars believe he was the King Ahasuerus who made Esther his queen. The Book of Esther describes events very similar to those in Persia's historical records of King Xerxes (see *Ahasuerus*).

Where to find it: *Esther 2:16-17*

YOKE was a wood frame that harnessed two animals together for heavy work. Oxen were often yoked to pull a plow, wagon, or other farm equipment.

The yoke was also a symbol of obedience for people. Jeremiah told the Jews to put yoke-bars on their necks as a symbol that they had to obey King Nebuchadnezzar of Babylon.

The Israelites told King Rehoboam that his father's "yoke" (meaning his demands) had been too heavy. But Rehoboam followed the foolish advice of his younger advisers and told the people, "My father made your yoke heavy, but I will add to your yoke."

In the New Testament, *yoke* is usually a word picture that means demands, requirements, or burdens. Jesus invited people to join themselves to him and his work. "Take my yoke upon you, and learn from me . . . for my yoke is easy, and my burden is light." He meant that loving and serving him may look hard, but it is really easy because he makes our lives so different.

Other passages speak of the yoke of slavery, or the yoke or burden of trying to keep the Old Testament Law.

Where to find it

Rehoboam increases demands   *1 Kings 12:4, 14*
Jeremiah's message   *Jeremiah 27:2, 6-8*
Jesus' invitation   *Matthew 11:28-30*
Trying to keep the Law   *Acts 15:10*
Slavery   *Galatians 5:1; 1 Timothy 6:1*

YOKEFELLOW *(YOKE-fell-oh)* describes a close relationship between two people. Paul once addressed a friend and fellow worker as his "true yokefellow." He meant they were working closely together for Jesus Christ.

Where to find it: *Philippians 4:3*

YOUTH in the Bible seems to refer to a broad period of time. Although no clear statement is given, it probably includes persons up to age 20 or 25. A man was counted in the census for army service at 20. A Levite could begin service in the Tabernacle at age 25. So the upper age limit of "youth" is not clear.

Where to find it: *Exodus 30:14; Numbers 1:1-3; 8:24*

People got upset when Jesus called Zacchaeus, the short tax collector, down from his tree and headed toward his house.

ZACCHAEUS *(zak-KEY-us)* was the chief Jewish tax collector in Jericho. Men such as Zacchaeus were hated because they worked for the Roman government and were not always honest.

Zacchaeus was so short he had to climb a tree to see above the crowds and look at Jesus as he walked past.

Jesus surprised Zacchaeus by stopping beneath the tree to say he'd be staying at his house. The crowds were surprised that Jesus would go to the house of a tax collector. But Zacchaeus was overjoyed. He said he would give half of his riches to the poor and repay those he had cheated with four times the original amount. It was his way of showing he was sorry for his sins.

Where to find it: *Luke 19: 1-10*

ZACHARIAH, ZACHARIAS (see *Zechariah*)

ZADOK (ZAY-dok) was a priest who was loyal to both David and Solomon. When Zadok was young, he joined David in his war against King Saul.

Later, when David prepared to bring the ark of God into Jerusalem, he asked Zadok and other priests to sanctify themselves and carry it.

When King David's son Absalom revolted and tried to take over his father's kingdom, Zadok fled with David, carrying the ark. David told Zadok and Abiathar and their two sons to take the ark back into Jerusalem and act as his spies. Zadok stayed loyal to David.

When Zadok was old and David was dying, Zadok anointed Solomon king as David told him to do. Solomon soon made him high priest.

Where to find it

Carries the ark for David   *1 Chronicles 15: 11-13*
Becomes spy for David   *2 Samuel 15: 24-36; 17: 15, 17-21*
Anoints Solomon king   *1 Kings 1: 18-45*
Becomes high priest under Solomon   *1 Kings 2: 35*

ZAREPHATH (ZAIR-uh-fath) was the town where Elijah stayed during the second part of a 3½-year drought. A widow offered him a room in her house. God miraculously fed the widow, her son, and Elijah during the drought through one jar of meal and one jar of oil that never ran out.

Zarephath was 8 miles south of Sidon and 14 miles north of Tyre on the Mediterranean coast in what is now Lebanon. The modern village of Sarafand is near the old ruins of Zarephath.

Where to find it: *1 Kings 17: 8-24; Luke 4: 25-26*

ZEAL (zeel) means an eager interest and determination. David said he had a zeal for God's house. Paul said the Jews had a wrong kind of zeal. They were determined about the wrong things.

Paul admitted with sorrow that he once had zeal to persecute the church. However, Paul praised the Corinthians for their zeal in giving to needy Christians.

Where to find it: *Psalm 69: 9; Romans 10: 2-3; 2 Corinthians 9: 2; Philippians 3: 6*

ZEALOTS (ZEL-uts) were a group of Jews at the time of Christ who were so determined to overthrow the Roman rulers that they sometimes used violence.

One of Jesus' disciples, Simon, was once a member of this group. He is called Simon the Zealot. He is not the same person as Simon Peter.

The work of the Zealots eventually helped to bring about the terrible war with Rome in A.D. 68 that destroyed Jerusalem and the Temple.

Where to find it: *Luke 6: 15; Acts 1: 13*

ZEBEDEE (ZEB-uh-dee) was the father of James and John, two of Jesus' disciples. When Jesus called James and John to follow him, they were mending fishing nets with their father.

Zebedee was a fisherman on the Sea of Galilee, probably near Bethsaida. Since he had hired servants, he may have been wealthy.

Where to find it: *Matthew 4: 21-22; Mark 1: 19-20*

ZEBULUN (ZEB-you-lun) was the tenth son of Jacob and the sixth and last son born to Leah.

His descendants became the tribe of Zebulun. When Moses counted the men over 20 years old who could go to war from the tribe of Zebulun, the number totaled 57,400.

Later, a second count was made in Moab. By this time, the number had increased to 60,500 men.

When the Hebrews got to Canaan, the tribe of Zebulun was given a section of land between the Sea of Galilee and the Mediterranean.

When Jesus visited the territory of Zebulun, he fulfilled a prophecy recorded in Isaiah 9: 1-2. "The land of Zebulun . . . the people who walked in darkness have seen a great light."

Where to find it

Son of Jacob and Leah   *Genesis 30: 19-20*
Moses counts men in the tribe   *Numbers 1: 30-31; 26: 27*
Boundaries in Canaan   *Joshua 19: 10-16*
Jesus visits Zebulun   *Matthew 4: 12-16*

ZECHARIAH (ZEK-uh-RYE-uh) was the name of 28 people in the Bible. Five have some importance—one king, three men who were prophets and priests, and the priest who was the father of John the Baptist. The Old Testament Book of Zechariah is named for one of the prophets.

1. Zechariah, the priest and prophet whose prophecies are recorded in the next-to-the-last Old Testament book, was from a family of priests. His family returned to Jerusalem from the Babylonian exile to help rebuild the Temple.

He began prophesying about 520 B.C. and may have continued on and off for many years. The first part of his ministry was during the same period as the prophet Haggai. He helped encourage the people to rebuild the Temple.

2. Zechariah, the fourteenth king of Israel, reigned about six months in 753 B.C., about thirty years before Israel was conquered by the Assyrians. He sinned against the Lord like the kings before him.

After six months as king, Shallum murdered Zechariah and became king in his place.

Zechariah's short reign fulfilled a promise the Lord had made to King Jehu, his great-great-grandfather. The Lord had told Jehu that four generations of his sons would be kings after him. Zechariah was the fourth and last king related to Jehu.

3. Zechariah, a priest and prophet during the reign of Joash, king of Judah, told the people God had forsaken them because they had turned from God. King Joash commanded that Zechariah be stoned to death, and he was killed in the courtyard of the Temple. This may have been the Zechariah that Jesus mentioned as the last martyr in the Old Testament.

4. Zechariah was also the name of a prophet during the early days of Uzziah, king of Judah. (Uzziah is called Azariah in 2 Kings.) Zechariah instructed him in the fear of the Lord, and "as long as he sought the Lord, God made him prosper." Uzziah later (perhaps after the death of Zechariah) turned away from God and did great evil. Eventually God struck Uzziah with leprosy.

5. Zechariah, the father of John the Baptist, was a priest during New Testament times. He and his wife, Elizabeth, both followed God's commands, and they were childless until their old age.

One day while Zechariah was burning incense in the Temple, an angel appeared and said that he and Elizabeth would have a son. Zechariah couldn't believe it, so he asked for some sign that it would happen. The angel told him he would not be able to speak until his son was born.

When the baby was born, friends and relatives came to congratulate the parents. They thought the boy should be named Zechariah after his father. But Elizabeth said, "Not so; he shall be called John."

Then they gave Zechariah something on which to write what the baby should be named. He wrote, "His name is John"—and suddenly Zechariah could speak again.

Zechariah and Elizabeth's son, John, was a cousin of Jesus. John was the prophet who helped prepare the way for Jesus' ministry.

Where to find it

Priest and prophet *Ezra 5:1-2; Zechariah 1:1-3*
King of Israel *2 Kings 10:30; 15:8-12*
Priest stoned to death *2 Chronicles 24:20-25; Matthew 23:35; Luke 11:51*
Prophet to Uzziah *2 Chronicles 26:5*
Father of John the Baptist *Luke 1:5-25, 57-80*

ZECHARIAH *(ZEK-uh-RYE-uh)*, **BOOK OF**, includes the prophecies of Zechariah to the group of Jews who had come back to Jerusalem after 70 years of exile in Babylon. Their goal had been to rebuild the Temple. However, soon after they began, the work was halted by the king of Babylon.

Twenty years later, in 520 B.C., Zechariah began to prophesy. He and another prophet, Haggai, encouraged the Israelites to go back to their work on the Temple. Four years later, in 516 or 515 B.C., the Temple was completed.

The Book of Zechariah contains five prophecies. The first prophecy, in Zechariah 1:1-6, called the people to repent.

The second prophecy, spoken one year later, is in Zechariah 1:7—6:15. It consists of eight symbolic visions to encourage the people to complete the Temple. The meaning of the visions is not always clear. The following list is a suggested meaning.

1. The first vision pictures horsemen who patrol the earth for the Lord. This vision, in 1: 8-17, assured the Israelites of God's care for them.

2. The vision about four horns and four smiths in 1: 18-21 taught that Israel's enemies would be destroyed.

3. Chapter 2 describes a man with a measuring line. It showed that Jerusalem would grow outside its walls and God would defend the city.

4. In chapter 3, a high priest is wearing dirty clothes to symbolize Israel's sins. This vision looked forward to a Messiah who would take away all sin and bring peace.

5. Zechariah's vision in chapter 4 is of a seven-branched candlestick connected to two olive trees. It taught that the leaders of the people would help bring success in the work of rebuilding the Temple.

6. Zechariah 5: 1-4 tells the vision of a flying scroll that would bring God's judgment on those who lie or steal.

7. A woman, symbolizing wickedness and the sins of Israel, is carried away to Babylon in Zechariah 5: 5-11, showing that sin would be banished.

8. Four war chariots in Zechariah 6: 1-8 show that God rules the earth.

These visions were followed by a scene in 6: 9-15 where gold and silver were fashioned into a crown for Joshua, the high priest. This pictured the Messiah, who would be both priest and king to his people. Zechariah called this Messiah the Branch.

Chapters 7 and 8 were spoken two years later. Here Zechariah answered questions about fasts observed in memory of the destruction of Jerusalem. He urged the people to be fair and honest with each other.

Chapters 9—14 were probably written much later. In these chapters, the prophet looked into the future and made many references to a coming Messiah. Pagan nations were to be destroyed. The Shepherd-King would be rejected but would return victoriously. God's triumphant Kingdom would be set up.

ZEDEKIAH *(ZED-uh-KY-uh)* was the name of the last king of Judah and two false prophets.

1. After King Nebuchadnezzar of Babylon captured Jehoiachin, the previous king of Judah, Nebuchadnezzar appointed Zedekiah to be king.

Zedekiah was 21 years old at the time, and he ruled for 11 years. He did not follow God's commands, nor would he listen to the advice of the prophet Jeremiah. He permitted Jeremiah to be placed in an empty cistern with muck at the bottom.

After Jeremiah was rescued from the cistern, he told Zedekiah that the Lord wanted him to surrender to the Babylonians so the city could be spared from destruction. The Babylonian army had surrounded the city, and all food supplies were cut off. Instead of following Jeremiah's advice, Zedekiah and his soldiers tried to flee. He was captured and his sons were killed. Zedekiah was blinded and the city was destroyed in 586 B.C.

2. Zedekiah, a court prophet of Ahab, king of Israel, delivered a false message. When Ahab wanted to fight the Syrians, he asked Jehoshaphat, king of Judah, to help him. Jehoshaphat wanted advice from a prophet. So Ahab gathered 400 of his prophets, including Zedekiah, and all of them said, "Go up; for the Lord will give it into the hand of the king."

Zedekiah even made horns out of iron and told the kings, "Thus says the Lord, 'With these you shall push the Syrians until they are destroyed.'"

However, a true prophet of the Lord named Micaiah said Zedekiah was lying and that Ahab would die in battle.

Zedekiah was so angry he hit Micaiah. But Micaiah's prophecy came true.

3. Another false prophet named Zedekiah is mentioned in Jeremiah 29: 21-23. He prophesied among the people of Israel exiled in Babylon.

Where to find it

King of Judah   *2 Kings 24: 17–25: 7; Jeremiah 34: 1-22; 37: 1–39: 7*
False prophet of Ahab   *1 Kings 22: 1-24; 2 Chronicles 18: 10, 23*
False prophet in Babylon   *Jeremiah 29: 21-23*

ZELOPHEHAD *(zee-LOW-fuh-had)* was a Hebrew man who died in the wilderness leaving no sons, but five daughters. His daughters asked Moses for the land in Canaan that would have belonged to their father's sons if he had had any.

The Lord told Moses their request was right. They were given the land of their father.

This became the basis for a law in Israel: If a man died without sons, his inheritance went to his daughters.

Later, Moses added that daughters who inherited land should marry men who belonged to the tribe of their father so the inheritance would not pass to another tribe.

Where to find it: *Numbers 27:1-11; 36:1-12*

ZELOTES (see *Zealots*)

ZENAS *(ZEE-nus)* was a Christian lawyer who apparently traveled and preached the gospel with Apollos. Paul asked Titus to see that they had everything they needed for their work.

Where to find it: *Titus 3:13*

ZEPHANIAH *(zef-uh-NY-uh)* was a prophet and great-grandson of Hezekiah, king of Judah. His prophecies are in the Old Testament Book of Zephaniah.

He lived in Jerusalem and prophesied in the royal court of Josiah, king of Judah, between 641 and 609 B.C. His prophecies seem to refer to the time before Josiah tried to turn his people back to God. Other prophets during his time included Nahum, Habakkuk, Huldah, and Jeremiah.

Zephaniah fearlessly denounced the evils of his time and told of God's approaching judgment. His prophecies also spoke of the hope that Israel would be restored as a strong nation.

ZEPHANIAH *(zef-uh-NY-uh),* **BOOK OF,** was written by the prophet Zephaniah during the reign of King Josiah, probably about 625 B.C. Perhaps Zephaniah's prophecies helped urge King Josiah to make some of his reforms.

When Zephaniah prophesied, Assyria had been a world power for 50 years. Josiah's grandfather, King Manasseh, had paid tribute each year to Assyria. He encouraged idol worship and even persecuted those who worshiped God. Josiah's father, Amon, did the same things.

Zephaniah prophesied judgment for Judah and for other countries that ignored God's demands for righteousness. He also offered hope for Israel after the judgment that was coming.

Zephaniah spoke of God's judgment as the "day of the Lord." This judgment would affect not only Judah but also Philistia, Moab, Egypt, and Assyria. He said the Israelites perhaps could escape judgment if they would seek God and do his commands.

The last section of the book describes the glory that would belong to Israel when God restored his people and saved them from their oppressors.

Where to find it

The dreadful coming Day of the Lord *Zephaniah 1*
All nations will share God's judgment *Zephaniah 2*
The glory that is coming   *Zephaniah 3: 9-20*

ZERUBBABEL *(zuh-RUB-uh-bull)* was appointed governor of Jerusalem by Cyrus, king of Persia, after the Jews' 70-year exile in Babylon. Zerubbabel was a Jew who was the grandson of King Jehoiachin. He traveled back to Jerusalem with Joshua, the high priest, and other returning Jews who wanted to rebuild the Temple.

In the years that followed, Zerubbabel showed great leadership ability. He and the others first set up an altar to God and offered sacrifices on it.

Then they laid the Temple foundation. As they worked, people from a neighboring area who had not been in exile in Babylonia came and offered to help build the Temple. Zerubbabel refused their offer, saying, "You have nothing to do with us in building a house to our God; but we alone will build to the Lord."

The other people then wrote a letter to the king accusing Zerubbabel and his workers of being troublemakers. The king ordered the work halted.

Not until Darius became king of Persia

could Zerubbabel go back to building the Temple. The work was resumed in 520 B.C. and completed in 516 or 515 B.C. A great celebration was held when it was finished.

Zerubbabel's name is listed among the ancestors of Jesus.

Where to find it

Returns to Jerusalem   *Ezra 2:2*
Sets up altar to God   *Ezra 3:2-3*
Lays foundation for Temple   *Ezra 3:8-11*
Begins work again   *Ezra 5:2*
Temple celebration   *Ezra 6:16-22*
Is an ancestor of Jesus   *Matthew 1:13; Luke 3:27*

ZEUS *(zoos)* was the chief of the Greek gods. The Romans called him Jupiter. His sign was a thunderbolt, and the rainbow was supposed to be his messenger.

In 168 B.C., the Syrian king Antiochus Epiphanes IV dedicated the Jewish Temple at Jerusalem to Zeus. The Jews were outraged at this idolatry, and it became part of the reason for the Maccabean revolt (see *Maccabees*).

When Paul and Barnabas were on their first missionary journey, they healed a crippled man in the town of Lystra. The people were so amazed they said, "The gods have come down to us in the likeness of men." They called Barnabas "Zeus" and Paul "Hermes." The priest of Zeus wanted to offer sacrifices to them, but Paul and Barnabas made them stop.

Where to find it: *Acts 14:8-18*

ZIBA *(ZI-buh)* was a servant of King Saul. After David became king, Ziba told him that Jonathan's crippled son, Mephibosheth, was still alive. David wanted to do a kindness in memory of Jonathan, so he appointed Ziba with his 15 sons and 20 servants to farm for

Mephibosheth the land that once had belonged to Saul.

Several years later, when King David was forced to flee from Jerusalem, Ziba met David with gifts of food. Ziba told David that Mephibosheth had rebelled. So David gave all of Mephibosheth's land to Ziba.

However, Ziba's story was a clever lie. David learned the truth when he finally saw Mephibosheth again.

Where to find it

David makes Ziba Mephibosheth's servant
   2 Samuel 9:1-11
Ziba tells a clever lie   *2 Samuel 16:1-4*
David discovers the truth   *2 Samuel 19:24-30*

ZIDON see *Sidon)*

ZIKLAG *(ZIK-lag)* was a city in southern Palestine where David lived for 16 months while hiding from King Saul. Achish, king of Gath, told David that he and his men and their families could live in the city.

Once while David and his small group of warriors were gone, the Amalekites raided the town and captured all the wives, children, and possessions. David and his men went after them and rescued their families and their possessions.

David was still living at Ziklag when he received word that King Saul had been killed in a battle.

Ziklag became one of the cities of Judah.

Where to find it: *1 Samuel 27:1-7; 30:1-26; 2 Samuel 1:1-4; 1 Chronicles 12:1-20*

ZION *(ZI-un)* is one of the hills on which Jerusalem stands. At one time, a Jebusite fortress stood on the hill. David captured the fortress and called it the "city of David." After David brought the ark of God to Zion, the hill was considered sacred.

When King Solomon moved the ark of God into the Temple on Mount Moriah, the name *Zion* was extended to include the Temple hill.

Later *Zion* came to mean all of Jerusalem. *Zion* also became another word for the nation of Israel.

Finally, in the New Testament, *Zion* came to mean "heaven." Hebrews 12: 22 says, "You have come to Mount Zion and to the city of the living God, the heavenly Jerusalem."

Where to find it

A Jebusite fortress   *2 Samuel 5: 6-9*
Zion refers to the city of Jerusalem   *Psalm 48: 1-3*
Zion refers to the nation of Israel   *Psalm 126: 1*
Zion represents heaven   *Hebrews 12: 22*

ZION, DAUGHTER OF, is a phrase used often in the Old Testament to mean the city of Jerusalem and all the people who lived there.

ZIPHITES *(ZIF-ites)* were people who lived in the town of Ziph or in the wilderness around Ziph, about 25 miles south of Jerusalem. Although the people in this area belonged to the tribe of Judah as David did, they were loyal to King Saul. Twice when David was hiding near their city, the Ziphites told King Saul about David's hiding place.

Each time Saul went out with his army to capture David, but David escaped.

One of the Psalms explains how he felt when the Ziphites betrayed him.

Where to find it: *1 Samuel 23: 14-28; 26: 1-25; Psalm 54: 1-7*

ZIPPORAH *(zih-PO-rah)* was the wife of Moses. Her father was Jethro (also called Reuel), a priest of Midian.

Moses met Zipporah after he fled from Egypt. She and her six sisters were drawing water for their father's flock, but some shepherds drove them away. Moses protected the sisters and helped them. Their grateful father invited Moses to eat and live with them and eventually gave Zipporah to Moses as his wife.

Zipporah and Moses had two sons, Gershom and Eliezer.

When Moses returned to Egypt after 40 years in Midian, Zipporah and their two sons went with him. However, at an inn along the way, Moses became very sick. Zipporah realized that the reason for his sickness was that they hadn't circumcised one of their sons as God had commanded, beginning with Abraham. So Zipporah circumcised her son.

Sometime during the conflict with the Pharaoh or the beginning of the Exodus, Moses had sent Zipporah and their two sons back to her father's home. After Moses and the Israelites crossed the Red Sea, Zipporah, her two sons, and her father came to the Israelite camp near Mount Sinai. The Bible states that after a short visit, Jethro returned home. It does not say whether Zipporah and her sons stayed with Moses or went back to Midian.

Where to find it

Meets and marries Moses   *Exodus 2: 15-22*
Circumcises her son   *Exodus 4: 24-27*
Returns to Moses in wilderness   *Exodus 18: 1-7*

Throughout its creation, this encyclopedia was reviewed and criticized by a distinguished panel of respected theologians and educators. Upon completion of their work, they made the following comments:

"I feel confident in recommending this long-needed and important biblical resource tool. The encyclopedia provides a wealth of easily accessible information to those desiring to increase their biblical knowledge.

"As an educator I am particularly pleased with the commitment by the authors and editors to insure that the definitions are both easy to read and to understand. The authors' ability to explain difficult concepts clearly in language familiar to readers is an outstanding hallmark of this set. Equally important is the care taken to insure that anyone with intermediate reading ability can easily use this encyclopedia. As I reviewed the drafts of materials for this set, I was continually surprised and delighted by the authors' evenness in writing at an appropriate level. The method of indicating correct pronunciations of words, unique to David C. Cook, provides an excellent, easily used aid to the reader.

"For both church and home use this resource is excellent. Children and adults can turn to the encyclopedia and rejoice in learning!"

Dr. Donna Ogle
Director, Reading Clinic
National College of Education
Evanston, Illinois

"This is a unique book about the Bible. It contains a lot of information which can be found only in works beyond the reach of children. Yet it is interestingly written and does not go above the heads of children. Its use will enable them to learn a great deal about the Bible—its background, its separate books, its teaching and the people in its pages—and it will help them grasp its meaning for their own lives and learn the power of its message today."

Dr. G. R. Beasley-Murray
Professor of New Testament
The Southern Baptist Theological Seminary
Louisville, Kentucky

"I am impressed with this project for several reasons: (1) an extensive resource tool about Bible facts has long been needed in the vocabulary of this age group, 9-12-year-olds—this set at last makes such a tool readily available; (2) the encyclopedia not only provides general knowledge about the Bible, answering countless questions raised by "Bible jargon" and otherwise strange terms, but it does this in a responsible accurate fashion by a distinguished biblical scholar and his learned wife; and (3) the encyclopedia, at least that part I checked, gives straightforward, simple, but not simplistic answers to complex theological concepts. I heartily endorse it.

"I look forward to purchasing a set for my 12-year-old."

Dr. Gerald F. Hawthorne
Professor in Greek
Wheaton College
Wheaton, Illinois

"The idea of producing a Bible encyclopedia for children is a commendable concept. Such a work could easily be of rather poor quality.

This one, however, is a splendid achievement in terms of the quality of the material for the level of the intended audience. Such a volume should help children study the Bible in a responsible way. In this light, the use of this volume should definitely be encouraged in families and churches."

David M. Scholer
Associate Professor of New Testament
Gordon-Conwell Theological Seminary
South Hamilton, Massachusetts

"I am most favorably impressed with the work and eagerly anticipate its publication. The encyclopedia unites the commendable features of clarity, easy readability, and scholarly insight. Each brief article is carefully written to include the important facts on the subject without confusing the young reader by insignificant details. A helpful linguistic pronunciation guide aids the child in pronouncing any biblical word which is hard to say. Well-chosen cross-references direct the reader to key biblical passages where more information can be learned. This consistently biblical encyclopedia is strongly recommended for church and Christian day school libraries, for children's Sunday school teachers desiring to communicate effectively to their pupils, and for Christian families concerned about knowing God's Word better."

Kermit A. Ecklebarger
Assistant Professor of New Testament
Conservative Baptist Theological Seminary
Denver, Colorado